Nine Lives

Memoirs and Occasional Papers
Association for Diplomatic Studies and Training

In 2003, the Association for Diplomatic Studies and Training (ADST) created the Memoirs and Occasional Papers Series to preserve firsthand accounts and other informed observations on foreign affairs for scholars, journalists, and the general public. Sponsoring publication of the series is one of numerous ways in which ADST, a nonprofit organization founded in 1986, seeks to promote understanding of American diplomacy and those who conduct it. Together with the Foreign Affairs Oral History program and ADST's support for the training of foreign affairs personnel at the State Department's Foreign Service Institute, these efforts constitute the Association's fundamental purposes.

J. Chapman Chester
FROM FOGGY BOTTOM TO CAPITOL HILL
Exploits of a G.I., Diplomat, and Congressional Aide

Robert E. Gribbin
IN THE AFTERMATH OF GENOCIDE
The U.S. Role in Rwanda

James R. Huntley
AN ARCHITECT OF DEMOCRACY
Building a Mosaic of Peace

John G. Kormann
ECHOES OF A DISTANT CLARION
Recollections of a Diplomat and Soldier

Armin Meyer
QUIET DIPLOMACY
From Cairo to Tokyo in the Twilight of Imperialism

William Morgan and Charles Stuart Kennedy, eds.
AMERICAN DIPLOMATS
The Foreign Service at Work

James M. Potts
FRENCH COVERT ACTION
IN THE AMERICAN REVOLUTION

Daniel Whitman
A HAITI CHRONICLE
The Undoing of a Latent Democracy

Nine Lives
A Foreign Service Odyssey

Allen C. Hansen

Association for Diplomatic Studies and Training
Memoirs and Occasional Papers Series

  Books

Washington, DC

Library of Congress Control Number: 2007936672
ISBN 978-0-9794488-6-7 paperback (alk. paper)

 An imprint of New Academia Publishing
P.O. Box 27420 - Washington, DC, 20038-7420

 NEW ACADEMIA PUBLISHING | info@newacademia.com
www.newacademia.com

To Charmaine
and our five children
Robert, Annette, Katherine, Alicia, and Mark
who explored the world with us

Contents

Preface		*ix*
Acknowledgements		*xii*
1	The Launching	1
2	Calypso in Caracas	13
3	Mexican Mosaic	69
4	Guyanese Gumbo	103
5	Spanish Sojourn	133
6	Dominican Detour	159
Photo Gallery		*189—204*
7	Murder in Montevideo	205
8	Breathless in Bolivia	245
9	Peruvian Panorama	305
10	Passage to Pakistan	355
11	The Landing	417
Notes		*429*
Abbreviations		*431*
About the Author		*432*
Index		*433*

Preface

In 1953, during the administration of President Dwight Eisenhower, the United States Information Agency (USIA) was established as an independent agency that worked closely with the Department of State and other U.S. government agencies. Its information, cultural, and educational exchange programs eventually became known as "public diplomacy" to distinguish USIA activities from traditional diplomacy.

Many Americans became familiar with its international radio service, the Voice of America (VOA), and its major educational exchange activity, the Fulbright program, but few were aware of its other programs which explained U.S. Foreign Policy through its many media services and "told America's story to the world" utilizing cultural and educational exchanges as well as media activities. USIA programs were conducted in more than a hundred countries where USIA offices overseas were known as the "United States Information Service" (USIS) and were attached to American embassies and consulates.

In 1999 USIA was abolished, in the mistaken belief by some government leaders that with the end of the "Cold War," public diplomacy, a major activity that contributed to the Cold War's end, was no longer important enough to be maintained as an independent government entity. Most of its varied activities were either transferred to the Department of State, or terminated. An exception was the VOA which was left separate from the State Department and placed under the supervision of a presidentially appointed Board of Governors whose public title is the "Broadcasting Board of Governors." (Such a title lacks any identification as to what this Board does or that it is a U.S. Government entity, which also occurred when USIA briefly became the International Communication Agency (ICA).)

After the terrorist attack September 11, 2001 that caused the destruction of New York's World Trade Center, and especially the invasion of Afghanistan and Iraq by primarily U.S. armed forces, many

Congressional and Executive Branch leaders re-evaluated the activities formerly conducted by USIA and now more widely known as "public diplomacy." In the years that followed the demise of USIA, but especially in the last few years, it has become increasingly clear that public diplomacy is just as important today as it was during the Cold War.

Since USIA was abolished, there have been few calls for re-establishing a separate entity like USIA, although that idea has crossed the minds of those who seek to increase the effectiveness of current and future public diplomacy programs. Beginning in 2005 a few public voices have suggested that it may be time to think seriously about re-establishing a separate organization like USIA to conduct America's public diplomacy.

Seven years after USIA was abolished, the importance of public diplomacy activities in furthering U.S. foreign policy objectives seems to have become better understood by U.S. Government leaders, yet public diplomacy can only contribute so much. Its successes or failures depend greatly on the policies it is designed to explain and advocate. Equally important for effective public diplomacy efforts are adequate tools of that profession (media, cultural, and educational programs), sufficient funding, and organization that permits 100% focusing on the purposes for which USIA existed. As a "public diplomat" for 32 years, I believe strongly that when USIA existed as a separate entity, of utmost importance was the ability of both field officers and Washington headquarters to focus on the means and goals of public diplomacy since that was their only function. It remains to be seen if, in a larger bureaucracy concerned with many other diverse programs and objectives, the focus necessary for successful public diplomacy can be achieved as effectively as when it was managed by an independent agency devoted solely to conducting public diplomacy programs.

Re-establishing a separate entity similar to USIA, even if U.S. government leaders decided to do so, would take considerable time and effort. Like successful public diplomacy itself, this could not be accomplished overnight. An alternative to consider would be to give the public diplomacy organization in the Department of State the same relative independence that the Agency for International Development (AID) had when I was on active duty with USIA.

Nine Lives depicts some of the programs conducted in the nine countries and Washington, D.C. where the author was assigned from 1953 to 1987, as well as some of the glamour, excitement, frustrations and satisfactions of working overseas as a "public diplomat" for USIA. It was a time when the U.S. Information Agency operated independently though always in concert with the Department of State and under the guidance of the U.S. ambassador in each host country.

Nine Lives is a memoir about how one USIA Foreign Service Officer and his colleagues sought to gather support for U.S. foreign policies and to explain U.S. culture in its broadest sense to the people of nine nations. Those who shared my overseas adventures or served in a similar capacity will be reminded of similar or greater challenges in the countries where they served "Uncle Sam." And hopefully, anyone thinking about a career in the Foreign Service will be inspired by the inside view depicted here and seek to do so.

A.C.H.
McLean, Virginia
2007

Acknowledgements

The first draft of NINE LIVES was completed after writing it from 1994 to 1998. It was considerably edited before submitting it to the Association for Diplomatic Studies and Training (ADST) for possible inclusion in their relatively new memoirs series. Prior to completing the initial manuscript, my brother Henrik Hansen, my son Robert Hansen, my daughter Alicia Hatcher, and a friend, Norma Rathner, an American Foreign Service Officer's spouse, who, with her husband, shared some of our adventures, read it in whole or in part and offered valuable edits and comments.

I am indebted to ADST for sponsoring the book's publication and particularly to Margery Thompson, ADST's Publishing Director, for her advice and assistance; Stephen Grant, ADST senior fellow who meticulously and superbly edited the manuscript; and to four ADST interns: Dan Mallinson who prepared the photos and covers for printing and Katie Frink, Kate Tussey, and Brian Moran, all of whom worked on the electronic version. My thanks also go to my son-in-law, Monte Hatcher, for designing the cover for NINE LIVES as he has done for some of my other books. From the above it is clear that much of this has been, like the adventures depicted herein, "a family affair."

I would also like to acknowledge the people mentioned in these pages whose company, both at work and socially, contributed to the enjoyment and welfare of my family and me during those 32 years of adventurous living as a public diplomat in the USIA Foreign Service.

Nine Lives

1
The Launching

The first chapter of a journey is always detailed and slow.
Its middle hours are drowsy, and the last ones swift.
—Valdimir Nabokov, *King, Queen, Knave*

The four-motored Constellation, on its weekly flight from Madrid to New York, landed at the Azores for refueling at approximately 3 a.m. The young man in seat 27A was wide-awake. There was little to see through the aircraft windows except the airport lights, a deserted runway, and the fuel truck waiting to move into position after the propellers stopped spinning. But the mind of the passenger in seat 27A was filled with exciting thoughts. He was returning to his native land earlier than anticipated because of a telegram he had received a week ago. Visions of serving his country in important assignments in exotic places offset his melancholy about leaving behind the fun and excitement of Madrid. But he rationalized, surely with my three months' experience in Spain, if the USIA hires me they'll probably send me back due to my familiarity with the country.

The telegram he had received in Madrid ten days before read:

PREPARED TO OFFER YOU APPOINTMENT AS
PUBLIC AFFAIRS TRAINEE, FSS-11, $3,927
PLUS ALLOWANCES UPON SUCCESSFUL COMPLETION
PANEL INTERVIEW AND PASSING MEDICAL EXAMINA-
TION. TRAINING CONSISTS OF ONE MONTH AGENCY
WASHINGTON AND ELEVEN IN AN OVERSEAS POST.
WIRE ANSWER IMMEDIATELY.

He cabled back: ARRIVING OCTOBER 17 FOR INTERVIEW.

In 1954, Spain was a military dictatorship ruled by one man— Generalissimo Francisco Franco. The Spanish economy, not yet recovered from the Spanish Civil War, and suffering from Franco's decision, initially at least, to favor the losing side in World War II, was enduring a depression comparable to that experienced by the United States twenty years earlier. Productivity was down, unemployment was rampant, and poverty was plentiful. Still, one could get a glass of table wine for the equivalent of one U.S. cent; Spanish song and dance were as popular as ever; Spanish cooking had recovered its élan after the dark days of the Civil War when some Spaniards had to eat cats to stay alive; and the bullfights still provided gutsy entertainment every Sunday afternoon. For the young American who had arrived in Spain a few months before, it was an exciting place to be. But there could be no doubt that the Spanish economy, nearly a decade after the end of World War II, was in bad shape. Spaniards still suffered from the effects of the Spanish Civil War and Spain's isolation from the WWII victors, an isolation which was only now about to end. Even so, despite the suffering of its people, Spain was still, as James Michener would write later, one of the world's most exuberant civilizations.

This was the period when the American Containment Policy with respect to the Soviet Union was in full swing. Port Lyautey, French Morocco, was the location of a major French-American airbase designed to provide one of that policy's deterrents in the form of American bombers stationed there which were within striking distance of Moscow. But with Morocco soon to gain its independence from France, agreements made with the French government for maintaining U.S. bombers at the Port Lyautey airbase were about to be terminated. Even if the new government were to agree to let the Americans stay, its stability and future policies were questionable.

In view of the changing situation in North Africa, the U.S. sought other alternatives to keeping U.S. bombers in Morocco. As a result, a major effort was made to forge links with the Spanish caudillo in order to replace the possibly vulnerable Moroccan military bases with bases in Spain. The Generalissimo undoubtedly saw this situation as the salvation of the Spanish economy, which it proved to be. Because of the mutual advantages for both the Spanish and American governments, an agreement was signed to begin construction of a number of Spanish-American air bases and other military facilities on Spanish soil, including a major naval base in southern Spain for the U.S. Sixth Fleet, watchdog of the Mediterranean. The howl of liberal American and European writers who expressed outrage at the thought of democratic America under Eisenhower going to bed with Franco's fascist Spain echoed and re-echoed for more than a decade. Some thirty years later Spain, by then ruled by a democratic government, would be invited to become a full partner of Western Europe and the U.S. in the North Atlantic Treaty Organization.

It was the above scenario that had brought me to Spain, for I was, of course, that young man who was flying back to his homeland. I could not have guessed at the time how that flight would change my life and, in effect, provide me with nine adventurous lives before my foreign service odyssey came to an end.

Upon getting out of the Navy after the Korean War I intended to knock around Europe as a tourist before settling down, but through some navy contacts I obtained a job in Madrid with Brown-Raymond-Walsh, prime contractor for the construction of the Spanish-American military bases. I had just become accustomed to what, for a foreigner on a dollar salary, was the good life in Madrid. This included a growing attachment to an attractive Spanish girl who was slightly my junior. Equally exciting were the almost-weekly dinner parties at the home of a Condesa, a widow who had seen better days, and who, in the sudden mixing of traditional Spanish culture with modern America which the base agreements had brought about, welcomed contacts with Americans as adding excitement to her life. I suspected she was also interested in the possibility of getting jobs for friends and relatives, and maybe an American husband for her teenage daughter, so there were always a few American guests invited to her parties. I became a regular because I was in the personnel division of Brown-Raymond-Walsh, although I didn't stay there long enough to be of any benefit to her even had that been possible.

Also making Madrid an exciting place to be was the camaraderie of other young bachelors, both Spaniards and foreigners, who savored, as I soon learned to do, the Spanish lifestyle of the times. Eat, drink and be merry, for the food and wine are good, the women are beautiful, the bullfights are thrilling, and the art and history of Spain almost overwhelming! British author John Masters in his novel, *Fandango Rock*, presents the new Spanish and American cultural coziness of the times as a clash rather than a melding, but this had not yet occurred, at least not to my Spanish friends and me. As one of my Spanish colleagues commented when we discussed the new Spanish-American relationship, "Spaniards consider Americans as being their rich relatives. We get along together so well because we Spaniards think we're smarter than you Americans."

When I entered the USIA building at 1776 Pennsylvania Avenue in Washington, about a block from the White House, I felt I was about to begin not only a new career, but to enter a new world and begin a new life. I had only one worrisome thought: that I might fail the test I was about to undertake with the USIA panel.

In a seventh floor office I was greeted by a gray-haired man in his late fifties who exuded cordiality.

"We're glad to see you, and glad you could come back for this interview. How was your flight?"

"Not bad," I replied. "I got into Washington yesterday morning."

"It will just be a few minutes. One of the members of the panel has been delayed but he'll be here shortly. You understand the process. We're very favorably impressed by your credentials as a former naval officer and a reporter, but until you're paneled and we have the opportunity to discuss with you face-to-face your experience, your knowledge, and how you perceive current U.S. foreign policy, among other things, we can't offer you a definite job. I hope that was clearly understood from our telegram as I know you've gone to a lot of expense to fly back here for this interview."

"Oh yes. I understand," I said in a subdued manner. "But the opportunity to work with USIA is why I'm here, and no matter how the panel goes, I welcome the chance."

Ten minutes later I was ushered into a conference room where five neatly dressed and somewhat severe-looking men were seated around a table. I was asked to sit down in the chair at the end of the table. After introductions, the middle-aged man at the opposite end of the table who acted as chairman said, "Mr. Hansen, suppose we begin by you telling us a little about yourself. I understand you're thirty years old. What have you been doing for the past thirty years?"

I smiled. "Well, I was born in New Jersey where I went to school and went into the navy at age eighteen in World War II. When I got out of the navy I went to Syracuse University where I received a B.A. degree in political science, and then went to work as a reporter for the Perth Amboy Evening News, covering Metuchen, New Jersey, my hometown. But as I remained in the Naval Reserve, I was recalled when the Korean War broke out and later was commissioned a Lieutenant, Jr. Grade and ended up here in Washington with the Potomac River Naval Command. When I completed my tour last June and was discharged, I went to Spain. In Madrid, through navy contacts, I got a job with the prime contractor building the Spanish-American air bases." Then I quickly added: "But I would much prefer the kind of career in the Foreign Service that working for USIA seems to offer."

There followed a battery of questions by the various members of the panel. I had the sunken feeling that I didn't field the questions very well, but I tried to keep up a good front and plowed on despite my growing belief that I was ill prepared for the type of questions I was being asked. I answered them as best I could but the sinking feeling that my answers would not satisfy the panel persisted.

There were questions about American history and government, the American economy, and what did I think about Eisenhower's containment policy? Why did I want to join USIA? Why did I go to Europe when I got out of the navy? What are my views about communism? Where had I traveled in the U.S. and overseas and with the navy, and what did I do in the navy and did I like it? Although the panel fired these questions at me in something like a thirty-minute period, to me it seemed like I had missed both lunch and dinner, and still the questions came. Furthermore, despite being honest, earnest, and answering to the best of my ability, the feeling of not having done my best remained with me. If anything, I believed I did worse as time went on. At last the inquisition ended and I was asked to step outside.

I sat down in the outer office and began to perspire. The palms of my hands were wet. I've come all this way, I thought, and I've goofed. I've done so terrible in answering those questions that they're sure to say that they made a mistake in asking me to come in for this interview. Fortunately, they'll take me back at Brown-Raymond-Walsh, but it really cost me to fly here and then to go back there in defeat. What a blow to my ego!

Minutes passed which seemed much longer as I awaited the verdict of the panel.

"What's taking them so long?" I thought. "They've surely decided that I'm not qualified to be a USIA officer. I must still be tired from the long trip, or else I'd have done much better."

These thoughts were interrupted by the gray-haired man whom I had met when I first came into the office. As he approached me he was smiling.

"Congratulations! The panel has approved you for our training program. You did very well," he said, extending his hand and shaking my hand vigorously. I was not sure that this wasn't all a dream.

"They were particularly impressed that you would fly all the way here from Madrid at your own expense to be interviewed, and they weren't disappointed in meeting you and seeing how well you did in answering their questions."

I remained torn between reality and fantasy.

"Is this really happening to me?" I mused. "This must be a dream. How could they possibly think that I did so well when I was so sure that I did poorly?" It was hard to shake the thought that I would probably wake up tomorrow back in Madrid with my new-found friends, and find myself rushing across town in those old Spanish cabs, trying to get to the bullfights on time.

The training program for "junior officer trainees" (JOTs) of the United States Information Agency consisted of one month at USIA headquarters in Washington and eleven months at an overseas embassy. The Washington part of the training was a whirlwind course which introduced the novices to the mysteries of the American government bureaucracy and the mission of USIA. As difficult as it was to understand the workings of the bureaucracy, learning the mission of USIA, though more exciting, was even more of a challenge. USIA had just been created the year before. Exactly what its mission should be and how it was to go about accomplishing that mission were to be debated in the Congress and through various administrations for at least the next two decades.

On my first day at the prestigious address of "1776 Pennsylvania Ave. N.W.," I met the eight other trainees who comprised "JOT Class 2" and with whom I would spend the next two months of intensive training. Three of the "JOTs" were women, and none was over the age limit of thirty-one, a rule which, like so many others, would be abolished in later years.

The nine trainees came from diverse backgrounds. Their new careers, while they lasted, would be equally diverse. I still believed that my first overseas assignment would surely be Spain and that before long I would again be making the rounds of my favorite Madrid haunts, on and off the Gran Via.

USIA investment in two of the three women in my class was ill fated. One was sent to a Western European country for her overseas training. She had hardly completed it when she married a State Department officer whom she met at the embassy to which she was assigned, and had to leave the Service. The U.S. Foreign Service had not yet accepted the concept of "tandem couples," where both the wife and the husband could be Foreign Service officers. The other equally attractive female member of my junior officer training class, assigned to a Latin American post, met a local medical doctor, married him, but shortly thereafter contracted a disease which her Christian Science upbringing prohibited her from treating with modern medicines. She left the Foreign Service to return home, and her husband left her, perhaps because she refused to take his medical advice. The third woman in the class was older, a lawyer, and went on to a presumably satisfying career for many years, serving mainly in the Far East, until, after a few decades, she went on to other things.

The histories of the five other men in my class can be told in a few words which is no reflection on their merits or the value of their contribution to USIA. One, for example, served at a number of posts, but when his mother-in-law, who was a child psychologist, convinced her daughter that the foreign service is no place to raise children, his wife returned home to mama with their two small children, presumably in order to raise the children in the approved child psychology methods of that era. Needless to say the breakup of his family distracted his concentration on his career.

Another member of USIA's second JOT class was to continue to cross my path for the rest of our careers. Eighteen months after our first meeting in Washington and after we both had completed our overseas training programs, he replaced me as a public affairs assistant. He served the agency in Asia, Europe and South America, and then was placed by USIA's management into an untenable position that forced him to resign. Soon after his marriage to an American girl he had met when stationed in Caracas, he was slated to be sent immediately to Zaire [now Democratic Republic of the Congo] at a moment in history when world attention was focused on that country. Zaire, the former Belgian Congo, was in the throes of post-independence convulsions. White women had become an endangered species; the raping and murder of some European nuns having made the headlines in the American media during the weeks just prior to my classmate's wedding. Thus he was faced with the dilemma of either leaving his new bride behind, or taking her with him to that fabled land where the fable had soured. USIA officials also faced a dilemma when he asked, under the circumstances, to go to another corner of the globe. But the Agency's personnel management took the view that if his assignment were cancelled, others might justifiably ask for similar treatment, and in those days a Foreign Service officer was expected to be available for service anywhere in the world. Twenty years later that stipulation would be followed at times more in the breach than in practice. In the mid-sixties, however, when ordered to fulfill his assignment or resign, he believed he had no option but to resign, which he did.

Another colleague was a Norwegian-American from Minnesota, a bachelor like me but one who had a sharp eye for good real estate investments. One of his favorite topics among his fellow trainees was how he was going to become wealthy by investing in old townhouses on Capitol Hill, have them repaired, and rent or sell them for a considerable profit. In this he probably was right, as the surge to renovate that area close to the nation's capitol building was, in 1953, just beginning. Capitol Hill is unique for being one of those relatively few neighborhoods, a part of which, once inhabited mainly by American blacks who were living on or below the poverty line, was eventually reclaimed and rejuvenated by relatively wealthy whites. Twenty years later the transition was almost complete, and forty years later it was a racially mixed community, but one which, despite its proximity to the U.S. Congress, shares some of the dangers common to the inner cities of most American urban communities.

His overseas training assignment was Oslo. After that choice tour of duty he was sent half-way around to the world to Laos. There he performed well, but Laotian law and the rules of his own government brought about his fall from grace. He had already left the country and was en route home for his end of tour leave when an untoward incident, which adversely affected his career, occurred at dockside in Vientiane. A river steamer was loading his household effects which were to be shipped back to Washington, his next assignment, when one of the crates containing his worldly goods slipped in its cradle and fell to the ground, split open, and some cartons fell out onto the wharf.

Several of the cartons now on the pier appeared to be liquor cases. This raised the curiosity of the U.S. government inspector who was present and who, in exercising his prerogative, requested that those cases be opened in order to examine their contents, since U.S. government employees, like their fellow citizens, must declare any sizable shipments of alcohol to the U.S. for tax purposes. To the surprise of the inspector, what were uncovered were not bottles of brandy or other alcoholic beverages, but, mixed with sundry other things were two ancient Laotian pistols! This discovery took my colleague out of the frying pan into the fire. Laotian officials had long professed grave concern about the loss of Laotian antiques, so shipment out of their country without a permit of anything in that category was considered by them to be a heinous crime. The Laotian inspector present confiscated the pistols, and the next day the U.S. ambassador was called to the Foreign Office to explain the affair. Needless to say, our colleague's career was not enhanced by this incident. This may have been what influenced his decision to leave the agency, or it might have been that his Capitol Hill investments had become too important to him to handle from abroad. In any event, another Foreign Service career ended abruptly.

Another of my classmates, like a few others in "JOT Class 2," was a Californian. (It was still a time in American history that whenever two Californians met, no matter where, they considered themselves blood brothers or sisters and would exchange praises about the paradise they left behind.) In later years it was said that his hair turned gray because of the heavy responsibilities of a Foreign Service officer, but that's not true because, as a JOT, just starting out in the Foreign Service, his hair was already gray. This, combined with a serious mien, gave him status and a certain amount of prestige among his peers as they looked upon him as being older and, therefore, presumably wiser. He was sent on his first assignment to the Far East, found both the Foreign Service and the exotic East to his liking, and thus had a long and generally satisfying career with USIA. His career might have lasted even longer if, more than two decades later, one of the directors of USIA had not been influenced by Secretary of State Henry Kissinger's "GLOP" Program.

For a Foreign Service officer to be "glopped" during Kissinger's tenure as Secretary of State was to be transferred from one geographic area, where years of study, language capability, and experience had been developed, to another where the culture and the language often had to be learned from scratch. The idea behind the "Global Outlook Program," from which the term "GLOP" was derived, was to broaden the views and experience of career officers and to bring new ideas to the different geographic areas where U.S. interests are represented. In this case, after about twenty-five years of specialization in Far Eastern affairs, my former JOT colleague was ordered to learn Portuguese and was sent to Brazil. The place, the language, and the timing were all factors sufficiently strong, taken together, to convince him that the time had come to retire from USIA, though he would gladly have continued his career for many more years had his superiors continued to take advantage of his broad knowledge of, and experience in, the Far East. Of course, after he and others were adversely affected and the Kissinger era ended, "glopping" became passé. Some officers may have benefited from being "glopped" and the State Department and USIA effectiveness may have been enhanced in some instances, but in this instance the "glop" convinced this highly capable USIA officer that it was time to terminate his foreign service career. He was probably among a number of experienced, qualified Foreign Service officers lost to the U.S. government because of the "glop."

The ninth member of this historic class was a young, handsome, but very quiet man and his career was equally quiet. After a few years and a few assignments, he decided that life in the foreign service was not the lifestyle for him, so he resigned.

The four weeks of intensive training passed rapidly and the information we were expected to absorb was almost overwhelming. The alphabet soup of the Washington bureaucracy was thrown at the trainees as they were exposed to the great variety of activities that USIA conducts. There were sessions about the mission of USIA; the "wireless file;" the educational and cultural exchange programs, including the famous Fulbright Program; the functioning of the Voice of America and the Motion Picture Service of the Agency; the importance of "personal contact;" security concerns; and a myriad of administrative matters, some knowledge of which is necessary, they were told, "if you are to survive the moves back and forth between the U.S. and foreign cultures."

At the end of the training period, the great day came when individual country assignments were to be announced. While it was known that our assignments could be any place on the globe where the U.S. maintains diplomatic relations, I continued to believe that there was only one place where I would surely be sent, given my three-month sojourn in Spain, especially since Agency officials were fully aware of my experience there.

It was November 20th, 1954, when the phone rang at the house in the Washington suburbs that I was sharing with six other bachelors I had known from my navy days. The phone call was from my training officer.

"Congratulations Al! You've been assigned to Caracas!"

When I recovered from the shock enough to speak, I said, "But why do we have a USIA operation there? Isn't that a small Dutch island off the north coast of South America? What does USIA do in such a small place?" I asked with noticeable disappointment in my voice.

Now it was the training officer's moment to sound perplexed, as he replied, "But that's a very important country these days from a foreign policy viewpoint." There was silence on both ends of the line, and then I heard, "Say, you're not thinking of the Dutch island of Curaçao, are you? That isn't where you're being assigned. It's Caracas, the capital of Venezuela."

"Oh, I guess I misunderstood," I answered, but my voice could not hide my disappointment at the thought of being assigned to a post in South America, where I would be even farther from Spain and my friends than I was right now. Surely fate was conspiring against me by sending me off to a country about which I knew absolutely nothing. But if that's the way the ball bounces, I reflected, I suppose that I'll have to bounce with it. In the navy when faced with diversity, I had learned to say "T.S." and to move forward to do whatever was required under the circumstances. In the Foreign Service the same philosophy would have to apply at times, and this seemed to be one of those times.

There was very little time left before the members of "JOT Class 2" would split up and head for their overseas assignments. Part of this time was devoted to learning about the country and area where one was headed. Knowing little or nothing about Venezuela, I was now resigned to my fate and took very seriously the concept of learning everything possible about the country I had been assigned. This intensified research and the paper I produced as a result made me such a walking, talking expert on Venezuelan statistics that I would soon astound my new colleagues in Caracas shortly after my arrival, for few of them, busy at their respective jobs, had the time or inclination to become walking encyclopedias of the host country.

When the day of departure arrived, I was ready for the big adventure which was about to begin. I and my fellow JOTs, confident, excited, and having been exposed to the delights as well as the dangers of being a part of the American government's bureaucracy, were ready to take on the world, or at least that part of it where we were being sent.

If any of us experienced some trepidation at the thought of going abroad to officially represent our country for the first time, we didn't show it. We were all smart enough to know that we had much to learn in our new profession and in our new environments, but young enough to enjoy the excitement and the challenges the Foreign Service had to offer. Though still disappointed at the fact that I was going south instead of east, I would find that my new job, a new environment, and a girl named Charmaine would gradually eliminate my immediate interest in Spain.

2
Calypso in Caracas

"The young Foreign Service officer, full of uncertainty about himself and wonderment about everything else, was not the same man as he was (later in life)..."
—George F. Kennan, *The Last Wise Man, Sketches From A Life*

"If a Venezuelan is a friend of yours,
he'll give you the shirt off his back."

"It's the same foreigner with a different clay pipe."
—Venezuelan proverbs

As my plane landed at Maiquetia airport on the Caribbean coast, about twenty miles north of the Venezuelan capital, I was thrilled and excited. The thought of living and working in a new, strange country in a job that promised to be as interesting as it would be satisfying, made me think of how fortunate I was.

Venezuela was, as it had been for many years, a military dictatorship. The country had been the private fiefdom of Dictator Juan Vicente Gómez for twenty-seven years, from 1908 to 1935, and although Venezuelans experimented occasionally with elected representatives after the Gómez era, military coups and political assassinations had taken their toll. For the previous two years a military man was again in charge. President Marcos Pérez Jiménez, an army colonel who had led the latest successful coup, was known to all Venezuelans as "P. J." He was not a charismatic leader, being short in stature and not particularly attractive, but he and his army cohorts controlled the guns, and thus the government, and he was credited in his relatively short reign at the time with creating the economic boom the country was then experiencing.

As I stepped out onto the hot, sunbathed tarmac of the airport, my attention was drawn to the startling beauty of the nearby verdant foothills of the Andes. The lush green tropical forest, glistening in the sunlight, was just a stone's throw from the airport runways. The march to the sea of the Andean hills seemed to have stopped just far enough from the coastline to allow the airport to be built at that spot, though not without bulldozing a few hills whose scars were still evident. Also attracting my attention was the presence of a number of heavily armed soldiers near our plane and at various points around the airport.

"What threat to Venezuela is so imminent," I wondered, "as to require armed guards to be posted all over the place?" My musings were interrupted by the hearty "hello" and handshake of Harry Kendall, who greeted me just as I was about to enter the terminal building.

"Welcome to Venezuela," Kendall beamed, looking directly at me and extending his right hand in welcome. He quickly surmised from my appearance that I was the young and eager "JOT" he had come to the airport to meet. I would soon learn that he was a Cajun from Louisiana and a former newsman who now, as a USIS[1] officer, was the embassy's hardworking, personable press attaché. Kendall would quickly become my mentor in the art of "public diplomacy." My diplomatic passport and the friendship that seemed to exist between Kendall and the airport officials expedited the airport clearance procedures. "Or perhaps," I reflected, "the speed of my exit from the airport is an example of the well-known efficiency of dictatorships." But I soon dismissed this reflection as I noted the noise and chaotic appearance of hundreds of travelers milling about, some looking for lost luggage or friends and relatives, a scene hardly warranting confidence in the way in which Maiquetia Airport was organized and managed.

Kendall introduced me to Juan, the USIS driver, who then rushed off to bring the car from the parking lot to the platform where my baggage had been deposited. In a few minutes we were speeding up the *autopista*, one of P.J.'s most notable legacies to his country. The autopista, truly an engineering feat of the first magnitude, is a four-lane highway built in the Andean mountains to carry traffic between the coast, where the airport, the harbor, and numerous beach resorts are located, and the 3500-feet high mountain valley in which Caracas is nestled. While the distance between the airport and the capital is only about twenty miles, the challenge for the road builders was the pristine ruggedness of the terrain, conquered only by constructing numerous tunnels and bridges. Surrounding this modern technological feat, which the highway represented, are the stark, rugged, green-covered mountains through which the road wends in its steep rise to Venezuela's capital city. Before the autopista was built, this trip took up to three hours on an old, narrow, two-lane road, which wound itself endlessly through the coastal range that separates Caracas from the sea.

Juan said little as we hurtled up incline after incline, passing more than a few cars and only occasionally being passed by still-faster vehicles. It was clear that he was keeping the accelerator on the floorboard. Juan was typical of many USIS drivers I would meet in the years ahead—almost all of them drove as if they had to catch a plane, even when leaving the airport. What little he spoke was difficult for me to understand since many *Caraqueños,* like their English-speaking cousins around the Caribbean, tend to clip their words.

"Well, here's your hotel," Kendall announced as we arrived in front of a five-story building in the San Bernardino section of Caracas.

"The Hotel Potomac—makes me feel at home," I replied, thinking of the river of the same name which borders Washington, D.C. Kendall laughed. "Not 'Po-toem-ick.' Here it's pronounced 'Poe-toe-mack,' with the accent on the last syllable."

After the baggage was unloaded and I signed the register, Kendall explained the virtues and pitfalls of a few nearby restaurants and how to get from the hotel to the U.S. Embassy, located a few blocks away. He gave me some phone numbers to call in case of any difficulties, said he would see me in the office in the morning, again told me how welcomed I was here since there was more work to do then a three-man USIS post and one secretary could handle, and asked his leave as he thought I would want to retire after the long flight. Thus began the Venezuelan adventure that was to change my life.

Early the next morning I had breakfast in the hotel and, with great anticipation, walked the few blocks to the embassy. San Bernardino, the neighborhood where the U.S. chancery was located, was predominantly a residential area with scattered neighborhood stores and eating-places. Caracas had about one million inhabitants and was experiencing a building boom stimulated by Venezuela's burgeoning oil wealth. It was also experiencing a population boom, both from rural migration to the capital and an influx of Italian and Spanish workers. Many Italians emigrated from Italy thinking that by getting to South America, and thus being geographically closer to the United States, they would be able to get into the U.S. more easily. This was not the case, but Italy and America's loss was Venezuela's gain, for most of the Italian immigrants and their children became hardworking Venezuelan citizens who contributed greatly to national growth during the following few decades (as did the Spaniards, though they seemed to be greatly outnumbered by the Italians.)

Venezuela even today is an underpopulated country, with large, sparsely settled mountains and plains; thus immigrants were welcomed. Its capital city, however, located in a beautiful though narrow, elongated valley bordered by green, tree-covered slopes on both sides, was limited in its growth by the steep sides of the valley.

The valley runs in an easterly-westerly direction. Its northern side is much more precipitous than the southern one. It is the northern mountain range which has to be crossed to reach the Caribbean coast where the international airport is located. This was why the construction of a super, four-lane highway—the autopista, from the city to the airport and its neighboring coastal towns, was such an important achievement. In later years the solution to the growth problem facing Caracas was found by bulldozing the tops of some of the hills on the valley's southern side, and by building vertically. The steep inclines surrounding the city in the north were left for the poor. Not infrequently, during the rainy season, the huts and shacks on the steep, northern slope are swept away, some of their owners with them.

Despite its tropical location, the altitude of Caracas provides the city with an ideal climate. Seldom is it too cold in the winter or too hot in the summer. The combination of the bright blue tropical sky, brilliant white cumulus clouds, and dark greens of the towering mountains, which hover over the city, provides views never to be forgotten.

As I walked to the embassy I was filled with awe at the beauty of this city in the mountains where the air was so clear and fresh. I felt inspired and excited at the thought that I was about to begin my career as a representative of my country in a foreign land!

The embassy was a five-story building built to be an apartment house but now used as the U.S. chancery. Next door was a small, one-family house, painted green with vanilla trim, where the USIS press office run by Harry Kendall was located.

At the entrance to the embassy I was stopped by a Marine guard who asked for my identification and then directed me to the second floor office of the public affairs officer (PAO). Here I was greeted by George Butler, the Director of USIS (the PAO), a thin, wiry, red-headed man in his late forties who ushered me into his office and, as had Kendall the day before, expressed his delight that USIS Caracas now had a JOT on board.

"There'll be plenty of work for you to do and we'll try to see that you don't get bored," he said with a smile.

"What I want you to do first is to get settled in—take all the time you need, find a place to live, get your administrative matters taken care of, and then you'll be ready to work full time. I'm going to put Harry Kendall in charge of your program. You'll start on the information side, then work with the cultural affairs officer (CAO), and then get into administration. I want you to learn everything from the bottom up, including the files. Now I want you to meet the rest of the staff."

He pressed a buzzer on his desk and his secretary appeared at the door. She was Rose Capachione, a pleasant, Italian-American woman who was in her late twenties. A few minutes later Andy Wilkinson, the CAO, came into the PAO's office and we exchanged greetings. A smiling, hypo-energetic, cultured man, warm-hearted and sincere, he was everyone's friend and enjoyed to the hilt his role as the guardian and propagator of American culture in Venezuela. The personalities and philosophies of the PAO and the CAO were so different that they were bound to hold divergent views as to what USIS should be doing and how. The PAO, cool, efficient, and politically savvy, was most at home on the information side of USIS activities. As an experienced TV producer before joining USIA, he personally created one of the first locally produced television programs of any USIS post. It was also the first educational TV program to be shown on Venezuela's new (and only) TV channel. He not only produced the program but personally directed it as well, until he was able to train someone else to take over.

The CAO, as noted above, was a warmhearted and gentle person, willing to help anyone who asked for his help. Thus any request, regardless of its uniqueness, but which to him appeared to be of merit, would find a sympathetic response. One such request came from an American citizen who had written a letter to the ambassador and which, like most unique requests sent to the U.S. Embassy in Caracas, eventually found its way to the in-basket of the CAO.

"Dear Ambassador," the letter stated, "I have a hobby of collecting soil from the birthplaces of famous people. Could you please send me some soil from the birthplace of The Great Liberator, Simón Bolívar?" The letter was signed by a presumably elderly woman from a small town in Nebraska. While filling out some papers in Rose Capachione's office, I overheard the PAO and CAO discussing this somewhat strange request from a lady in Nebraska.

"Where were you all yesterday morning?" Butler asked Wilkinson.

"I needed you here and no one knew where you were."

"Well," Wilkinson answered, "I was trying to get permission from the Venezuelan authorities to take a little dirt from Bolívar's birthplace to fill the request made in this letter that came in." Butler fussed and fumed. "Andy, how can you spend your time like that? You have more important things to do. If you have to answer that damn letter, why not just go outside and pick up some dirt in the street and put it in the envelope? She'll never know the difference."

It was time to go next door and meet the staff of the information section, all of whom worked under the supervision of the Information officer, Harry Kendall. To reach that office one had to go out the front door of the embassy and walk around the building, through the garden, and into the yard of the house next door. In rainy weather, and especially during the heavy tropical downpours which occurred during the rainy season, rain gear was needed to survive the journey. One USIS Officer wanted to buy an umbrella for the office for these frequent expeditions to and from the chancery, but he was unable to convince the embassy administrator who had to approve such purchases that this was a legitimate government expense.

A young, attractive blonde greeted me in the downstairs reception hall. She introduced herself as Harry Kendall's secretary. She was from Canada and taught English part-time at the Venezuelan-American Cultural Center in Caracas. Since only one American secretary was assigned to each small or medium-sized USIS post, and since Venezuelans with a good knowledge of English willing to work at such jobs were hard to find, she was hired when she showed up one day looking for work. Caracas was, in fact, a haven for expatriates looking for employment overseas. The living was easy, there were good-paying jobs in many different fields in the expanding, oil-based economy, and the combination of city life in the capital and the easy accessibility of the mountains and the sea were great enticements to the young and adventurous, both men and women. Thus Venezuela in the mid-fifties was, for many, a "land of opportunity."

She guided me upstairs to the master bedroom, which was now part of the information section of USIS. Here I met the press chief, Aristides Moleon, and his assistant. Moleon, an Argentine journalist distressed with the current Argentine president, Perón, had left Buenos Aires to seek his fortune, as did many others, in booming Caracas.

The information section received news stories, backgrounders, and feature articles from USIA Washington on a wireless teletype, the antenna for which was a prominent feature on the roof of the embassy building next door. Whenever Moleon, a highly talented journalist, discovered a passing reference to Venezuela in the daily file, he would rewrite the article to highlight the local angle before sending it to the local press. As a result he often had the satisfaction of seeing his rewritten stories on the front pages of the leading local dailies.

One such story which was received on USIA's "Latin American file," and which made the front pages, was a backgrounder on the peaceful uses of atomic energy, a highly popular subject at the time. Buried in the article were a few lines which noted that the Caracas medical center was among the institutions which would soon receive radio isotopes from the U.S. for medical research. This became Moleon's lead with the result that every major daily newspaper in the capital used it as a front-page story the next morning, some making it the major story of the day. Needless to say, such talent was greatly appreciated by his superiors, and helped the American officers at USIS to demonstrate to Washington how well they were doing their job. This story had particular significance for USIS since peaceful uses of atomic energy was a major U.S. foreign policy theme at that time.

I spent the first three months learning the techniques of USIS press operations as patiently taught to me by Kendall and Moleon. Except for PAO Butler's personal television production, a field in which USIS became heavily involved only much later as television grew in importance, Kendall supervised all other "information activities". The USIS motion picture operation, for example, was a major activity with many 16mm films from the USIS film library constantly placed on loan to Venezuelan schools and institutions. There were also two mobile motion picture units that carried portable electric generators for visits to towns and villages throughout the country, many of which did not have their own dependable electrical supply. In some villages these showings, often presented in the main square of the town, became the big event of the week, although what impact they had on village life other than to provide entertainment continued to be debated among USIS officers for many years. When television came into its own the debate ended, for so did the mobile unit programs.

Another element supervised by Kendall was the post's radio section, which, like its film section, was an extremely busy activity. As Jorge Luis Borges, the Argentine writer and philosopher once remarked, "English is the language of literature; Spanish the language of real life." Real life is talking, and radio is the talking medium. Certainly Latin Americans love to talk, and their language enables them to say almost anything in more different ways, and in a longer time, than comparable thoughts in English. Their love for the spoken language may be why even the smallest of Latin American countries is inundated with radio stations. Venezuela in the fifties was no exception. The numerous stations, hungry for suitable programs, were easily fed by taped *Voice of America* programs distributed by USIS. The post also produced a few of its own programs, including a weekly news feature highlighted on about thirty stations. The producer, a dynamic young Venezuelan named Renny Ottolina, later made good use of experience gained producing USIS shows for radio and television. He went on to wealth and fame as "Mr. TV" of Venezuela, until his tragic death in a jungle plane crash at the height of his professional career.

A woman in her late twenties whom I shall call "Maria," was in charge of the USIS radio section. Dark-haired, attractive, but ultra-serious, she was entirely dedicated to her job as the supervisor and controller of the post's taped radio programs. She maintained an elaborate accounting system for the hundreds of taped programs which were loaned to radio stations throughout the country, more than fifteen stations in Caracas alone, and she kept in contact with dozens of radio station managers and program managers, cajoling them when necessary to return USIS tapes after the programs on them had been aired. Her intense devotion to her work may have been due to her efforts to cope with her husband's accidental death about a year prior to my arrival in Caracas. In the tradition of old Spain, she wore black as a symbol of mourning, although not for the customary weeks, months, or even one year. As the years passed friends tried to influence her to place her emphasis on the living and the future, but she continued to dress only in black as she carried out her role as a "mourning widow" for more than a decade. She is "mas papa que el papa" (more like the Pope than the Pope) said one of her friends, commenting on how this attractive woman held on to tradition while the world around her was rapidly changing. However, "Maria" was an excellent and effective supervisor of the post's extensive radio programming.

My introduction to USIS press, radio, and motion picture operations in an environment highly receptive to USIS information programs was a fascinating and exciting experience. My enthusiasm was unbounded, for almost daily I could see or hear the results of the information activities produced under Kendall's overall direction and in which I was participating. Interesting as this was, I had to heed the PAO's words, "Get settled, find a place to live." So I began my search for suitable living quarters "appropriate for a vice consul of the United States government."

I soon learned that the search for housing in Caracas was not going to be easy. The embassy housing office offered a few leads, but my best chance of finding a suitable place to live that was not too distant from the embassy, was to trudge from building to building throughout San Bernardino and to visit the few apartments I learned about through the local newspapers or by word-of-mouth. More than a month passed and hotel living was getting stale when I chanced upon an apartment within walking distance of the embassy. Since I had no car, and public transportation was terrible, being able to walk to the office was an important asset. Furthermore, it was within my small housing allowance as an unmarried junior officer.

The apartment was on the second floor of a new, rather narrow building. Downstairs on the ground floor was a butcher shop. The smells from the shop occasionally reached the balcony of the apartment, but except for this minor distraction, it was suited to my needs and my pocketbook. The balcony was large, even if the living room and the single bedroom were tiny. The kitchenette had a counter which could also serve as a bar, and among the apartment's attractions was a separate entrance on the ground floor next to the butcher shop. It consisted of a winding outdoor staircase used to reach the second floor. All in all, I thought the place was quite exotic.

"It will be great for parties," I surmised, except in inclement weather when I would be unable to use the large, uncovered balcony which faced the street and was as wide as the building. Most of the time, though, the balcony would provide plenty of room for the large number of guests I hoped to entertain once I was settled.

It was because of this apartment, into which I moved a few weeks later, that I met Charmaine Rostant and, once again, my future took a radical turn. Charmaine was a friend of an adventurous American woman, Marie Tilley, who was about to vacate the apartment. She was a woman with some claim to fame in local circles. Typical of the adventurous types drawn to the frontier atmosphere of Venezuela in the 1950s, Tilley worked for an American firm in Caracas but her real purpose for being in Venezuela was to partake of adventure on the frontier. She had recently been featured in the local press as "the first white woman ever to reach the base of Angel Falls."

Angel Falls, the largest waterfalls in the world, was discovered in the mid-1930s deep in the jungle of southeast Venezuela by American bush pilot Jimmy Angel. With two Indians and a local guide to help carry her canoe over various rapids as she went up the Caroni River south of Ciudad Bolívar, after more than a week of canoeing and walking, Marie Tilley managed to reach the bottom of the escarpment where the waters of Angel Falls plunge into the jungle after plummeting in a steady stream more than three thousand feet. She returned safely to Caracas with spectacular photos, some of which the local press printed with articles describing her exploits. After that adventure, and having spent seven years in Venezuela, she decided to return to the U.S. Because of her imminent departure from Caracas, I would soon be able to move into her old apartment and, not long thereafter, because she introduced me to a friend from Trinidad, I would soon also acquire a wife.

As I prepared to move into my new living quarters, my work and training at USIS went on. After my exposure to the information section I worked for a few months in the cultural section under the supervision of CAO Andy Wilkinson. Here I learned how USIS exhibits were handled, how American performing artists were programmed, how educational exchange programs were administered, and I had my first contact with the "*Centro Venezolano-Americano*," the binational cultural center which received financial grants and other support from USIS.

Prior to the arrival of a new center director six months earlier, the center was the scene of some strange and spectacular events. The librarian had been murdered, her body found a week later in the outskirts of the city. There were also dark rumors that involved questionable financial dealings and sex scandals. When the new director, Melvin Niswander, arrived, it was said that he had "an easy act to follow." Under his direction the center, whose main source of income came from funds generated by the teaching of English, thrived and expanded. The scandals of an earlier era disappeared into history. Instrumental in changing the image of the center was not only the assignment of a new director but a change of venue from an old, dilapidated, downtown building in the colonial section of Caracas to a bright, new building in the expanding eastern section of the city.

By any standard the "Centro Venezolano-Americano" was an orphan as far as USIS was concerned. USIA policy with regard to such centers was such in those days that JOTS like me knew little if anything about them until arriving overseas. Even then I and most other JOTS at the time were never sure as to how closely associated these centers were or should be with USIS. They were run by boards of directors, half of the members being local nationals and the rest resident Americans, often including the PAO or CAO. Control was never vested in USIS, although USIS provided funding and other support, including grants for American directors and, at some large centers, an American director of courses. Later USIS officers would become directors of many larger centers. The goal of these centers, to foster mutual understanding between the U.S. and the host country, through cultural programs and the teaching of English as a second language, clearly served USIS objectives, a fact fully acknowledged by many USIA officials only as the Agency matured.

With some cultural affairs experience under my belt, my next training assignment was to learn about the administration of the post: such things as budget considerations, personnel matters, and expenditure of funds. Also during this period one of the highlights for a young JOT was an invitation to lunch one day with Ambassador Fletcher Warren and his wife. As the sole guest, I was much impressed and concluded that the chief of mission was, after all, a human being. I also assisted in the arrangements for a press conference of a visiting U.S. cabinet officer, Secretary of Agriculture Ezra Taft Benson. My minor involvement on that occasion was the first of what were to be many press conferences of distinguished or well-known Americans that I would attend, and often direct, in the years ahead. Accompanying a senior Agency official, James Opsata, on a visit to the branch post in Maracaibo as part of a routine inspection of USIS operations in Venezuela, was also a highlight, as was a series of meetings with a "Washington wheel," USIA's Latin American area director who flew into Caracas for consultations with the PAO. This was heady stuff for a JOT, as were the meetings with the movers and shakers of Venezuelan public opinion—newspaper editors, radio station managers, government officials and leading educators, among others.

I moved into my new apartment a few weeks later. The tall, thin, black maid who had cleaned the apartment for Marie Tilley agreed to work for me a few days each week. Though there were a few things I had to buy, my new living quarters were partially furnished so it did not take long before I was ready to host my first party, slated to be a personal rather than an "official" affair.

The "singles" in Caracas who were from abroad were of differing nationalities and backgrounds and were there to make money, for adventure, or because they had been assigned to Venezuela by their government or company. They soon managed to find each other as the foreign community was still relatively small, the recreational areas in the city limited, and congeniality flourished.

The group of young people that I spent most of my recreational time with had one thing in common: they were all "Musius." A "Musiu" in the Venezuelan lexicon is a foreigner. It was not long before the

"Musius" with whom I associated most frequently and who shared my youthful interest in partying and adventurous expeditions to the beaches and the mountainous hinterlands began calling themselves "The Musiu Gang." Occasionally a Venezuelan youth would join us, but this was infrequent despite the popular local saying that "When a Venezuelan is your friend, he will give you the shirt off his back." I couldn't help but reflect each time I heard this, which was often, "What friend wouldn't?"

Venezuelans, even younger Venezuelans, were difficult to get to know, probably because their country in the early 1950s was still a nation suffering from a lack of identity. The early Spanish invaders, with no knowledge of the black gold that Venezuela possessed, went elsewhere in search of real gold, leaving Venezuela as a backwater province. Even with later immigrants from Europe it remained only slightly populated compared with many other Latin American countries. It was even less populated by indigenous Indian tribes, all of which were so small that they lacked any impetus for cultural change, thus they maintained their primitive ways well into the modern era.

In the south, in the state of Bolívar and the Amazon region, native Indians still poisoned their arrows and lived much as they did centuries before. In the west, where the border with Colombia meant nothing to them, the "Motilones" occasionally murdered oil prospectors who approached their camps in the "Sierra de Perija," not far from the booming oil city of Maracaibo. In Maracaibo itself, the less ferocious Guajira Indians, while frequently seen on city streets, still clung to their traditional ways in such things as painting the faces of their women to indicate their marital status (black for widows, red for virgins). So neither from the indigenous culture, nor from the culture superimposed upon them by the Spanish *conquistadores,* did the modern Venezuelan have a cultural nail on which to hang his hat. The result was that the camaraderie which comes natural to people who believe, whether true or not, that they are equal to all other nationalities, was difficult for many Venezuelans.

While they had one great national hero, Simón Bolívar, this was not enough, apparently, to overcome a sense of cultural inferiority that permeated Venezuelan society in the first half of the twentieth century. This would eventually change somewhat when Venezuelans as a people overcame tremendous odds to adopt a more democratic society. Their courageous stand to grasp and hold a democratic form of government against Castro-inspired threats in the 1960s gave them a degree of pride not obtained earlier, but which is required to meet strangers as equals. And while the discovery of oil in the 1920s provided the country with wealth far beyond that of most of its neighbors, wealth alone is no guarantor of cultural equanimity. In short, Venezuelans, at least young Venezuelans, were difficult for young foreigners to get to know, so those with whom I found recreational rapport were, for the most part, fellow "Musius." Professional contacts that I established were, of course, a different ball game.

As the Musiu Gang expanded, there was never a shortage of volunteers to join expeditions to the nearby beaches and mountains on weekends and holidays, or for impromptu partying. There were soon more than a dozen "regulars" who were almost always ready to leave Caracas for a weekend or a few days to explore other parts of Venezuela. Members of the gang included two girls from the Canadian Embassy; two Swiss boys who provided entree to the Caracas Swiss Club, a favored watering hole, and an Argentine who was the Lucky Strike representative in Venezuela. Also in the "gang" was a young Dutchman who was the Heineken representative in Caracas and who led us through many a "Heineken Club" tour, which consisted of having a Heineken "on the house" at each of four bars before settling down in the fifth one for the evening. Others included a girl from the British Embassy who was later to marry a young member of the gang from St. Maartin, the latter being greatly adept at composing and singing calypsos and whose guitar playing and singing enlightened many a Musiu gathering; an American woman lawyer who later married a Norwegian businessman from the gang; a Spaniard who later married an American girl who was in Venezuela on a painting scholarship; an American accountant with one of the oil companies; and a French girl from the French Embassy. In addition to these stalwarts of the Musiu Gang expeditions, there were an assorted number of other Britishers, Canadians, and Americans who came and went depending on events. There also were two girls from the Caribbean island of Trinidad, one of whom was Charmaine Rostant.

Almost every weekend became a time for adventurous journeys to the Caribbean beaches, most of which were now only an hour away on the autopista or into the mountains. The one-day expeditions usually ended back in Caracas at someone's house or apartment where a "farewell party" was held—farewell until next weekend. The house where the Marine guards of the embassy lived was also a popular meeting place for singles since there always seemed to be a party going on there anyway, or one could easily be started.

One memorable weekend the Musiu Gang went to Chichirevichi, a Caribbean beach that was well off the beaten track. Chichirevichi was an idyllic tropical paradise, accessible only by driving for three or four hours over a torturously narrow, unpaved mountain road and through jungle landscape at the approaches to the beach. Except for a few fishermen, the Musius had the entire expanse of white, sparkling beach to themselves. Numerous swaying palm trees a hundred yards or so from the water's edge provided shade. It was the perfect place to hang hammocks and set up camp. The whole scene was enveloped by a bright blue tropical sky punctuated by startling white cumulus clouds. With the soft greens and blue of the sea in front and the dark greens of the jungle jostling the mountains to the south, this was as romantic a spot as any Musiu would ever see.

We pitched camp, which meant putting up our *chinchorros* (hammocks) among the palm trees, covering them with mosquito netting, and building cooking fires. An unwritten rule had been accepted by all—the men were to provide the transportation for this expedition; the women were to provide the food, enough to feed at least one guy. It was then that I learned for the first time what a good provider and cook Charmaine Rostant was, for she had agreed to supply the food for me, the thin young American from the U.S. Embassy who always looked like he could use a square meal.

One of the Swiss boys, Frank, had been "assigned" to Mary, an American secretary at the embassy. It soon became obvious that Mary was not well versed in the frying of eggs or other cooking chores. Aside from this lack of cooking talent, when Charmaine saw the pittance Mary provided her dinner guest, she felt sorry for Frank. She offered him some of her bounteous supply of meat and potatoes that evening at supper, and bacon and eggs at breakfast. I could not help but be impressed, not only at the quantity of food Charmaine brought with her on this overnight expedition, but her cooking abilities and her concern for the welfare of others. This was the beginning of an awakening in my mind that this young lady from Trinidad—while she might talk a bit differently than the British or the Americans, given her Trinidadian accent and sometimes colorful expressions—had qualities that set her apart from a great many others.

The first time I met Charmaine, I would often recall later, was when, on a lark, Marie Tilley (the woman who was vacating the apartment I would move into) invited her and me and other friends and acquaintances to go roller skating at Caracas's only outdoor rink. During a break in the skating we were all standing around chatting when the discussion turned to the ability to speak various languages. I could not resist saying, "Oh, I speak every language but Greek." Charmaine's reaction to this, she would tell me later, was "Oh my

God, another wise guy American showing off as usual," and she skated away. One of the Canadian girls, without giving the idea much thought, said, "Oh, really! Well, speak Ukrainian," to which I replied, "That's Greek to me," and skated off, chuckling to myself.

Charmaine and I became better acquainted after I learned that she was a member of the Caracas Sports Club. Actually, it was her sister and her sister's husband who were members. This enabled her to use the club's facilities. After learning this, tennis became the name of the game, for with Charmaine as my partner, I was able to play tennis at the club. The salary of a "JOT" would never have enabled me to join the capital's most exclusive club that welcomed foreigners. Neither of us were particularly good at tennis, but the game brought us together. I remained convinced for a long time that my only interest in her was as a tennis partner.

One day a Polish acquaintance of mine who also played tennis at the club was having a cup of coffee at the snack bar of the new eastern branch of the Venezuelan-American Cultural Center. I was also taking a coffee break after a visit to the center's director so I sat down at the same table and chatted with him.

"Who's that attractive girl I always see you playing tennis with at the club?" he asked.

"Oh, just a friend," I replied.

"She is really pretty," he said in a way that indicated that he really meant what he said.

"Do you think so? I really hadn't noticed, but now that you mention it, yes, she is pretty, isn't she?" I honestly hadn't thought along those lines earlier, but now that my Polish acquaintance mentioned it, I focused my attention on my tennis partner's appearance. "Yes, by God, I guess he's right," I thought. "Maybe I've had my mind too much on tennis."

In March of that year I learned that a Canadian Embassy official was about to be transferred to another country and was selling his car for $500, a good buy if the car ran all right. On my annual salary of about $4,000, that was about all I could afford. I examined the car, satisfied myself that it ran O.K., and became the proud owner of a small, four-door black Vauxhall, 1948 vintage. As the owner of a car my horizons were about to greatly expand. Where it was necessary to walk before, to bum a ride or take a bus, I would now be able to drive my own car. Things were looking up!

I had arrived in Caracas in November of 1954. By April I decided that I was ready for a small vacation and, if granted, I would use my leave to explore the interior of the country in my new car. I began to formulate a plan to drive from one end of Venezuela to the other, assuming the roads in the interior would enable me to do so. I estimated that to drive from Caracas, which is centrally located, and return to the capital from the eastern and western ends of the country, would take about fifteen days. In that underdeveloped nation, the roads could, of course, be a problem. But with the optimism of youth, and because fools rush in where angels fear to tread, I believed the roads would be a challenge, not a problem.

The trip from Caracas to Ciudad Bolívar, the major town in eastern Venezuela, could be made only by taking the highway that ran east-west across the Venezuelan *llanos*, the low-lying grassy plains which swept east from the foothills of the Andes to the Atlantic. This road was frequently washed out by torrential tropical rains. Such minor inconveniences, however, would not dampen my adventurous spirit or deter my determination to see Venezuela "from inside." All that was needed, in my view, were some companions to share the adventure, and the expenses. If all went well on the trip east, my plan was to return to Caracas in eight or nine days, then head west to Maracaibo. Looking at the map, this could easily be accomplished in a two-week period.

I began a diligent campaign within the Musiu Gang to get two or three persons to join me. Initially this campaign was unsuccessful. Many of the Musius professed a desire to share in such an adventure, but for one reason or another found it impossible to leave Caracas at that time, or for that length of time. I began to despair. Without companions it would be foolhardy to travel in the Venezuelan wilds, even if I could afford to do so financially. But just as I was about to give up all hope, there was a show of interest by a Trinidadian girl, Gloria Chandler, and the American art scholar, Joan Gold, although these glimmers of hope presented complications which would have to be faced if the trip was to succeed. Gloria could get enough vacation to go on only the eastern portion of the trip. As for Joan, she also could get away only for a week, and she wanted to go only to Maracaibo in the west. The solution, which seemed far from certain only a few days before the expedition was to begin, came when Charmaine decided to join the group, though she could not say why. She knew her friends and relatives would be shocked if they learned that she planned to travel with an American "youth" to the far corners of Venezuela, despite the presence of another woman. Yet Charmaine did agree to accompany Gloria and me on the trip to eastern Venezuela, and Joan and me on the western segment. So the trip was on, a trip which none of the participants would ever forget.

The day we left Caracas was like most days in Venezuela's capital city—clear, bright, and sunny. Soon we were passing sugar cane fields, banana and bamboo trees, and coffee plantations in the Araguan Valley south of Caracas. We spent the first night in a government-run tourist inn in San Juan de los Morros, a place noted for its hot, spring-fed sulfur baths.

The drive from San Juan de los Morros to the Socony Oil Camp at Anaco, where we planned to spend the second night, took us across the hot frying pan that is the Venezuelan llanos. The roadbed, built high above the swampy lowlands in many sections, was paved only as far as El Sombrero, about sixty miles east of San Juan. From there to Valle de la Pascua, a distance of eighty miles, the road was under construction and not yet hard-surfaced. We ate the dust of passing vehicles and were constantly threatened, our windshield occasionally hit by stones from the roadbed that flew up at us whenever a speeding car passed in the opposite direction.

A few hours after leaving San Juan the engine of my car began to misfire. Fortunately we were within sight of one of the few gas stations on that main east-west highway. The problem turned out to be merely a cable shaken loose from a sparkplug. The mechanic refused to take any money for fixing it, so we gassed up and continued on our way.

About forty miles down the road we encountered our first obstacle—a stream that ran across the highway. It appeared to be fairly shallow, and indeed it was, for we reached the other side before the flooded engine died right in the middle of the road. Our little car was light so the three of us were easily able to push it to the side, thereby enabling the traffic behind us, comprised mostly of large trucks, to move on. Some fifteen minutes later the motor dried out and I was able to start the engine. Once again on our bumpy way, we were soon eating the dust of passing vehicles, mostly trucks.

At Valle de la Pascua a newly paved section of the highway greeted us like a cold beer in the desert. After bouncing up and down for the previous four hours, the sensation of riding on a newly paved road was like taking a sulfur bath, an experience that has to be tried to be appreciated. However, our joy at riding smoothly did not last. An hour later we ran onto the older section of the highway where no work had been done. Then the sport of the day again became the dodging of potholes, any one of which, if hit hard enough, might easily have broken a spring or stopped us completely. In any event we had to stop completely whenever encountering the largest holes. Then we backed up and sought a safer route. All this stopping, retreating, twisting and turning slowed our progress, but by mid-afternoon the oil city of El Tigre was in sight and we began passing the first of the many wells which make up Venezuela's eastern oil fields.

From El Tigre the road was much better, and by late afternoon we arrived at our destination, the Socony Vacuum Camp at Anaco. We had traveled on the main road connecting eastern and western Venezuela and now knew the reason for the emphasis on air travel in this country. I had read that in 1950, of Venezuela's 5,667 miles of highway, only 2,000 miles were "in fairly good condition," and of these, only 600 miles were concrete surfaced. The Pérez Jiménez regime had recognized Venezuela's need for road building if the country were to prosper, and we now saw evidence of this need as well as the government's new policy in this regard.

When we pulled into the Socony camp at Anaco, Bob Fondes, a fellow "Musiu Gang" member who had recently been transferred from Caracas, greeted us with great surprise.

"What in the world are you doing here?" he exclaimed. "How did you get here? Why didn't you let me know you were coming?"

"Didn't you get our telegram?" we said in unison.

"Telegram? No. If you sent one I'll probably get it in a few weeks. It would go to the nearby town, and they might decide not to bring it here until someone was coming out to the camp. Anyway, it's great to see you all!"

As darkness fell the flares of burning gas which dot the landscape at Anaco became visible, appearing along the horizon in some places like a number of rising suns. The flares burn off excess gas that comes to the surface with the oil as it is piped from the wells to vacant fields. There the pipeline ends in a vertical section rising about ten or fifteen feet above the ground. At that point the escaping gas is ignited as it leaves the pipe and comes into contact with the air, just like a pilot light on a gas stove.

Anaco was the site of Robley's Flare, once the world's largest. That evening we drove out to see it at close range, though it was already reduced in size from what it had been some years earlier. The government had just recently initiated a conservation program not yet in full effect. A large circle of scorched earth about a hundred yards in diameter surrounded the flare, providing an indication of how large it was when "Robley" was the biggest pilot light in the business.

Jaguars, which are fairly common in this region, often approach the flares at night to stalk other animals that are also attracted to the light. However, that evening the only animals present at Robley's were about three dozen cows who were lying on the scorched earth, looking very philosophical as they gazed at the bright, steady flame shooting high into the air.

The Venezuelan government's gas preservation law was intended to preserve gas for future use, but by pushing the gas back into the ground there are other advantages. The gas helps maintain the underground pressure released by the removal of oil, thus forcing the remaining oil to the surface. When the right combination of gas and oil is present, the oil is brought to the surface by the release of pressure already existing below the surface, or by attaching a pump, known as a "jack," to the producing well.

The terms "flare" and "jack" are easy to understand, but the story was often told in Anaco about a woman, new to the oil business, who was hired by the procurement department of the New York office of Socony. Upon receiving a requisition from Anaco for 200 "Christmas trees" she proceeded to place the order with a Washington state firm, delivery to be made in December. She thought it was a somewhat strange order, especially since it was dated early June, but she assumed the order had to do with the company's policy of providing "a home away from home," and the long lead time was needed to get the trees to Venezuela in time for the holidays. Only later did she learn that a Christmas tree in petroleum parlance is the name given to the conglomeration of pipes, valves, and gages, which decorate the surface directly above a producing oil well.

Actually a genuine Christmas tree order for Venezuela was not at all strange. There were insufficient local trees to supply the demand made each December by the growing number of foreigners living and working there, so thousands of pine trees were imported annually from Canada and the U.S. for the Christmas season.

Early the next morning we were on the road again, en route south to Ciudad Bolívar, the capital of Bolívar State. Often referred to merely as "C.B.," this town of 35,000 inhabitants in the mid-fifties is on the southern bank of the lower Orinoco River, 165 miles from the Caribbean coast city of Puerto de la Cruz. From there to C.B. a generally north-south paved road runs past Anaco, which is itself 120 miles north of Soledad, the town on the Orinoco's northern bank opposite Ciudad Bolívar. Built with the aid of the foreign oil companies who were its main users, the road widens out into a four-lane highway as soon as it reaches one of the flattest sections of the llanos, just south of El Tigre.

Despite the paved road, or because of it, the landscape was strewn with many wrecked automobiles left at the sides of the road near their crash sites. These mechanical corpses, rusting in the wind and rain, remained where they had fallen because neither the owners nor the government appeared to be interested in them anymore. Most were useless wrecks. They served as reminders of what excessive speed can do, but not everyone got the message. Just south of El Tigre, where the highway broadens out into four lanes, there was a special reminder. The remains of a totally demolished automobile had been placed on a pedestal about twenty feet high for all to see, a grim notice to motorists of what can happen on the El Tigre-Soledad road.

"That monument hardly seems necessary," Gloria commented. "There are plenty of reminders on the side of the road."

At Soledad we had to get out of the car and walk through a hoof-and-mouth disease prevention path while the tires of the car were sprayed with disinfectant before we drove aboard a small ferry which took us across the Orinoco River to Ciudad Bolívar. After a quick tour of the town we settled down for the evening in the Gran Hotel Bolívar.

We had intended to spend only one night in C.B. as the town held few attractions. But that evening, as we were dining, the hotel manager approached our table, introduced himself, and asked if we would be interested in going on a special flight the next morning to see the highest waterfalls in the world. The flight was leaving from the C.B. airport and three seats were still available. This was an opportunity that was not to be missed, we agreed, so our plans to head east the next day were quickly changed.

Ten a.m. Wednesday, August 17, 1955: we are flying over Ciudad Bolívar in a one-engine converted cargo plane heading south for some of the wildest, most isolated sections of Venezuela. The plane we are flying in has the face of a cow painted on its motor cowling, and underneath it, the words "La Vaca" (The Cow). There are five other passengers — three adventuresome Venezuelan girls from Caracas who are on vacation, an Italian waiter and a Spanish desk clerk, both from the Gran Hotel Bolívar. Visible to the south are giant cliffs and bluffs that rise up out of the jungle greenery, the outstanding landmarks of the Gran Sabana. Angel Falls lies about 200 miles to the south.

"Imagine, all this for only 100 Bolívares," I said to Charmaine.

"And sustained faith in the plane's one engine," Gloria added. Below us there was no place to land if it became necessary to do so.

About forty-five minutes out of C.B. we passed over "Iron Mountain," aptly named for its iron ore deposits reputed to be the richest in the world, a mountain of iron which had been inaccessible until foreign capital and skills were brought in for development. Also visible was the newly constructed railroad which carries the ore ninety-three miles through the jungle to the new town of Puerto Ordaz on the Orinoco River, from where it is loaded aboard ocean steamers bound for the smelting mills in the U.S. and Europe.

The weather was perfect; only a few clouds occasionally blocking our view of the rich, green tropical vegetation a few thousand feet below. Finally, about two-and-a-half hours later, we reached the "Lost Continent," the "island in the sky" where Angel Falls spills its silvery streak of water down a sheer cliff for 3,212 feet, a distance twice the size of the Empire State Building and fifteen times higher than Niagara Falls! As we neared the falls and flew by and above them, the shadow of our plane appeared like a small moving dot against the giant landscape.

Above the falls Auyantepuy (sometimes spelled Auyan-Tepui), known also as "Devil's Mountain," overlooks the vast reaches of the Gran Sabana. A short distance beyond the brink of the escarpment the pilot Captain Romero takes his plane low for a good view of Jimmy Angel's plane, which is still lying there as if it had touched down only yesterday. Yet it has been twenty years since Jimmy Angel attempted to land on what he thought was a smooth landing area. It turned out to be a boggy marsh. He and two others, including his wife, survived the crash and walked out of the jungle six weeks later after negotiating the 3,000-foot-high cliff in a perilous descent. Angel's plane has since been removed from the spot where he crashed and placed in a museum.

After a last look at the great falls and after flying a short distance parallel to the cliffs, we headed north. At various places along the escarpment a few other falls were visible, but none equaled the king of them all. It is said that in one place along that giant ridge there is a falls slightly greater than Angel Falls, but it is not considered to be a true falls, since the water evaporates in the hot tropical air before it reaches the bottom.

With the mysterious wonders of Auyantepuy fading quickly into the background, Captain Romero shouted back to his passengers through the open door leading to the cockpit, "Would you like to land at Canaima?" "Sure," everyone answered in unison. The din in the cabin from the plane's engine made it necessary to shout to be heard.

We had all heard of Canaima, the Venezuelan "Garden of Eden," but had never expected to see at first hand the place reputed to be a jungle paradise. Few Venezuelans, and fewer Musius, knew the meaning of the word "Canaima," though they rightfully assumed it was an indigenous Indian name. To the local tribes, Canaima is the name of the supreme being who is responsible for and controls the destiny of all things. He is known as a just but terrible god who protects the good but delivers misfortune upon the evil. The Indians believe he lives in the mysterious plains above Auyantepuy where, from his sky-top dwelling, he watches over all things. It seemed to be a suitable name for a tropical paradise located in the center of the Green Hell that surrounds it.

"The Cow" dropped swiftly down onto a pasture, a single landing strip hacked out of the surrounding jungle. The plane bounced along on the ground almost to the end of the strip, and just before running into some trees, turned sharply in a small space intended for that purpose and headed back to the point where we had landed. When the propeller stopped spinning the silence was deafening.

As we stepped out of the plane a six-foot, red-bearded, rustic-looking man who was obviously not a Venezuelan stepped forward to welcome us. He introduced himself as "Bryan." We soon learned that he was an American who worked for Captain Vaughn, the American bush pilot who was well known in Caracas and in the Gran Sabana for his aviation activities in eastern Venezuela, and for his efforts to eventually develop Canaima as a major tourist attraction. But that development was many years away, for at this time Canaima was only a rustic camp in the jungle with a dirt landing strip and little else. Besides working for Vaughn, Bryan said he was prospecting in the area, presumably for gold and diamonds. A small group of curious, lightly clad Indians stood behind him, staring silently at us with expressionless faces as we emerged from the plane.

"Would you like to stay for lunch?" he asked after the introductions were over and after he had exchanged a few words with Captain Romero, whom he obviously knew. While the invitation was unexpected, I surmised that Bryan would welcome our company, especially that of the charming young ladies in the group, and the opportunity to obtain news of the outside world.

"We've got plenty of wild pig and rice that my boys have been cooking for three days if you'd like some." He did not have to ask twice. We had been flying for more than three hours and it was now well past our usual lunch hour. He led the way and we followed him to a clearing at the edge of the river where a few Indian huts had been erected. Also visible in this "Garden of Eden" was a long, roughly hewn wooden table which was under a rectangular-shaped matted roof, held up by wooden poles and open on all sides. Nearby were a couple of open-ended wooden and grass shelters where hammocks with mosquito netting had been strung. A large bubbling pot of meat and rice simmered over an open fire. Although the weather was extremely hot and thus enervating, the excitement of the morning flight had whetted our appetites. We sat as best we could on logs and at the makeshift table. Although the pork was still not tender despite days of cooking, it tasted delicious.

After lunch we explored the edges of the dark lagoon beneath the thundering falls. The darkness and silence of the lagoon contrasted sharply with the light cast by the sparkling, cascading water and the thundering noise, which increased as one approached the falls. The Caroni River at this point drops several hundred feet. In a setting of lush tropical foliage, with a bright blue, sunlit sky spotted with giant, white cumulus clouds as a backdrop, the scene was idyllic.

The water of the Caroni River as it flows through Canaima after escaping over the falls was clear but tea-colored from the vegetation and minerals of the region. The sand at the edges of the river in some places was a startling pink; in other places it was black from its volcanic origin. The sounds of tropical birds and insects and the steady hum of the falling water in the background did indeed give one a feeling of a tropical paradise. Palm trees swaying in the light breeze heightened the effect of a Garden of Eden.

When Captain Romero informed us it was time to leave we reluctantly left the river's edge and headed back through the jungle path to the landing strip, led again by Bryan. As we reached the side of the plane and turned to say goodbye and to thank our host for his hospitality, he said, "Well, that will be twenty-five dollars each."

I could not believe what I thought I had heard. "What did you say?" I asked.

"I said that will be twenty-five dollars each."

"What are you talking about?" I and others answered in various stages of shocked surprise. "What do we owe you twenty-five dollars for?"

"It's a rule Captain Vaughn has laid down," Bryan responded. "There's a landing fee of $25 per person for everyone who comes to Canaima."

I still could not believe what I was hearing. "You mean your invitation to lunch had a price tag on it?" I asked. "Why didn't you tell us when we first arrived instead of leading us to believe that this was merely the kind of hospitable treatment we would expect to find in the jungle?"

"Didn't Captain Romero tell you?" he replied. "I assumed you knew the rules here."

"No, he didn't tell us. He only asked us if we wanted to land here and we all said 'Sure, why not?' as we had heard about how Captain Vaughn was trying to develop Canaima." The others chimed in that they were not told either and did not intend to pay.

Finally, just before boarding the plane, I took a card out of my wallet and handed it to Bryan. "Here's my card," I told him. "I'm with the American Embassy in Caracas. You can tell Captain Vaughn he can contact me there if he wants to discuss this any further, but we're not going to pay you anything now. And in the future I hope you make it clear to anyone who lands here like we did what you're up to."

The shock of being asked for monetary remuneration for what we assumed to be merely typical hospitality in a land where visitors were few and far between, had still not left me and my colleagues even when we were airborne once again. None of us had planned, nor did any of us agree, to fulfill Bryan's demand.

Afterwards I often thought about our visit to Canaima, and expected to get a call from Captain Vaughn or someone from his office in Caracas demanding payment. But what others and I did not know at the time was that because of a series of events, which would take place a few weeks later, our farewell to Bryan had a finality about it which was the end of the issue.

The day after we returned from our flight to Angel Falls and Canaima, we drove eastward toward the juncture of the Orinoco and Caroni rivers, the site of the Puerto Ordaz and Palua iron ore loading operations. Cattle and burros soon became a part of the flat landscape and occasionally we passed groups of vultures busily engaged in cleaning up the carcasses of animals that had fallen in their tracks. Although a small village had existed there since Bolívar's time, Puerto Ordaz was now a new, bustling town constructed at the river's edge where iron ore from Cerro Bolívar, brought by rail from the iron mountain, is transferred to cargo ships. The Orinoco River had been dredged for about 170 miles to enable ocean-going vessels to reach the Puerto Ordaz dock. This mammoth project, in the midst of the Venezuelan jungles, had been completed only the year before, the first ore shipment having arrived in Philadelphia in January of 1954. Soon some three million tons would be shipped annually from the new port to the U.S.

We hoped to be able to spend the night at the El Pao mining camp, but not before we visited the Caroni Electrification Project. The work on that project was well underway, the main aspect being a dam, now under construction, across the Caroni River. When completed in 1958, some 110 million kilowatts of hydroelectric power would become available for the new industries being developed in eastern Venezuela. We met and were briefed by the chief engineer at the site of the dam, Dr. Alberto Rodriguez, who enthusiastically explained the project to us. As we drove over the top of a temporary earthen dam built to allow work to go forward on the permanent dam, we had a rare view of the dried-up river bed. It was pitted with many large, black shiny boulders. In the near-distance we were also able to see the beautiful and bountiful lower falls of the Caroni. In a few years that whole area would be many feet under water.

As we neared the iron mine at El Pao we passed numerous villages and a number of banana plantations. The recent abundant rains gave the tropical vegetation, with its varied hues of green, a special brilliance and brightness when in the sunlight. For some distance the rail line from the river to the mines paralleled the road, and often the road crossed and recrossed the tracks. At each of these crossings there was a familiar X-shaped sign with red lights and warning bells and, incongruous in a Spanish-speaking country, the familiar statement in English, "Stop, Look, Listen." About 2 p.m. we reached the mines and were welcomed by the assistant manager who arranged for us to visit the pits. All mining at El Pao is the open-pit variety.

Our guide was the engineer in charge of the shift. Tall and well-tanned, he spoke with a distinct British accent, bubbling over with enthusiasm when explaining the mining operation. This same enthusiasm was evident in almost everyone connected with this formidable task of removing iron ore from the wilderness, though this fellow sometimes also spoke in apologetic terms. "There's really nothing to see," he would say, then proceed to speak with pride at how, starting from scratch, forty-three miles inland from the mighty Orinoco River, in the midst of the jungle, they were now able to send forth a steady stream of iron ore that flowed north by rail and ship.

Beneath his mining hat, which, given his British accent and the jungle environment, took on the appearance of a pith helmet, his blue eyes moved with nervous energy. He said he had been there several years and expected to spend his lifetime in El Pao. What intricate complexities in a man's history, I thought, so shapes his character that he finds happiness so far removed from civilization!

The engineer explained how the small mountain on which we stood contained high-quality ore in a huge streak that formed the shape of a giant bowl. For every ton of ore carried off the edges of this "bowl," tons of dirt also had to be carried away. While a steady stream of trucks capable of carrying thirty tons each dumped the dirt over the southern side of the mountain, another stream of trucks was loaded with ore which was then carried a short distance down the mountain to where a special device lifted the load and dumped it into a crushing machine. From there the ore was carried further down the hill by a conveyer belt, which pushed it into waiting freight cars. We could see where the streaks of ore existed, where they thinned out, and where common earth began. The soil, a light reddish color, contrasted with the ore which sparkled brightly in the late afternoon sun.

After the blasting operation, which takes place every afternoon, giant cranes scoop up the ore and load it into the waiting trucks. Everything was dry and dusty that day. One truck was kept busy watering down the roads. During tropical rainstorms, however, the work all but ceases as the mountain turns into a sea of mud. At times the giant cranes sink into the mud until the tops of their treads, which are about seven feet high, are no longer visible. When this happens a ramp is dug leading to each tread and all possible mobile equipment is used to push and pull the cranes back to the surface. In two or three years, our genial guide said, the bottom of the "bowl of iron" would be reached and the problems of mud could be expected to diminish. And at that time, he said, no longer would it be necessary to remove two tons of dirt for every ton of iron. "And then," he added, "when the ore at El Pao is finally exhausted, many years hence, this iron-rich area will still be providing ore from other veins which have been discovered nearby but which have not yet been tapped."

The next day we left El Pao and headed south on a road which led us through more lush, green forests, tiny villages, and banana and sugar farms. A few hours later, at a juncture in the road where we had to decide whether to go farther south, to Upata and the gold mines of El Callao, or to return to Ciudad Bolívar, we decided on the latter. The road leading to the south appeared to be as bad as any we had yet driven on, and we were already three days behind the schedule we had set for ourselves, so we decided to forego the gold mines and try, instead, to make Puerto de la Cruz on the Caribbean coast, some 250 miles to the northeast, our next destination.

After crossing the Caroni once again on a small ferry, and just missing a rainstorm that would have turned the dusty road to Ciudad Bolívar into a quagmire, we arrived back in C.B. As I was parking the car in front of the Gran Hotel Bolívar where we had decided to stop for a late lunch, I failed to notice that the curb, instead of going up like a conventional curb, went down, for almost a foot. Both the front and rear wheels on the right side of the car fell down into this area, so I was unable to get the car back on the road. Four men who were standing nearby observing the scene saw my dilemma, walked over and asked if they could be of any help.

"Sure," I replied, " but what do you suggest?"

Without saying another word the four men walked to the front of the car, picked up the front end, and placed it gently on the pavement.

They then did likewise with the rear end. My pride excepted, nothing was damaged.

The sun was setting as we crossed the Orinoco for the last time. By nightfall we were rolling quickly and smoothly north on the highway leading to Puerto de la Cruz, where we arrived about midnight after passing through the eastern oil fields with their hundreds of flares glowing eerily in the dark landscape. Although I had to apply the brakes dozens of times to avoid hitting cattle that were strolling or sleeping on the highway, we took no toll.

The Gulf Oil Refining Camp, near the end of the pipelines that paralleled the road for mile after mile, was a welcome sight after the long day of driving. Gloria's brother, the chief accountant at the camp, met us and arranged for us to stay at the camp's guest house. Since the camp's recreational facilities included a motor launch for fishing and Playa Colorado, a white sand, palm-lined beach nearby for swimming, we wanted to linger before starting the grueling trip back across the llanos to Caracas. After one more day of savoring the pleasant surroundings of Puerto La Cruz, we packed up and headed for home.

Our return trip back across the llanos was relatively uneventful. A short distance from Puerta La Cruz a motorcycle policeman motioned for me to pull over to the side of the road. He alleged that I was speeding and after discussing the situation and being threatened with all kinds of delays, he said that we could go on if I paid him a fine of 200 Bolívares. When he saw that I only had 190 Bs in my wallet, which, I told him, was all we had to get back to Caracas, he relented and said he would reduce the fine to 100 Bs. With tongue in cheek, I asked him for a receipt. He smiled and said it would be mailed to me.

Occasionally we were delayed by minor motor troubles caused by the poor roads, and once we found ourselves stuck in midstream when the motor died while navigating through a small river which crossed the road after some heavy rains. We were rescued by a passing jeep, which pulled us to dry land. The motor started as soon as it dried out. As it took two days to reach Caracas, we spent the night at a village inn where hammocks were strung for the guests and where we shared the patio with pigs and poultry, but arrived back in Caracas the following day.

After a day's rest in the capital, Joan Gold, the American art student who was in Venezuela on a one-year scholarship, replaced Gloria as the third member of our party. As we headed west I wondered if this portion of our trip would be as adventuresome as our visit to the eastern part of the country, and if Joan would be as good a traveling companion as Gloria. I would soon find out. Meanwhile, my knowledge of, and interest in Charmaine was beginning to grow.

If the roads were bad at times in eastern Venezuela, they were infinitely worse in the west. Although we arrived in the oil city of Maracaibo, our most western destination, within a few days and after a minimum of difficulties on the road, our attempt to return to Caracas along the coast resulted in our being trapped between two swollen rivers which flowed across the road, forcing us to spend the night outdoors waiting for the water to subside. When the water subsided late the following morning, we reversed our course and headed for the main east-west highway well to the south of us in the Andes.

I had received another ticket for speeding just as we were leaving Los Teques, a town on the outskirts of Caracas, at the start of our trip west. On that occasion my license had been taken from me and I was told to return the following week to retrieve it and to pay the fine. By the time we arrived at the outskirts of Los Teques it was about 1 a.m. so we found a small hotel to spend the night and planned to settle my latest caper with the local law in the morning.

After breakfast we went to the main square of town and asked the first policeman we saw for directions to the office of the inspector of motor vehicle transportation. We were politely directed with a knowing smile. While I went into the designated office, just a block away, to settle my account with the law, Charmaine visited a nearby church to settle her account with the Lord who had, no doubt, been with us as we traveled through the Venezuelan heartland.

After entering the building I was directed to a small room where several men were lined up in front of a desk. A middle-aged man was leisurely but efficiently making notations in a large book. On his desk, carefully stacked in two neat piles, were the stubs of tickets in one pile and drivers' licenses which, evidently, had been impounded, in the other. I patiently awaited my turn, then produced the necessary paper required to retrieve my license. The clerk took it without comment and began writing in his big book. Suddenly he stopped writing, looked up, and said, "How do you spell your name?"

I took out one of my calling cards and handed it to him.

"You're with the American Embassy?" the clerk queried.

"Yes," I replied. The man resumed writing. Then he tore two pages from the book and handed the card back to me along with the torn pages. "You take this to the agency for official papers and pay your fine there. Bring the receipt back here and you'll get your license."

I thanked him and went to do as I was told. I paused to look at the papers I had just received and read, "For the infraction of Article 32, Allen Hansen is fined fifty Bolívares." "Well," I thought, "it could have been worse—that's about fifteen bucks."

After getting directions to the Agency for Official Papers, located three blocks from the "*Inspectoria*," the necessary paperwork was arranged, the fine paid, and I returned to retrieve my license. The line I had been in before was now much longer, but when the clerk looked up and saw me, he called to me, searched for my license, and handed it to me in exchange for the receipt. I was elated. I left feeling like I was once again a free man.

At precisely 12 noon we arrived back in Caracas. During more than 3,000 miles of travel under conditions that tested our stamina and wit, Charmaine and I had become very well acquainted. It was an acquaintance which was to blossom into the kind of love which would change our lives.

When I arrived at the office I learned that some important changes were about to take place at USIS. Harry Kendall had received his transfer orders as his tour of duty was about to end. He would be replaced some months later by an officer who was new to the Foreign Service, Bob Amerson. Although ideally there should have been an overlap between the arrival of Amerson and the departure of Kendall, this was not to be. Instead, the scheduling provided me with the opportunity to fill in as the acting information officer for a few months, though as PAO Butler told me, "I'm reluctant to put you in charge because you haven't had much experience, but I'm going to give you the opportunity to prove yourself."

"From JOT to information officer in five months! That will look great on my record," I thought. "And besides, Butler is right there and, more important, so is Moleon. I can handle it."

During the last week that Harry Kendall was in town, the farewell parties for him which began a month or two earlier were now carried out in earnest. One memorable night the Venezuelan men on the staff with whom Harry had worked for four years, and whose confidence and respect he had gained, took him on a tour of "the real Caracas"—nightspots not frequented by "Musius." I joined them and we ended the barhopping evening about 2:30 a.m. in a small bar-restaurant in the old section of the city. There we drank Mondango soup and ate *arroz con pollo.* I found that early-morning meal so delicious I insisted that the Venezuelan staffers join me for lunch there a few weeks later. In the daylight the place looked dirty and dingy, and the food was horrible!

For the next few months I was kept busy with my "on the job" training. I thrived on the work and the responsibility, keeping Kendall's advice in mind, working closely with the PAO, and, above all, accepting most of Moleon's generally excellent suggestions. Placement of USIS articles in the Caracas dailies remained as high as ever.

It was at this time that Austria gained its freedom from the Soviet Union by becoming independent, an event that was looked upon with some amazement as the Soviet Union was in those days seldom known to release anything within its grasp. Until then, Austria had not gained its post-World War II independence. In doing so this miracle was, of course, widely reported in the world press.

The USIA wireless file, received by radio teletype, provided the information upon which most of the news releases of USIS Caracas were based. Thus comments by U.S. government leaders and others about this historic event were included in what was the major story on the file that day. When I read that Secretary of State Dulles was quoted as saying that "the Austrian example will be followed by others," I could not believe what I read.

"That just isn't going to happen," I told Moleon. It didn't, at least not until the Soviet Union itself disintegrated many years later.

When Bob Amerson arrived a few months later a new wave of USIS-sponsored parties was initiated to introduce him to media leaders and the diplomatic community. I accompanied him on calls to editors and writers of the leading newspapers, to the television station managers, and to other key media people. After a few weeks he took over the information operation and I moved to the cultural section of USIS to continue my training, this time under the supervision of CAO Andy Wilkinson.

After being back in Caracas many weeks after our visit to Angel Falls, Canaima, and western Venezuela, I still had heard nothing from Captain Vaughn about the fee Bryan had demanded when we landed at Canaima. Then one morning, as I read the newspapers, I was shocked to learn that Bryan had died. The burly prospector whose company we enjoyed, until he asked for the bill, had gone fishing above the falls at Canaima with another prospector, an Italian, in an Indian dugout canoe and the canoe had been swept over the falls. The body of the Italian had been recovered by the Indians, but Bryan's body was still missing. The body that had been recovered was reduced to a skeleton, presumably from having been caught in the whirlpool at the bottom of the falls and scraped against the volcanic rocks bordering that swirling basin. But because of the violent deaths and the need to locate Bryan's body, which was found a few days later, the government ordered an investigating team to go to Canaima and report on the incident. This team made headlines in the Venezuelan newspapers the following day.

The team was composed of six government investigators. They boarded Captain Romero's plane, "The Cow," that morning at the Ciudad Bolívar airport for the relatively short flight to Canaima. It was a normal takeoff until the plane reached about 300 feet of altitude. Then the motor stopped and the plane plummeted to earth. A moment later it started burning. Before anyone could reach it, a tremendous explosion rent the air. The plane was completely demolished, killing all on board.

Some months later still another tragedy was to strike those associated with Canaima. Captain Vaughn had spent the weekend there as he often did while continuing with his plans to develop the area as a major tourist attraction. While flying back to Caracas on a Sunday evening, accompanied by his wife and another American couple, the authorities at Maiquetia Airport radioed to him that he would be unable to land at Maiquetia because of weather conditions. The alternate airport was at Higuerote, about eighty miles to the east, so he headed for Higuerote. It will never be known how or why Captain Vaughn overshot the airport at Higuerote, but the last time he radioed the tower at that airport he was heading back toward Caracas in a westerly direction. Shortly thereafter his plane ran out of fuel and crashed into dense jungle somewhere between Higuerote and Caracas. The Venezuelan army searched for a week before they located the wreckage. There were no survivors. Years later I would be reminded of the events surrounding Canaima when that name came up again in an entirely different context.

While the Musiu Gang continued its many weekend excursions to the beaches and mountains, which Charmaine and I joined as often as we could, we also were spending more time together, seeing each other almost daily. Love was in the air, and not only for us. Several other Musius in the Gang who found themselves to be mutually attracted to each other were similarly stricken, although I thought my case was the worst, but this was only because of my intimate knowledge of my own emotions. Suddenly, like a revelation of a great truth, the moment arrived when I decided that it was time to get married. The woman I wanted to marry, of course, was Charmaine. Although we had known each other for only six months, the adventures we had shared in our travels in the jungles of Venezuela had ignited sparks in both of us that were electrifying and hardly controllable. We were in love. And Charmaine made no bones about it. If I wanted to share the ultimate experience, I would have to get married.

I was more than ready. "After all," I mused, "if they send us bachelors abroad we're going to meet foreign women and eventually want to get married to them." I wasn't sure who "they" were, but I knew that USIA regulations required that a Foreign Service officer who wanted to marry a non-U.S. citizen had to resign from the Agency. The Agency would then either accept the resignation, or, if the proposed spouse was considered "suitable," the resignation would not be accepted and the young man or woman could get married and continue with his or her career.

I had never really given the momentous step which marriage entailed much thought before. Now I could hardly think of anything else. I recalled, however, that many years before, discussing with my mother the subject of marriage in general terms, she scoffed when I told her that I probably would never marry. "Don't worry," she said. "When you're ready to get married, you'll get married." "Yes," I now reflected, thinking of her words, "I'm now ready."

When my decision to get married was announced, the most important requirement as far as the U.S. government was concerned was the initiation of a security investigation of the potential spouse, the results of which would determine whether or not my resignation from the Foreign Service, as required, would be accepted. Until a "routine background investigation" of the type required of all U.S. government employees was completed on Charmaine and was "satisfactory," the Agency would not authorize me, as a U.S. Foreign Service Officer, to marry a foreigner. To have done so without authorization would have meant immediate dismissal. With the engagement announced and the ring bought, the date of the marriage could not yet be set because I did not want to lose my job. Not only would it soon be necessary to provide for a wife and, eventually, I expected, a family, but my introduction to life in the Foreign Service had convinced me that this was the career for me—exciting, enjoyable and satisfying.

All now hinged on Charmaine's security investigation. Since I had already received word that my next assignment, following my training period in Caracas, would be Mexico, I prayed that the investigation would be expedited. If it were not, I might have to leave for Mexico City, then return to Caracas later to get married. This was not an option for which there was any enthusiasm by either Charmaine or me. Aside from what fate might have in store should the marriage be delayed, travel to Mexico as man and wife would be at the government's expense.

If I returned to Caracas from Mexico to get married, that round trip would be at my expense.

Being sympathetic to my dilemma and wanting to keep me on his staff if at all possible, PAO Butler cabled Washington headquarters requesting that I be assigned to a new position in Caracas following my period of training. His request was denied. "JOTs are to be transferred to other posts after their period of training," the return cable read. The theory behind this policy made sense—JOTs who had finished their training period were expected to arrive at new posts as full-fledged officers with all the authority and prestige that that designation implied.

With no alternative but to wait, Charmaine and I decided to join an expedition of some fellow Musius to neighboring Trinidad to participate in that island's famous carnival. In addition to being introduced to one of the most unique experiences in the western hemisphere—the traditional Trinidad carnival with its steel bands and calypso music, Charmaine would introduce me to her relatives.

The "steel bands" for which Trinidad is famous and which, along with calypso singing, make the Trinidadian carnival unique, are a legacy of World War II. When the island was unable to import musical instruments during the war, an ingenious West Indian saw the tremendous possibilities of making music with a set of old, empty oil drums. By hammering in the ends of the drums and heating them to form different tones, notes are distributed around what becomes the head of the steel drum. The different tones are then outlined with a cold chisel and white paint by the tuner. The other end of the drum is cut off. The resulting length and diameter determines whether it is "tenor pan," alto, baritone, or "bass-boom." Played with rubberized or padded sticks, all the orchestral voices and ranges of accompaniment, melody and countermelody are represented in a group of fourteen to sixteen men, complete with maracas, gourds, and wood blocks to round out the music.

The music of the steel bands stimulates the major action of carnival in Trinidad—the "Jump up." Inspired by the steady melodic beat of the bands, the streets are filled with people performing the "jump up"—a solo dance performed much like a rock and roller. Of course no one moves, or "jumps up," like a Trinidadian, but the chanting rhythms of the bands affect staid, elderly British subjects just as it does the most conservative Musius. No one can resist the beat of the steel drum, especially when the world around you is shaking to the same beat.

A Trinidadian carnival "band," as distinguished from a "steel band" which makes music, is a group of dancers who have joined together under one director and under a central theme organized to march and dance in the streets of Port-of-Spain during carnival. Among such "bands" that year was a group which depicted the 1956 Olympics; skeletons conniving in the city's most famous graveyard; long-nosed clowns; a group dressed as Peruvian Indian dancers; and an 18th century ballroom group. One of the most impressive bands was a group of sixty-four men and women dressed as chess pieces. These human chessmen, as part of their repertoire, periodically simulated a fourteen-move game of chess every few blocks as they marched along. Resplendent in blue, black, and gold costumes, the Black King was mated after a beautiful but bloodless battle by the two opposing queens, supported by their respective knights, rooks, bishops, and pawns.

The King of Carnival '56 was "Shaver Man"—a character inspired by an infamous, real-life villain who became known by that name because of his penchant for collecting the hair of Trinidadian women unfortunate enough to become his victims. The "Shaver Man" of real life made a habit of breaking into the bedrooms of sleeping damsels where, with a quick slash of his razor, he collected samples of hair from their heads and quickly fled without doing anything else! By the time carnival began that year, he was no longer collecting hair. He had been caught and jailed. But such bizarre incidents, which quickly become widely known throughout the island and are relished as entertaining gossip by those not victimized, often become the subjects of popular calypso songs.

Trinidad is a multiracial society, though the majority of the population is composed of blacks, followed by East Indians (whose forefathers came from the subcontinent), a designation which can be confusing since all the inhabitants of Trinidad are known as "West Indians." Chinese form the largest minority, and the white population, the smallest. While the whites and blacks mingled to a certain extent during carnival of '56, each generally socialized only with its own kind, as did the other racial groups. Three decades later, and after many years of governance by the black majority, the preference for socializing with one's own racial stock was still generally maintained among the vast majority of Trinidadians.

Concerned about Charmaine's security investigation, I visited the U.S. consulate in Port-of-Spain to inquire about the status of the background investigation of my fiancée.

"Oh, our part here in Trinidad was completed weeks ago," the vice consul told me. "That should have been mailed to Caracas and Washington by now. But if you want me to check, I'll look in the mail room. We haven't had a mail clerk for about three weeks, so some things have been delayed, and you know, during carnival nothing gets done."

In a few minutes the vice consul returned to his office where I awaited him.

"Well, I think I found what you were looking for," he announced. "It was in the in-box of the mail clerk but hadn't moved because he's been away like I said. Sorry about that. I'll see that it goes out in the next mail."

I was flabbergasted. It was almost mid-February. I had already received my orders transferring me to Mexico. I was to report to Mexico City in April. That left only a month or so for my fiancée to be given the stamp of approval so that we could get married before leaving Caracas. Until the security investigation was completed, the plans for our marriage could not be finalized—unless, of course, I was ready to write an early finish to my new career in the Foreign Service.

"But if I hadn't come here," I blurted, more to myself than to the vice consul, "that report might have stayed in that box another month or two! I would have had to leave on my transfer to Mexico and would have to return to Caracas to get married!" I shook the vice consul's hand. "Thanks for your help," I said. "I'm sure glad I decided to come to Trinidad for carnival." I left and hurried back to tell Charmaine the good news—and the bad news—that the major part of her investigation was completed but the results still hadn't been sent to Caracas. We both shuddered upon realizing that if I had not personally intervened, our plans might have gone astray simply because of the absence of a mail clerk in our embassy in Trinidad!

At midnight of the Tuesday before Ash Wednesday, a startling silence descended upon the Trinidadian capital. The steel bands struck their last note for Carnival '56; the people in the streets and at the clubs stopped dancing; and the calypsonians stopped singing—at least for the next twenty-four hours. An exhausted but happy populace staggered home to their beds. The carnival was over, and the next day we and our fellow Musius flew back to Caracas as did hundreds of other tired revelers.

Aside from the sounds of the steel bands emblazoned in their memories, the "Number One" calypso on the Carnival Hit Parade also reverberated in the minds of the Musius as they reflected on their carnival experience. Composed and sung by "The Mighty Sparrow," it was entitled "Yankee Gone." It commemorated the fact that the American naval base at Chaguaramos, about ten miles from Port-of-Spain, was finally about to close. A decade after World War II when it had been established as part of the "ships for bases deal" with the British government, the Americans were finally leaving Trinidad. "Yankee Gone" noted this as follows:

Well, the girls in town feeling bad,
No more Yankees in Trinidad.
They going to close down the base for good
Them girls have to make out how they could
Is now they park up in the town
In for a penny, in for a pound,
Is competition for so,
Trouble in town when the price drop low.

CHORUS
So when you bounce up Jean and Diana, Rosita and Clementina,
Round the corner posing, bet your life,
Is something they selling.
And if you catch them broken,
you can get it all for nothing
Don't make no row, Yankee gone,
Sparrow take over now.

-2-
Things bad, is to hear they cry
Not a sailor in town, the night clubs dry
Only a West Indian like me or you
Can celebrate the way we do
Since we have things back in control
Ah seeking revenge with me heart and soul
And as we spread the news around
Is to see how them cave men floating in town
CHORUS

-3-
When the Yankee was in full swing
Just imagine how I was suffering
Mavis tell me straight to me face
How she find I too fast and out of place
No, No, No, they would start to fret
Money or not, poor Sparrow can't get

Because with the Yankees they have it cool
Calypsonians too hard to fool.
CHORUS

-4-
It's the glamour boys again
We are going to rule Port-of-Spain
No more Yankees to spoil the fete
Dorothy have to take what she get
All of them who used to make style
Taking their two shillings with a smile
No more hotel and simonds bed
By the sweat of thy brow thou shall eat bread.
CHORUS

Upon our return to Caracas the number one priority for Charmaine and me was to finalize our wedding plans and prepare to leave Venezuela. Less than three months remained before I had to be in Mexico on my new assignment. Assuming that Charmaine's security investigation showed her to be neither a criminal nor a communist, and that USIA would thus reject my required resignation, the date for the wedding would soon have to be set.

Like all weddings, this one would be different, or at least unique, although it would be similar in the sense that those involved in the planning, and some of those at the fringes, all had their own ideas about how that momentous ceremony should be conducted. Since Charmaine was Catholic and I, nominally, Protestant; and since she was from Trinidad and I was from New Jersey; and since we were to be married in Venezuela and the reception was to be held in the Venezuelan home of Charmaine's brother-in-law, two religions and three cultures were represented. There was a great opportunity here for the clash of ideas, though this was generally avoided, with minor exceptions, due primarily to the strength of Charmaine's will and determination, and the fact that she was Catholic born and bred.

Under the circumstances, once the couple in question had decided to wed, not only did the American government have a part to play, but the Venezuelan government as well. In Venezuela, as far as the state is concerned, a civil ceremony is what counts for two individuals to legally become "man and wife." And while, theoretically, the civil ceremony is free of cost, in reality, as we soon learned, our civil marriage would cost more than a simple two-dollar fee.

My first contact with the church authorities who would be involved in blessing my marriage to Charmaine was Father Butterly, an Irish priest who eventually agreed to perform the wedding ceremony. He had a very pleasant personality and was the type of person, I readily observed, with whom one could easily and freely discuss things. However, he was one of the few English-speaking priests in Caracas, thus was overloaded with responsibilities in meeting the needs of a large English-speaking Catholic community among the large number of foreigners who now lived and worked in the Venezuelan capital. In these circumstances he was always pressed for time. He always seemed to be on the run whenever we consulted him. Yet he was willing, and in the end, extremely helpful in assisting us to meet the stringent requirements of the Venezuelan Catholic church (which seemed to be closer to the nineteenth than the twentieth century in its outlook), and the interested governments.

Among the complicating factors, from the church's point of view, was the fact that I was a Protestant, yet Charmaine insisted on a church wedding, which meant getting a "special permit" as the marriage would be "mixed." Thus one of the first steps that had to be taken was to contact a priest at the church in the San José Parish where Charmaine wanted to get married. There we met Father Van de Velde, the parish priest, a Belgian who had the same pleasant personality and aura of helplessness that marked Father Butterly. In consultation with Father Van de Velde, May 5th at 4 p.m. was determined to be the best date and time for the wedding—contingent upon getting the Archbishop's approval to get married in the church (being "mixed" as we were). With this decided, Father Van de Velde then asked me to sign the vows pertaining to noninterference with my future wife's religious practices, and the agreement to raise any offspring in the Catholic manner. As I took out my pen the priest said, "But where are the witnesses?"

"The witnesses?" I answered with surprise.

"Yes, the witnesses. Didn't Father Butterly tell you that each of you need two witnesses to your signature?"

"I don't think so," I said. Neither Charmaine nor I had been aware of this requirement. Perhaps we simply had not understood Father Butterly's hurried explanation of the need for witnesses at the initial planning session.

Faced with this requirement and worried about any delays, we remembered that a party was taking place about a half-mile away to which we had been invited and where a number of our Musiu friends might be found. I asked to use the phone and quickly contacted the party goers. I asked if four of them could come right away to the Rectory of San José to act as witnesses. "Delighted to," came the reply, and within fifteen minutes four Musius arrived to be witnesses—two American girls who were to become Charmaine's bridesmaids, and Frank and Bruno, two Swiss boys from "the Musiu Gang."

Father Van de Velde spoke no English, so all of the above was carried out in Spanish. But when our Swiss friends, Frank and Bruno, arrived, they were able to carry on a stimulating conversation with Father Van de Velde, half in French and half in German. With that phase of the preliminary arrangements with the church successfully completed, Charmaine and I joined our partying friends to celebrate.

About a week later Father Butterly made arrangements for us to call at the Archbishop's office in downtown Caracas in order to apply for permission for a church wedding. We arrived at the appointed hour at the appointed place where we were to meet Father Butterly but by noon, after waiting several hours, there was still no sign of any activity in that office or of Father Butterly. I tried to phone him, but the phones in that part of the city were out of order.

"These churchmen are hard to pin down," I complained to Charmaine. "I wonder if we'll ever get all the permissions we need in time to get married before I have to leave for Mexico."

"Keep the faith," she replied.

Several days later, when I was finally able to contact Father Butterly, he apologized profusely for having failed to keep the appointment. Something urgent had come up, he said. At that point I decided to try another tactic to get through to the Archbishop's office in order to get the needed permission for the church wedding before it was too late. I knew that the consul general at the embassy, Ray Phelan, was an old friend of the priest who was the personal secretary of the Archbishop. By using these connections I felt sure I could cut through the red tape. A few days later, with a letter in hand from the consul general to the Archbishop's secretary, we went again to the Archbishop's office.

This time we found the office open. After the Archbishop's secretary read the letter I handed him we were escorted, with utmost consideration, to an office on the ground floor where doors flew open for us.

"Wait here for a few minutes," the secretary said as he turned and went into the Archbishop's inner sanctum. In a few moments he returned.

"It's all arranged," he said with a smile. "Can you come back with three witnesses Thursday afternoon at four o'clock?"

"Sure," we said in unison. Thanking him profusely, we left. Years later, on a country road in British Guiana, we met a nun Charmaine had known when attending a school in Barbados run by Ursuline nuns. She told us about her difficulties in getting a visa for the U.S. When she added that "It's harder to get into the United States than into heaven," I recalled the difficulties I had encountered in marrying a Catholic in Venezuela.

"Getting married in a Catholic church, if one of the parties is not Catholic, is even harder," I countered. At the time, however, my thoughts were on witnesses. "All these witnesses!" I mused, "The church doesn't trust anybody!"

The following Thursday, shortly before 4 p.m., Charmaine and I arrived at the Archbishop's residence with three witnesses, and a fourth for good measure. Mrs. Giusto and Mrs. Corbin, middle-aged Catholics of good reputation; Mary Healy, who would be the maid-of-honor, and Bob Fondes, best-man-to-be. The delegation was ushered into an inner office by an elderly priest who gave me the impression that he had been given a disagreeable task to perform by his superiors, and aimed to do it as quickly and efficiently as possible. The priest directed everyone to sit in the chairs that were lined up in front of his gigantic desk. He then quickly moved behind the desk and sat down.

On his desk was a book of huge proportions, perhaps in keeping with the size of the desk that held it. He began to read from this tremendous book in a hurried but methodical fashion, in Spanish. At the appropriate places Charmaine and I and the witnesses responded to questions. The entire ceremony lasted about fifteen minutes. When it was concluded, all the questions presumably having been answered satisfactorily, the priest moved to the front of the desk, wished Charmaine and me the best of luck, and even chanced to smile, now that his work was done. At this stage I was still wondering how many more witnesses and signings would be required before we would be able to go to the altar.

Though the witnessing of signatures in several places was now behind us, one more consultation was needed with Father Butterly and Father Van de Velde. We met in the latter's office in the San José Rectory and all seemed ready at last when Father Butterly casually remarked, "Now all you need is the permission from Rome."

"What!" I exclaimed in so loud a voice that it sounded like a shout. "You mean we need the permission of the Pope to get married? But we have the permission of the Archbishop!" But then I thought, "He must be kidding."

"Yes," Father Butterly replied in a calm voice, "but you still need permission from Rome. Whenever a non-Christian wants to marry a

Catholic, the Church requires that permission be granted by Rome. I'm sorry, but that's the law of the Church."

"A non-Christian!" I said in a slightly less agitated tone than when I had first reacted to what I was now learning about the ways of the Church. "A non-Christian! But I'm not a non-Christian. I'm not a Catholic, but I consider myself to be a Christian."

"Oh, I didn't realize that. I thought you said that you weren't a Christian in one of our earlier talks. Forgive me. In that case, you're all set. Do forgive me," Father Butterly repeated.

That was the last time I saw Father Butterly until the day he performed the marriage ceremony. No more misunderstandings or difficulties arose between us—until the day of the wedding—perhaps because we had no further communication until then. The important thing, however, was that the Church had given us our "exams," and we had passed. Now all that was needed was for us to pass the exams of the two interested governments.

Although we weren't officially engaged until December 27th, by the middle of November we were "engaged to be engaged." When that happened I thought it prudent to immediately begin my dealings with the United States government, so at that time I obtained the numerous forms that Charmaine had to fill out for a background investigation. When the forms were filled in, they were submitted to the post security officer. But as I found out in Trinidad, the most important part of the investigation, though completed by mid-February, was lingering in the outbox of a mail clerk. A week or so after I returned from carnival in Trinidad I was happy to learn that the necessary documents from Trinidad had finally arrived in Caracas.

"Well, we're all set now, eh?" I remarked to the embassy security officer.

"Not quite," came the reply. "I have a little more to do here in Caracas, and then I have to write up the report."

Two or three more weeks passed before the investigation was fully completed. But, when I checked, it had still not been written in the approved form by the security officer.

"I'll get to it as soon as I can, Al," he told a more-and-more anxious groom-to-be. "But I've got three urgent cases pending that I have to complete first. And now I don't have a secretary. I asked Washington for a secretary two months ago. You know how they replied? They sent me a dictaphone machine. I call it 'Miss Gray.'"

While I appreciated the heavy workload the security officer faced, my frustration at not seeing the investigation finalized continued to gnaw at me, for until the completed report had been received in

Washington, I would not receive Uncle Sam's permission to marry a foreigner. The possibility of my having to leave Charmaine behind and then return to Caracas to get married later loomed ever larger.

During the week that followed, every time I met the security officer in the corridors of the Embassy or on the street, I asked him about the status of his report on Charmaine.

"Just as soon as I can get to it," came the constant reply. Time continued to run out. My boss, the PAO, offered to lend his secretary to the security officer in order to expedite the report, but for some reason this did not appear to be a solution to the problem. I was getting more and more nervous.

While waiting for the U.S. government regulations to be surmounted, there remained those of the Venezuelan government. At the time it was said that at least fifty percent of all Venezuelans were bastards because they were born out of wedlock. This may have been true simply because the average Venezuelan could not easily get married legally. Furthermore, it was relatively expensive, thus the lower economic classes—the majority of the people—simply skipped the so-called "civil ceremony."

The "civil ceremony" was a term completely new to me, though I quickly learned about it as soon as I became interested in the subject. I also learned that if I were to marry Charmaine in Venezuela, I would have to get married twice—first by the state, then by the Church. When the time came I consulted a Venezuelan acquaintance, a veteran of Venezuela's marriage laws, since he had already been married a few times. I assumed that he was in a good position to provide some firsthand knowledge and advice given his experience.

"I have a friend who works in the office of the *'Jefatura Civil'* in San José," he told me. "I'll give her a call and you can go there and find out how to do it." I followed his advice immediately, but soon learned that his friend could not help me since her office dealt only with cases concerning people who lived in her district. My wedding was to take place in another district. I was told that I would have to apply there.

The following day I arrived at the second "Jefatura Civil." The receptionist smiled at me kindly and said, "Yes, you've come to the right place. But you have to bring three witnesses with you." I was beginning to think that I should never leave home without witnesses.

Having by now learned of the importance of having friends in high places and of the value placed in Venezuela on letters of introduction, I decided to once again ask the consul general for advice. Again the "CG," who had been in Venezuela many years and knew anyone who was anyone, came to my rescue. He immediately dictated a letter to his secretary, which, he suggested, should be hand-carried to the president of the Municipal Council. "This should expedite your civil ceremony arrangements," he told me.

The following Saturday morning, a relatively normal working day for Venezuelan government offices, I was ushered into the president's inner chamber.

"So, you plan to get married," the president of the Municipal Council said after completing the usual niceties of a first meeting.

"Si, Señor Presidente," I replied.

"Well, that's easy. Enrique, give Señor...Señor... (he looked at the letter again) Han-sen a card of introduction to the president of the 'Junta Comunal.'" Then, turning to me he said, "Señor Gonzalez will take care of the matter for you. It was a pleasure meeting you and I wish you the best."

"Gracias, Señor Presidente," I replied gratefully. Señor Gonzalez escorted me to a side office, typed out a short note on the back of one of the president's cards, and gave me an address indicating where I should go. I thanked him and left.

When I finally located the office of the president of the Junta Comunal, I entered and prepared for my fourth attempt to arrange the civil wedding ceremony. Upon entering the office, I saw a man sitting behind an impressive desk and immediately walked over to him.

"Ah, are you the Presidente?"

"No, I'm the secretary to the president. Can I help you?"

"Well, I have a note for the president of the Junta Comunal which I would prefer to give to him personally. Will he be here shortly?"

"No, he's gone for the day. Why don't you come back on Monday?"

"Well, perhaps you can help me. You see, I want to get married, and. . ."

"Oh, then you'll have to see the president. Can you come on Monday morning?"

"I guess I'll have to. Thank you."

The following Monday I returned to the office about 10 a.m. The president arrived about 11:30. I was told that I would need three witnesses to fill out certain papers which would be posted on the window of the building for ten days, after which the civil ceremony could take place, providing no objections to the marriage were voiced during that time. At the ceremony, two witnesses would be needed. A few days later Charmaine and I returned to the office of the Junta Comunal, accompanied by three witnesses (the new USIS Information

Officer Bob Amerson; his wife, Nancy; and Charmaine's sister, Marion).

"Now you understand," the President's secretary informed me, "that there is no cost for the ceremony. However, these papers have to be filled out." He pointed to an impressive stack of papers on his desk.

"You can fill them out yourself, or we can arrange to have them filled out for you. You understand now," he reiterated, "it costs nothing to get married. There is a fee for clerical work, however, if you don't wish to bother filling all these papers out yourself."

I took a second look at the pile of papers. "How much will it cost?" I asked. "Eighty Bolívares," he said.

I made a hurried mental calculation. That was about the equivalent of $24 U.S. I also thought, "You can't lick City Hall; City Hall just won't be beat." I gave him the 80 B's, and though tempted to ask for a receipt, decided it probably was better not to.

Ten days later, no one having voiced an objection to our marriage, Charmaine and I returned to the Junta Comunal. We were accompanied by Charmaine's sister as well as Mary Healy, Bob Fondes, the two ladies who had earlier acted as witnesses at the Archbishop's residence, Bob and Nancy Amerson, and Consul General Raymond Phelan who, by now, had taken a personal interest in our marriage. In a five-minute ceremony with Charmaine and me saying "Si" whenever we thought it appropriate, we legally became man and wife. "We're making progress," I whispered into Charmaine's ear as I kissed her.

There was still the U.S. government to contend with. Until I received word that Charmaine's clearance had been granted and my request to resign was denied, I could be sent to Mexico being, in a way, only "half married," legally by the Venezuelan government but not married in the eyes of Charmaine and her church.

USIA's Atomic Energy exhibit, which emphasized the peaceful uses of atomic energy, a major USIA theme, was scheduled to open in Caracas a few weeks later. It is thanks to this fact, and PAO George Butler's creative thinking, that my problems about the church wedding were able to be resolved. The exhibit gave the PAO a good reason to request Washington headquarters that I stay on in Caracas an extra thirty days to help mount the exhibit. Such exhibits almost always require considerable extra work and manpower, and this one was no exception. By delaying my departure to Mexico by at least a month, the security officer could conceivably complete his report on Charmaine. In fact, by the time the exhibit completed its first week in Caracas, the report was completed and on its way to Washington.

"You're a lucky guy," the security officer told me. He was certainly in a position to know.

The main obstacle was overcome. Additional paperwork required for a young Foreign Service officer to marry a person who was not a citizen of the United States was compiled and rushed to Washington. This consisted of my request for permission to marry; my letter of resignation (in case the Agency rejected my request); biographical data and a photo of the prospective bride; etc. The reply came back in record time for a U.S. government agency. The cable giving me the green light included congratulatory letters from the director of personnel and the area personnel officer. The wedding could proceed as planned on May 5th, just a few days after the Atomic Energy exhibit ended its Caracas showing. Charmaine and I were ecstatic! To add icing to the good news that Charmaine had received the "stamp of approval" of the U.S. government, my travel orders to Mexico would include my wife and we would be able to honeymoon for a few days in Jamaica and Miami en route to Mexico City.

I knew that once the state had sanctioned our marriage, by virtue of the civil ceremony, there was no turning back. A few nights before, as I passionately kissed my bride-to-be good night as we stood under the stairway leading up to the apartment where she was boarding with an elderly couple at the time, my doubts about whether or not I was doing the right thing in taking on the great responsibilities of marriage seemed to loom larger than ever. "Once married," I thought, "what will happen to my freedom? Am I really ready to take on the tremendous burden of supporting a wife? And, afterwards, there would probably be children to be taken care of. What then?" Of course, these thoughts were normally kept to myself. But on that evening I said something that sparked an immediate, startling reaction from Charmaine. My self-doubts became exposed when, standing face-to-face with my beloved, between kisses as I hugged her, I said something to the effect that perhaps we should wait awhile longer before getting married. Charmaine's reply was immediate and violent.

"Don't think you're doing me any favors, Allen," she exploded as she stepped back, visibly upset. "We don't have to get married, you know, if you don't want to."

I was taken aback. Her reaction to the mere suggestion of some delay produced fire in her eyes and her temper flared. I had not expected such a violent reaction. Now my emotions went to the other extreme. I loved her all the more—especially since she looked so lovely when she got excited in this way. "What if she backs out?" I momentarily thought. Now I began to panic, not from the thought of getting married, but from the thought of not doing so!

"No, no, no, Charmaine," I said, "I'm only kidding. Calm down. Everything is on track. Honest."

She calmed down, but the magic spell was broken for the moment. "I'm going up," she said. "Good night."

We came out from behind the stairs, not realizing that an elderly couple who lived on the third floor had just entered the foyer and was walking toward the stairs. The couple looked at us with alarm and disapproval. "What had they been up to under the stairs?" was written all over the woman's face as she and her husband passed by us.

"Buenas noches," I said, trying to be cheerful, but received a vacant stare in reply.

"They must think we're awful," I said to Charmaine, "cause they've seen us here before. Oh well, it won't be long now. In two days we'll be married," I remarked, referring to the civil wedding.

"Oh no we won't. We're not married until the church wedding, my love. And are you sure you still want to go through with it?"

I answered with a kiss. "I'll see you tomorrow. Good night, love." She disappeared up the stairs to the second floor apartment. As I watched her from the bottom of the stairs I thought, "This is one of my last nights as a 'free man'." But this thought now did not greatly disturb me. I was now at peace with myself. The thought of losing her if we did not get married was now much more disturbing.

It was now less than two weeks until the church wedding, and Charmaine had much to do before then. She had already developed formidable plans for the wedding ceremony. The supporting cast had long ago been chosen—an organist, a vocalist, a flower girl, a ring bearer, three bridesmaids, the best man and three ushers. Although the details of the ceremony were more or less settled, the plans for the reception, to be held at the home of Charmaine's sister, were still to be completed. It was in planning the reception that Venezuelan, Trinidadian and American cultures might be expected to clash. However, I took the optimistic view that rather than causing problems, the presence of three cultures might be a blessing.

"Take the timing of the cake cutting, for example," I told Charmaine's sister and her husband, Alberto, as we sat around the kitchen table at the Carvallo home, discussing plans for the reception for the tenth time.

"If we decide to cut the cake early, though it's the Venezuelan custom to cut it only when we're ready to leave, and we stay around, the Venezuelans will think we're merely following the American custom.

If we decide to follow the Venezuelan custom, our American and Trinidadian guests will be right in thinking we're doing it Venezuelan style. So, however we do it, it'll be right! We can't lose."

In the many discussions concerning the very serious business of how to conduct the wedding, only one issue created a major point of dissension. This concerned the mode of transportation for the bride and groom.

My boss, George Butler, and the political officer at the Embassy had both agreed to lend me their late-model, black Buicks, which, I thought, were sufficiently dignified to carry my bride and me and our entourage to and from the church. It was two nights before the big day when the subject of transportation, which had been left for last, came up around the kitchen table.

When informed of the transportation arrangements I had made, this being one of the few responsibilities of the groom, Alberto, almost shouting, indicated his great shock at learning, for the first time, of my plans for the transportation: "Black Buicks! Black Buicks at a Venezuelan wedding! Impossible! That's like getting married in dungarees! You have to have the wedding car."

"The wedding car?" I thought he was kidding, but soon learned that he was completely serious. "The wedding car?" I then turned to my old argument that this affair was between a Trinidadian and an American, thus our customs should prevail. "For example," I said to Alberto, "We've invited everyone to come to the church while the Venezuelan custom, as you know, is that only a few close friends attend the church ceremony while everyone goes to the reception. Why can't we do the same thing here—follow American custom?"

But Alberto was adamant. "Inconceivable!" he again almost shouted. Charmaine and I were equally adamant that the black Buicks were fine by American standards, even though we were being married in Venezuela and the reception was to be held in a Venezuelan home. But it soon became clear that this issue could cause greater friction in the family than it was worth, so, reluctantly, I relented and said, directing my remark to Alberto, "O.K. Where do we get this Venezuelan wedding car?"

Later that night, following Alberto's instructions, Charmaine and I drove into a big downtown garage that specialized in car rentals. Lined up in neatly-parked rows were about two dozen brightly polished, late model Cadillacs, Buicks, and Chryslers.

"Let's take this one," I said to Charmaine, pointing to a 1956 Cadillac. "Looks fine to me," she replied. I filled out the necessary papers, paid the hundred Bolívares rental fee, and left with the belief that our final hurdle had been overcome.

"Well, at least we'll ride in style," I told Charmaine as we headed home. "And Alberto will be happy."

The next evening we again visited Marion and Alberto for a final review of the wedding plans. While some believe that the bride and groom should not see each other the day before the wedding, and we were aware of this, we felt we just had too much to do not to meet one final time with our sponsors, especially since everything fell on their shoulders since Charmaine's parents were no longer living and my family—my widowed mother and my brother, would not be present.

"Well," I confidently told Alberto, "everything is set for the transportation. We've rented a spanking new black 'Caddie'."

"What!" Alberto exploded, "A black Cadillac! That's no better for the occasion than a Buick! You've got to get the special wedding car."

"The special wedding car?" I replied with amazement. "What's that?" Alberto began to explain to me what he thought he had explained the night before, but which obviously we had not clearly understood. So, once again, I dashed off to the rental car agency downtown. And sure enough, there was such a vehicle as Alberto had described—a superduper, deluxe chauffeur-driven, British-manufactured limousine of about 1930 vintage. A plate-glass window separated the driver from the passengers. When I saw it, I thought to myself, "That'll probably be the fanciest car Charmaine and I will ever ride in." But that we would ride in style on our wedding day there could be no doubt. There were two of them parked next to each other, a white one and a black one.

"I'll take the black one," I told the attendant. I paid an additional 45 Bolívares, and left satisfied that the car crisis was concluded. When I phoned Alberto later to tell him the good news, I imagined the smile he would have on his face and the sigh of relief when I gave him this good news, since Venezuelans are, in some respects, like the Chinese. Face is important.

"You got a black one!" Alberto shouted back at me. "The black one! You should have gotten the white one!"

"I just can't win for trying," I thought to myself.

Then Alberto said. "No, that's fine Allen. I'm just kidding." He said that he was pleased now that his sister-in-law's wedding would be a proper one.

I returned to my hotel room about 10 p.m. I was too tired for a nightcap, even though this was the final eve of my bachelorhood. My best man, fortunately, had foreseen this happening, thus had wisely arranged for the bachelor's party to be held a week earlier. It had been held at the Swiss Club and a few other places around town, and was now just a pleasant memory.

A few days earlier I had moved out of my apartment and back into the Potomac Hotel where, seventeen months earlier, I had stayed upon my arrival in Caracas.

"How things have changed," I thought, "not at the hotel, but with me. In those days Charmaine and I didn't know each other existed," I reflected, "and now we're about to spend the rest of our lives together!"

The afternoon that I moved into the Potomac I drove over to the Hotel Avila to make arrangements for renting the bridal suite where I planned to spend my first night with Charmaine. A little shy about asking for that particular room, I first asked to see a few other rooms, none of which were to my liking, before confessing to the desk clerk, "Well, actually, I'm getting married that day."

"Oh!" the clerk responded enthusiastically. "Then you want the wedding suite. Juan, show Mr. Hansen the wedding suite." This conversation attracted the attention of the few people who were in the lobby at the time. They all turned and looked in my direction. I blushed. One elderly man even put down his newspaper and stared directly at me. I was glad to escape from the lobby to view the wedding suite. It was, of course, highly satisfactory. When I left the hotel I glowed with the feeling that everything was now all set for the Big Day.

My best man Bob Fondes, determined to get me to the church on time, arrived at the Potomac Hotel about an hour and a half before I was scheduled to depart for the church. Bob carried with him a bible and a pamphlet entitled "Duties of the Best Man." He obviously took his responsibilities seriously.

As I was getting dressed, Bob remarked, "Take it easy, you still have about an hour to go."

"Plenty of time," I replied. ". . .eh, . . .eh, what's her name doesn't leave Marion's until quarter to five."

"What's her name! Boy, you're not nervous, are you Al? Her name's Charmaine, remember?"

About ten after four we were ready to leave the Potomac, picked up the boutonnieres for ourselves and the ushers at a nearby flower shop, and drove to the Hotel Avila to drop off my luggage. We went up and inspected the bridal suite. All was in readiness. Then we went down to the bar. "You might as well have your last drink as a bachelor," Bob said. I had two and felt strengthened.

Our arrival at the church was unheralded. Fortunately we found a parking place on the street directly behind the church. This was an auspicious sign, for generally a parking place in that part of town was all but impossible to find.

Bob left me sitting in the car and went into the church to see if everything was all right and to distribute the gardenias to the ushers. When he returned he reported that all was fine. "All ushers are present and accounted for, Al, and the organist is playing soothing music which is keeping the guests entertained. I didn't know you had so many friends."

"I don't," I replied. "Most of them are Charmaine's."

"Let's sit here for another minute or two, then ease up along the side of the church so we're in a good position to see when Charmaine and her entourage come into sight. That could make for perfect timing."

"O.K." came the docile reply. I was depending on Bob at the moment to take the lead. After the wedding I would depend more and more on Charmaine, though not necessarily to take the lead.

Bob and I were on station in front of the church when the cars carrying Charmaine and her brother, Cecil, and the bridesmaids rounded the corner. This was the signal for us to enter the church and head for the altar. It was a long, long walk, I reflected, but to my surprise discovered that I was not the least bit nervous. My nervousness had left me! When I thought about it later, I concluded that "there must be a little bit of 'ham' in everyone. I really enjoyed being the center of attention." But then the real center of attention entered the church — Charmaine and her entourage. The bride looked happy and lovely, smiling to her many friends as she walked down the aisle accompanied by her brother, preceded by the ushers, two bridesmaids, the maid of honor, the flower girl and Marion and Alberto's small five-year old son, who was the ring bearer.

When I, who perhaps should have been thinking only of my lovely bride at the time, thought about how I was enjoying the moment and felt not the slightest tremor of nervousness, I remembered how, at my brother's wedding, about ten years earlier, I had had the job of lighting some of the candles in the front of the church and could hardly do so because my hands shook so from the excitement. I marveled that here I was at my own wedding, cool and collected.

Charmaine moved down the aisle as if she had not a care in the world, which was true compared to what lay ahead in the years to come. Her good humor and relaxed manner were genuine. She too recalled participating in the wedding of a friend and exhibiting the same kind of excitement and nervousness that had affected me at my brother's wedding. We spoke about this later. I reasoned that while the wedding ceremony officially marked our marriage, the decision to get married had long been made. It is in reaching decisions, not in carrying them out, that one is most inclined to waiver.

If it was a long walk to the altar for Bob and me, it seemed an even longer wait, once we arrived there, before the bride and her party entered the church and the wedding procession began. Father Butterly was at his duty station in front of the altar. He gave Bob and me a friendly nod. While we stood side-by-side facing the altar, I turned my head several times to see if the bride was coming. After several minutes I heard one of my friends call out from one of the pews, "Al, are you sure Charmaine hasn't changed her mind?" This produced in me a fleeting thought: "She can't change her mind. We're already married legally." A moment later the organist struck up that old familiar tune which notified everyone that the bride was about to come down the isle. It was time for everyone to stand. The ceremony was finally beginning!

With the arrival of the bridal party at the altar, Bob and I moved to the side to make room for them. Little Alberto Jose, the ring bearer, was ready to sit down in one of the pews as soon as he arrived at the front of the church. The timely intervention of one of the bridesmaids coaxed him into standing there with the rest of the bridal party.

Some time later I tried to recall what went on during the next five minutes. I drew a blank. "All I remember," I told someone, "is that Father Butterly made a good case for God, the Church, faithfulness, and marriage, and that Charmaine and I said 'I do' at all the right places."

What I did remember was that never in my life, before or after, had I said "I do" with such firmness and conviction in my voice. I wanted the whole world to know that I was declaring my love for Charmaine. Yes, I would love and cherish her "until death do us part." The ceremony was the result of a decision which was made at what now seemed like a long time ago. The mechanics of swearing, before God and man, the results of that decision, were easy to perform.

The bride and groom and the congregation (at least the Roman Catholics among them) knelt in prayer. The ceremony was about to end. Charmaine and I were now truly man and wife!

"Now if you'll just step behind the altar and sign the book," Father Butterly said.

"Sign the book!" I said in a rather loud voice. "Sign the book! But we've already signed two or three documents."

"But you have to register now," the priest said calmly but with just the slightest hint of irritation in his voice.

"But we've already signed," I insisted, truly believing that with all the signatures demanded by the Church en route to the altar, I had signed all the papers that were necessary. I surmised that Father

Butterly just didn't know what Father Van de Velde had had me sign, or the Archbishop for that matter. So I held my ground, while Father Butterly looked more and more perplexed. This had never happened before at any of his ceremonies. The people in the pews began to wonder what was happening, for this seemed a strange time and place for a discussion between the priest and the bridegroom.

We were at an impasse. Silence reigned while the world waited. Then I had an idea.

"Would it be all right if the best man and the maid of honor sign?" I asked Father Butterly. "After all, we've already signed church documents so many times."

Father Butterly looked defeated. He accepted my solution as a way out of the dilemma. The best man and the maid of honor followed him to the back of the altar and into a side room. Emerging a few minutes later, they resumed their positions in the wedding party. The organist began the recessional. Mr. and Mrs. Hansen walked, hand in hand, down the aisle, smiling with happiness at their friends and relatives.

As we went through the front doors of the church and out into the late afternoon sun, the two chauffeurs who came with our "wedding car" stood at attention beside the open rear door of that spectacular vehicle. I helped Charmaine step up into the car, closed the door and went around to the other side. The driver, who had moved to that side of the vehicle by then, opened the door for me and I got into the back seat alongside Charmaine. Rice was pelting the car and a swarm of neighborhood children had gathered around. I opened the window on my side and the altar boy stuck in his head.

"Don't you have something for me?" he asked.

Irked by this unexpected request, though only momentarily, I reached into my pocket and gave the boy some Bolívares. "These Venezuelan customs," I thought to myself. Later I learned that the local custom was not only to give money to the altar boy, who participates in the wedding mass, but also to the children who swarm around the wedding car.

"Where to?" asked the driver after opening the window that separated him and his colleague from the newly-weds.

Charmaine told him the address of her sister's home in La Florida.

"But don't go there directly," I chimed in. "We want to ride around a little bit. We don't ride in a car like this every day." So we took a circuitous route though it still took only about twenty minutes. After delivering us to Marion and Alberto's home, the wedding car left, its role completed. Despite some disappointed children who received no coins at the entrance to the church, because this Musiu was ignorant of that custom, all other aspects of a traditional Venezuelan wedding ceremony had been followed to the hilt.

The wedding reception, designed to celebrate the blessed event of holy matrimony, was at first affected by the fact that a relative of the hosts, Marion and Alberto, had died some weeks earlier. Although this occasion was designed, in a sense, to celebrate the continuation of the species, if Venezuelan standards were followed there could be no singing and dancing at this reception. To do so, despite the fact that neither the bride nor the groom, nor most of the guests, personally knew the deceased, would be seen as being in poor taste. This view held for the first hour or two, but then the youthful energies and ebullience of the Musiu Gang could no longer be constrained. Nor was this discouraged by Charmaine, who held that while there should be all due respect to the departed, this was her party and had nothing to do with the earlier sad event. Thus, before long, the proper joy in the current event expressed itself in song and dance among the celebrants, and the party began in earnest.

The star attraction was, as always at gatherings of the Musiu Gang, Julian Conner, the big Dutchman who was from the Caribbean island of St. Maarten, and his guitar. On this occasion he, of course, had to sing the calypso he had written a few months earlier in our honor. Entitled "Blackmail in the Musiu Gang," his booming voice reverberated throughout the Carvallo home and out into the neighborhood as he strummed on his guitar and sang:

> I turning and I tossing, I cannot sleep
> All night long just counting sheep.
> The news just reached me yesterday,
> they hanging Al Hansen on the 5th of May!
>
> CHORUS
> Blackmail in the Musiu Gang, blackmail,
> Blackmail in the Musiu Gang, blackmail.
> This is the end of a happy life,
> for a man is hanged when he takes a wife.
> What make you want to do Al bad?
> Girl, pack up, and go back, to Trinidad!
> -2-
> Young Hansen is a good old pal of mine,
> I've known the man for quite some time,

and it breaks my heart to hear them say,
they hanging Al Hansen on the 5th of May!
CHORUS
-3-
Without any talk of judge nor jail,
Al is the victim of pure blackmail.
It's even too late now to pray,
Lord spare Al Hansen from the 5th of May
CHORUS
-4-
If I were the judge with hammer in hand,
I could do something to save the man,
O'er rule the court and then proclaim,
To banish the woman to Port-of-Spain
CHORUS
-5-
They spreading the rumor all o'er the town,
They going to hang Al Hansen like old
John Brown.
And our children shall learn in their history
They hanged Al Hansen on the 5th of May.
CHORUS
-6-
Bring out your sack-cloth and your purple wreath,
In the shadow of the gallows-rope I shall weep,
There's nothing left for us to do,
But mourn for the loss of our brother Musiu.
CHORUS
-7-
Now there ought to be a society,
For the prevention of cruelty,
To poor young bachelors like me,
To save us from the curse of matrimony.
CHORUS

The reception continued far into the night, and while there was much joy, there was also a gnawing feeling that the golden era of the Musiu Gang as it had existed for the past 18 months in the glorified cow town of Caracas of the mid-1950s was about to come to an end. This would occur with the departure of two of its major participants, plus others who were preparing to head for other climes. Other changes were also in the offing, like those which took place for Charmaine and me, which would affect a number of fellow Musius, not least of whom was Julian Conner. Despite his line "to save us from the curse of matrimony," he too would wed another member of the gang, a lovely English lass, and soon thereafter settle down in St. Maarten, his native Dutch island in the Caribbean.

In a sense the wedding reception was a double occasion—the beginning of a new life for Charmaine and me and the ending of the exciting, sometimes glamorous, and always enjoyable association of the young men and women of more than a dozen nationalities who made up "The Musiu Gang." Together we had roamed the beaches and mountains of Venezuela, a country of raw tropical beauty that beckoned the adventuresome spirit of youth and, for better or for worse, still waited to be developed. To have partaken of that scene, with that group of young people, at that time, was to partake of an adventure that would never be forgotten by the participants.

As with Charmaine and me, other matrimonial ties would develop within the Musiu Gang, some more lasting than others. But the bottom line was that with our May 5th wedding and our departure from Caracas, the golden era of the Musiu Gang was coming to a close. For this reason as much as anything, we wanted to savor the event for as long as we could and did not want to leave until our last guest had departed. It was about 4 a.m. when the music stopped and the last guests, except for best man Bob Fondes, said their goodbyes. Bob, always the "perfect best man," tried to follow his instruction book to the letter. This included the duty of driving the newlyweds to the hotel where they would spend their first night together.

En route to the Hotel Avila we stopped off at an all-night cafe for coffee and snacks. About 5 a.m., when we arrived at the hotel, it was the dawn of a new day, and, for Charmaine and me, the dawn of a new life together. My first overseas tour with USIA had certainly been a memorable one in so many ways. Given the challenges, glamour, excitement, frustrations (at times), and many satisfactions of a career in the Foreign Service, we looked forward with much anticipation to whatever Mexico held in store for us.

3
Mexican Mosaic

"Once the dust of Mexico has settled on your heart,·
you have no rest in any other land."
—Mexican proverb

It was a bright, sunny day when our plane touched down at the airport in Mexico City. Before landing we caught a glimpse of Mount Popocotepetl, one of the two snow-covered guardians of the Mexican capital, and as the plane swept over the sprawling metropolis, its vastness impressed us. The sheer size of this city, as seen from the air, reminded us that our beloved Caracas was a small town in comparison. The excitement of arriving in a new country, a new culture, and a new environment, and not least of all, the anticipation of living in one of the largest cities in the world, quickened our heartbeats and made us think that we were among the luckiest people in the world.

We had enjoyed our honeymoon in Jamaica and Miami en route to our new post. An incident we were to recall with a smile while staying at the Tower Isle Hotel in Jamaica was when we were awakened about ten o'clock one morning by a knock on the door.

"Who can be calling on us at this hour of the morning?" I asked Charmaine, my sleepy voice hardly audible. I got out of bed and walked over to the door, though I did not open it.

"Who's there? What do you want?"

"It's 'shyour daily cleaner sir," answered a male voice. "It's my what?" I asked.

"It's 'shyour daily cleaner sir," the man outside the door repeated.

"We didn't ask for anything to be cleaned—leave us alone please," I responded. A few hours later when we finally opened the door to our room and went to have brunch, we saw what the mystery man had in mind. On the floor outside our door was the hotel's complimentary copy of Jamaica's leading newspaper, *The Daily Gleaner.*

But our honeymoon was now over and the challenges of living and working in Mexico lay ahead. Upon our arrival at the airport we were met by the information officer, Joe Ravotto, who would be my immediate superior on my new job. Ravotto, an Italian American who was an ex-newspaper reporter, had joined USIA at its inception and considered himself a professional newsman, which he was. He welcomed Charmaine and me to Mexico, accompanied us in an office car to a second-class hotel a few blocks from the embassy, and explained that this hotel was chosen for newcomers because of its convenience to the office. He left us at the hotel after giving us his best wishes and a "welcome kit" which weighed about half a pound and would require the whole weekend to read if we were to digest its contents. But Charmaine and I were too excited to do much reading. We rested for awhile, then went out into the city streets to explore our new environment. Our thoughts were not on such mundane things as finding a place to live and settling into a new routine; nor did I focus on what my responsibilities might be in my new job. Rather, we young newlyweds thought mainly about how we would enjoy the music of the Mariachis, the romance and glamour of the Mexican environment, and Mexican cuisine. The more serious concerns about getting settled into our new environment could wait at least until Monday morning.

Monday morning came sooner than we might have wished, but excited about tackling my new job and meeting my new colleagues, I was anxious to get to work. The main office of USIS was located on three floors of the embassy. The entire embassy occupied the sixth to sixteenth floors of a sixteen-story office building and was about three blocks from our hotel. As I walked briskly through the busy, bristling streets of the Mexican capital en route to the first day on my new job, my thoughts returned to a similar occasion in Caracas when I was walking from the Potomac Hotel to the embassy—reporting to work on my first day in a new job in a new country. The San Bernardino neighborhood, mostly residential with small shops, had been quiet and relaxed. It was symbolic of the Caracas I came to know fairly well by the time I left a year-and-a-half later. Now I had to keep alert so as not to bump into anyone on the crowded sidewalks and to exercise caution when crossing the busy streets. Only the large statue of a golden angel which was perched on a huge pedestal at the center of a mammoth traffic circle near the embassy seemed to remain aloof from the hustle and bustle of the busy streets below.

I took the elevator to the sixth floor and stepped out. I was greeted by a Marine guard and after showing my credentials was directed to Joe Ravotto's office. Ravotto, who was obviously involved in the crisis of the day, smiled briefly at me and motioned for me to sit down until the crisis subsided. The information activities of USIS are always involved in meeting deadlines since the issues of the moment are the stock and trade of the information section, and the main vehicles for their messages, the mass media, wait for no one. After awhile, during which a number of Ravotto's subordinates dashed in and out of his office, consulting rapidly with him, calm returned and he came over to where I was patiently waiting and ushered me into his inner office.

"Sorry I couldn't get to you sooner, Al. The ambassador was misquoted in the Mexican press this morning and we have to get out the straight story for the afternooners or there'll be hell to pay. How are you?"

"Oh, I'm fine," I replied. "I'm looking forward to getting to work and Charmaine and I are thrilled about being here in Mexico. What little we've seen so far sure substantiates what we'd heard about Mexico City."

"I'm glad you've already found it to your liking, and I'm sure you'll love a tour here like we all do. What I want you to do first is meet the people in the office, and later, today or tomorrow, you can visit our other establishments. The radio/TV office and the library are located in other buildings, and the print shop you're going to be in charge of is a block from here. I've got to go to the country team meeting because the PAO's visiting Guadalajara today, so I'll turn you over to the PAO's secretary and she'll show you around. Tomorrow, when we chat some more, I'll tell you what I want you to focus on in the coming months. You'll also have to make your calls and go house hunting, so let's go upstairs and I'll leave you in the good hands of Liz Brown for a few hours." Ravotto spoke in a rapid fire fashion which coincided with the way he moved. He was going to be an interesting fellow to work for, I thought.

Compared to my Caracas experience, USIS Mexico was the big time. Caracas had three officers, plus a JOT and an American secretary. In Mexico, with the country public affairs officer at the top, the American staff alone consisted of the information officer and three American assistants (AIOs), the cultural affairs officer and two American assistants (ACAOs), an executive officer, a JOT and two American secretaries—12 Americans in all. In addition there were two other Americans who were USIA employees—the book translation officer and a regional librarian, both of whom did not report directly to the USIS director but to their Washington offices. The Mexican employees of USIS totaled about 75.

After meeting the USIS staff on the sixth and seventh floors of the office, I was escorted on tours of the motion picture/TV section located across town, as well as the large Benjamin Franklin Library that USIS operated. The library was a valued source of information about the U.S. and the world in general for many Mexican educators, students, and intellectuals. But the most exciting introduction was, of course, the introduction to my own staff in the print shop that I would supervise.

Joe Ravotto had already alerted me to the delicacy with which he expected me to handle my staff, since the senior Mexican employee in the print shop was not only a temperamental artist, but of Spanish background. In addition, he was about twenty-five years older than me. I got the point. And while Dan Nuñez, the artist, merited special consideration, so did the second senior employee of the twenty-six employees in the print shop, Manuel Pardo. Sr. Pardo, of Indian background, was a master printer. He had learned his trade before joining USIS and had gained much knowledge since. Undoubtedly he shared Dan Nuñez' qualms about a young American officer, fresh from JOT training, coming on board to supervise their work. However, I had no qualms about meeting the challenges of the situation in which I now found myself. I knew that I knew nothing about managing print shops and would have to rely on the expertise of these two men to assure a smooth and effective operation. But I did feel that I knew something about human nature. Very much aware of the sensitivities of Spaniards, Latin Americans, and native Americans, I was determined and confident that the three of us could work together effectively.

One of the first duties required of a "husband-wife team" just arriving at a major Foreign Service post such as Mexico City in the 1950s was to follow traditional protocol and "make calls." Each post was different, depending on how traditional-minded the ambassador and his deputy chief of mission were and other factors, but in the 1950s calls were generally an integral part of the early activities required of new arrivals at an American embassy. In the seventies and eighties, this tradition died. As American missions abroad greatly expanded and life became more hectic, informality, always an element of American mores, became even more a part of our culture. A good example of this was the growing trend toward first-name usage in government and business.

Although time consuming, "making calls" had several advantages. It provided valuable information and guidance to newcomers, enabled them to get a better idea of the local geography as they visited different neighborhoods, and they met many more colleagues and their families with whom they would live and work than occurred in later years when the system of making calls was all but abolished. The instructions about calls for personnel at the American embassy in Mexico were specific. For example:

CALLS
Upon the ambassador. Cards should be left upon the ambassador within three days after arrival. For this purpose, the officer and his wife (or the wife alone) will call at the embassy residence sometime between 4:30 and 6:00 p.m., and will leave three cards for the husband and two for the wife (or two "Mr. and Mrs." cards and one for the husband). On the uppermost card there should be indicated, in pencil, the local address of the callers.

Similar specific instructions were provided about calls on the minister-counselor and the counselors of embassy and their wives, upon the service attaches and their wives, and upon the members of the section of the embassy to which the officer was assigned and their wives, if senior in rank. Calls were to be returned within ten days. The delivery of cards was often sufficient, though many senior officials and particularly their wives welcomed the opportunity to greet and become acquainted with new arrivals and to give them the benefit of their experience at that particular post. The main burden for the calls fell upon Charmaine, as I, like most husbands, was generally excused from most personal calls as I had "my labors to perform." The growing influx of women into the Foreign Service in later years was another reason for abandoning the time-consuming traditional calling system.

Second only to the obligation of making calls was the necessity to locate living quarters. The embassy administrative office provided some leads and some guidance as to what residential areas were desirable and relatively convenient to the embassy, but each person was on his or her own to locate suitable quarters. That office also provided the latest regulations as to limitations on size and cost of overseas housing, which the independent wealthy might ignore, but given my salary as a junior officer I had to make sure that whatever house or apartment Charmaine and I rented would have to be within the limits of our allowance.

After looking at a number of furnished apartments, for we had practically nothing in the way of furniture, we found one that met our needs. It was only a few blocks from Avenida Insurgentes, a major thoroughfare where I could get to the office by boarding one of the frequent cabs which picked up as many customers as possible, charging a peso per person as it sped toward the downtown area of the city. We soon became friendly with our landlady, a charming middle-aged Spanish woman whose family had emigrated from Spain to Mexico a decade or so earlier. She was a great help to Charmaine with advice on how to master the peculiarities of shopping and keeping house in Mexico.

The landlady's maid came with the apartment if we wanted to hire her, and we felt obligated to do so. Every middle-class family in Mexico had at least one maid, but Mexico at that time was going through a period of transition. Many of the women who formerly could make their living only as domestics were now being employed as factory workers in Mexico's expanding industries, thus maids were increasingly difficult to find. Among those who still worked as maids, more and more preferred not to "live-in" as had been the custom for generations. In the neighborhood where our apartment was located, most "live in" maids were quartered in one-room shelters located on the roof of the apartment buildings. The penthouse idea had not yet come to Mexico or else the maids would certainly have been relegated to the basements. But now I had a new responsibility—the care and feeding of a maid in my household. While at first blush this addition appeared to be a great advantage, unlike dishwashing machines, which might break down occasionally, maids are often subject to problems and emotions—part of the baggage of most domestic employees. These problems tend to involve their employers at one time or another. Thus I soon learned that among the subjects of discussion when diplomats get together at cocktail parties and other social or quasi-social gatherings, strange as it may seem, was the latest household problems brought about by the household servants. Yet most middle-class Americans living in the continental U.S. might argue that such problems are the kind with which they would be pleased to cope.

Meantime, back at the office, I was getting acquainted with my staff, my colleagues, and the office routine. I met the PAO who had returned from a short visit to Guadalajara, the location of one of USIS Mexico's three branch posts. Orville Anderson, the PAO, was a former war correspondent. He had an excellent professional reputation and, at the same time, was a humane, warm-hearted individual, traits that do not always go together.

"We're glad to have you on our team," Anderson told me when we met for the first time. "I've already heard good things about you.

George Butler wrote to me from Caracas. He says you're mature, versatile, and imaginative and that he gave you an intensive and varied training program. Coming from George those are solid recommendations. Needless to say I'm happy to welcome someone so highly recommended. There's plenty of work around here to stretch your imagination and energies. How's your wife adjusting to Mexico?"

"Oh, she loves it, just as I do," I answered.

After discussing the role of the print shop in USIS operations and what he expected of the publications officer, he reminded me that his door was always open and that if I had any problems or concerns of any kind to feel free to call on him.

"And by the way," he added just before closing the interview, "several guys are going on leave in the next few months. We'll probably be calling on you to fill in while they're gone. This will broaden your experience." I thanked him and made my exit. I returned to my office to continue reviewing with Nuñez and Pardo the details of the print shop activities. The USIS print shop provided for all the printing needs of USIS MEXICO, but the bulk of the work was the design and printing of pamphlets for distribution throughout the country and by USIS posts in Central America. Dan Nuñez's artwork graced the pages of many of these pamphlets, the themes of which were predominantly political, economic, and cultural subjects.

For a few months prior to my arrival the shop had been without an American officer directly in charge. There was a considerable backlog of work and a very serious morale problem, two items which I knew would have to receive priority attention. The problem of the backlog was complex and would take considerable time to resolve. As for the morale problem, I soon learned that it stemmed primarily from the fact that a young, recently-married Mexican employee had, in recent months, habitually reported for work an hour or two late. He had ignored repeated verbal warnings that he would be disciplined if he continued to arrive late to work, and yet no visible action was ever taken against him. Observing this, his colleagues, most of whom were hardworking and highly dedicated, concluded that if the supervisors didn't care about this fellow's work habits which adversely affected production, why should they? The American officer nominally in charge spent most of his time at his regular job in another building and visited the print shop only occasionally. Both he and Dan Nuñez, who acted as the immediate supervisor, were apparently waiting for the new American supervisor to arrive to perform what could be the onerous task of firing the wayward employee.

Within the first few weeks on my new job I gave the young man two warnings. When both were ignored, I fired him. This led to a violent confrontation whereby he claimed that I was "unfair," "cruel," unaware that he had recently been married and had a wife to support with a child on the way, etc. But I remained adamant.

A few days later I was called into the office of the public affairs officer.

"Al, how could you fire this guy? He's been to see the ambassador and he's seen me. He just recently got married. Can't you give him another chance?"

I was amazed at the young man's resiliency and efforts to regain his job. As I told the PAO, such energy had not been noticeable on the job, where not only was he consistently late in arriving to work, but lackadaisical in his duties. I was further amazed that the PAO would consider overruling my decision. Finally I said, "We have to stick with this decision under the circumstances. Either he goes or I go. If we bring him back the morale of my employees will sink even further than it has after seeing what this fellow was getting away with at our expense for so many months!"

"O.K.," the PAO replied. "I agree, but I hope you don't go around firing too many of our employees, Al. We're here to make friends with the Mexicans, not to get them upset with us."

The interview was ended. Following the decisive action taken with regard to an incompetent and abusive employee, morale shot sky high among the remaining employees of the print shop. And although word came back to me that the dismissed employee threatened to physically attack me for causing his dismissal, nothing untoward occurred. The former employee disappeared into the anonymity of Mexico's millions. Perhaps he took my advice when I told him to wake up to reality by being more conscientious at his next place of employment, perhaps not. But the change of morale among the other twenty-five print shop employees convinced me that, when the situation requires it, firing is a management tool that should always be considered. In later years I would say, with some validity, "I tend to fire at least one person at every place I've worked. It's good for morale." As for the backlog, that was not as quickly and cleanly resolved, yet in due course I was able to report that substantial progress had been made.

I had hardly begun to learn the intricacies of my new job as publications officer when I was called upon to fill a position that was to be vacant for about three months between the transfer of one officer and the assignment of another. This was just what the PAO had told me would happen, although I had not expected to be assigned extra duties so soon. For the next three months I would be the post's radio and TV officer.

"I know as much about radio and TV as I know about printing," I mused. But I knew I could learn, and among the things I was learning was that the Agency I worked for wasn't kidding when proclaiming that its Foreign Service officers were expected to be "generalists." They were supposed to be able to assume any assignment, be it informational or cultural, and were expected to rely on the national staff for the expertise required to carry out their mission. This meant that what was really required of these "generalists," aside from basic intelligence and ability to get along with people, was to be good managers. Relying on the professional qualifications and the intimate knowledge of local customs and mores of their senior nationals, their job was often one of supervision and administration. Those who knew how to lead and how to get the most out of their subordinates, succeeded. However, the new USIA had initially employed a number of former war correspondents and others who were more accustomed to working alone as writers and reporters than to supervising people. In such cases personnel problems were more apt to arise between the American supervisors and their subordinates, than between those American officials who already had managerial experience or who had studied good management techniques, and their staffs.

It was just such a situation that I noted with regard to my boss, Joe Ravotto, who, as an individual, was a pleasant, likable person. However, as a supervisor of three American assistants and, indirectly, some fifty-five Mexican employees, his management style often resulted in considerable frustration and bickering among his subordinates. The situation had become so intolerable that, by the time I arrived on the scene, two of his American assistants were extremely embittered toward him. This became obvious from their comments to me and their efforts to enroll me in their cause. My reaction was that in no way did I want to join their unhappiness. To do so would have meant spending time in such negative pursuits as endlessly discussing the alleged faults of the information officer. Rather than getting caught in that trap, I mused, I want to think positively. "I enjoy my work too much," I reasoned, "and relish the satisfaction which comes from seeing positive results to want to get sidetracked by becoming involved in their vendetta." This proved to be a wise decision. What added to the discomfort of the AIOs who were so unhappy with their lot is that they had been branch PAOs prior to being assigned to Mexico. Now each had been relegated from being his own boss as a BPAO to being the subordinate of someone who was always right there to tell them what to do, and who was not shy about providing instant criticism. This was a hard pill to swallow and the cause of much of their frustration. As for me, I was new, eager, and anxious to learn, and as I was experiencing so much fun and excitement in my new job, I had little difficulty remaining aloof from office politics. Eventually Ravotto's tour as head of the information section ended and he was replaced by Earl Wilson, another professional communicator but one who operated in a much calmer mode than his predecessor.

My new responsibilities as radio and TV officer brought me in contact with Mexican radio and TV managers and producers, including the famed Mexican TV mogul, Manuel Escarraga, whose office was the largest one I had ever seen and whose impressive desk was three or four times the size of an ordinary desk. His office contained a model of the new Mexican TV complex which would soon be under construction, a modern Mexican version of New York's Rockefeller Center. I also found myself discussing USIS TV services with a producer who confided to me that he was making so much money in TV that he had purchased three miles of the Mexican coastline on the Yucatan Peninsula and was now marketing coconuts as a sideline.

This same producer phoned me a few months after we had first met and asked me if I had seen a recent story in the news magazine *Time,* concerning the tragic blinding of a young Mexican medical doctor. This doctor had performed a cataract operation on a professional boxer who was spending the night at the clinic where the doctor had his practice. When the patient awoke from the operation in the early morning hours, he naturally could not see as his eyes were bandaged. But thinking that the operation had left him blind, he rushed out of his room in search of the doctor, stumbling as he felt his way along the corridors of the clinic and shouting and swearing in a fit of rage. The nurse on duty screamed and called for help. The doctor, awakened by the noise from his quarters nearby, rushed into the clinic and was met by the enraged boxer who attacked him. Before anyone knew what was happening, the boxer stuck his fingers into the doctor's eyes and tore them out. I had indeed read about that unique, tragic occurrence, reported to the world by *Time* and in the local press.

"Well," the TV producer told me, "Dr. Medina is a friend of mine. I was just wondering if it would be possible for the American Embassy to help him in any way. I understand they do marvelous things for the blind in the United States, and I thought maybe the embassy could help in some way to get him a scholarship to one of those schools for the blind. He's an educated person and does not want to end his constructive role in society because of this personal tragedy, but he's also not a wealthy person, having sunk all of his savings into his clinic. Do you think you can do anything for him?"

I responded with the sympathy that sprung within nearly everyone who heard or read about this case. After informing my superiors and consulting with Washington, arrangements were made in the United States for a grant to enable the doctor to attend a special training course for the blind. USIS further arranged that he and his wife should personally receive the grant from the ambassador. All of this, of course, took time, but in a few weeks all was arranged and a ceremony was to take place in the ambassador's office where the doctor would be awarded a grant to a rehabilitation center for the blind in the U.S. I met him when he and his young wife arrived at the embassy and escorted them to the ambassador's office.

The courage and positive outlook of the doctor were greatly admired by everyone who came in contact with him. Only the ambassador seemed to be unaffected by the human tragedy so evident in this incident. From what he commented later it appeared, much to my chagrin, that the ambassador's main interest was in the public relations aspect of the grant, for it was clear that he was totally unaffected by the plight of the doctor. Idealist that I am, such an attitude was disheartening to me. But from this experience I learned that being a "generalist" in USIA can also include activities far beyond the agency's cultural and information missions.

When I first arrived in Mexico, the American ambassador had been a career officer. He was transferred shortly after my arrival and replaced by a political appointee, the man mentioned above. Political appointees have often been bugaboos for career foreign service types, since they fill jobs which career officers would otherwise fill, and some of them act in questionable ways or ways which disrupt traditional systems, which often displeases the professionals. Many, however, are highly regarded and respected, and like their career counterparts, come in all sizes and shapes with varying degrees of competence.

Although I was new and inexperienced as a Foreign Service officer, I felt that the current ambassador was a person with attitudes that left much to be desired. My negative opinion of him was reinforced sometime after the incident with Dr. Medina. Using his ambassadorial prerogative, he caused the transfer to another post of the USIS cultural affairs officer, a highly qualified, dedicated and capable officer. The rumor making the office rounds was that the ambassador simply didn't like the CAO's face—he didn't want to see him at his periodic staff meetings. Others, years later, contended that it was anti-Semitism on the part of the ambassador that caused him to have this particular USIA officer transferred. The CAO was Jewish. Had I been told at the time that this occurred because the ambassador was anti-Semitic I would have thought it to be incredible. But this was 1956. If, indeed, such was the case, such ambassadorial power and such prejudicial actions were much less apt to be exercised a decade or two later as American society and the Foreign Service matured. In fact, the innocent victim in this case went on to serve with distinction elsewhere, eventually becoming a deputy assistant secretary of state, a level few USIA officers ever reached.

When the new radio and TV officer arrived at the post I went back to work full time at my publications duties. A few weeks later I was asked to fill in as the motion picture officer while he was on home leave. I had had some experience in running the motion picture operation of USIS in Caracas so I felt somewhat at home in this position. However, I was not prepared for a complaint the office received from a Catholic girls' school that had borrowed a USIS film on the American educational system. In the middle of the film someone who had borrowed it earlier had spliced into it a short sequence that was hardly germane to the subject. As the students were watching the screen and learning about the U.S. school system, suddenly a belly dancer appeared, doing her thing. Apologies were made to the school authorities and I ordered that all USIS films loaned across the counter should hereafter be carefully cleaned and screened before being placed on loan again. Although this had been standard practice, "it obviously needs to be done more thoroughly," I told the motion picture staff. We never learned who the culprit was, or whether the sabotaged film resulted from political or humorous motives.

After completing my "mopix" experience, I was next asked to fill in as the acting executive officer for a two-month period while the "exec" went on home leave. This turned out to be one of the greatest learning experiences of my Mexican tour because the "exec" at any USIS post must be involved in the planning and execution of all of the post's varied programs. The "exec" controls all the funding, must approve all payments, and consults frequently with the PAO and other officers with regard to nearly every aspect of their activities. He also gets involved in housing, travel, and other allowances affecting every American employee. He is almost in a better position than the PAO to know and understand the intricacies of the post's operations, though the decisions, and the policies, are the PAO's prerogative. Thus

I felt fortunate to be given the opportunity of temporarily filling this key position. I could not help but be pleased that the "old man" (the PAO) had expressed sufficient confidence in me to assign me to that position. I was also fortunate, I thought, in having such good men in the print shop as Nuñez and Pardo who could keep that operation functioning smoothly with a minimum of supervision on my part, particularly now that morale in the shop had hit a new high following the dismissal of the one rotten apple.

Charmaine and I had been in Mexico about three months and were enjoying the Mexican *ambiente* to the hilt, while my work at the office strengthened my belief that being a "foreign service information officer," as we were called in those days, was without doubt one of the most exciting professions in the world. We missed not having a car, however, and waited anxiously for its arrival by ship from Caracas. We had decided to ship my old faithful Vauxhall to Mexico. After all, it had taken us through so many miles of Venezuelan hinterlands and had, in a sense, brought us together. Though old and beaten, we reasoned that it would provide us with reliable transportation until I received a few raises and could buy a new car. When the word finally arrived that our car had been unloaded at the port of Vera Cruz, we arranged to go to the port, a one-day drive from Mexico City, with one of the Mexican employees in an office car. We would then drive our car back to the capital. Looking forward to seeing the Mexican countryside and the Gulf of Mexico on our first outing outside the city limits, we left the weekend after receiving word that the car had been unloaded in Vera Cruz.

Arriving in that port city at dusk, we checked into a hotel on the beach that had the trappings of a building that might have been there before the Mexican revolution. Our driver had relatives in Vera Cruz, or so he said, and disappeared with the car. He returned about 7:30 a.m. the following day to help us get our car released from customs.

With the same anxiety, thrill, and expectation that one might experience in going to pick up a new car, Charmaine and I approached the pier where a number of cars, recently unloaded from coastal steamers, were parked. The customs official took us to a small yellow Volkswagen and smiled at us as if to share, in a small way, our pleasure at a reunion with our wheels.

"But that's not our car" I said. "Our car's a Vauxhall. And it's black." The customs official was not the least bit disturbed. "That's the vehicle that's on the manifest," he said, but on looking at his papers a little closer he noted, "Yeh, you're right. Your car is a Vauxhall. They unloaded the wrong car."

Back in Mexico City a few days later, with the knowledge that the ship which had delivered cargo from Caracas was headed for Havana, I drafted a cable to the embassy in Cuba informing them about the Volkswagen sitting on the dock in Vera Cruz and asking them if they knew of the whereabouts of my Vauxhall. A week or two passed before a reply came back. The return cable informed me that the Volkswagen in Vera Cruz belonged to a secretary assigned to the American embassy in Havana and my Vauxhall had been unloaded in Havana. The embassy administrative officer, the cable said, would take action to switch the cars but it might take some time before shipment could be arranged. In the meantime, Charmaine and I would have to rely on cabs, friends, and company cars. Another three months would pass before our car finally arrived in Mexico, and since we had already been to Vera Cruz we decided to let the embassy arrange to have the car sent to the capital from there.

Having arrived in Mexico on a direct transfer from Caracas, after about six months in Mexico I became eligible for home leave. Thus we left Mexico en route to my childhood home in New Jersey on my first home leave since entering the Foreign Service. In addition to meeting my widowed mother for the first time, Charmaine would meet many of my relatives and a few friends. One of my aunts, knowing that we had met in Venezuela, and unaware that Charmaine's homeland of Trinidad was a former British colony, assumed her native tongue must be Spanish. "My, where did you learn to speak English so well?" she asked after they met and had talked for a few minutes.

Being new in the Foreign Service, I followed the typical home leave pattern of systematically visiting friends and relatives after an absence of several years. Only when I became a more seasoned FSO did I give up this custom, for by then I learned that regardless of the interesting places we had been to and the exciting adventures we had experienced, there was little inclination on the part of most of my relatives and friends to listen to our tales for more than a few minutes. They had their own problems and concerns which left little room for hearing about life in the Foreign Service. Furthermore, no matter how well or how often I explained that USIA was in the business of distributing information rather than collecting it, there were those among my acquaintances, even after thirty years, who remained convinced that I worked for the CIA.

Aside from buying new things available only in the U.S. and replenishing some items for our Mexican household, we had a major item of business to complete while on home leave. As the wife of an

FSO, Charmaine would not have to wait the usual five years to become an American citizen. The waiting period was waived. In fact, we had been encouraged to apply for her citizenship as soon as possible in order that she might more adequately represent the United States in her capacity as the wife of an American diplomat. So we made an appointment with the district court in Newark, New Jersey to obtain her American citizenship while on home leave.

Charmaine took the oath of citizenship with about forty other immigrants though she was concerned, until the moment of her swearing in, that the judge would ask her a question about American history that she would be expected to answer—and before all these people. What she knew about American history was about as much as I knew of Trinidadian history at the time. But the judge asked no questions. He merely made a statement about the significance of American citizenship, had the applicants raise their right hands and swear allegiance to their new country, after which he came down and shook hands with the new citizens and wished them well.

When the judge came to where we were standing he soon learned that we lived in Mexico City.

"I have a friend who lives in Mexico City," he remarked.

"Where does he live?" I asked.

"On Rio de la Plata."

"Rio de la Plata!" That's where we live. 'What number?"

"59."

"59! That's where we live," both Charmaine and I answered in unison. As it turned out, the judge's friend, a writer from Eastern Europe, lived in the same apartment building where we lived, in the apartment across the hall from us. "Small world, isn't it?" Charmaine reflected.

Shortly after our return from home leave in the U.S. our landlady notified us that she did not plan to renew the lease as she had decided to move back into her apartment. We would have to look for another place to live.

We began our search for a new home by looking at houses in several preferred neighborhoods where many diplomats lived, but each house we saw that we liked was too costly for us newlyweds. Finally, after several weeks of searching, we located a house in a residential neighborhood known as Guadeloupe Inn. The house had three bedrooms and a large yard, and was only a few blocks from Avenida Insurgentes where, if necessary, I could catch one of the frequent *puestos*, the ubiquitous taxis which ran up and down major thoroughfares picking up passengers and dropping them off along the way for a peso per person. Usually, however, I drove to the office in about half an hour.

We had only a few small pieces of furniture, so the first thing we had to do after signing the contract for the house was to get a bed for the master bedroom, a kitchen table and a few chairs. Other items would be added as time went on and as my salary permitted the expenditure of funds for capital investments. In the meantime we agreed that with the house so empty, especially the living and dining rooms, we would be able to give great parties where everyone could dance without worrying about knocking over the furniture. Nor would we be concerned if anyone spilled wine on the packing cases we would use as tables.

The neighborhood of Guadalupe Inn, where our new house was located, was about five miles from the embassy and the USIS print shop. I had been aware of the pollution problem in Mexico City, which people had only just begun to talk about, but it was not until I started commuting to work from my new home that I realized how serious that problem was becoming. Each morning, shortly before 8 a.m., as I turned into Insurgentes and headed toward the downtown area, I could see a dark cloud of smog far ahead of me, the darkness of which increased the closer I came to the downtown area. It would take several more decades before the Mexicans would become concerned enough about how their city was being choked by pollution to begin to do something about it. Thirty years later, for example, Popocatepetl and Ixtacihuatl, the two snow-covered 17,000-feet high volcanoes which overlook the city and which were often visible when I drove to work, could seldom be seen from the downtown area of Mexico City. By the early 1990s, by midday, often earlier, the downtown area was covered by a thick grey ceiling which thickened as the day wore on. Some environmentalists contended that even if all the factories in Mexico City were closed, the air would still remain stagnant and unhealthy because the main polluting culprits were the thousands of automobiles on the streets of what had by then become the world's largest city. None of those thousands of cars were required to carry anti-pollution devices. Complicating the efforts eventually made to combat polluted air is Mexico City's location on a plateau about a mile and a half above sea level.

It took years for the Mexican government to acknowledge the pollution problem, let alone to take any action to alleviate the situation, given so many other social problems Mexico faced. Yet it was obvious to anyone who drove from the periphery of the city into that black cloud every day, as I then began to do, just as it was to anyone who looked out the window of their plane just before landing at the Mexico City airport, that that dark cloud silently hovering over the sprawling metropolis below presented a problem which would get only worse as time went on. As an indication of this growing problem, the collars of my white shirts, after a day at the office, were black by the time I returned home in the evening.

In the wee hours one morning in July, I thought I was back in the Navy, aboard ship. We were riding out a rough storm, and it would soon be time to get out of my bunk and back up on the bridge, though I really felt as though I had just turned in. Then I realized that I wasn't aboard a ship. It was just that the room seemed to be rocking. The Venetian blinds were swinging violently back and forth. A few more seconds passed before I convinced myself that this was no dream. I was in my bed with Charmaine who also had been awakened, but why were the blinds swinging like that?

"What's happening?" I shouted in alarm. "Why are the blinds moving like that?"

"What's the matter?" she asked in alarm.

"The blinds, the blinds—they're moving"! I answered.

Charmaine stared at the blinds, which had begun to slow down in their movement back and forth across the window. "Oh, it's only an earthquake," she said matter-of-factly. She was used to minor quakes in Trinidad, which normally lasted only a few seconds. Nor did Port-of-Spain have any tall buildings to worry about when a quake hit. For me, however, I was at that moment experiencing my first earthquake.

"Let's get the hell out of here," I shouted at Charmaine as I jumped out of bed, grabbed my glasses from the side table and quickly slipped into my slippers. Charmaine was right behind me as we headed for the stairs.

The staircase leading from the ground floor to the upstairs area was one of the outstanding features of our new home. The stairs were of marble with wide, heavy marble railings. But as we fled down these stairs with the intent of getting out of the house before it disintegrated, another shockwave struck. The steps beneath us, and the railing which we grabbed for support, felt like jelly. We were fearful that the whole staircase might collapse before we reached the bottom, but it still held as we dashed into the kitchen and headed for the kitchen door which led to the outside.

We had a problem with the lock on the kitchen door so we had tied a rope to the door from the inside to prevent it from being opened from outside while we slept. Despite our relatively empty house being a poor target for a potential thief, we were very security conscious. But as I tried to untie the rope that held the door closed, my fingers shook so much that I couldn't untie the knot. Charmaine grabbed a kitchen knife and slashed the rope. We pushed the door open and moved quickly into the doorframe and stood there, huddled together, for we remembered that that is what is recommended under the circumstances — the theory being that if the walls of the house collapse the doorframes would remain intact and thus protect us.

As we stood there and looked out there was an eerie silence. In that silence we could hear our hearts pounding and our own deep breathing caused by our efforts at fleeing and our anxiety. The sky above us was black, as all the lights in the surrounding area had been extinguished when the quake disrupted the electrical power. Yet the sky was pretty, for with the city in darkness, thousands of stars were visible. Looking skyward from our backyard it was a tranquil scene. Still, we remained quiet and anxious, unsure about whether or not the earth would now settle down or if another shockwave was going to occur. Twice we heard a rumbling sound in the distance that grew louder as it approached us and diminished after it passed. These aftershocks were brief and mild compared to the initial shock that had awakened us.

Little by little lights appeared in the distance as people began to move about and as emergency crews began to search for victims and to assess the damage. We had no way of knowing how bad the quake was. Our phone was dead and the radio was useless without electricity. The first sounds we heard in the eerie darkness were of dogs howling. It was a mournful sound. After a while we went back into the house as the aftershocks seemed to have ended. We tied our back door again and went back to bed. The next day we would see just how much damage the quake had caused. I checked my watch. It was about ten minutes to four. I judged the tremor must have hit Mexico City about 2:30 a.m.

We overslept the next morning, exhausted by the experience of the night before. When we awoke it was a bright sunny day, typical for that time of year. After breakfast I got into my car and left for the office. I was amazed at what I saw as I drove down Insurgentes en route to the downtown area. Some sections of the city appeared to be completely unscathed, but here and there buildings had been heavily damaged. Many looked as if they had been bombed the night before.

As I passed a familiar theater on Insurgentes, which was on the ground floor of a ten-story building, I was shocked at what I saw.

Each floor of the building above the theater had collapsed so that the floors were now stacked like pancakes, all the supporting walls having disintegrated. The building was allegedly owned by the great Mexican comedian, Mario Moreno ("Cantinflas"). During the day the floors above the theater were filled with women garment workers, all of whom would have perished had the quake occurred during working hours. As the quake occurred in the early morning, only the guard who lived on the third floor lost his life at that particular site. Later the government announced that about 500 people had died in the quake, but no one who lived through it and saw the devastation accepted those figures. Everyone assumed the government had its important tourist trade in mind when the official statistics were released.

When I reached my office Nuñez and Pardo had already arrived. The outside wall by my desk had collapsed, leaving a hole big enough to drive about five cars through. The print shop itself was a mess, with paper and pamphlets strewn about and pulverized plaster covering the presses, the collators, and other machinery. No one was permitted to enter the building and it was, in fact, declared uninhabitable a few days later. With the building condemned, the search for a new site began immediately. We found suitable space on the ground floor of a new building a few blocks away that had withstood the quake with little damage, but several months passed before we were able to install our operations at the new site and our presses were able to roll once more.

The cleanup of the old site was tedious and had to be exercised with caution because of the condemned status of the building. But as our move to a new site happened at a time when we had just received, but had not yet installed, a large Harris press for our printing plant, the timing of the quake was, in a sense, propitious. If this act of nature had to occur, it could not have happened at a more suitable time for our printing operation. Had the large, new press already been installed and operating, our losses and the difficulty of the move would have been much greater.

Miraculously, none of the embassy's American and Mexican staff had been killed or seriously injured, though some relatives of Mexican staffers were not so lucky. The embassy itself had suffered major damage, and as the stories of individual experiences unfolded, the extent of the damage wrought by the quake became apparent.

The two Marine guards on duty in the sixteen-story embassy building at the time of the quake had their mettle tested. Sergeant Ronald Walker was on duty at the guard desk on the sixth floor when the building began to rock violently. The wall he was facing split open and cracks appeared suddenly in all of the walls around him, followed by a burst of white dust as the plaster along the lines of the cracks disintegrated. He caught just a glimpse of all this as almost immediately the lights went out and he was in total darkness.

His colleague, Sergeant Joe Woolery, was treated to an even greater shock. He was in an elevator, coming down from one of the upper floors after routinely inspecting the various offices, when the swerving building caused the elevator to swing back and forth against the walls of the elevator shaft as it plummeted down to the ground floor after the electricity was lost. As the elevator shaft was located on the back outer side of the building, the force of the elevator hitting the outer side of the shaft as it bashed into the brick walls of the building sent hundreds of bricks flying into the street below, leaving huge gaps in the side of the building. When the surprised Marine reached the bottom, he had to force open the elevator doors. He stepped out and turned on his flashlight, but could see absolutely nothing. The same swirling chalk-like dust from the cracked walls, which enveloped his partner on the sixth floor, enveloped him. Despite the difficulty in breathing caused by the dust, especially in Mexico City's thin air, he ran to the stairwell and dashed up the stairs to the sixth-floor guard desk in order to return to his duty station and to assist his colleague if needed.

Just prior to 2:40 a.m. when the quake hit, a Saturday night party at the Marine House was winding down, though it was by no means stalled. The quake brought it to an abrupt halt. Bricks from the high walls surrounding the house tumbled down and a goldfish from the fountain in the patio was sloshed out onto the ground. The lights of the house went out as they did elsewhere. The "Gunny" ordered two of his Marines to head for the embassy immediately and told the others to stand by. The party was over.

The embassy security officer, awakened as Charmaine and I were, tried to call the embassy but the phone was dead. He dressed hurriedly and rushed to assess the damage at the chancery and to assure himself that the embassy offices were secure. Passing through streets filled with frightened people and strewn with shattered glass and debris, he wondered if the embassy building was still standing.

At the ambassador's residence, an old, sturdy building which had survived other earthquakes, the ambassador and his wife were awakened by the sound of falling plaster. They had arrived in Mexico only the week before, thus earthquake relief would become the ambassador's first major order of business at his new post.

The consul general, driving home along the Paseo de la Reforma in the center of the city, suddenly felt his car swerve as if blown by a strong wind. He had gone to the airport to pick up two visiting officials who were his friends and had just dropped them off at their hotel. He pulled his car to a halt as soon as he could. The streetlights suddenly went out while the headlights of his car could hardly penetrate the dust that arose and covered the street.

The administrative officer, describing his experience to his colleagues the next morning, said that he and his wife awoke to find their bed rolling across their bedroom floor. This was accompanied by the crash of a Chinese jade screen in their living room, a cherished Hong Kong memento which broke into pieces. To get out of his apartment he had to kick down his front door.

The embassy's communications supervisor and his wife had just gone to bed after returning home from the Marine party. The force of the quake threw them completely out of bed.

One of the book translation editors, whose home faced the "Glorieta" which holds Mexico's beloved twenty-foot high gold-colored "Angel," looked out of his window to see the tall pedestal which holds the "Angel" sway back and forth. Then the statue fell from its 150-foot perch, striking the pavement and breaking apart.

In her third floor apartment of the Casa Latino Americano near the embassy building, a clerk from the legal attaché's office awoke from the sound and the movement of the first shake. Her roommates were on a trip so she was alone in the apartment except for the maid. She clambered over fallen chunks of plaster and was pushed from wall to wall by the shock waves. Once she was knocked completely over before managing to reach the maid's room. Together they lighted a candle and, working with a hammer and a screwdriver, forced open the jammed front door.

When the security officer first arrived at the embassy the elevators were out of order, there were no lights, debris was strewn about, and the air was thick with dust. Escorted by one of the Marines, he began an office-by-office inspection of the building.

His inspection revealed large cracks in the walls, and in some places the walls had collapsed. Chunks of concrete had fallen here and there and the tops of desks and office equipment were littered with plaster. Some of the office doors were jammed and had to be forced open.

In the nearby Casa Latino Americana where the legal attaché's clerk had finally managed to escape from her apartment, the authorities ordered everyone to evacuate the building, fearing that it might fall down at any moment. Unable to find a telephone to call friends for assistance, the clerk went to the embassy building and climbed the stairs in the dark to the guard's desk on the sixth floor. She shook so much from her experience that she had to ask the Marine guard to dial the phone for her.

By sunrise some of the telephones were working and the flood of calls from friends and relatives began to arrive, swamping the embassy switchboard. When the duty officer answered one of the first callers to get through, the sister of an embassy employee who was calling from Los Angeles said, "Is my sister dead?"

"Where did you get such an idea?" he answered. "Because you've had a tremendous earthquake," she responded. "It's in the headlines of all the papers."

At daybreak the ambassador arrived and climbed the eleven flights of stairs to his office. Orders went out for all section heads and all of the Marines to report for duty. A check on the safety of American and Mexican employees was the first order of business. Reports also had to be prepared immediately on the extent of damage to the embassy, the need for assistance, the safety of American residents and visitors, and an estimate of the extent of damage that Mexico had sustained. A special task force was immediately established under the ambassador's direction to expedite the reporting and to initiate the activities needed to enable the embassy to operate again. But first a determination had to be made as to the safety of the shaken embassy building. Unlike the nearby Casa Latino Americana and the USIS print shop, the embassy building was soon declared safe for habitation. The cleanup and repairs began immediately thereafter.

Some fifty-odd minor tremors succeeded the main quake, keeping everyone alert to the possibility of personal injury or additional damage to those buildings already hard hit.

Communication with Washington was essential under the circumstances. Normally the landline teletype from the embassy to the State Department was not in operation on weekends, and that Sunday morning was no exception. However, the embassy communications officer had had the good fortune to reach the chief watch officer in the Department by phone and the teletype was switched on. Communication with the resort city of Acapulco, a popular American tourist spot, was a different story.[1]

First reports were that the epicenter of the quake was near Acapulco, but with the phones dead the situation there was unknown. The naval attaché was instructed to fly to Acapulco, along with a vice consul, to make a complete check on the welfare of the hundreds of American tourists that normally vacation there. When they arrived, they found the town virtually undamaged, though hundreds of American citizens were at the airport. Many expressed their gratitude for the embassy's concern and prompt action in looking after their welfare.

Considerable responsibility for the smooth functioning and security of the embassy offices, even in normal times, fell upon the embassy's administrative officer. Under these unique circumstances he worked long hours to initiate the cleanup and repair work and to assure that extra guards were on hand until the physical security of the various offices of the mission could be reestablished. My print shop, for example, with large holes in the walls, was tempting for looters and had to be guarded night and day until arrangements could be made to close the gaps in the walls.

The following day the few employees living in the Casa Latino Americana were permitted to briefly return to their apartments to retrieve their belongings. Only one person at a time was allowed to enter the building, and then only for ten minutes for fear that it might collapse.

After being assured that all was being done to reestablish the functioning of the embassy, the ambassador called personally on the Foreign Office to express condolences and offer assistance, if desired, of the United States government. He was informed that the Mexican government could handle the situation very well by itself, thank you, though the foreign minister expressed his appreciation for the prompt offer of assistance. How much Mexican pride was involved in turning down this offer of assistance is not known, though nearly thirty years later, in 1985, when an even more devastating quake struck Mexico City, assistance was again proffered by the American ambassador, and at that time, was accepted.

Monday morning, less than forty-eight hours after the earthquake, the embassy opened with a skeleton staff. That afternoon the ambassador cabled the department: "Staff morale high in spite of original shock and strain of continuous work. I have commended all for a steady and courageous performance of duty during the last 48 hours."

Many observers of the July 1957 earthquake that shook Mexico City so violently wondered why it affected principally the taller buildings, with one notable exception. Few buildings under five stories high were damaged if they had good foundations and were not struck by neighboring buildings collapsing on them.

Experts concluded that faulty design and questionable construction practices accounted for much of the damage, but another reason was the considerable variation in the intensity of the quake in various parts of the city. The one notable exception was a newly constructed 43-story building in downtown Mexico City, which was virtually unscathed. Not one of its hundreds of windows was broken. This building, nearly twice as tall as any other building in the city at the time, was designed to behave as a floating concrete box set upon piles. It had some 360 concrete piles driven more than a hundred feet into the earth, and though records showed that it swayed considerably during the quake, the building's design proved its worth.

The Mexican capital is built on an old lake bed in a zone of volcanic action. The mountain peaks Popocotepetl and Ixtacihuatl, southeast of the city, though dormant, are constant reminders of the geological forces that shape the central Mexican plateau where Mexico City is located. As every tourist visiting Mexico's capital soon learns, the *Museo de Bellos Artes*, with its heavy baroque-style architecture, has, since its construction, steadily sunk into the unstable soil beneath it. As a consequence one enters the second floor at street level, where the third floor may be by the time this is published.

Another factor which affected the severity of this particular quake was that it was the worst shock the city had received since records were kept beginning in 1900. In the capital the Richter scale measured it at between seven and eight and the waves had peak periods of 0.9 seconds and 1.8 seconds. According to later reports the quake hit the town of Chilpencingo, fifty-five miles from Acapulco on the Pacific coast and 145 miles from Mexico City, even harder, measuring an estimated ten on the Richter scale. Some geologists speculated that the quake was caused by the formation of a new volcano on the southwest coast of Guerrero near Chilpencingo, but at the time the tectonic plate theory had not yet been fully developed. Whatever the cause, another similar major quake would not occur until nearly three decades later.

As the months passed and the big quake receded into memory, we found Mexico City life and the Mexicans much to our liking. Like so many before us, we adapted well to Mexican food and music, especially the loud, joyful sounds of the mariachis, and the Mexicans themselves. I was busily engaged in reestablishing the print shop while Charmaine went about the challenge of shopping for furniture and furnishings for our still relatively barren house.

Like a bolt out of the blue a letter arrived addressed to me from the area director in Washington. It read, in part:

Dear Al,

I'm happy to inform you that you have been selected to be the first USIS officer to serve in British Guiana. This is an important assignment and there are those in Washington who believe we should send a much more senior officer. However, I am fully familiar with the outstanding record you have made to date both in Venezuela and in your current position, so I have complete confidence in your ability to take on this challenging assignment.

You will be receiving additional information shortly about the situation in Georgetown and what will be expected of you. In any event you should now contact the Desk officer for B.G. as soon as possible, and make preparations for your departure from Mexico.

I know you are doing well there and would possibly prefer to stay on since you have been at that post scarcely 18 months. However, rest assured that this new assignment is a particularly important one and one which will receive special support and attention from headquarters. Congratulations to you and the best of luck.

I found it difficult to believe that, just as we were about to begin getting settled in our new home, we would have to pack up and leave for South America. Charmaine accepted the news I brought her that evening with mixed emotions. There would be an advantage in being so close to her homeland in Trinidad. On the other hand, her knowledge of B.G., as British Guiana was commonly referred to, was based on growing up in Trinidad. There, B.G. was looked down upon as being a backward country, even by Trinidadian standards, far out of the mainstream. It was called "mudland" by the Trinidadians because the muddy rivers which emptied their coffee-colored waters along that country's Atlantic coast made mudflats of B.G.'s beaches, in stark contrast to the white, sandy beaches of the Caribbean islands. Furthermore, she felt she was just beginning to enjoy the marvelous Mexican ambiente at her first post as a Foreign Service wife, and we were now very much at home in Mexico City. To suddenly move into a new, unknown situation was not something to be happy about. But she had signed on "for better or for worse," so where her husband went, she went. And it did sound like a marvelous opportunity for a young officer.

When the news circulated among the print shop employees who had grown accustomed to working with me, especially Nuñez and

Pardo, they too had mixed feelings. My two top employees knew it was a great opportunity for me with respect to my Foreign Service career, and in this they shared my delight, but we had enjoyed excellent rapport in working together so they would have preferred maintaining the status quo to the inevitable change that would come with a new supervisor. They had been through this before—the American Foreign Service officers came and went all the time. When the Americans are difficult to work with, or fail to understand the Mexican mentality, as occasionally occurs, they looked forward to a change. But when they had good rapport with their American supervisor, they viewed a change from a known to an unknown element as a cause for concern.

The area director's letter had arrived shortly before Christmas. I was assured that while I should get to British Guiana as soon as possible, we would be able to spend Christmas in Mexico. Christmas is special everywhere in the Christian world, but few places can surpass the posadas in Mexico—the nine days of Christmas celebration in commemoration of the journey of Mary and Joseph from Nazareth to Bethlehem, begging for lodging each night along the way.

The posadas like many things that were brought to Mexico by the Spaniards, have assumed an Indian-Mexican character, such as the breaking of the piñatas during the posada nights. By midnight, with fireworks, whistles, and bells joining the celebration, the *Misa de Gallo* ("Mass of the Cock") is held which is followed by a banquet for some, the traditional lamb and wine by others. Nativity scenes *(nacimientos)* abound in Mexican churches and homes, and the custom is to go from church to church to view them during the Christmas holidays. Charmaine, as a staunch Catholic, was exhilarated by the Mexican fervor during the Christmas season.

We were to leave for South America shortly after New Years, and while the holiday partying and Christmas spirit prevailed, we began to get our few worldly possessions ready for the trip to British Guiana. Because of the holidays and our imminent departure, we invited all of my print shop employees to our home for a party. There would be music and dancing, using the empty dining room for the latter, and there would be no concern for spilling wine on the carpets as there weren't any.

The Mexican party was over and it was time to move on. I requested two days leave en route to our new post in order to briefly visit Charmaine's sister and our friends in Caracas, especially since we would be changing planes there. I was surprised at the cable that the public affairs officer in Trinidad, who would be my new boss, sent back in response to my request. It said that I was urgently needed and should not delay my arrival by two days. I brought the cable home and showed it to Charmaine. "How is it that they have not filled this new post for at least three or four months," I told her, "and now, when they finally have someone assigned, the PAO contends that they can't wait two more days"?

"What happens if you don't follow that order?" Charmaine asked.

"Well, I guess we'll just have to see," I responded. "I can't conceive of two days making that much difference in the establishment of a new post for the first time. I know it won't set well with my new boss, but I'll just have to work like hell to convince him what a good officer I am. We're not going to fly into Caracas without stopping at least for a day to see Marion and our friends."

A week later our goods were packed and shipped to Georgetown. It was impossible to take our dog Kazan with us, but fortunately the Venezuelan family who lived nearby who had given him to us was willing to take him back. Our last look at Mexico came as we drove our car north to the border, where a disgruntled Mexican customs officer made us take everything out of our overloaded trunk for inspection, a process which took well over an hour by the time we unloaded and reloaded. We were driving to New Orleans from where a ship was to take our car to Georgetown and where we would catch a plane to Trinidad via Caracas, and then on to Georgetown.

As we were about to leave Dallas, en route to Louisiana, our old car gasped and quit. Our old friend had finally run out of steam which was probably just as well. We traded it in at a nearby used car lot for a larger and nicer looking second-hand Ford that cost us $400 in the bargain. Our new car was a much more appropriate vehicle for the new vice consul and branch public affairs officer of the American consulate in Georgetown.

Mexico had been, for us, a mosaic of impressions, many good and some bad. It marked the first phase of our life together, as well as my first experience as a full-fledged Foreign Service officer. It would remain in our memory as our first exciting and enjoyable experience of married life in the Foreign Service. The dust of Mexico "had settled on our hearts." Some day we hoped to return, *si dios quiere* ("if God wills it").

Before boarding the plane in New Orleans shortly after midnight, the airline clerk at the desk informed all passengers planning to debark in Caracas that they might not be able to land there.

"There was a big riot in downtown Caracas today," he said. Apprehensive but unwilling to change our plans, we boarded the plane.

The flight's first stop was in Havana where we were on the ground for about twenty minutes, just long enough to pick up a local newspaper. The main headline read: "24 KILLED IN STREET RIOTS; HUNDREDS INJURED." The dateline was Caracas. As the plane took off from Havana, the pilot announced that we might have to land in Montego Bay (Jamaica) as it was still undecided whether or not we would go on to Venezuela.

We tried to sleep as we flew over the blue Caribbean, which at that hour of the morning, 3 a.m., was black, but we only tossed and turned. Not knowing where we would be landing added to our anxiety. I was beginning to think that perhaps a day or two layover at Montego Bay, with its beautiful white coral beaches, would be an adjustment that could be made without too much difficulty. On the other hand, the thought of seeing the Caraqueños once again brought forth nostalgic memories, making sleep impossible. And then, far below, a large, darker shadow in the dark sea appeared—Jamaica, with a few glimmering lights. We continued to fly inland, across the island. Apparently the captain had decided to continue on to Caracas. I finally dozed off.

We arrived at Maquetia airport shortly after sunrise on a sunny day similar to the day I had arrived at that same airport three years earlier. On that occasion I was alone. This time, with Charmaine at my side, it was a real homecoming as her sister, Marion, and her sister's husband, Alberto, were there to greet us. But there was obvious tension in the air as the airport runways and the terminal were more heavily guarded than usual. Armed guards with carbines at the ready seemed to be everywhere.

"Let's get out of here as soon as we can," a nervous Alberto said as soon as the welcoming formalities were over. "After we get to town we'll have to take some back roads to get home. There could be some more rioting this morning and we want to be back home before it starts."

The main subjects of conversation in the long drive up the autopista were how we had enjoyed our tour in Mexico and the tense situation in Caracas. For days, Alberto said, there had been rumors that the Perez Jimenez government was about to fall at any moment.

"The situation is not good," Alberto added. "For a week now there's been talk of a military coup. You know I have nothing to do with politics, but it's obvious that P.J.'s position is getting weaker and weaker. He could be leaving any day. The problem is we don't know what will come next."

The tunnels and bridges between the airport and the city were all under heavy guard. Before we could leave the airport Alberto, who was driving, had his *cedula* checked by a guard at the exit who carefully looked over the passengers in the car before permitting us to proceed. There were also road checks at several points as we reached the outskirts of Caracas.

As much as we would have liked to avoid the center of town, it was necessary to pass through a portion of the downtown area before heading for the suburbs. Here and there we saw signs of the rioting which had occurred the day before—broken walls and windows, twisted bus stop signs, a few burned-out buses and autos, and piles of debris, including burned tires, at various places. Some buildings, streets and sidewalks had been splashed with a liquid that left an ugly red stain—a liquid chemical used by the police to disperse rioters. When coming in contact with people it stained their clothes and their bodies like some of the buildings had been stained, and caused vomiting and other ailments. It also enabled the police to easily identify rioters.

In the main square of El Silencio, in the center of Caracas and in the shadow of Edificio Bolívar, the two skyscrapers that visitors often describe as "the Rockefeller Center of Caracas," truckloads of heavily armed, steel-helmeted soldiers were on guard. They seemed to be waiting for something to happen.

Several hours after we had left the airport we arrived at Alberto and Marion's home, a trip which normally takes about an hour. It was now almost noon.

"Time for a siesta," I announced, suffering as I was after a sleepless night on the plane. Charmaine did not join me right away. She had too much to discuss with her older sister. But she too was worn out from the excitement and lack of sleep, so a few hours later she also collapsed. We had to be awakened from a sound sleep for dinner. The evening of reminiscences and enthusiastic tales about Mexico passed rapidly.

It was 5 a.m. when I was awakened by a knock on my door. Even though I had slept soundly the afternoon before I still had not caught up on my sleep after the flight to Caracas.

"Allen and Charmaine, get up. Something is happening." It was Alberto. I threw on a robe and, still half asleep, went into the living room.

"What's up?" I asked Alberto, who was pacing up and down in front of the radio in the living room. The announcer was saying, "Citizens of Venezuela. Remain calm. The military junta is in full charge. Keep tuned to your radio for further announcements." A few hours later radio and television reporters announced that President Marcos Perez-Jimenez had fled from the capital about 3 a.m., having flown out of the small Caracas airport, La Carlota, to seek exile in the United States.

With only a few days to spend in Caracas, we decided that, despite the revolution, we would venture out to visit friends whom we otherwise would not see. We planned to avoid the troubled downtown area where more rioting and lawlessness were most likely to occur if the new government was not yet in full control. As I drove Alberto's car to the La Florida neighborhood almost every car we passed blew its horn. Often the driver would stick his hand out of the open window on the driver's side and flash the Churchillian "V" for Victory. Although we were neutral observers, I thought it wise to at least smile back politely.

"It might be prudent for us to blow our horn also," I said to Charmaine after we noticed that some of the horn blowers weren't smiling back at us. "Otherwise they may think we're supporters of 'P.J.' " But when I pressed the horn, nothing happened. "We're going to have to talk to Alberto about this. The horn doesn't work."

With typical Venezuelan humor, that day became known as the day of the *Batalla de las Cornetas* (the battle of the car horns). This horn blowing, an expression of joy at the termination of the Perez-Jimenez dictatorship, was particularly significant because during P.J.'s reign anyone who used a car horn in downtown Caracas was subject to a heavy fine. As a result, automobile drivers pounded the sides of their vehicles with their fist or the palm of their left hand as a substitute for blowing their horn, a custom that never failed to amaze visitors from abroad.

The first day of the junta's rule did not pass, however, with mere horn blowing and victory signs to mark the change in government. The headquarters of the hated and dreaded National Security Police was stormed and its political prisoners released, though this was done without bloodshed. At 5 p.m. a curfew was imposed, bringing the city to a standstill. We had been able to visit with a few of our old friends during the day, but we made sure that we were back home well before the curfew began.

The following day, continuing our visits, we were at the home of a friend when a telecast from the National Palace captured everyone's attention. The new president of the military junta, Rear Admiral Wolfgang Larrazabal, addressed the nation and introduced other members of the junta and the new cabinet.

Admiral Larrazabal was a strikingly handsome man, young and dynamic in appearance. Compared with the man he had just replaced, who was short and stocky, the admiral looked and acted like a television star. This image, combined with his apparent sincerity and seriousness of purpose, struck a sympathetic chord among many Venezuelan viewers.

Although television had been initiated in Venezuela only four or five years earlier, it had already developed into a powerful influence on Venezuelan society, particularly for the Caraqueños. The new government was savvy enough to recognize its importance and to take full advantage of it. Thus they were able, in effect, to invite the public into the National Palace to see for themselves the stripe of the new regime. By being able to state his case in person, via the television tube, in so many Venezuelan living rooms and other places, the new president quickly gained the confidence of most Venezuelans. As a result the aftermath of looting and violence probably subsided much more quickly than if the new leaders had to rely on radio alone to reach the people. As Venezuelan coups went, the use of TV in this manner was a "first."

Yet not all was peaceful and quiet immediately after "P.J." fled from his disenchanted people. On the second day of the new regime, many Venezuelans, at the urging of the new government, attempted to return to their offices and workplaces. Some managed to do so but skeleton staffs were the rule. "Normality" remained elusive for a few days more.

A friend of ours related later how he attempted to return to work that Thursday but found it impossible to get to his downtown office because the streets were still crowded with people celebrating. Unable to drive, he parked his car some distance from where he normally parked and started to walk. He had gone only a few blocks when, about fifteen feet ahead of him, three men stepped in front of another man and asked the man they had detained for his identification.

"You're a National Security Agent," one of the three insisted. "No I'm not, I'm not," came the panic-stricken response.

"Then what's this?" demanded one of the three men, producing a revolver from the clothing of the man who had been stopped. There was no time for a reply. Two bullets fired at close range entered the chest of the victim and he fell to the ground. Witnessing this, our friend said that he halted in his footsteps, frozen with fright. The trio, ignoring the fallen man, stopped another man who was walking by at that moment.

"You're a National Security Agent," they insisted again.

"No I'm not," the white-faced man replied, "and I can prove it. I have my papers."

"Well, put out your hand. If it shines we know you're guilty," said one of the trio.

Our friend didn't wait to find out what happened. By now he recovered enough to retreat to his car where he placed the gears in reverse, made a quick U-turn and headed for home. "I was afraid they were going to stop me next and ask if my hand trembled. I knew that not only would my hand tremble—my whole body would shake."

One family we knew lived near one of the reportedly nine mansions of the former president. This family was concerned that if the looters who were now working overtime invaded the former president's mansion near their home, as was expected, they would not stop there but might enter neighboring homes as well. While some of the mansions were looted, including that one, the junta moved fast to restore order so that general looting was not as widely spread as originally feared.

By Friday, January 24th, the *Junta Patriótica* had the support of almost all organized factions of Venezuelan society, the university students, and the rest of the military. However, there was still no effective police control in the city. With the disappearance of Perez-Jimenez, the police had disappeared also, fearful of vengeance from the public. It was the police who had been charged with dispersing the mobs when they first appeared in downtown Caracas four days earlier, a dispersal that ended with twenty-four announced deaths and hundreds of injuries.

We were visiting old friends at the embassy when word was received that the curfew, which the day before had been extended to 7 p.m., was now suddenly changed back to 5 p.m. This was intended to cut down the scattered violence. At the same time the embassy received a report that the central police station was being stormed by people seeking to avenge the deaths and injuries of relatives and friends. The embassy staff was ordered to close for the day, and along with thousands of others, we headed home. The result was a massive traffic jam throughout the city as thousands rushed to get home before the curfew. Several times as I drove home at an excruciatingly slow pace due to the traffic, the tenseness and anxiety of many of the drivers seemed ready to explode into panic. But despite the tension, not a single driver failed to stop for the traffic lights when they turned red. Then as soon as the light changed, a moment's hesitation by the lead car brought the tumultuous roar of dozens of car horns beeping from behind. This time they were not the sounds of victory, but the nervous, frantic efforts of frustrated drivers who wanted to beat the curfew.

By Saturday morning a new phenomenon appeared. A simple sentence expressed the desire of the majority of Venezuelans to return to their normal living habits. They wanted the "party" to end—to get back to work and their daily routines. Suddenly appearing throughout the city, posted on automobiles and buildings, and written on leaflets distributed by university students who patrolled some of the major thoroughfares, was the phrase *Los saquedores son enemigos del pueblo* (Looters are the enemies of the people). This same phrase was repeated on radio and television throughout the day. Its effect was electric. The sought-after "normality" began to return.

By Monday, January 27th, as we sat in the back of a cab in which we were being driven through the downtown area en route to the airlines office to catch the limousine to the airport, "normality" had definitely returned. At a street corner, while waiting for a traffic light, a friend of the cabdriver stopped a moment while crossing the street.

"Well, Pepe, how goes it with you?

"Reg-u-lar" the cabbie replied.

"What do you think of the situation?" his friend asked.

"I think it's back to normal," the cab driver replied."

"At last!" his friend exclaimed with a sigh of relief as he waved good-bye.

4
Guyanese Gumbo

"These rivers know that strong and quiet men drove back a jungle, gave Guiana root against the shock of circumstance, and then history moved down river, leaving free the forest to creep back, foot by quiet foot, and overhang black waters to the sea."
— A. J. Seymour, Guianese poet, *There Runs a Dream*

The flight from Caracas to Port-of-Spain, Trinidad, was a little more than an hour. The tropical island of Trinidad would be a part of the South American landmass were it not for a few miles of water which separate it from neighboring Venezuela.

We were met at the airport by my new boss, Public Affairs Officer Garland Routt and his wife. They welcomed us warmly but it was clear that Routt was irritated with me for not following orders by coming directly to my new assignment instead of stopping off in Caracas. It was an irritation that would cloud our relationship for a long time but eventually would be put aside.

For the first few days I was briefed steadily by Routt on the importance of British Guiana to U.S. interests. The leading politician, he told me, was Cheddi Jagan, of East Indian background and a dentist by profession. Jagan had studied in the U.S. and was married to an American woman, Janet Jagan, considered to be a communist with great influence over her Marxist-leaning husband. The general view among American government leaders was that Jagan would surely lead B.G. into replicating Castro's Cuba when Guyanese independence, due to occur in a few years, became a reality.

"The last thing (President) Eisenhower wants," Routt told me, "is a second Cuba on the South American mainland." Setting up a USIS operation in Georgetown, he said, was, at a minimum, designed to shed a little democratic light into Guyanese[1] society. Of course the

British had been doing that for years, though they maintained certain anti-democratic traditions, such as keeping the "Georgetown Club" off bounds for blacks and East Indians. As a result of this and other colonial traditions racial resentment against the British among the predominantly black and East Indian population smoldered. The embassy political officer and the embassy's economics specialist also briefed me about my new post.

The U.S. Government maintained a consulate in Georgetown. Just as the consul reported to the embassy in Trinidad, I as a branch public affairs officer (BPAO) would report to Routt as the director of USIS in Port-of-Spain. I would also be responsible to the consul who, as the U.S. government's chief representative there, had veto power over any USIS programs I might wish to initiate.

British Guiana was often referred to as "The Land of Six Peoples." The six peoples were composed of the descendants of Africans who had been brought there as slaves and constituted the largest ethnic group; the East Indians, whose forefathers had come as indentured laborers; Chinese, who made up about four percent of the population; Portuguese, whose forefathers had arrived from the Madeira Islands to work in the canefields but adapted poorly and their immigration was soon stopped; the indigenous people, known as Amerindians to distinguish them from the East Indians; and the "whites," mostly British, who made up one percent or less of the population and controlled the economy.

Although antagonism between the blacks and the whites existed in this highly class-conscious society, the most serious antagonisms existed between the blacks and the East Indians. They were the two largest ethnic groups. If they could not learn to live with each other, disastrous results could be expected when the British left. Although the British were criticized as being racist in some of their attitudes, their presence and power had generally kept extremists in the two most antagonistic racial groups from cutting each other's throats.

In 1956 the blacks were more numerous than the East Indians, but with the East Indian population multiplying much more rapidly, they represented a threat to the black politicians. Because the blacks represented the major racial group, and because most Guyanese cast their votes along strictly racial lines, the blacks could expect initially to gain control of the new, independent government. They would be unable to maintain control, however, when the day came when there were more East Indian voters than black voters—unless they could devise ways to do so, which is apparently what happened for at least two decades following independence.

The leading political leader among the blacks was Forbes Burnham, an Oxford-educated lawyer and a former Jagan ally in the days when independence was being sought from the British. He was now Jagan's leading opponent, and because Jagan's leftist ideology threatened to turn Guyana into a second Cuba if Jagan became the prime minister of the newborn country, the U.S. government, as well as Americans with family ties to Guyanese blacks, of which there were a number, sought to help Burnham in any way they could.

A third political party was headed by Guyanese businessman Peter Deguiar. Although generally well respected by most Guyanese and praised for bringing employment to the colony, DeGuiar was of Portuguese descent and thus would never be able to garner enough votes from the two leading racial groups for his followers to have more than a minority representation in the local legislature. He tried to work with Burnham for a while but soon became disillusioned with that arrangement, to no one's surprise.

The East Indians were more family-oriented and generally more willing to sacrifice for the education of their children. Not only would they eventually outnumber the blacks, but because of their emphasis on education, they threatened to become the economic as well as political leaders of an independent Guyana. In contrast many of the black Guyanese came from broken homes and were raised by single parents, generally a working mother, thus were disadvantaged by not having a father figure to provide a model and support. Many also tended to identify physical labor with slavery, thus sought low-paying white-collar jobs as commercial or government clerks, which kept their hands clean but earned minimum wages. The blacks were also urban-oriented, so they constituted the majority ethnic group in Georgetown, whereas the East Indians were predominantly agricultural workers who lived in the countryside and worked on the vast sugar estates or were independent rice farmers. Many of their sons and daughters, often through great parental sacrifice, went abroad to became educated as doctors and lawyers. Cheddi Jagan, for example, was an American-educated dentist although he was born and raised in a small village on the Courantyne coast of B.G.

The economy of British Guiana was based on sugar. Large sugar estates existed close to Georgetown and up and down the coast. At some of these estates, because of the low water table, the cut cane was hauled to the factories in barges that floated through man-made canals. Mules were used to haul the cane-laden barges to the factories though they were being slowly replaced by tractors. The factories were becoming fewer in number as estates consolidated. They produced brown sugar, which was then shipped to England to be refined into the white table sugar so familiar to Americans and Europeans. Of course, rum was also a major product. The second major industry was bauxite, the source of aluminum. Like the brown sugar, the brown bauxite was also shipped abroad for further refining. Small steamers picked up the bauxite and hauled it to Trinidad, which unloaded the bauxite for transshipment on larger vessels to refineries in the U.S. and Canada.

Trinidadians often referred to British Guiana as "mudland" for a good reason. South of the country the mighty Amazon River carried the silt of South America far out to sea and the currents brought some of it back to the shores of the three Guianas—French Guiana, Dutch Guiana, and British Guiana.

North of "B.G." was the Orinoco, the second largest river on the South American landmass. It also deposited some of its silt on Guianese shores. British Guiana itself had major rivers flowing down to the sea, such as the giant Essequibo, the Cuyuni, the Demerara River on which Georgetown is located, and the Berbice River, which separates British Guiana from Dutch Guiana, now known as Suriname. The result of all of these silted rivers was that the beaches in "B.G." were like no other beaches in the world—covered with brown, sticky mud rather than sand.

"Gumbo" is an Americanism for a fine, silty soil of the western prairies of the U.S. It becomes sticky and nonporous when wet. Thus "Guyanese Gumbo" is a fitting phrase to describe the brown, muddy beaches of British Guiana, as well as the shores of the Guiana's silt-laden rivers.

While I was taking my crash course in the political, economic, and social factors of Guyanese society, Charmaine visited friends and relatives in her old hometown. We had not been back to Port-of-Spain since our carnival adventure in 1956, nearly two years before. As it was now the end of January, Trinidadians were revving up for Carnival '58, now only a few weeks away. We, however, had our minds on more serious subjects.

The more I learned about the mysterious land across the muddy waters to the south and east of Trinidad, the more excited I became and the more anxious to get on with my new assignment. Remembering our good times in Mexico and aware of British Guiana's unfavorable reputation in Trinidad, Charmaine continued to have mixed feelings about living in Georgetown. But the time was at hand to head into a new unknown. On the last day of January 1958 we left Piarco airport on PanAm's hour-and-a-half flight to Georgetown.

We left Piarco airport on a southeast heading that took us diagonally across the island. As we gained altitude we could see the lush green hills popping up between the low-lying clouds covering Trinidad. Most of Venezuela lies to the west of Trinidad, but the east coast of Brazil and the three Guianas are to the southeast. Leaving the island behind, the clouds thinned out and we could see the muddy waters of the Orinoco River spreading far out to sea, staining that part of the Atlantic for many miles. Within the hour we were flying over the northwest corner of British Guiana and caught our first glimpse of the mammoth South American jungle.

From 25,000 feet the jungle looks like a continuous patch of celery stalks and broccoli. There were few signs of human habitation and, in fact, this area, like vast regions of British Guiana, is uninhabited. The clouds along the coast were scattered, permitting good views of the ground, but not far to the west solid cloud cover hid the escarpment which marks the giant plateau that runs from western Guiana to southeastern Venezuela; from Kaiteur Falls in "B.G.", the seventh largest waterfall in the world, to Angel Falls, the largest. The coastal area is interspersed with rivers, the largest being the Essequibo. As we crossed a large island in the center of the Essequibo, the Guyanese passenger sitting next to me proudly pointed out that that particular island is 19 miles long, comparable to the island of Barbados in the Caribbean. "You know," he added, "the name 'Guyana' in one of our Amerindian dialects means 'land of waters.'"

British Guiana in the mid-fifties had only about 500,000 inhabitants in a country of 83,000 square miles, equal in size to the state of Idaho. Ninety percent of the population eked out their living on a narrow strip of land along the northeastern coast. Except for isolated mining, ranching, and Amerindian settlements, most of the interior was inaccessible tropical jungle.

Atkinson Field, the country's only international airport, was located inland about 27 miles from Georgetown. It was the penultimate stop on the Caribbean run of the Pan American Airways flight which ended in Suriname. The airport was built by the U.S. during World War II to ferry aircraft to Africa. Now, more than a decade after the end of the war, the runways were still in relatively good shape despite questionable maintenance and the constant exposure of the concrete to the tropical sun and rains.

As we disembarked we were met at the ramp by Cecil Squires, second in seniority of USIS Georgetown's current three-person staff. He was an amiable, light-skinned black who had worked for USIS in

Trinidad and Barbados and had now been "seconded," as the British say, to Georgetown to help establish a full-fledged USIS operation soon to be under the direction, for the first time, of a branch public affairs officer. He had arrived in Georgetown a few months earlier and was handling information matters until the American officer arrived to supervise expanded activities. Four months earlier the post had been established as a USIS library and "information center" under the direction of Mrs. Betty Drayton, an East Indian with an apparent taint of African heritage. In this "Land of Six Peoples" there was no getting away from describing individuals by race. The third USIS employee was an East Indian who used the sole name of Samaroo and who worked as a messenger-clerk.

The administrative officer at the consulate, Fred Washer, was also at the airport when we arrived. It was his turn to deliver the classified diplomatic pouch to the plane's captain for delivery to the State Department on the return trip to the U.S. The few American officers at the Georgetown consulate had to take turns in performing this duty, a chore that few relished, including me when it became my turn, which was all too frequent. Although it was nice to be out of the office on a sunny afternoon, the pouch run which required handling by an American officer meant an afternoon wasted as the fifty-four mile round trip took more than an hour each way. Sometimes the trip took even longer as traffic from Georgetown to the airport on the narrow two-lane road was frequently held up awaiting the passage of the sugarcane barges in a canal that crossed the road at one point. When this happened a small bridge had to be raised, stopping traffic in both directions. Elsewhere on the road there were numerous pedestrians, cattle, and slow-moving carts. Although there were far fewer automobiles than what I was accustomed to in Mexico City, Guiana's airport road was in some ways more dangerous than entering the fast-moving traffic of a Mexican *glorieta*.

Before starting the long trip back to Georgetown in the consulate car with Washer and Squires, and with Walter, the tall, elderly, thin black driver, we drove to the other side of the airport.

"Have to pick up some fresh vegetables," Washer said. The concrete roads we drove over at Atkinson Field, built like the runways by the Americans, also seemed to have held up well despite their age and punishment from the tropical sun and rains.

"The Guyanese think very highly of American technology," Washer commented. "They can't help but compare the roads and buildings here at Atkinson with their own. It's no wonder, as you'll soon find out, that they think the quality of American products is outstanding."

A few miles from the terminal, but on the grounds of the former air base, the Correias, a farm family of Portuguese descent, had taken over a hydroponic farm that the Americans had developed during World War II to provide vegetables for the soldiers and airmen stationed there. Now the Correias grew vegetables in the same hydroponic installation and raised chickens, which they sold in Georgetown. Whenever someone made the pouch run from the consulate they invariably stopped at the Correia farm to pick up chicken, eggs, and vegetables for the consulate staff. The markets in Georgetown continually suffered from shortages, and those rare times when supplies were plentiful, the local fruit and vegetables offered were generally of mediocre to poor quality. Thus consulate staffers had come to depend on the Correias for edible chicken and better quality produce. Unfortunately, as B.G. moved toward independence, and as the Correia farm began to prosper, particularly with chickens and eggs, when the newly independent government was installed it hindered rather than helped their enterprising food business. A few years later, with a local government unwilling or unable to encourage local business, success evaded them so they quit farming and moved to England.

As we headed for Georgetown we found the first three miles or so on cement roads to be a smooth drive. However, when we passed an unmanned gate that marked the end of the old air base, the road became noticeably worn and weathered.

"You're now off the old air base," Washer commented. "If we don't get held up by the sugar barges we should be in Georgetown in about an hour." The road stretching ahead in the direction of Georgetown was flat and narrow. On either side were unkempt grassy areas and soon single, roughly hewn wooden houses, many of them on wood or cinder block piles, began to appear. At many of the houses bundles of long poles with white or colored cloths tied at the top were stuck into the muddy soil in a corner of the front yard. These were the homes of Hindus who made up the majority of Guiana's East Indians. The poles with the cloths hanging in the breeze had a religious significance.

A few head of cattle were in the fields around the houses. Most appeared scrawny and underfed. Soon more houses became evident, and as we proceeded toward the coast more and more people appeared. The number of small children was striking. "No television sets here," I thought. Though I had never been in India, I assumed that this must be what parts of the subcontinent look like. The East Indian men, like their cattle, were noticeably thin. The women, despite the heat, were heavily clothed.

Walter drove fast past people walking in the streets and only occasionally did he get stuck behind a mule-drawn cart. There were very few cars on the road but traffic increased the closer we came to Georgetown. Since all cars were driven on the left-hand side of the road, English style, Charmaine and I felt sure we were going to crash into oncoming cars every time we rounded a curve, but this was only an illusion. There were no sidewalks out here in the country, and drainage ditches on both sides of the road meant that everyone—people, cars, carts, and cattle—had to share the road.

Some sections of the road were replete with potholes so bad that Walter had to maneuver over them very slowly. He seemed to know where the worst ones were as well he should. The airport trip was a ritual three to four times a week.

We passed a big pile of what looked like red dirt on the side of the road where a group of workmen were standing.

"That's burnt earth," Washer said. "They use it to fill the potholes."

"Burnt earth? Is it effective?" I asked.

"It generally washes away after one or two rains, but it's cheap," he replied.

Soon we came to a narrow bridge that crossed one of the many streams that empty into the Demerara River. The river could occasionally be seen through the foliage to our left. The road ran roughly parallel to the river, which, at Georgetown on the coast, contributes its muddy waters to the Atlantic Ocean.

"They've been working on this little bridge ever since I arrived here about eighteen months ago," Washer explained. "It seems that they keep putting piles down to stabilize it, one on top of the other, and the piles just keep sinking down into the soft mud. Jim Cheatham, the USAID highway engineer who you'll meet later, says if they would use an American method of flotation he could solve their problem in a week, but that's not going to happen, he says, because they'll never ask him."

The coastal plain of B.G., which generally stretches from the ocean to the equatorial forests to the south and the mountains to the west, is mainly composed of white sand and clay, a combination that is not good for farming. The narrow silted sliver of land on the coast was long recognized as being the best area for farming, so it was there that the sugar plantations developed as well as Guiana's second crop, rice.

Sugar cane fields that stretched to the horizon began to appear on both sides of the road. In the distance was the factory that processed the cane. As we passed near the factory the strong scent of molasses permeated the air. In some areas the cane had not yet been cut, its green stalks glimmering beautifully in the afternoon sun as they swayed in the wind. Elsewhere the cane had been burned, the method used to remove the chaff before cutting the stalks, which are then gathered and sent to the factory.

Many canals, some with empty barges, others with barges brimming over with cut cane, could be seen in the distance. But when Walter stopped behind a small line of cars and carts and turned off the motor, he explained that we would have to wait for some barges to be moved.

"You mean traffic on this main road to the airport can be held up while the sugar cane barges move by?"

"You've got the picture," Washer replied. "They plan to build a new bridge here, but until they do, you just have to hope that you never miss a plane because of this bridge. The interesting thing too is that this drawbridge is raised by hand. See those two men over there turning that winch?" We looked in amazement. If Charmaine and I did not realize it before, we did now — we had arrived in a truly "underdeveloped" country (though diplomats called it "developing"). I could not help but think, "Whatever one calls it, a country which repairs its roads with dirt and uses manpower to raise and lower a drawbridge has a long way to go to reap the benefits of twentieth-century technology."

After a twenty-minute wait, which seemed longer, the two men lowered the drawbridge and the traffic moved ahead. It was another thirty minutes before we had our first glimpse of Georgetown. The streets became more crowded and wooden buildings appeared on both sides of the street. Most remarkable were the canals that ran parallel to the road. Washer explained their significance.

"When the Dutch ruled B.G. they utilized the silty soil near the coast for their agriculture, and being accustomed to building dikes, they built them here and slowly moved back the sea. Now Georgetown can get inundated from either the front or the back. Since the sluice gates can be opened only at low tide to drain the water when we have heavy rains, sometimes too much rain comes before low tide and Georgetown gets flooded. Then at times there are breaks in the seawall that protects the town and most of the coastal farms at high tide. When that happens we get flooded from the sea. You see, most of the coast is at least four feet below sea level. That's why this is one of the few places in the world where you can be practically six feet under and still breathing."

Maintaining the country's sea defenses along the coast where most of the population lived meant caring for about 140 miles of seawall. The many sluice gates in this sea defense system, which lets the tropical rain waters flow out to sea, were generally opened and closed twice a day at low tide. In addition, the seawalls kept the sea from inundating the land. Maintaining all this added a tremendous cost to the government and private coastal enterprises in a country that was already poor by any standard. Such was the legacy left by the Dutch of a country, which, by 1803, became the only British possession on the South American landmass.

Another remarkable thing about Georgetown was the change in racial makeup from the hinterland, where East Indians predominated. On the streets of Guiana's capital the people were overwhelmingly blacks. Many were government workers, office workers, and clerks in the downtown stores.

By late afternoon we pulled up in front of one of the only two hotels in town, the Tower Hotel, a three-story wooden structure with the bar and restaurant on the ground floor. The lobby was on the second floor. The rooms were located there and on the third floor. I glanced at the swimming pool at the side of the hotel. I saw insects floating on the surface of the water, but said nothing.

"The office is just down the street," Squires explained. "Do you want to wait until morning to go to the office?"

"Sure," I replied. Washer had already been dropped off with the pouch mail that he had picked up at the airport. Before leaving he told me that the consul would see me in the morning.

"We'll take it easy tonight and get some rest. Thanks a lot for meeting us," I said to Squires. "See you in the morning."

Tomorrow our life in Guiana would begin.

The sun comes up early in the tropics, and people generally rise early to take advantage of the relatively cool air of the morning.

Shortly after sunrise we went down to breakfast, which was served on the patio near the swimming pool. The pool was a recent addition to the Tower Hotel but the management had not yet worked out the intricacies of keeping the water in the pool clean.

We ordered scrambled eggs, toast, and coffee for breakfast, leaving the exotic tropical fruit for another day. The food did not arrive for quite some time, a harbinger of the torpidity which one might expect in a tropical country far removed from the mainstream of human affairs.

When our eggs finally came, I reached for my fork. I was hungry and anxious to get going on my new job. Just before lifting my loaded fork to my mouth, however, something caught my eye. I looked at my plate more closely.

"They seem to have already put pepper on the eggs," I thought. "How strange." But just before bringing my fork to my mouth, I paused and examined it minutely.

"By God!" I exclaimed to Charmaine. "That's not pepper. It's ants! Little black fried ants!"

"Waiter, waiter!" I called. The waiter, an elderly Guyanese black, came over to our table. "Yes sir?" he asked.

"Waiter, there's ants in my eggs!" I exclaimed, unable to keep the shock I felt out of my voice.

The waiter looked down for a moment at the plate on the table, then back at me. "Yeah," he said, emotionless and without any indication that he was concerned about the ants, let alone planning to do anything about them.

"I don't want fried ants in my eggs!" I declared, visibly upset at the waiter's lack of interest. "Take these away and bring me some others," I demanded. The waiter, who seemed to shrug his shoulders, though I may only have imagined this, picked up the plate and headed for the kitchen. He returned about thirty minutes later with a new plate of eggs. By then Squires had appeared, ready to escort me to the office. He joined us for a cup of coffee and briefed Charmaine on the shopping situation in the downtown area where the hotel was located. With breakfast finally finished, he and I left for the office, a five-minute walk down Main Street. Charmaine returned to the room, which would be our home for a few weeks while searching for a permanent residence.

The USIS office and library were located on the ground floor of the American Consulate building, a three-story wooden frame structure that had originally been built as a private residence. The center of town where it was located was one of the few areas in Georgetown where the ground floor could be utilized since the central area of the city had been built up and the drainage system in that part of town meticulously maintained. Many other areas of the city were too damp to use what would normally be the ground floor of a house.

The consulate building was painted white as were most buildings in Georgetown, except the tall wooden cathedral, which was painted a startling bright blue. The canary yellow shutters of the consulate building were also exceptional, though this gave the building a special personality and made it easy to locate along Main Street. Most Georgetown buildings were designed to reflect the hot sun, a sun that never failed to appear every day of the year. Many older buildings, however, had not been maintained. They had long ago lost their paint. These older structures were mainly in the older sections of the city and in the poorer suburbs. They looked weatherbeaten and forlorn. Since most of the populated areas of B.G. lie between six and seven degrees of latitude north of the equator, the sun is an important factor in everyone's life. Tropical downpours shut out the sun for a short while, but it always returns to heat the earth and generate more rain.

As Squires and I walked into the USIS library, Betty Drayton greeted us at the door.

"Welcome to Guiana," she said. "I hope you're going to like it here. We've been expecting you for some time."

I knew from what I had heard in Trinidad that Betty Drayton was an excellent, enthusiastic employee. But I also knew that she would need to be treated with circumspect as the charter member of USIS Georgetown and after being her own boss for the past four months. She had established and supervised USIS in British Guiana after only a short introduction to the goals and programs of the U.S. Information Agency. What she knew about USIA she learned during one brief visit to USIA headquarters in Washington; a visit to USIS Port-of-Spain; and from a few brief visits to Georgetown of PAO Garland Routt.

The library, already a popular cultural entity in the community, was created and functioning apparently very well under her supervision. It was her "baby," and while she reported to the American consul while awaiting my arrival, the consul, busy with other matters, did not attempt to micromanage her activities. Starting today, however, now that I was on board, she would have a supervisor looking directly over her shoulder. I could appreciate the possible effect on her of this changed situation and was determined to be as understanding and helpful as possible in order that we would work together as an efficient team.

Mrs. Drayton's husband, a well-educated, soft-spoken mulatto, was a senior civil servant in the Department of Labor. The minister of labor at the time was Mrs. Janet Jagan, the wife of Prime Minister Cheddi Jagan. It was because of the professed communist leanings of the Jagans that the U.S. government had such an interest in this backward British colony that was about to gain its independence. This made for an interesting situation as far as the American consulate was concerned, and led to accusations some years later, never substantiated, that Mrs. Drayton's political ideology was the same as the Jagans. I always doubted such accusations based on my experience with her and the evidence of her years of dedication to the USIS program in her native land.

She showed me the small library which took up most of the space on the ground floor of the consulate, and three small offices—mine, hers, and Squires's—and she introduced me to the two contract employees, Samaroo, a young East Indian boy of about eighteen who ran the motion picture projector and acted as messenger and janitor, and a young lady who worked part-time as a librarian. Afterwards I called on the consul, John Cope, a career State Department Foreign Service officer like his replacement, Carroll Woods, who arrived a few months later. Both were excellent officers to work with.

The next few days were taken up with calls on various government officials, the newspaper editors, the few educational and cultural leaders in the city, and the one radio station. Television had not yet come to Guiana, and for reasons peculiarly Guyanese as well as political, did not come for many years.

Several weeks went by while Charmaine and I looked at the few potential houses available for rent which would be satisfactory to us and suitable for an American diplomat to entertain Guyanese officials. The offerings were slim and nothing considered suitable came to our attention. When Agency for International Development officials offered to let us use one of their four furnished apartments, one of which was temporarily vacant, we were elated. Two weeks at the Tower Hotel was close to a lifetime, even if no more ants appeared in my morning eggs. Since no suitable alternative to the AID offer developed, we readily accepted and moved into that apartment. From time to time we were urged by the consul and AID officers to seek other quarters in order that the apartment would be available for any new AID officers assigned to Georgetown, but the AID program remained stagnant primarily because Cheddi Jagan, the prime minister of the pre-independence government, wanted as little to do with the U.S. government as possible.

The apartment was to have been a temporary solution to our housing problem. It turned out that it was not really needed by AID during the eighteen months we lived in Georgetown. Nevertheless, we continued our search for suitable housing. Once, six months later, we almost closed a deal with a Portuguese family who had decided to rent their house to us but the negotiations broke down after the U.S. government had agreed, at its own expense, to install a hot water heater in the rented house for bathing and cleaning. The owners could not understand the reason for this.

"You don't need hot water in the tropics," the owner argued. "We've managed without it all our lives." They then informed us that they had decided not to rent their house and that was the end of our search. As we had arrived in Georgetown on "direct transfer," my assignment was only for eighteen months. With about twelve months to go, and by then comfortably ensconced in the AID apartment and accustomed to our neighbors, and with the U.S. economic assistance program still stalled, there seemed little reason to continue to pursue the search for other housing.

While hot water was considered a "must" for American diplomats, air conditioning had not yet become essential. Although some of the offices in the consulate were air conditioned and the chief of the U.S. mission was granted such a luxury in his home, air conditioning had not yet arrived in force neither in Georgetown nor in the mindset of USIA administrative officials in Washington who made the decisions as to what should, or should not, be sent to overseas posts. In 1956, the view of Washington bureaucrats was that air conditioning at overseas posts was an unneeded luxury. It had a low priority, or more usually, no priority.

Because Georgetown was an area where malaria could be contracted and because the windows had to be left open at night to catch whatever breezes might stir, we slept under mosquito netting. This cut down the number of mosquito bites we suffered, but interfered with whatever cool breezes might develop during the night. One just had to get used to perspiring all night. Some years later, when air conditioning became more common in the United States, it became acceptable to install air conditioning in American living and working quarters in tropical countries. Initially, however, proponents of air conditioning argued that a.c. units should be sent abroad to demonstrate American technology. Eventually, of course, air conditioners in homes of Foreign Service personnel became not only acceptable, but essential.

As the first USIA officer to be stationed in British Guiana, I thought I ought to introduce myself and the new library to the leaders in Georgetown in a spectacular way if possible, one which would capture their attention and demonstrate that the services USIS provides could be highly beneficial to them. About that time I received word from Washington that a new motion picture was available to the agency, which seemed to be an ideal instrument for this purpose.

The American singer Marian Anderson had become famous the year before when the Daughters of the American Revolution did not allow her to sing in Washington's Constitution Hall because she was a Negro. She later sang at an outdoor concert before thousands of people at the Lincoln Memorial.

Miss Anderson's highly successful tour of India was filmed in an hour-long documentary entitled "The Lady from Philadelphia." USIA had just acquired the film and a few copies were being "bicycled" around the various posts that requested it. I put in a priority order to receive a copy as it seemed to be an ideal film for showing in British Guiana. Given the racial animosity existing between Guyanese blacks and East Indians, I believed that this film of an American Negro in an Indian setting should interest both groups while demonstrating that the two races can be friendly and cooperative.

When the film arrived, invitations to view it were sent to about 200 of Georgetown's government, media, educational, and intellectual leaders. About seventy-five showed up in the USIS library where chairs had been rearranged for the film showing. Although the prime minister did not attend, his wife, Janet Jagan, the minister of labor who was often described as "the power behind the throne," did. She stayed a short while during the reception afterwards, no doubt surveying the capitalist camp, having seen the new USIS library only from outside, although certainly aware of it as the wife of her chief civil service assistant was the USIS librarian. Perhaps, having been born and raised in Chicago, she also wanted a nostalgic look at the rack of American magazines in the far corner of the library, magazines with which most Americans are familiar.

The film was a great success, received by an appreciative audience who left feeling it had been made for the Guyanese. The following day the local media praised the film and the event, and so, on this upbeat note, my professional career in Guiana was launched.

Although the USIS operation in Georgetown was tiny relative to many posts, with only one American and four national employees (counting a new secretarial position), personnel administration, as at larger posts, required much of my time as director and occasionally posed major problems.

The librarian, Betty Drayton, was efficient, hard-working, amiable, and dedicated. Her only problem, in the minds of some Americans, was that with her husband on the staff of the communist minister of labor, "could she be trusted?" The consul and I felt that she could be, and the proof was in her hard work and dedication. She considered the library to be her creation, and rightly so. Some critics in far-off Washington could not understand that her husband's position was that of a civil servant and nothing more; that chance had placed him where he was, not ideology. As far as I was concerned, Mrs. Drayton was not a problem. On the contrary, she was a valued asset.

When Cecil Squires, the acting information assistant, returned to Trinidad a few weeks after I arrived, he was replaced by a young black newspaperman, Stephen Leacock. Unfortunately, although Leacock was likable, well-intended, and capable of performing his assigned tasks, he could not manage the responsibility of having the USIS van at his disposal (which he was to use only for official purposes such as film showings, visits to newspaper editors, etc., and to garage at his home for his convenience. When he damaged it in an accident one weekend while driving his family to church, I reluctantly fired him — not for the accident but for the unauthorized use of a government vehicle.

When interviewing a young East Indian girl who was applying for a job as my secretary, I questioned her as to why she seemed to want to put a "u" into words where I thought a "u" didn't belong. She must have thought I was crazy. After the interview she indicated that she would not work for me under any circumstances and no matter what the salary. Only later did I discover the difference between written American English and English English, which is the written language of Guiana. I finally hired a middle-aged Chinese woman, Ena Chee-a-Tow, who was so efficient she could have managed much of the entire operation. "The best secretary I ever had," I told all in later years. She was too efficient for Guiana, however, and she and her family emigrated to the Bahamas a few years later.

Mrs. Chee-a-Tow was in the habit of leaving loose change in her desk with which she bought soft drinks occasionally. One day, after being with USIS a few months, she told me that someone was taking things from her desk, including her loose change, and that she suspected the culprit was Samaroo, the young East Indian clerk-messenger. Confronted a few days later with a situation that could be explained only by Samaroo's actions, he denied the accusations at first, then begged forgiveness. Reluctantly, I felt compelled to discharge him. In both cases I had empathized with the young men who were likable and capable in their own way, and had great opportunities to advance as USIS grew, but they blew it.

Samaroo had not been what the U.S. government terms "a regular employee." He was a "contract employee," a person who theoretically was not to work on the premises but was under a contract to provide specific services. This is the way American bureaucrats the world over stretch their personnel ceilings. Countless hours have been spent seeking ways to eliminate this category of employee who normally has little or no retirement benefits, let alone leave and other amenities of regular employees. Yet were it not for this system, one like it would probably have to be invented to accomplish the tasks many government offices confront. It was also under the contract system that Betty Drayton obtained a library assistant.

The media operations of USIS in Georgetown were not elaborate and only partially successful. There were three daily newspapers: the anti-government *Daily Chronicle,* the *Daily Argosy,* and the tabloid *Guyana Graphic.* All were limited in size thus short on space but the *Chronicle,* being most ideologically in tune with American values, used USIS articles much more frequently than the other dailies. The editor of the *Argosy* was a sociable, well meaning and friendly man as far as USIS was concerned, who seemed to be constantly apologizing to me for not using articles which he said were interesting but could not be printed due to space limitations. At times the *Argosy* and others used USIS materials in their editorials or as background for special features. These "evidences of effectiveness" would always be reported to Washington headquarters to demonstrate how well USIS was doing. The *Graphic,* owned by British interests, tended to be leftist and uninterested in American-sponsored articles except for occasional health, scientific, or technological items.

The editor of the *Chronicle* was a man we shall call "Bill," a friendly black man who considered himself to be the sharpest editor in Guyana, and probably was. Unfortunately, he was an alcoholic. On one occasion when I was entertaining media editors at my home, he was in his cups and fouling the air with the most vulgar language imaginable. I faced a dilemma. If he continued raving he would insult all the guests. He was on the verge of becoming violent as his emotions became increasingly volatile. If I threw him out of my house, as I was about to do, the *Chronicle* might no longer welcome USIS and its articles. If I didn't get him to leave, someone or something in my home would surely suffer. Finally, by cajoling him to leave, he staggered out and somehow reached his own home. The *Chronicle's* friendship with USIS and me survived.

The leading cartoonist in Georgetown was a young East Indian chap named Rashad. His cartoons appeared frequently in the *Chronicle* and dealt with both local and world events, always from a democratic view. I developed a friendship with Rashad and we would meet periodically over a beer at which time I would pass on to him various ideas that the cartoonist might wish to use. Some of them were used which always pleased me and gave me another opportunity to report to Washington on the effectiveness of USIS.

Guiana had only one radio station, owned and operated by the local government and run by the B.G. Information Services. While its director, Rafiq Kahn, was amiable and would occasionally use music or items about American music provided by USIS, there was no way, initially at least, to get USIS items into local radio programming, no matter how hard I tried. Like the local press, limited space was a factor in keeping USIS programs from gaining entrance into this medium. Any efforts to encourage establishment of TV was met with negative political concerns. The two major political parties apparently believed that if TV were available it would benefit the opposition party more than themselves, so both sought to keep television out of the colony.

Given the limitations of press and radio, I sought to use as additional information tools the USIS library, pamphlets, and magazines, the latter being particularly popular among Guyanese recipients, and motion pictures. I had a large wooden screen constructed in the backyard garden area of the consulate, directly behind the library, where chairs could be placed on the lawn for film showings. We showed USIS films several evenings each week in our "outdoor theater," weather permitting. This proved to be popular except when it rained, which, unfortunately was rather frequent. Still, these screenings were useful and a relative success. But if the information outlets were limited, there was no limitation on what might be offered in cultural fields except for the amount of funds available to USIS for cultural programs and the limited number of programs that Washington was able and willing to send to this tiny, isolated post.

Periodically arguments were made in Washington that U.S. government cultural and educational programs should be removed from USIA, the organization principally responsible, at the time, for U.S. government overseas information programs (or what some refer to as "propaganda"). Proponents of this line of thinking maintained that cultural and informational programs are unrelated. Others argued that both were designed to foster U.S. interests and complement each other, and thus could and should be under one roof.

The cultural and information programs of USIS Georgetown, under my direction, complemented each other, as they did elsewhere. But since the former were generally viewed as being less ideologically oriented, they were often acceptable even to those who criticized U.S. policies.

USIS Georgetown functioned in a relatively hostile political environment, given Prime Minister Jagan's anti-U.S. views. Despite his wife's American heritage and his own university and dental school experiences in the U.S., he viewed the colossus of the north as being the world's worst capitalist criminal and the Soviet Union and Cuba as his friends. Jagan also knew that the American government was concerned enough about Guyanese independence under Jagan's leftist leadership to have beefed up the U.S. foreign service staff at the local American consulate. And while Jagan had been able to hold the number of AID types now working in Georgetown down to a bare minimum, USIS began operations in B.G. under an agreement with the British government, which still controlled most things prior to independence.

The exchange of persons program, usually an important aspect of cultural programming at USIS posts, was slow to get underway. The consul and I had our eyes on some political leaders whom we would like to see exposed to the U.S. system of government by providing them with grants to visit the U.S., but whenever government officials were selected, the Jagan administration usually found reasons to prohibit such candidates from accepting our grants. Thus most of our grantees were educators or professional people, including writers, poets, and newspaper editors, who did not need the permission of the local government to accept U.S. government grants. Often those invited were already sold on democratic philosophy.

Among the individuals I thought could really benefit from a visit to the U.S. was a leftist writer on the *Graphic* who lambasted the U.S. in his newspaper articles at every opportunity, although he had never set foot on American soil. My efforts to get him to accept an invitation from the U.S. government to see the United States firsthand were never successful. He interpreted such efforts as attempts to "brainwash" him.

There were, however, other media personalities who accepted our invitations to visit the U.S. so that before long a cadre of media editors and writers soon had a first-hand view of the country that played such a dominant role in world affairs, and whose influence reached all the way to their own poverty-stricken, isolated colony. When they returned from their visits their experiences and observations were reflected in their newspapers and in other ways, generally to our satisfaction.

Occasionally I would receive exhibits of various kinds, mostly inexpensive poster-type but occasionally other types. A collection of about 500 American high school and grammar school textbooks, for example, was placed on exhibit at Queen's College, the leading high school in Georgetown and one where some of the teachers had "come out," as the British say, from England to teach. The textbooks generated a great deal of interest, both as to content and the quality of the printing, which was extraordinary by local standards. One of the British teachers, admiring the plush use of color and white space of some of the volumes, remarked, "With books like these, you Americans make learning too easy!"

Another aspect of USIS cultural programming was to bring American specialists to Georgetown to lecture or hold seminars. The Director of the film department at Ohio State University, for example, demonstrated various film techniques and showed a film taken of Alec Guinness rehearsing for his famous final scene in "The Bridge Over the River Kwai." Seeing Guinness being shot and spun around in his death throes about five times as he played and replayed the scene until the director was satisfied, is something Guianese audiences would not soon forget. More importantly, the "American specialist" who talked with those who attended the showing of his films and lectures exuded a charm and an interest in the Guyanese that created the type of empathy for Americans that the program sought to encourage.

Visits of American specialists always provided opportunities to invite local counterparts or individuals interested in a particular specialty to a social gathering either at my home or at the USIS library. Occasionally the consul would host the affair, but compelled as the chief of mission was to entertain so many Washington visitors who seemed suddenly to have discovered Georgetown (now that B.G. had become politically interesting), he was always happy to share the entertaining responsibilities of the mission with other members of the consulate.

On one such occasion Guyanese novelist Jan Carew, who had just published a new book, was attending one such function for a visiting American at my home. Carew had grown up in Georgetown but, like so many other successful Caribbean writers, now lived in London. His latest book, *Black Midas,* was a story about a "porknocker," the local term for independent gold prospectors who searched for riches in the Guyanese hinterland. The hero of Carew's novel struck it rich several times and each time returned to Georgetown to lead a brief but exotic life of rum and ruinous women, before losing all and being compelled to head back to the jungle again to seek more gold. Despite repeated rich strikes, he dies as broke as when it all began. I had recently read the book so I told the author how much I enjoyed it.

"Were you trying to tell the reader," I asked, "that your hero is just like Guiana — abounding in wealth, because this really is a wealthy country, but reduced to living in poverty because all that wealth wasn't handled properly?"

Carew smiled. "Well, I never really thought of it that way," he replied. "I just wrote the story as it came out of me. I had no political motive."

The USIS film program, usually a part of the "information section," more often than not was a "cultural event" because of the predominantly cultural content of the films shown. Since the major entertainment medium in the country was the movies, USIS films, though mainly documentaries designed to educate and inform, were always popular. The schools and other institutions borrowed our projectors along with the films and only occasionally did USIS send out its own projectionist for films shown outside the USIS premises.

The library, however, was the centerpiece of USIS cultural programs. It soon became well known and well used. The only other public library in the city was located a block away. It also had a connection with the U.S., for it was originally the gift of the Carnegie Foundation. Though still well used and providing a great service to the community, a low budget and other problems limited its activities. It could not possibly keep up with the tremendous volume of books being produced in the modern world and the revolutionary changes in library science underway in the developed countries. We worked closely with the Carnegie library's head librarian, and supported that library with books and advice from trained specialists whenever the latter visited Georgetown under USIS auspices. Under the circumstances the USIS library became an equally important cultural center, allowing many Guyanese to experience for the first time the joy of being allowed to check out a book to take home and read at their leisure.

Public entertainment and recreation were practically nonexistent in Georgetown, unless one enjoyed watching the national pastime, cricket. Aside from that there were the movies, eating in one of the two or three acceptable restaurants in town, or walking along the seawall to catch the evening breeze. Thus the main recreation among the expatriate community of Georgetown was home entertainment. At a continuous round of parties in private homes, where rum was the preferred drink of the Guyanese and Scotch or gin and tonic the preference of the expatriates, one tended to meet the same people again and again.

On Sundays, traditionally a family day, we often joined British friends who lived next door to us where Sunday brunch at their home, served as soon as church services ended, had become a local tradition. By mid-afternoon most had eaten and drank so much in the oppressive heat that that party seldom lasted beyond 3 p.m. By then everybody headed home to take their Sunday afternoon siestas. Half the city was sleeping soundly by 4 p.m. on any Sunday afternoon, especially those who had attended after-church parties.

Among the Guyanese whose company I enjoyed and with whom we became good friends, was the deputy chief of the B.G. information services, Lloyd Seawar. An East Indian by descent, he was intellectually stimulating with a good sense of humor. Although he would win no beauty contests as he loved food and this showed, he was very friendly and always willing to be of help. He told Charmaine and me that he was of the Catholic faith and never tired of reminding Charmaine that they were coreligionists. Most East Indians in B.G. were, of course, either Hindus or Muslims like their ancestors.

Seawar was an astute observer of Guyanese culture. He was fond of saying that the great Caribbean novel yet to be written would be about how those with black skins keep trying to marry someone with whiter skin than themselves in order to eventually turn their family into Anglo-Saxons, or equivalents. "Only then will they have it made and feel satisfied with themselves," he remarked. He himself was a dark-skinned East Indian, well aware of the attention given to skin color in the Caribbean. But he had the intellectual attributes and sense of humor to overcome feelings of inferiority that affected many of his countrymen.

Despite the general desire to lighten one's complexion among many dark-skinned individuals, and the sometimes explosive racial-oriented frictions with the few local whites and expatriates, the real problem then and as accentuated later was between the blacks and the East Indians, as noted earlier.

Once, when I was waiting for a plane at an airport on one of the Caribbean islands, I chanced to meet an East Indian government official whom I knew in Georgetown. During the long, tiresome wait for our plane to arrive, we chatted about a number of things. I was surprised to hear this presumably well-educated East Indian vent his disdain and derision about the capabilities of Caribbean blacks.

Appalled at this government official's blatant condemnation of a large segment of Guyanese society, I said to him, "If you, as an educated man, believe Negroes to be so inferior, what must less-educated people believe?" And I added, "I think you're wrong because environmental factors, education, and culture have a great deal more to say about how a person develops than the color of his skin." Yet this particular East Indian's view of the Guyanese majority, I soon learned, was typical of many of his race, as it was of many Caribbean whites.

In the Guiana of the 1950s, no one could escape the race factor in the local society. Although professing pride in their claim to be 'The Land of Six Peoples," nowhere in my experience had I witnessed the element of racial characteristics to be such a constant, conscious element of daily life as was evident in Georgetown. Psychological, sociological, and economic factors were at work in making race such a dominant factor in Guyanese culture, but also a political factor stimulated animosity between the two major racial groups. The blacks knew that in time they would be outnumbered by the East Indians because of the latter's larger families. Some blacks felt, therefore, that at all cost they must maintain their preindependence control of the political power for as long as possible. This above all else endangered the development of democracy in B.G. Cheddi Jagan would miss taking the reins of power of an independent Guyana more for the simple fact that he was an East Indian, which estranged him from the Guyanese blacks, than his communist leanings which estranged him from the influential American government and, to a lesser extent, the British government.

The editor of the pro-communist, anti-U.S. weekly newspaper of Cheddi Jagan's Peoples Progressive Party, *Thunder,* was a young man named Ranji Chandisingh. He had been educated in England and the U.S. Perhaps the only thing I had in common with him was that we were both young men. In any event there is always the belief on both sides of an ideological curtain that perhaps one side can influence the other. Thus when I saw Ranji, as I did from time to time at various places around town, we were courteous to each other and occasionally chatted. One day he invited me to his home, ostensibly to listen to some of his jazz records (he was a jazz *aficionado)* and to taste some homemade East Indian cooking. He was a bachelor and lived with his mother.

I accepted the invitation and the date was set. Like the Russians and the Americans during the Cold War, many antagonists seem to have a love-hate relationship. They enjoy the battlefield of ideas, wonder what makes the enemy so strange as to believe the things he advocates, and there is always the hope that, perhaps, with a little effort, the opponent might become enlightened. Of course this rarely occurs, but the game must be played.

I drove my car that evening to the neighborhood where Chandisingh lived and found a parking place on the street a few houses away. It was with some trepidation and, of course, curiosity, that I was about to enter the den of the communist writer who was so critical of the

U.S. and such a staunch supporter of the Jagans, the Cubans, and the Russians. What would some of my friends or those Guyanese who were vehemently anti-Jagan and anti-communist think if they knew that I was being entertained by Ranji Chandisingh! Of course I had informed the consul about the invitation I had received. He urged me to accept, being as curious as I was as to why the invitation had been extended and what I might learn from the experience.

Ranji met me at the door and ushered me into the small living room. It was a very modest home, indeed. I met his mother, a thin, elderly, grayhaired woman who, after we had been introduced, excused herself and returned to preparing the meal in the kitchen. "Just like anybody's mother," I thought. The family had undoubtedly sacrificed to send Ranji to college abroad. I wondered what had happened to Ranji's father but didn't ask and wasn't told. I surmised that he had probably died, as one of the strengths of the East Indians was their allegiance to family. If he were alive he probably would have been there.

Ranji had an impressive array of jazz records which he had collected over a number of years. Most, of course, were by American musicians. He professed his interest in jazz and praised the American development of jazz.

"It's your economic system that I disagree with," he said. "It's exploitative. The rich get richer and the poor get poorer." I took up the challenge and presented my case for capitalism, or, as USIA called the American version of capitalism in those days, "People's Capitalism." The editor of *Thunder* smiled and renewed his attack. It was obvious that we would both leave from the same door through which we entered.

Ranji's mother did not join us for dinner but afterwards came to say goodbye as I was getting ready to leave.

"I'll walk you to the car," Ranji said.

We shook hands and I got into my car, turned on the motor while Ranji stood across the street to see me off, when suddenly he started yelling and ran back to my car. "Stop! Stop!" he shouted, "There's a man under your car!"

I turned off the motor and got out. I looked under the car. Sure enough, someone was sleeping there. If I had started the car to maneuver out into the street my wheels would have gone right over the man who was lying on the pavement.

Ranji reached under the car and shook the man, who despite all the noise of the motor and the shouting, had not stirred.

"What are you doing there?" Ranji shouted. "Get up! Get up! You almost got run over!"

The shaking and the noise finally revived the dark, prostrate shadow. It stirred, then moved slightly, and slowly a man crawled out on the road from underneath my car.

"Wha' you say, man? Wha' happened? Where am I?"

"You almost got run over. What a heluva place to sleep! You've been drink'n, man. You better get out of here and get on home. You're lucky to be alive!"

I was flabbergasted. The drunken man had somehow crawled under my car and gone to sleep while I was having dinner with Ranji. If Ranji had not spotted the prostrate body, the wheels of my car would surely have run over the sleeping drunk as I maneuvered to get out of a tight parking space. Thinking about the incident later, I visualized what the local media and others would say if the man had been killed or even injured. I could just see the headlines in the *Daily Chronicle*: "VICE CONSUL ON VISIT TO COMMUNIST EDITOR KILLS SLEEPING MAN."

"I must have a guardian angel watching over me," I thought. I thanked Ranji profusely for being so alert. The evening had turned out to be interesting as expected, but my adrenaline was all used up as I thought about what might have been but for the good eyesight of my host.

Maintaining good health is always a special problem in a developing country like British Guiana. In B.G. malaria was the greatest concern of most expatriates. In the mid-1950s, malaria suppressant pills, which were routinely issued to Foreign Service employees in later years, were not yet available. The risk of getting malaria, or elephantiasis, or some other tropical disease, was always present. Yet this risk was generally accepted, when thought about, as being part of the challenge to an officer and his family that goes with life in the Foreign Service.

The only hospital in Georgetown was run by the Seventh Day Adventists. These wonderful, dedicated people were tremendously helpful to the local population, though the Americans who ran the hospital could do only so much, limited as they were in financing and equipment. Many of their patients were unable to cover the cost of their treatment, which added to the hospital's lack of funds and consequent difficulties in maintaining high standards. Americans on the consulate staff who required medical treatment were strongly advised to seek medical assistance elsewhere unless an emergency situation developed. The nearest available medical treatment meeting American standards was at the U.S. naval base at Chagaramous in Trinidad.

Charmaine and I were fortunate that during our tour in Georgetown we contracted nothing more serious than a few colds, with few exceptions, and when Charmaine became pregnant we thought it advisable to make use of the hospital facilities at the U.S. naval base in Trinidad.

In early June Charmaine's time was quickly arriving so we left for Port-of-Spain where I would spend a few days and return to Georgetown to await the big event. She stayed with the PAO and his wife prior to my return. At the first sign of any action I would be immediately notified and would catch the daily flight to Trinidad to be at her side when the baby arrived. Unable to stand the anxiety any longer, I returned to Port-of-Spain several days before our son, Robert, made his appearance. All went well and I was able to return to my post. About ten days later I combined the chore of delivering the diplomatic pouch for the consulate in Paramaribo to the PanAm plane arriving at Atkinson Field from Trinidad with greeting my wife and baby son upon their arrival on the same plane. It was a joyful reunion.

Having come to Georgetown on a direct transfer from Mexico, where I had already spent six months after my first home leave, my tour of duty in Guiana would be less than the standard two-year period of regular assignments. I had now been there fifteen months, so I expected at any moment to receive a cable from Washington informing me of my next assignment and naming my replacement.

As the days went by and the cable I was expecting didn't arrive, I began to wonder if they had forgotten about me in Washington. I had talked by radio telephone with Gar Routt in Trinidad, but he had not heard anything either. "If I hear anything," he said, "either about your assignment or your replacement, I'll call you right away."

Another week went by and still no news. Charmaine was also getting anxious, wondering if the next country we would be going to would be good for Robert. Up to a point it was exciting not to know where one might be living next, but as our departure date would soon be less than sixty days away, we both felt that it would now be nice to know what the future had in store.

In the official mail that came in the pouch one afternoon the following week, a letter arrived addressed to "BPAO Allen Hansen, USIS GEORGETOWN." The letter had apparently gone to Suriname by mistake and had been forwarded to Georgetown from there. The return address indicated that it had been sent by "F. Corey." My heart skipped a beat. I knew that Frank Corey was the personnel officer for

Latin America at USIA headquarters. Perhaps this would have some information about my new assignment.

I opened the letter gingerly and began reading: "Dear Al, You'll be pleased to learn that you have been assigned to Madrid." I stopped reading. I couldn't believe it. Madrid! I was being sent to Madrid, to Spain, to the country and the people I had enjoyed so much! "Unbelievable." I thought. "Simply unbelievable. Won't Charmaine be thrilled!" I read on. "You are being assigned to a new position being established as the assistant cultural affairs officer in charge of a new textbook translation program." The rest of the letter covered some nitty-gritty, expressed confidence in my ability to fill the new assignment based on my record in Georgetown and Mexico, and wished me well. I was elated. I could hardly wait to tell Charmaine. "I guess I've done my penance at this hardship post and Madrid is my reward," I thought.

When I told Charmaine the good news she fully shared my enthusiasm for the new assignment. She had always had mixed feelings about our tour in Guiana. It was a culture with which she was familiar, having grown up in Trinidad, and it enabled her to visit relatives in her hometown, but it was, in many respects, what it was supposed to be, a "hardship post."

I had enjoyed our stay in Georgetown much more than Charmaine since my work had been challenging to say the least and I had found my professional contacts to be generally friendly and, at times, stimulating. I would leave Guiana with the feeling that I had established the new post on a solid foundation and that the USIS officers who followed would find fertile soil in which to expand their contacts and programs. At the same time I believed that USIS resources could contribute to the social and intellectual growth of this country, at least among those interested in such growth and who had not turned themselves completely away from "Yankee capitalism."

Looking at the history of British Guiana years later, however, after it became the independent country of Guyana, I wondered what might have happened if the U.S. had shown "benign neglect" rather than becoming so concerned about the rise of Cheddi Jagan and his espousal of communism.

The British had been much less concerned, but, as usual, were willing to listen to their American relatives. Whether the U.S. government's interest in British Guiana during the Eisenhower and Kennedy administrations made any difference to Guyana's future is difficult to say. More than thirty years later, however, as this is being written, that history is sad. Cheddi Jagan and his Cuban-Soviet support were neutralized but the country which became independent May 26, 1966, after 163 years as a British colony was saddled for nearly two decades with an Afro-Guyanese leader, Forbes Burnham, the former Jagan ally and head of the People's National Congress (PNC). Burnham never was able or willing to lead his country out of poverty and neglect, though he lived very well himself. While Guyana did not become "a second Cuba" as had been feared, neither did it prosper.

Nearly three decades later, in June, 1987, Dr. Cheddi Jagan was still head of the Marxist People's Progressive Party (PPP) and Ranji Chandisingh, who saved me from driving over and probably killing the inebriated man who had fallen asleep under my car, was by then the vice president of the PPP. Forbes Burnham had been removed from office by his death a few years earlier following unsuccessful surgery on his throat by a Cuban doctor. The PNC still controlled the local government after Burnham's death but eventually the PPP returned to power.

For years, the opposition political leaders denounced the Burnham government for its corruption. In 1987, a three-member commission advocated mechanisms for dealing with corruption in public life and for "protecting and preserving the country's socio-economic and moral fiber", as the *Barbados Advocate* reported from a safe distance. The PPP, alleging that all elections under the PNC for the last eighteen years had been rigged, contended that this "has set the tone in our national public life" and went on to say: "Corruption in public life grew from rampant into endemic proportions, with high officials having lifestyles and levels of consumption their salaries could not provide. A vast number of them have become landed proprietors, farm owners, businessmen, traders, property dealers, and engage in lucrative activity in full view of the public without any indication of the source of their capital." While advocating methods to assure fair elections, the committee also questioned such practices as a minister of the government being president of a company that accepts government contracts, or a chairman of a government commission who, as a private lawyer, defends his staff in court, presumably for a fee!

Poor Guyana! It was but an episode in our lives, an episode which would soon be left behind. But for the Guyanese, their country was the reality with which most would have to live—along with the Obeahs and the Kanaimas, in spirit at times, if not in practice. As for Charmaine and me, we had partaken of "Guyanese gumbo" for eighteen months. We would never forget our Guyanese experiences, though whenever we thought about preindependent Georgetown, it was with mixed feelings.

On November 18, 1978, Guyana captured world headlines when U.S. Congressman Leo J. Ryan and others investigating mistreatment of American followers of the Reverend Jim Jones' People's Temple cult were murdered, triggering a mass suicide execution of 911 cultists. No Guyanese were involved in this truly American tragedy that happened in the Guyanese jungle.

Near the turn of the century, Guyana remained a country with mammoth problems. A World Bank country study published in 1993 noted that prior to 1988, Guyana followed a set of economic policies characterized as "cooperative socialism." The report said that these policies "led to the domination of the public sector in the economy, and severely distorted incentives for the private sector. Existing private investments were nationalized, particularly the critical sugar and bauxite sectors, and government control extended to most financial institutions and consumer marketing." By 1991, the per capita income of Guyana was only US $290, the lowest in the western hemisphere.

The report further noted that "most public sector infrastructure necessary to support the private sector has deteriorated to the point of nonexistence. Power and water supplies are so erratic that many large private sector firms have invested in their own generators and water sources. The road system has deteriorated, particularly critical farm-to-market feeder roads. The sea wall system, which protects the most productive agricultural land, has been breached in several places, and patched temporarily, but needs major reconstruction. Schools lack basic repairs, books, equipment, and supplies. Hospitals operate with most equipment not working, with no drugs to dispense, insufficient budget for food, and the inability to carry out simple diagnostic tests, such as x-rays or blood tests."

It also stated that "the tax system is badly administered, and the level of collection is far below the potential in the system. Evasion, avoidance and corruption are everyday occurrences. . . It is difficult to know exactly the nature and extent of poverty in Guyana. Since 1980, however, out-migration has kept the total population roughly constant at about 750,000 people. . . An estimate made by the International Development Bank in 1989 indicated that 67 percent of the population was poor."

As with most reports of this type, it ends on a hopeful note: "Despite its many problems, Guyana remains a country with much potential, including a productive agricultural sector, vast timber resources, and mineral resources that include bauxite, gold and diamonds. With recent massive devaluations, the relative cost of labor in Guyana is one of the lowest in the world." The World Bank study concluded:

"Guyana is a country blessed with tremendous resources, but also burdened with tremendous problems."

Some years later, long after I had left Georgetown, the political situation in what was by then an independent Guyana deteriorated to the point where bombings and killing became all too common. Though normally the violence was between black and the East Indian political factions, on one occasion someone placed a bomb in the USIS library which had maintained neutrality and provided the country's best library service to both factions. The bomb destroyed the library and part of the consulate offices upstairs. A young girl who worked as a part-time librarian would have been killed had she not, by chance, been behind a pillar when the bomb exploded. However, she was deafened by the noise of the explosion and, I was told, never regained her hearing despite the best efforts of American doctors in the U.S. Fortunately for Charmaine and me, during our tour in B.G. the traditional "Demerara hospitality," which Guyanese were always quick to mention and which most lived up to, was still operative. The terror, including bombings, developed much later. Like a water faucet, it was turned on suddenly and eventually turned off.

We shall always wish Guyana better days in the twenty-first century than it experienced in the latter part of the twentieth century. And in a footnote to Guyana's twentieth century history, by the early 1990s Cheddi Jagan was again prime minister. Following the breakup of the Soviet Union, he dropped his former association with Soviet-style communism and became an advocate of democratic politics and a free-market economy.

5
Spanish Sojourn

"The difference between an American and a Spaniard is that an American takes himself lightly, and his work seriously, while a Spaniard takes himself seriously, and his work, lightly."
— Author unknown

With home leave to look forward to and visions that we would soon be living in the land where wine, flamenco music and dancing, and the fighting of bulls were national symbols, we had no regrets upon boarding the Pan American plane at Atkinson field. Our long journey from the jungles of South America would take us to one of the cradles of European civilization. I would be going back to the Spain I had learned to love, though now with a wife and a baby son. Things might be a bit different from my bachelor days in Madrid, but Spain was still Spain—a country of romance and enchantment.

After our second home leave in New Jersey ended, it was with light hearts and the spirit of adventure that we prepared for our next overseas assignment. A neighbor drove us to the pier in New York City where we boarded the S.S. *Independence* bound for Spain (Foreign Service regulations in that era often allowed families to travel by sea, a job benefit that, along with many others, eventually disappeared).

We were about three days at sea when we passed the Azores. We had been invited the night before to sit at the Captain's table for dinner. After dinner he took his dinner guests to the bridge to show us how the *Independence* maneuvered. While there he showed us some photos taken from the bridge of his ship as it was passing the Azores a few years earlier. The photos showed black volcanic ash coming out of the sea as a volcano erupted near the islands just as the *Independence* steamed by! They were dramatic photos and the captain was understandably proud of them.

Young Robert, now three months old, was an easy traveling companion as he couldn't run around and get into trouble and he was light enough to be carried without much difficulty. He slept most of the time, which also made our voyage easier. Thus the cruise across the Atlantic and into the Mediterranean on one of America's last traditional luxury liners, until their return more than a decade later, was thoroughly enjoyed. The voyage included a stop at the Madeira Islands for a day of sightseeing in which the major tourist attraction is to ride a sleigh drawn by two galloping horses down the steep cobblestone streets of Funchal, the capital city of these Portuguese islands. This, of course, we had to do. A day in Casablanca was also on the itinerary, which brought back memories of my visit there as a sailor aboard the U.S. Navy's *LST 533* about seven years earlier. Roaming the city with wife and child was fun, but somewhat less exciting than during my first visit there. In those days there was considerable social unrest as the Moroccans pressed the French for independence. Now it was peaceful and quiet.

A few days later the large liner pulled into the port of Algeciras and we and our new car, a small, British-made Ford Consul, which we had bought in New Jersey and shipped aboard the *Independence*, disembarked. We left immediately for the capital, stopping overnight along the way. Our Spanish adventure was about to begin.

Having lived in Madrid for three months before joining the Foreign Service, I had expected that the adjustment to our new post would be simple and stressless. How wrong I was. I had not reckoned with the fact that I now had two others to be concerned about: my wife and child. This was a new ball game. Despite my presumed knowledge of the culture and the city, the adjustment to Spanish mores and customs almost proved more difficult than any experience in settling into new surroundings which followed. Perhaps I had forgotten how different Spanish life is from what an American is accustomed to. Perhaps it was the new experience of having to take the baby into account in our every move. But although those first few months were difficult and stressful, before long we took to Spanish ways like a Russian takes to vodka.

The most difficult adjustment in our unsettled state those first few weeks was arranging our eating schedule to that of the Spaniards. While in the hotel all our meals were in restaurants; even after we moved into a temporary apartment we frequently ate out. Often if we arrived at a restaurant at 9 p.m. for dinner, the hour most restaurants opened for the evening meal, we found that we were the only ones there since most Spaniards ate much later. However, since I had to be at the office at 9 a.m. the next morning, I sometimes suffered from lack of sleep and indigestion caused by the late dining hours. The cure for this minor malady was to take a siesta during the long two-hour lunch break before returning to the office, which remained open from 4 to 7 p.m.

Some weeks later, with the help of the embassy administrative staff, we located a row house on a quiet, cobbled street about ten blocks from the embassy. It was ideal for our needs. I could walk to the office in fifteen minutes or drive in five. A small garden and driveway were fenced in at the front of the house. This provided ample privacy and turned out to be a pleasant place to enjoy the sun that spring and summer. Occasionally we would entertain guests or simply enjoy dining outside by ourselves by putting a card table in the driveway. The three bedrooms provided us with a room for the baby and a guest room. The rear of the house had a chute for bringing coal into the basement to feed the small furnace located there. Except for the remarkably small size of the furnace, it reminded me of growing up in New Jersey where, in the twenties and thirties, we also had a coal furnace in the basement of our home. It required not only the frequent shoveling of coal to keep the house warm in the winter, but also the slightly less frequent removal of the ashes, boyhood chores shared by my brother and me.

One thing about living in Spain while Generalissimo Francisco Franco ruled was that we slept well at nights. It was a real change from Georgetown, where we never knew when someone might crawl through our open windows and rob us, or worse. Here in Spain the Guardia Civil (civil guards) in their black, three-cornered Napoleon-style hats and green uniforms were ubiquitous. They were both respected and feared. In addition, every few blocks of the residential areas of Madrid had a *serreno,* a night watchman who was paid a small sum by each of the owners or tenants of the homes and apartments that he guarded, so crime against persons and property in Franco Spain was virtually non-existent. In parts of Madrid where apartment houses abound, the serreno carries the keys for all the entrance halls of the buildings. Many apartment dwellers seldom bother taking the building key with them, depending instead on the serreno to let them in.

While settling into our new home I became acquainted with my new colleagues at USIS and began learning my new duties as an ACAO. I felt somewhat inadequate for the title since it seemed to imply that I was a very cultivated person who knew a great deal about the culture of the United States and who would, on occasion, represent the U.S.

government in this magnificent country that was Spain—a country possibly more famed for its art and literature and general cultural achievements than anything else. I was concerned about living up to my own expectations. As I became more confident, however, I realized that not as much was expected of me as I had feared. I was also fortunate in that I was only one of three assistant cultural attachés and, furthermore, our immediate supervisor was a very decent fellow with whom I shared excellent rapport.

As we gradually settled into our new home, we adapted to the Spanish way of life and I soon began to feel at home in my new job. We also began to appreciate more than ever our good fortune at having been assigned to the Spanish capital.

My assignment to USIS Madrid as one of three assistant cultural affairs officers (ACAOs), or assistant cultural attachés, occurred because of a new textbook translation program. The new project required a full-time manager, the job I was to undertake. The program was slated to receive $500,000 of Public Law 480 funds in local currency, generated by U.S. economic assistance programs to Spain. USIS planned to carry out this new program in five years at the rate of $100,000 annually. The first hundred thousand had been transferred to USIS Madrid eighteen months or so prior to my arrival, but all the officers at the post were too occupied with other priorities to initiate the new project.

One of the other two assistant cultural attachés already assigned to Madrid administered the educational exchange program, a full-time job in itself, including an expanding Fulbright program. The other ACAO was fully involved in arranging exhibits, supervising the library operation, and handling the multitudinous other activities which fell under the category of "cultural affairs," all under the general supervision of the cultural affairs officer.

Since most of the major Spanish publishers were in Barcelona, this meant that I had to make frequent trips to that exciting city to arrange the publication of American textbooks in Spanish translation under the new program. Spain had long been the leading publisher of books in the Spanish-speaking world, thus the Barcelona publishers were a major source of books for all of the Spanish-speaking Latin American countries.

On my first visit to Barcelona to meet with a number of publishers who might be interested in this project, I found myself in a most interesting situation. I had had no experience whatsoever in the publishing field, yet here I was in Barcelona, planning to arrange the publication of $100,000 worth of American textbooks! I could not help but think how my personal fortunes had changed. About five years earlier, before becoming a Foreign Service officer with USIA, I had crossed the Atlantic in tourist class on an Italian ship and had arrived in Barcelona seeking adventure and the least costly way to travel and exist on the European continent. Now I was in the Catalan capital on an expense account with, in effect, one hundred thousand dollars in my pocket. That was a lot of Spanish pesetas in those days.

The Spanish publishers were not only eager to do business with USIS, but were, for the most part, charming, well-educated individuals with an excellent sense of humor typical of most Catalans, and more than ready to wine and dine a U.S. government official with money to invest in their field of interest. It did not take long or require much effort to sign contracts with a number of them for the translation and purchase of two hundred or more copies of each contracted title, to be delivered to USIS when published. This guaranteed that the American texts selected would be published and, by dealing with well-known publishers, distributed commercially throughout Spain and Latin America. The two hundred copies we obtained would be placed in our lending libraries and sent to book reviewers and teachers to encourage sales.

It quickly became apparent, as more and more contracts were signed, that the marriage of U.S. funding with the experience and skill of a number of Spanish publishers would soon result in the increased publication of American textbooks in Spanish. The program held great promise, but just after my successful launching of it, two factors intervened to kill it. Right after signing contracts for about twenty book titles and working on this project for a few months, the Spanish government devalued the peseta. As a result, the hundred thousand dollars worth of pesetas in my budget for that year shrank overnight to about $60,000. Since the funding for this project was the dollar equivalent in local currency, I suddenly found myself with far less financial resources than when the program had been initiated. The second blow came about three months later. Somewhere in the upper echelons of the U.S. government a decision was made that the remaining funds (originally the equivalent of $400,000 but now reduced to $240,000 because of the devaluation) could better be used for other priorities. The end result was that although we managed under this project to encourage the publication of forty-two titles that year, the new textbook program ended almost as quickly as it began.

Although I no longer had to concern myself with textbook publishing, other duties were soon thrust upon me. USIS work is like housework—it never ends and can always be expanded. My workdays soon became as filled as they had been when I was deeply engrossed in the textbook publishing business. Many Spaniards, particularly the educated classes, were, at that time, highly receptive to and interested in the culture, the people, the economy, and the technology of the United States. Through the Spanish-American base agreements and U.S. military and economic assistance programs, Americans had brought new jobs and considerable hope to Spain.

In the late 1950s, because of the Franco dictatorship and Franco's World War II association with Nazi Germany, Spain still suffered from the effects of its civil war and ostracism by its Western European neighbors. In this environment there was a great demand for information about America and things American that no USIS office, regardless of how large its staff or budget, could fully meet.

My colleagues at USIS were, generally speaking, wonderful people to work with though their personalities, as might be expected, differed considerably. The office environment was not without the customary personality conflicts and resulting tensions. The PAO was Frank Oram whose last assignment was as Assistant Director of USIA for Latin America. He was the one who had enough confidence in me to send me to British Guiana as the first USIS officer in that country, and though this meant leaving Mexico sooner than my wife and I would have preferred at the time, no doubt he was also instrumental in what could be called my "reward," an assignment to Madrid, a most highly desirable post. Though some of the senior USIS officers may have had their differences with him, the overall *ambiente*, at least from my perspective as a junior officer, was one of relative calm and excellent cooperation among the various elements of USIS.

The information officer was a Mexican-American who, when transferred at the end of his tour, was replaced by a former war correspondent. The new I.O., "Buck" Hutchinson, had a great sense of humor. He used to frequently take me aside after our periodic staff meetings with the PAO and jokingly say, "If you keep asking the boss why we do what we do, you're going to get in trouble. He's going to have you shipped out!" But rather than antagonizing the head of USIS operations, he seemed to accept the challenges occasionally raised by this junior officer with good humor. Furthermore, I don't believe I ever had any influence on his decisions when he finally made them, or on the programs he had already implemented despite my freely expressed reservations at various times.

The cultural attaché, my immediate superior, had been the CAO in Mexico for some time when I was there. An intelligent, hard-working man, he was always fair and understanding with his staff. Of my two fellow assistant cultural attachés, one had been a professor with a doctorate in Latin American history. A serious, industrious type with a dry sense of humor, he was easy to work with. The other had possibly also taught and was equally serious and devoted. I had no problem in working hard to keep up with these two and, at times, being serious, but I could not equal their academic qualifications.

We three ACAOs and our wives all became good friends. When the wife of one of them, who was a happy-go-lucky Uruguayan woman (quite the opposite of her very serious and businesslike husband), fell and broke her hip while playing ping pong in her home while wearing high heels, we all sympathized with her but were not too surprised about her misfortune. We knew of no one else who would even think of playing ping pong in high heels, but knew that she was quite capable of doing so. Her period of recuperation was, perhaps, longer than it might have been had she not insisted on dancing while still using crutches during the recovery stage!

The senior assistant information officer, Harry Kendall, was another former colleague, probably the one I knew best. He had been the information officer and my chief mentor at my first post in Caracas. His main job in Madrid was to organize and supervise "America Weeks" throughout Spain, a series of exhibits, lectures, concerts, and movies. These "weeks" were designed to portray contemporary U.S. society to the Spaniards who, prior to the signing of the Spanish-American base agreements about five years earlier, had been isolated from America and Americans. Americans were still a relatively unknown element among most Spaniards, yet increasingly visible because of the base agreements and the growing influx of American tourists. There was a growing interest in Spain in learning more about those strange, wealthy, and technologically advanced foreigners whose presence was stimulating the stagnant Spanish economy, even if their ways were sometimes difficult to comprehend.

The British writer John Masters astutely portrayed some of the differences in U.S. and Spanish culture in a novel he wrote entitled *Fandango Rock*. Fandango is a lively Spanish dance and type of music while the "Rock" in the title of his book refers to a well-known American phenomenon, Rock and Roll. In one scene he depicts an American driving in the Spanish countryside who accidentally crashes into a group of Spaniards on a rural highway in Spain. The ensuing melee exemplifies how each cultural group fails to understand the other, and, in fact, misinterprets the other. This was the problem USIS addressed in Spain in the late fifties as more and more American military, most of whom were little versed in the ways and mores of Spaniards, descended by the thousands on Spanish society. The "America Weeks" were an effort to enable Spaniards to better understand the Americans who suddenly appeared in their midst.

Another assistant information officer who worked on press and publications activities of USIS had been one of the nine members of my junior officer training class. He was also a likable person with a ready smile for everyone and a dedicated officer. But after his mother-in-law, a child psychologist from California, visited him and his wife and his two children in Madrid for a few months, his personal life began to change drastically. Upon his return with his family to California on home leave, his wife decided to leave him. She took their two boys with her and went home to mommy. When her devastated husband returned to Madrid, he told us that his wife became convinced by her mother (no doubt practicing her child psychology) that her children weren't being brought up properly by her husband in the Spanish environment.

Another key officer of USIS Madrid was the executive officer. He controlled the budget and finances of USIS and supervised the general administrative chores of the office. He therefore had knowledge and access to all USIS activities, whether cultural or informational. He was a likable man with whom everyone got along, and his wife was particularly fun to be around in social situations because of her frank and honest view of things and her reputation for calling a spade a spade, spiced with her own brand of humor.

Finally, as time passed, a couple of junior officer trainees passed through Madrid and left their marks after completing their training. Having been a "JOT" myself, I was especially willing to pass on my "vast knowledge and experience" to these younger officers. In so doing I learned a great deal. One was a graduate of the Columbia School of Journalism. The other was a family member of one of the great industrial giants of the Midwest who probably did not have to work but found satisfaction and enjoyment in government service. Both did well and eventually moved on to the higher echelons of USIA. These, then, were the Americans who carried out the plans and programs of USIS Madrid in the late 1950s. Helping us were about three dozen Spanish employees, many of whom were professionals in their own right and whose importance to successful USIS programs can never be overestimated.

One of the responsibilities of a USIS post, which generally involves every officer and employee in one way or another, is to provide press coverage and assist local and foreign correspondents in their coverage of presidential visits, and to support such visits in many other ways. So in December 1959 when President Dwight Eisenhower came to Spain on the tenth stop of a global trip to eleven nations, even this assistant cultural attaché became involved in the President's visit.

Eisenhower was known affectionately by millions as "Ike" which, in Castilian, was pronounced by the Spaniards as "E-kay." He was, that year, *Time* Magazine's "Man of the Year." Although I had seen him many times on the motion picture screen and too many times in the USIA press conference film series, which USIS distributed, I was totally unprepared for the warmth which he radiated in real life.

I was working in the press stand at the Torrejon air base when the president arrived. (Torrejon was a joint Spanish-American air base near Madrid, established under the Spanish-American base agreements.) Earlier a Boeing 707 Intercontinental jet, which looked huge to us at the time (long before the 747 came into being), landed and discharged about 90 reporters. They had left Paris shortly before the president did so that they could photograph and report on his arrival in Spain. By the time the president's plane arrived, the press stand was filled to overflowing with some of the most famous foreign correspondents in the business as well as local reporters and stringers. For some of the journalists who had traveled with "Ike" across Europe and part of Asia, these arrival ceremonies had become so routine they preferred the warmth of the press busses to the cold press stand. Most, however, chose to witness the arrival ceremony. As the wheels of the plane carrying the president and his party touched down, the motion picture and television cameras just above my head began to grind. I was standing with some USIS colleagues and a reporter from Washington who had arrived on the press plane.

"Imagine," the reporter commented, "breakfast in Pakistan, lunch in Afghanistan, and supper in India. We move about so fast it's hard to keep the countries straight, let alone the days. The president has remarkable stamina to keep going the way he has at his age."

The plane was now taxiing toward the crowd, coming closer all the time. It then turned in a narrow arc following the yellow line painted on the cement pavement almost directly in front of us, enabling us to appreciate even more the large size of this aircraft compared to what we were generally accustomed to. The roar of the jets subsided and quickly stopped. The front door of the plane opened while the gangway was rolled toward it. The first person out was the president. He waved, removed his hat, grinned his famous grin, and walked down the stairs to meet the Spanish Chief of State, Generalissimo Franco, who saluted him and then warmly shook his hand.

The rear door of the plane now opened and out stepped the presidential press secretary, Jim Hagerty, followed by several other officials. National anthems of the two countries were played and then the two chiefs of state reviewed the Spanish troops and a U.S. Air Force contingent stationed at Torrejon. After completing the review and shaking hands with a number of cabinet members and other top Spanish officials, the president and his host stepped up to a small, red-carpeted platform. The Generalissimo welcomed his guest to Spanish soil, and after the president's interpreter, Colonel Vernon Walters (who later became the U.S. ambassador to the U.N. and Germany) repeated Franco's address in English, the president replied with appropriate words.

As the president spoke I was looking at a typewritten note in the hands of one my colleagues. It was the president's official arrival statement. But he did not follow the "script;" instead, he ad-libbed. "He's a master of the cliché," commented one of the reporters next to me. "I've heard him say practically the same thing about ten times, but each time it goes over in a big way."

The welcoming ceremonies completed, Franco and his guest entered a specially imported "bubble car" for the short trip to Madrid. Before the presidential party departed, however, there was a mad scramble in the press stand. The reporters left as quick as they could and rushed to waiting buses so they could depart before the president and thus arrive in the city ahead of him. As soon as the car with the president and the Generalissimo left, the crowd dispersed. I went back to one of the hangers where a temporary press headquarters had been set up. The USIS driver was waiting for me, and as we rode back to Madrid, swarms of people still lined the fifteen-mile route even though twenty minutes had passed since the president went by.

All along the route Spain's famous Civil Guards in their black hats and green capes were much in evidence. They were stationed on the sides of the road at about fifty-foot intervals and beyond the road, on the hills and in the fields where they had a clear view of the road and the surrounding area.

"Que simpatico es ese señor, que simpatico es el presidente" ("The president is so simpatico, he is so simpatico!") the chauffeur said to me over and over again, as we drove back to town. These words were repeated time and again by many of the Spaniards who saw the American president. The Spanish newspapers, in reporting his visit, used the same expression. *Simpatico* defies easy translation into

English, for it means "sympathetic, pleasant, agreeable, likable, and congenial" all rolled into one.

From the moment word was received that the president would be visiting Madrid the embassy became a great hub of activity devoted to the visit. I personally was not affected until about a week before the visit, the nature of the work of an assistant cultural attaché being what it is, but many officers with different duties worked weekends, holidays, and nights on the multitude of tasks that the visit created. Such things as protocol; security; providing housing and facilities for the president, his party, and several hundred visiting newsmen; scheduling of events; publicity; selection of parade routes; and hundreds of other details had to be planned and coordinated by the two governments.

One particularly thorny problem involved protocol. In Spanish tradition the most important personages are greeted last. In the American tradition, the most important personages are at the head of the line, and are greeted first. The Spanish were insisting that when the president stepped off the plane, he would greet lower cabinet members first and, finally, the Generalissimo. "Impossible!" cried the Americans. He has to meet the Spanish chief of state first, then if there is time, the lesser notables. The American position won, but not without a struggle.

Several days before the visit, the streets of Madrid—on which the president's motorcade would travel, began to change their appearance. A number of ingenious giant arches arose, made from steel piping and covered with plywood and shrubs, each bearing huge portraits of Eisenhower and Franco, or Eisenhower alone.

New and brighter street lights were installed on one of the main avenues of the parade route. By the morning of December 21, an estimated 40,000 Spanish and American flags of cloth and paper were either flying from specially prepared staffs or posted on buildings from the outskirts of Madrid to the Palace of La Moncloa. La Moncloa would be the president's overnight home, and, therefore, the American "White House" in Spain for a day.

It seemed so strange, a few days before the visit, when on my way to work I would see the flag of my country flying so boldly on Spanish streets. A week or more after the visit some flags were still flying. On Madrid's famous Paseo de Castellano a short distance from the embassy, a giant portrait of "Ike" smiled down on passing motorists and pedestrians for several weeks after the president had come and gone.

Charmaine couldn't be at the airport with me but she was at the special area for embassy personnel and their families on the Paseo de Castellano just in front of the plaza where the president and Franco transferred from the "bubble car," which had carried them into the city, to an open car which was to take them through downtown Madrid.

The atmosphere here where the exchange of cars was to take place was charged with emotion and eager anticipation as the crowd waited for the arrival of the two chiefs of state. Suddenly two helicopters, which were preceding the presidential motorcade by a few minutes, arrived and hovered at rooftop height above the throngs of spectators.

"Here he comes, here he comes"! Someone in the crowd shouted. Necks stretched and people pushed forward to get a better view. Then, as the motorcade approached, a voluntary, thunderous roar of appreciation and approval broke out mixed with the noise of thousands of clapping hands. When the president stepped out, he raised both arms in his stylized "V," holding his hat high, and smiling as usual. "Que simpatico, que simpatico" could be heard again and again. After receiving the key to the city from the mayor of Madrid, the two leaders entered the open car and the procession moved on, now preceded not only by two helicopters and the usual press and security people, but also by a detachment of colorful lancers of the Spanish cavalry.

The same scenes were repeated again and again: the president forever smiling and waving, undoubtedly pleased at the warm reception he was receiving from the Spanish people. At his side, Franco appeared to be more serious but undoubtedly pleased with this visit of the American president, a clear expression of American support for him and his regime after years of isolation and ostracism.

When I returned to Madrid from the airport, I stopped off at the embassy for a few minutes then walked down the street to the Hotel Castellano Hilton where the Spanish government had set up special press headquarters for visiting newsmen. The place was buzzing with activity. Eisenhower's press secretary, Jim Hagerty, was due to arrive momentarily for a press conference. Reports had come that the entire presidential party was way behind schedule because the crowds that had turned out to welcome the president were so thick at Plaza España, in the center of the city, that the procession had to slow to a turtle's pace.

"We haven't seen such a large, warm reception since we left New Delhi," one of the traveling newsmen commented. The official estimate of the welcoming crowds released later was one and a half million, counting those who lined the road from the Torrejon air base to Madrid. The rest of the day I worked with USIS colleagues on press matters until about 2 a.m. I then went home and set the alarm for 6:30 a.m.

By 7:30 a.m. I was at the embassy again and a group of us walked over to the Castellano Hilton. I gave the USIA photographer, who was with the traveling press corps, a package of photos that our photo lab had worked on until 4 or 5 a.m. He would carry them back to Washington for worldwide use. At the hotel a number of correspondents were lined up to check out at the reception desk. Despite their experience by now on their whirlwind trip to three continents, one of them remarked, "Next time I'm going to check out at night so I don't have to go through this morning lineup again." Nevertheless, they all managed to get aboard the special buses taking them to the airport. They were scheduled to leave well before the president's departure at about 11 a.m. so they could be on hand to cover his arrival in Morocco that afternoon.

A small group of us drove out to the airport in the press attaché's car and took our positions again in the press stand. The weather was not quite as cold as it had been the day before, but it was still not what one could call a warm day in June. After all, we were in December.

About forty-five minutes after we arrived three large helicopters appeared in the distance. Two of them landed first, near the rear of the presidential plane. They discharged their passengers, including Hagerty, and taxied away. The third helicopter landed shortly thereafter, near the front of the Boeing 707, and Franco and the president stepped out. Again, as on the day before, there was a review of the troops and considerable handshaking followed by short talks by each chief of state. Franco then walked with the president to the end of the ramp, they shook hands, exchanged a brief *abrazo* (the Spanish hug or embrace), though I question my own memory on this point, and the Generalissimo, who was in uniform, saluted General Eisenhower, who was in mufti and again, ostensibly for that reason (though there were probably other reasons as well), did not return the salute. Eisenhower then went up the stairs of the gangway, paused a moment at the top, smiled, dramatically waved both hands, and stepped inside. The door closed behind him, the engines started almost immediately, and within seconds the plane taxied toward the runway. It was quickly airborne, trailing clouds of dark, black smoke as it climbed sharply into the gray sky. That afternoon the president would be in Morocco, lunching with the king of that country, and before midnight his wife would be greeting him at Andrews Air Force Base, just outside of Washington.

The "Pact of Madrid" was signed September 26, 1953, by Ambassador James C. Dunn for the United States and Foreign Minister Albert Martin Artajo for Spain. It included three separate but interdependent agreements: a defense agreement, an economic aid agreement, and a mutual defense agreement. The agreements created considerable criticism of the United States for "going to bed with Franco." By the beginning of 1960 there was still criticism about the agreements, both within and without Spain, and particularly in Western Europe. However, the American goal of having military bases within striking distance of the Soviet Union, if needed, had been achieved. As for the Spanish government and people, the American connection launched them on a journey that would eventually link them to the western democracies, particularly their Western European neighbors.

The Spanish-American agreements were economically pervasive. At their inception they saved the Spanish economy from near-collapse by the injection of funds and food (P.L. 480 surplus agricultural products) and the creation of jobs in connection with the building and later the maintenance of the military bases. In July 1959 when the country was again about to go bankrupt despite sizable amounts of American aid, the Generalissimo agreed to follow the advice of European and American economists, devalued the peseta and instituted sorely needed administrative and financial reforms. The result by 1962 was a billion dollar foreign exchange balance and a relatively prosperous, expanding economy compared to a decade earlier, though one that was still far behind the level of Spain's Western European neighbors (other than Portugal).

The Pact of Madrid also pervaded Spanish military life because of the millions of dollars of new military equipment, from tanks to ships, which the Spanish armed forces received from the United States. In addition, a large number of Spanish military officers and men received training in the United States. This must have influenced the thinking of many of them.

The pervasiveness of the base agreements on the political life of Spain was equally dramatic. Before the Pact of Madrid, Spain was not a member of the United Nations. After gaining membership in the UN following the agreements, the Franco government peacefully relinquished Spanish Morocco to the new Moroccan government and, unlike Portugal, reported regularly on the administration of Spain's African colonies as requested by the UN. Franco remained solidly with the West on the issue of Soviet communism and gave active support to the United States when needed. During the first of several crises involving Lebanon, for example, when U.S. logistical support was needed for military operations in that country designed to protect American lives, Spain allowed U.S. aircraft to land in Spain en route to and from Lebanon, despite criticism from anti-U.S. groups. The Spanish government also applied for associate membership in the Common Market of the six Western European democracies and was eventually accepted. Despite these actions, critics within Spain who opposed Franco argued that the U.S. should have been doing much more to influence the Franco regime toward greater political liberalization. Julian Marias, the liberal Spanish philosopher who was unquestionably a great friend of the U.S., writing in *Foreign Affairs* in October 1960 expressed his concern in this regard:

> Not too long ago most Spaniards were hopeful that the United States representing the greatest 'possibility' in the world at present would help to warm and melt everything frozen (in Spain), to set in motion after many years of war, everything alive, to open the future. Many people, especially among the youth, born to the present situation, are now turning in other directions ... Most would like and love the United States if only they had the right image of it, if they could visit it. But they cannot overcome the handicap of misrepresentations; they have no hope left. Paradoxically, the United States appears to be praised and supported by quite a few of its old (pro-Nazi) opponents and by other people who, in fact, strongly dislike it; meanwhile, anti-American feeling is growing among the potential real friends of the United States.

How much anti-American feeling was growing in Spain at the time was debatable, and, of course, public opinion polls were out of the question. But countering such attitudes was part of USIA's mission.

Unlike President Ronald Reagan's forceful call to support democratic growth worldwide nearly a quarter of a century later, American policy in the fifties and sixties was much more timid. In this respect Arthur P. Whitaker, author of *Spain and Defense of the West, Ally and Liability* (Harper, NY 1961) noted at the time:

> Generally intelligent and well-informed persons hold that the policy of nonintervention permits the United States to strengthen a dictatorship with economic, military, and political aid, but prohibits it from putting any pressure on the same regime to reduce the flagrant contradiction between its own character and the ideals of democracy and freedom which the

arrangements made between them profess to defend. Again, the same persons who unqualifiedly endorse the requirement of economic reforms as a condition of aid to a foreign country usually reject as 'intervention' the suggestion that the need for political reforms might similarly be pressed.

Clearly there were two schools of thought among Americans with respect to U.S. policy toward Spain. Liberals favored a much more aggressive policy in line with Julian Marias, Whitaker, and others while the conservative school felt that an attitude of "don't rock the boat," i.e., don't intervene in political matters, was the proper one. Whitaker argued in his book that the U.S. should revert to an attitude of "coolness and correctness" toward the Spanish dictator; secondly, the U.S. should persuade other nations to share the political liability that he felt any association with the Franco regime represented; and thirdly, the U.S. should have made known its disappointment with the failure of the Spanish government to give effect to the principles of "individual liberty and free institutions" that it endorsed by signing the economic aid agreement of 1953. Marias, in his *Foreign Affairs* essay, added that the U.S. should "at least make a gesture which would show that Americans really care for liberty and reject any crushing of it, from either side."

Time would tell how this issue would finally be resolved, but not fully so until the Generalissimo was no longer on the scene. In the meantime, Spaniards, like Americans, were divided in their thinking. While many Spaniards disliked and distrusted Franco, there were also plenty of "Francophiles." Many shared the view expressed in a story making the rounds in Madrid at the time. A friend tells his colleague, "Have you heard the news? Franco is on his deathbed!"

"Thank God!" remarked his friend.

A short while later the informant returned and said, "Have you heard, Franco's not going to die after all!"

"Thank God!" came the quick reply.

Although Spaniards under Franco were careful not to criticize their maximum leader in public, and press censorship prevented any criticism of his regime, in private he was the butt of many jokes. Given the Spanish sense of humor and the need to express themselves to offset the lid placed on public discussion by Franco's dictatorial government, they found release in stories about him that were widely circulated among friends and acquaintances. One such story was about the time the Generalissimo and his family were flying over the Spanish countryside in his plane when his wife said to him, "Francisco, why don't you throw out a thousand peseta note and make some poor peasant down below happy?"

Then his daughter interjected, "Papa, why don't you throw out ten one hundred peseta notes and make ten peasants happy?"

Then the pilot turned around and said, "Why don't you jump out and make everybody happy?"

This same joke, with Harry and Margaret Truman as the principals, circulated in the U.S. in the early days of the Truman administration.

Franco was as interested in obtaining favorable public opinion of himself and his policies as are American presidents who must cater to public opinion for their policies to be successful. Of course the Spanish caudillo had control of the media and exercised restrictions on freedoms generally enjoyed by American citizens. Nevertheless, because public opinion remained important to him, the visit of President Eisenhower was a large feather in his cap.

Franco's main support, according to Arthur Whitaker at the time, came first from the armed forces; secondly from the leaders in banking, industry, and commerce, including big landowners ("the oligarchy" as Whitaker calls them); and thirdly, the Catholic Church. The *Falange,* Franco's political party, while still one of his major instruments, was of little importance power-wise relative to the three groups just cited. Hugh Thomas, author of *The Spanish Civil War,* noted in his book that "the Falange proper is really no more than the bureaucracy which staffs the ministries, including old soldiers who use the *Falange* ideology to gather some popular appeal."

The Catholic Church in the late fifties, according to some observers, was attempting to extricate itself from the close identification it shared with the Franco regime for a quarter of a century. Dissatisfaction and criticism of the regime were growing among various segments of the church hierarchy. Nationwide strikes in the spring and summer of 1960 were treated by the regime with comparative leniency, due, some said, to the increasing support given the strikers by the church.

A large and rather impressive church directly faces, from the opposite side of the street, the impressive, modernistic building of the American Embassy in Madrid. Visitors to Spain were sometimes shown these two buildings and told, "These are the two pillars of Spain."

American policies and actions are always subject to criticism by someone. For example, the failure of Spain to receive anything similar to the Marshall Plan aid to Western Europe was viewed by some Spaniards as unfair treatment on the part of the United States, yet many of these same people condemned U.S. friendship with the Franco government, as if the U.S. government could deal directly with the Spanish people without dealing with their government. Julian Marias, for example, noted that the lack of a "Marshall Plan for Spain" was the first of three major disappointments experienced by Spaniards in their post-World War II relations with the U.S. The second disappointment came, he said, when the "quarantine" policy of the late 1940s kept Spain out of the United Nations. This "hurt Spanish pride and gave unexpected strength to the existing state of things," he contended. The third disappointment came when the U.S., after deciding to do business with Franco, failed to exact from him an agreement to move closer toward the ideals and principles espoused by his American ally.

Marias further believed at the time that three other factors contributed to increasing the wariness of many Spaniards toward Americans: the growth of anti-Americanism in Western Europe and Latin America; the effects of left-wing propaganda; and "the official relationship between the United States and Spain and the impression the public has of it." By this he meant that the "cool and correct" attitude toward the Spanish dictator disappeared with the signing of the base agreements. Yet how could it be otherwise?

Marias's views were overly pessimistic. He could not foresee that, thirty years later, an economically dynamic Spain would be governed by a freely elected government that is now a member of the political, economic, and military associations of the western democracies. Perhaps one of the major forces that Marias didn't reckon with was the influx of Americans and their ideas, which would, in time, help bring about the liberalizing effect he sought, just as what occurred in Eastern Europe and the Soviet Union by the last decade of the twentieth century. The interaction with the rest of the world contributed greatly to the remarkable changes in the Iron Curtain countries. This effect is why the long-standing U.S. policy toward Cuba of prohibiting American citizens from visiting that country is highly questionable in the views of many students of international affairs, including this one.

In 1962 some 700,000 Spanish workers were living in parts of Western Europe. Tourism, which accounted for one million visitors to Spain in 1951, reached more than ten million by 1963. This interaction rubbed against Spanish citizens and left its mark.

In 1959, prior to the end of the U.S. Information Media Guaranty Program (IMG) in Spain, American books and periodicals in quantities amounting to $750,000 were entering Spain annually, a fifteen-fold increase over the $50,000 worth of imports of similar materials a few years earlier, prior to the IMG arrangements. The IMG, administered by USIA, enabled Spaniards to buy U.S. books and magazines with pesetas instead of scarce dollars. By 1961 magazines and newspapers from the U. S. and other countries became so widely distributed in the major cities of Spain that Mingote, the famous Spanish cartoonist of the monarchist newspaper *ABC*, was moved to draw a cartoon showing a kiosk covered with foreign publications, including *Look*, *Life*, and *Time*. A farmer and his wife, recently arrived in the big city, stare uncomprehendingly at these publications. The wife remarks to her husband: "And you told me that you knew how to read!"

Left-wing propaganda which constantly attacked the U.S.-Spanish base agreements and other cooperative efforts between the two governments, and which Marias mentioned as a factor in shaping Spanish public opinion, included the programs of *Radio España Independiente (REI)*. *REI* broadcast from Prague. Except for Madrid, where the broadcasts were jammed, they were received with little difficulty throughout most of Spain. It was against the law for Spaniards to listen to *REI*, but, of course, many people did. In a country with a censored press, it was bound to be popular as a source of uncensored news, no matter how skewed. Its collaborators within Spain kept it surprisingly well informed and it, in turn, informed the people in Spain about things that they could not read in their own press, though with communist condiments added. *REI*, according to Hugh Thomas, pursued three main themes: (1) Reconciliation among anti-Franco forces; (2) opposition to the United States; and (3) a moderate rather than an extreme economic policy.

The American investment in military bases on Spanish soil was designed to provide a deterrent to Soviet expansionist plans. Small wonder that the communists were opposed to the establishment of the bases. But as Hugh Thomas noted, rather than seeking support among the masses, "the Communist Party has concentrated on gaining a few well placed followers. . . hard working and disciplined party workers exist in many villages in the south of Spain, among intellectual circles in Madrid, in the syndicates and even in the ministries." It was in this environment that USIS Madrid, with branch offices in Barcelona, Santander, and Seville, sought to further U.S. foreign policy objectives and offset the efforts of the Spanish communists and their Soviet supporters to thwart, or at the least denigrate, U.S. policies toward Spain.

Censorship of the media in Spain under Franco was a fact of life. It was one of the many aspects of the Franco regime that intellectuals like Julian Marias regretted and criticized in their own way. They could not openly criticize their government, but many, like Marias, did so by speaking about the foibles of former Spanish governments. On the surface this was history, but everyone knew that he was referring to the present regime. And as long as this was done in lectures, where the audience was limited, he was not bothered by government bureaucrats assigned to assure that the masses only heard or read what was considered "safe." The mass media had much tighter rules.

On several occasions I was reminded of how conditioned Spanish citizens had become to their government's broad and well-known censorship policies. For example, in June 1962 I was invited to present a lecture on American culture in a small mining town in Asturias, which was located in the center of an area that had been strike-bound a month or so earlier. Several incidents occurred in connection with that event that reminded me of how pervasive the idea of censorship had become among Spain's citizens.

First, I was somewhat taken aback when a Spanish employee who had been a USIS staffer for many years asked me in all seriousness if the talk that I was going to present had been censored, an outrageous idea from an American viewpoint. Although this employee had worked for Americans and should have known our position on this subject, she believed that somehow, and in some way, the American government might be willing to submit the comments of a U.S. government official to Spanish censorship! Such an action would, of course, be intolerable if not unthinkable.

After presenting to the group of assembled miners and mining officials my lecture that dealt with basic characteristics of Americans (a talk I developed in connection with the "America Weeks" programs of USIS), one of the local officials who was on the platform with me asked me why I had not presented all of my prepared speech. I asked him what he meant. He said, "Well, from where I sat, I could see that you skipped some parts toward the end." What I had left out were additional points which I dropped as I judged the audience had had enough. I explained this to him. But only later, as I thought about it, did I realize why he had raised that question. He had assumed that what I omitted was a "censored" portion, such was the extent of censorship in Franco Spain!

My talk included a discussion of various aspects of American ideas regarding competition, equality, separation of church and state, elections, and other concepts foreign to Spanish society under Franco. Afterwards a man who had been in the audience came up to me and said, "We liked the talk because you, as a foreigner, can say things which we Spaniards can't talk about."

In addition to the censorship imposed by the state in Spain, the Roman Catholic Church, which dominated the educational system throughout the country, was represented on all censorship boards for television, radio, books, and newspapers. But censorship in Spain as elsewhere was arbitrary and often appeared to be irrational. In 1960 several hundred of Spain's leading writers and intellectuals appealed to the government to provide them with guidelines concerning censorship but they could hardly have expected a reply. Inconsistencies were constant as foreign journals containing articles that must have infuriated Franco at times were permitted to enter Spain and be distributed. At other times, *Time, Life,* and *The New York Times* were kept off the newsstands for what appeared to an outsider as being nothing to get excited about.

I had occasion to learn how arbitrary Spanish censors could be by my close association with a number of Spanish publishers. For example, I had read something about Spain in a book by Princeton Professor William Ebenstein entitled *Today's Isms*. When a Spanish translation of this book, published in Barcelona, was given to me by the Spanish publisher, I looked for the passage about Spain which I had read in the original English edition. It was completely missing! Following a paragraph about Yugoslavia, which had been left untouched, the missing section (in the English version) read:

The case of Spain is similar. In 1939, the Franco regime was set up as an admittedly antidemocratic, authoritarian government, with strong sympathies for the fascist systems of Mussolini and Hitler. Yet despite such doctrinal sympathies, Spain refrained during World War II from entering the conflict on the side of Italy and Germany, thus enabling the British and American navies to win the Battle of the Atlantic with less cost and sacrifice than would otherwise have been the case.

After World War II, the Franco regime has gradually mellowed politically, toning down its authoritarian tendencies, although still being far removed from a liberal democracy. Since 1953, the United States has been building, with the cooperation of the Spanish government, vast naval and air installations on Spanish soil, and the impact of American aid, combined with the direct personal influence of thousands of American civilians and military, has been in the direction of bringing Spain closer to the western democracies.

As in the case of Yugoslavia, no one can seriously maintain that Spain is a democracy. Yet even more important to the free world is the fact that Spain is willing to play her part in the struggle against communist imperialism, and can be counted upon to be a much more reliable ally in the struggle than many other states, such as Yugoslavia or some Asian nations.

In January 1962 Blas Piñar, the director of the *Instituto de Cultura Hispanicas*, wrote an article in the Madrid daily *ABC* that denounced the United States as being hypocritical for many reasons. Filled with half truths and charges which could be made against any man or any society, the article contended that Americans were hypocrites doing one thing one time and saying another thing another time. Not only did *ABC* carry the article throughout the country, but it was picked up and widely circulated by other publications as well. Since Blas Piñar had been a respected Spanish government official prior to becoming director of the prestigious Hispanic Cultural Institute, he seemed to be out of character in what embassy officials considered his stooping to name calling. Yet, the fact that the article appeared in the heavily censored Spanish press made it appear that it had the approval, if not the blessing, of the Spanish government, despite immediate denials to the contrary.

I was reminded of the power of the press, even a heavily censored press, when, during my visit to Asturias, one of the local officials said to me: "Is it true that in the White House there is a plaque which says that Columbus was a great Italian explorer and doesn't mention Spain at all"? My only knowledge of this alleged plaque and in this context was the Blas Piñar article in which the author had written that this is so "despite the hypocritical Americans' expressed friendship for Spain."

I asked the Asturian official who raised this question if his source of information regarding this was the Blas Piñar article. It was. This was only one of many instances whereby the influence of a widely dispersed newspaper article in Spain in 1962 was evident, leading me to believe that even with the distrust most Spaniards had of their censored press, many still believed what they read in their censored publications.

When my tour in Spain was nearing its end many months later, I was tempted to request a second tour because we had come to love the Spanish people, their music, wine, and lifestyle. Strange as it may seem, one of the factors I weighed in my own mind was whether I wanted to live another few years in a society where the local media carried only what the government wanted it to carry. This grated against my belief in one of the most important freedoms that Americans take for granted—freedom of the press. Of course there were other reasons, when the time came, for wanting to give up what was really a good life in Spain and move on to other things, other "lives." But this was one of the factors in equating the advantages and disadvantages of requesting a second tour.

In Barcelona during my days as a USIS American textbook promoter, I became very friendly with a publisher of technical books who had spent some time in Spanish jails for his political views. Although that was now behind him as there had been some liberalization in recent years, he told me he still found it necessary to travel to France every so often for, as he said, "a breath of fresh air."

Our son Robert was about a year old when Charmaine announced that she was expecting again. She said she was hoping for a girl this time, but, of course, we would take whatever came along. This situation did tend to cut down on our social life a little bit, but not much. Our frequent visits to the *cantinas* and restaurants of Madrid continued. Although I was still a relatively junior officer in the foreign service and my pay reflected this, the exchange rate for the U.S. dollar with the peseta and our allowances for housing and other things made it possible for us to live very well in the Spanish economy.

One of our favorite pastimes was to dine at two well-known places in Madrid where flamenco singers and dancers performed. We would always take visitors to one of those places as the food was good and the entertainment spectacular. On one occasion we sat just two tables back from the stage. Sitting at the table directly between us and the stage and exactly in my line of sight was Ava Gardner of Hollywood fame. This was the woman who had appeared in more than fifty films in the 1940s and 1950s, playing opposite such stars as Clark Gable, Gregory Peck, Richard Burton, and Burt Lancaster. She had been married to three famous husbands—Mickey Rooney, Artie Shaw, and Frank Sinatra. She had been living in Madrid for a few years and I had seen her in the USIS library a few times. But that evening, when I wasn't watching the flamenco dancers, I found it difficult not to look at that beautiful woman directly in front of me. She was not far from being forty years old then, but her beauty was still stunning. I can see why she was considered, along with Marilyn Monroe and Rita Hayworth, one of Hollywood's leading sex goddesses at a time when the movies were America's primary entertainment, and why she attracted men the way she did. As for her being married to three husbands, she was once quoted as saying, "I don't know why the hell anybody should talk about my marital record. My three ex-husbands had twenty wives between them." (She died January 25, 1990, in London at age sixty-seven.)

As the months sped by for us in the delightful Spanish *ambiente,* Charmaine's time for the birth of our second child was fast approaching. Little did we know that the new baby would arrive faster than anyone expected. On February 13, 1961, I drove Charmaine to the British Hospital in Madrid where her doctor planned to induce labor because she was overdue. When we arrived at the hospital and Charmaine was settled in her hospital bed, she was given an intravenous injection of hormones to help induce labor. I was sitting in a chair alongside her bed, and noticed that the valve that was supposed to allow a drop of fluid to enter her arm periodically was not working properly. The fluid, instead of entering her system in droplets, was entering in an almost steady stream. By the time I called this to the nurses' attention, Charmaine was experiencing strong labor pains and the nurse was already signaling for help to bring her into the delivery room. As they wheeled her away I thought, "Well, now the long wait begins." Once again I was wrong.

In about ten minutes the doctor came out to see me. "Congratulations. You have a baby daughter. Both she and your wife are fine." Of course I was elated, but I could not believe that everything had gone so smoothly. Needless to say, I was extremely happy that all went well and that Charmaine had been granted her wish for a daughter. We would name her Annette Marie.

While waiting for Charmaine to return from the recovery room I phoned the office to report the good news. Then I phoned our maid, Victoria, to also let her know how everything was. When I told her that it was a baby girl born fifteen minutes ago she started laughing.

"Sr. Hansen," she said. "You are kidding me. You only left here about a half-hour ago. How could the Señora already have a baby girl?"

"Victoria," I said. "I'm not kidding. She just gave birth to a baby girl."

"Sr. Hansen," Victoria replied. "I do not believe you. That's impossible. My sister had a baby a few months ago and she was in the hospital for two days before the baby came." With such logic I gave up trying to convince Victoria that we now had a baby daughter in the family. She would just have to see for herself when Charmaine and the baby came home in a few days.

Our days in Spain were numbered as we neared the end of our three-year tour. USIA had instituted a new program designed to develop greater knowledge among Foreign Service officers of their own culture. President Kennedy had been quoted as saying that the most important thing a Foreign Service officer can know is his own culture. My agency took this to heart by starting an American Studies university program for its officers. For as long as anyone could remember there had been an academic year available to a few who applied for this program and were accepted, the theory being that such exposure to American university life would assist those lucky few in presenting American policies and culture abroad in later years. The new program, which meant spending an academic year on a university campus, was different only in that it focused on American Studies.

The first participant in the new program was Barbara White, a highly respected and experienced Agency officer who went to Harvard University for a year. I found the new program exciting and thought that if I were to be accepted, the timing would coincide with my departure from Spain so I applied for the second year of the program, not really expecting to be chosen. Oh me of little faith! I was chosen, possibly because no one else in the Agency applied, and thus I knew what I would be doing for a year after we left Spain, even if I did not yet know where I would be doing it.

In June 1962 our life in Spain ended with our departure from Madrid in our small Ford Consul. It had served us well on Spanish roads. We headed for France where we would visit Lourdes to bathe in that magical water which dries on your skin as soon as you step out of it, then meander down to Italy and on to Naples where we boarded the S.S. *Constitution* for the seven-day trip to New York.

In Naples we left our car at the pier to be loaded aboard the S.S. *Constitution* and then went on board ourselves. Among our fellow passengers were a young junior officer trainee from USIS Madrid, Phil Pillsbury, and his wife. They had left Spain one day before we did and were also heading back to the U.S. for home leave.

The *Constitution* stopped at the French Riviera and Gibraltar on its way back to the U.S., which was the icing on the cake. When we arrived in New York harbor and sailed up the Hudson River to Pier 97, the sight of the Statue of Liberty was as thrilling to us, after a three-year absence, as it has been over the years to the thousands of new and old Americans whom the Lady smiles down upon as Manhattan comes into view. To be greeted by the Lady of Liberty, her arm holding the light of freedom aloft, is to be welcomed home in grand style.

A few hours after arriving our car was unloaded and we were on the road headed south to Metuchen, New Jersey, where Grandma Hansen greeted us upon our arrival. Our Spanish sojourn, now ended, would often be recalled as a particularly enjoyable and exciting time in our lives. Yet the fresh air of a free society, symbolized by Lady Liberty, was a welcomed change.

6
Dominican Detour

"Only liberty fits men for liberty."
—Gladstone

"If we did help restrain the Dominicans from destroying their society, if we did pressure their free choice, if by what at this moment seems to require little short of a miracle an effective, freely elected representative and constitutional government does emerge, then we can take considerable satisfaction in what we did."
—John Bartlow Martin, *Overtaken By Events, 1966*

Our few weeks of home leave passed far too quickly. We could not linger because we had to be in Washington to make arrangements for my university assignment well before the academic year began. When I reported to headquarters, I was surprised to learn that nothing had been done about where and when I would be taking post-graduate studies for a year.

The assumption at USIA was that I would naturally want to go to Harvard like my predecessor. However, that was not the case. I wanted, if possible, to study at a university closer to New Jersey where we would be available to help my ailing mother. I also wanted to obtain a master's degree in the one-year reprieve from my Foreign Service duties. After exploring various options I settled on the University of Pennsylvania in Philadelphia, a few hours drive from my mother's home. I could easily fill the language requirement with my knowledge of Spanish and, if I worked hard, get a master's degree in one year. Harvard and most other schools, unlike the University of Pennsylvania, required a minimum of two years to obtain a master's.

We rented a furnished row house in a predominantly Italian-American neighborhood in Upper Darby on the outskirts of Philadelphia. I was able to take a trolley to the campus, about a forty-minute ride, so the location was good. Both Robert and Annette were still too young to attend school, so schooling for them was not a problem.

Being back in an academic environment after an absence of more than ten years was also a special challenge. For example, after writing a paper for an international relations course entitled "Public Opinion in Franco Spain," in which I expected to excel, I soon realized that I had to relearn the tricks of the trade.

When I received a "C" for the final grade in that course I was furious. For one thing I needed a "B" average to receive the degree I had set as my goal. For another, I considered my personal opinions based on my three years experience in Spain as being valid for that paper. The professor didn't. In conference with him he quickly pointed out to me that objective research requires beaucoup footnotes citing many other sources than merely the writer's opinions. I got the message. The more (footnotes) the merrier. Following his advice, I pulled some of my grades in other courses up to "A's" and earned the overall "B" average needed to obtain a master's degree.

In the fall of 1962 my mother's condition worsened and we made frequent trips to New Jersey to check on her. Finally, on the doctor's advice, we placed her in a nursing home not far from her home where friends could easily visit her. We hoped that after a few weeks she would recover her strength and be able to return home, but this was wishful thinking. She did return home after a few weeks, but was bedridden and near the end of her life. Both she and her doctor must have known that the end was near. She always said that she wanted to die in her own home, so at her insistence the doctor finally agreed to her return there.

My mother's sister, also a widow, lived in the house with her. She phoned us a few days after my mother's return to tell us that we should come home immediately as things had taken a turn for the worse. We arrived a few hours later, provided what solace we could, but saw in my mother's eyes that she knew the end was near. She died that evening, at age seventy-two, from heart failure. My father had died ten years earlier, at age sixty-two, after suffering a heart attack. Though both had been born in Denmark, they met in New Jersey, endured the 1930s depression, and led generally happy and productive lives. Now a generation and an era were gone.

After the funeral it took awhile to again concentrate wholeheartedly on my studies, but life goes on as it must. Also stirring was a new life—

Charmaine was pregnant again! After I received my master's degree in American Studies in May, our new daughter, Katherine, joined us in June. Her birth was much less hectic than the arrival of our last daughter. However, as I drove Charmaine to the hospital in nearby Darby, Pennsylvania, where her doctor was on call, a police patrol car stopped us. The officer asked me why I was driving so fast. When he learned why he said, "Follow me." With his lights flashing and his siren sounding, he led us to the emergency entrance of the hospital. All went well.

Upon Charmaine's return home a few days later, we arranged for my cousin Ellinor, who was visiting us, to hold the baby as we entered the house in order to introduce Robert and Annette to their new sister. When Annette saw the new baby, she threw herself on the floor and started a tantrum. We can only presume that she was upset at the thought of her mother's attention being diverted from her, which is why we had asked my cousin to hold the baby when we first came into the house. Robert, calm as usual, seemed to view the baby as a nice addition to the family. Despite the mixed reception, the Hansen family now numbered five.

With my academic year ending in June, we were looking forward to a much needed rest before beginning my next assignment, which would be in Washington. However, a call on behalf of my new boss, the USIA Area Director for Latin America, made it clear that I was needed to work on a special project that required my presence as soon as possible. So as soon as Charmaine could travel, we canceled our vacation plans, and went to Washington

My new assignment was as "desk officer" for the Caribbean in the Office of the Assistant Director of USIA for Latin America. Desk officers were specialists for a particular geographic region who maintained the major liaison between agency headquarters and the field posts in the countries assigned to them. The countries assigned to me were Jamaica, Haiti, the Dominican Republic, the French West Indies, Trinidad and Tobago, and British Guiana, which was soon to become an independent country. The change soon to take place in British Guiana was what brought me to this assignment. There was still concern that B.G. might follow Cuba into the Communist orbit. I was one of very few agency officers who had firsthand knowledge of that country.

I was on board only a few weeks when I was sent to Georgetown with instructions to review the current situation there with our PAO and consulate officials and obtain their thoughts about how USIS activities in B.G. might best be expanded at this time. Upon my return to Washington I wrote my report, recommending only that we increase our staff by one American officer and one local employee, in addition to minor increases in funding.

At first my superiors found it difficult to understand why my recommendations were so modest. I pointed out that the only important audiences in British Guiana were in Georgetown, a relatively small city of about 100,000 inhabitants, with only one radio station, no television, and two newspapers of any consequence. Therefore, I argued, for USIS to increase its operations more than what I recommended would be "overkill." They bought my arguments, but were still, in what might be called typical American bureaucratic fashion, a little uncomfortable with my recommendations. Some expected that any project that had White House interest should require substantial increases in funding, not the modest increases that I proposed.

Interestingly enough, I ran into a similar situation when I was later asked to design the initial USIS operation in Bridgetown, Barbados, when that country also obtained its independence from Great Britain. I recommended a staff of only one American officer and four nationals. Since Barbados is an island only nineteen miles long and five miles wide at its widest part, with a total population of about 250,000, it did not, in my view, require more staff than what I recommended. This would provide sufficient USIS activities, I argued, even though USIS Bridgetown would watch over the needs of some nine peanut-sized islands in the surrounding area, some of which would later also become independent. However, they would never grow much in size or importance.

After considerable discussion within the office about my plan and comments from others, I contended that "never has so much been said about so little." Still, there were those who believed the initial USIS post in that country should have been more grandiose. (Years later a second American officer was assigned to Bridgetown when U.S. attention focused for a short while on the Caribbean, as periodically occurs.) After the U.S. invasion of Grenada in 1983, an American USIS officer was also assigned to that little island until normalization returned and the position was abolished. Eventually the USIS operation in Barbados returned to the small size I initially suggested based on the area's size and relative (un)importance to U.S. interests. While I was immediately thrust into the issues and problems of the Caribbean as desk officer for that region, and would soon make periodic trips to each of the countries in my jurisdiction, adjustments to life in Washington went on.

Initially we thought that we would rent a house in the suburbs during our tour in the nation's capital. We assumed that to buy a house on my salary as a relatively junior Foreign Service officer, and with our living costs growing as our family grew, would be highly impractical. We soon discovered, however, that rents were so high that the only way to go, given Washington's real estate environment, was to buy. We located a house in the same neighborhood as a friend who had served with us in Madrid and Caracas. It was owned by a State Department officer who had just been assigned to Berlin and was anxious to sell. He was asking $26,000 for this three-bedroom house about a mile from the District of Columbia border in Maryland. We offered him $25,000 that he readily accepted.

After moving into our new home we lived close to the poverty line for about six months. Entertainment and recreation expenses were again put aside as they had been in Philadelphia, this time because most of our available funds were needed to maintain the household and to pay the mortgage. But with the passing of time my salary rose and we found ways to be entertained without going bankrupt. The investment in the house turned out to be a very wise move, the forerunner of similar investments in later years.

January 8, 1965. Sibley Hospital, Washington, D.C., just inside the District line and about a mile from our home in Glen Mar Park, Maryland. Alicia, the newest addition to the Hansen family, weighed in at about seven pounds. She would develop into a blue-eyed blonde child, energetic, creative, and generally very happy, but emotionally high-strung so that she could be on Cloud Nine one moment, and down in the depths the next—but not for long. She was almost always a joy to be with. Upon her arrival both she and her mother, who was by now getting used to this routine, were healthy. As a medical doctor might note, "the birth was uneventful." Of course, for us, it was very eventful.

We were settling into life in Washington quite comfortably. I was not at all anxious to ship out again, though inevitably the day for another overseas assignment would arrive. Having survived the heavy initial cost of buying a house, and having received a pay raise, things were looking up. Charmaine, however, missed the excitement and lifestyle of overseas living. She was ready to pack our bags at a moment's notice.

Among my extracurricular activities was the weekly meeting I attended at the old Naval Gun Factory in Washington. As a lieutenant in the Naval Reserve, I participated in training programs designed to keep Naval Reserve officers ready for the next war, if needed. The combination of credits for promotion, comradeship, and pay made it an enjoyable and highly worthwhile experience, as were the two weeks of training each year, generally at some military base. But my commission in the Naval Reserve would end when the nation's interest in maintaining the reserve units faltered and the reserve forces were drastically reduced. When assigned overseas again, I found it impossible to maintain this association and eventually had to drop out.

Early 1965 was a period of calm and complacency in the Hansen household. Alicia Lorraine had arrived and life in Washington generally agreed with her siblings and her parents, despite Charmaine's reservations about living in suburbia compared to living abroad. The neighborhood of single-family red brick houses with quiet, tree-shaded streets and friendly neighbors was symbolic of this period of our lives. But actions then taking place on the island of Hispaniola in the Caribbean, which culminated with the landing of U.S. Marines in Santo Domingo on Wednesday, April 28, 1965, were soon to interrupt our idyllic existence in Washington suburbia.

When hell broke loose in Santo Domingo in April of 1965 and the world's attention was momentarily focused on the capital city of the Dominican Republic, many readers, listeners, and viewers of the mass media throughout the world scurried to their atlases to locate the island of Hispaniola (which the Dominican Republic shares with Haiti). Long a backwater country of the Caribbean, the "DomRep" had a tragic history long before the events of 1965 occurred.

While the U.S. had so recently experienced the Cuban missile crisis of 1962; the assassination of President John F. Kennedy in 1963; and continued to be immersed in the increasingly controversial Vietnam holocaust, another small country was destined to involve the United States in a new adventure. This one, like Vietnam, also brought forth heated debate from various domestic and international quarters regarding the wisdom and morality of this new U.S. involvement in a foreign country.

U.S. entanglement in the affairs of the Dominican Republic was not new; though it had been about forty years since the last time that U.S. Marines had been sent there to presumably protect U.S. interests. In the mid-twentieth century, any U.S. intervention south of the border, particularly military intervention, was, for Latin Americans, a rallying cry against the Colossus of the North. No U.S. administration in Washington would ever take such a step lightly.

Generalissimo Rafael Leonidas Trujillo had ruled the Dominican Republic absolutely and tyrannically from 1930 to 1961. When he was assassinated on May 30, 1961, the Dominicans were in a state of shock. They had no experience in self-government. Those who survived Trujillo's rule were either among the oppressed or the corrupted. A month after Trujillo's death the U.S. sent a naval force to Caribbean waters because of threats to American lives and property in the turmoil following the dictator's demise. Again in November 1961, a U.S. naval force was dispatched to show support for the government of Joaquin Balaguer who became head of the Council of State established to govern the country. At that time Trujillo's son, Ramfis, who hoped to replace his father, was forced to leave.

Author Seldon Rodman in his book, *Quisqueya, A History of the Dominican Republic,* published in 1964, shows how Trujillo and his family ruled the country like their private domain. Citing the livestock industry, salt, gypsum, and iron ore among the Trujillos' investments, he wrote:

> A partial list of other investments in which the dictator and his family had a controlling share would include milk, alcohol, beer, firewood, pitch pine, baking, printing, fishing, shoes, marble, airplane and shipping transportation, matches, industrial gases, construction materials, cement, glass bottling, small arms manufacture, electric batteries, slaughterhouses and refrigeration plants, cigar and cigarette manufacture, hardware and plumbing, banking, rents, medicines, rice, sweets, sisal, and paint. The last two were handled with special tenderness. All export produce, it was decreed, must be packed in sisal containers. Every Dominican was required to paint his house twice yearly. Arismendi Trujillo was given control over the export of bananas, plantains, and poultry. Pedro worked the charcoal racket. Brother Romeo, appropriately acquired the concession for prostitution.

No wonder that with Trujillo gone, the economy was in turmoil.

Balaguer lasted only until January 15, 1962 when he was overthrown by General Rafael R. Echevarria. Two days later another coup took place, led by Captain Elias Wessin y Wessin. Both Balaguer and Echevarria went into exile. Wessin reconstituted the Council of State with Rafael Bonnelly at its head.

In December 1962 the first elections in several decades were held. Juan Bosch, head of the Dominican Revolutionary Party, won a landslide victory. As an orator he was brilliant. As an administrator, he was a disaster. Furthermore, he antagonized the military and the right wing by allowing the communist-oriented parties to continue to function freely.

On September 25, 1963, the military lost patience. Backed by civilian elements, they engineered a bloodless coup leading to Bosch's ouster. Bosch went into exile. Though the U.S. publicly deplored this latest coup and withheld economic assistance from the three-man junta that succeeded Bosch, there was a general feeling among many observers that Bosch's incompetence in economic matters and naiveté in politics doomed him to failure. After several months the civilian triumvirate was recognized by the Kennedy administration and U.S. economic assistance was resumed.

This new Dominican government was dominated by the former foreign minister, Donald Reid Cabral, an automobile dealer with a good reputation but little political experience. In late 1964 he announced that national elections would be held in September 1965 to return the country to constitutionality. But by early 1965 there were signs that the social explosion that might have been expected to take place at the death of Trujillo five years earlier, was fast approaching.

Stimulating the increasingly visible unrest in the Dominican population were a drop in the world price of sugar, the republic's principal foreign exchange earner, and Reid's policy of closing down the profitable smuggling business of most military officers. He also took other actions that adversely affected many of the privileges historically enjoyed by the military. With increasing unrest and the economy suffering, both the left and the right were becoming disenchanted with Reid.

In that kind of environment extremists of both the left and right became more and more active. Cuban radio broadcasts, heard in the D.R., became increasingly strident. On the one hand a "people's revolution" was demanded; on the other, some military officers wanted Bosch back while others wanted a new military junta. On April 24, 1965, Santo Domingo became a battleground.

Much confusion and great differences of opinion make it difficult to say what really happened in Santo Domingo that fateful Saturday morning of April 24, 1965, when what was to become known as the "Dominican Crisis" erupted. The version presented in the report of the Center for Strategic Studies, published the following year and entitled *dominican action-1965, intervention or cooperation?* [sic], is probably one of the best sources available to understand how the crisis developed.

On that April day the acting president of the governing triumvirate, Donald Reid Cabral, went from his home about mid-morning to the national palace to confer with General Marcos Antonio Rivera Cuesta, the army chief of staff. Rivera Cuesta had told Reid that he had learned of a rumored coup d'état against the government. The fact that there was plotting going on against the regime in power was well known, but neither Reid nor U.S. embassy officials who had heard about the plotting expected anything to happen in the immediate future.

A few days earlier the U.S. ambassador, W. Tapley Bennett, Jr., had been ordered to Washington for long overdue consultations, leaving the deputy chief of mission, William B. Connett, in charge of the embassy. En route to Washington the ambassador had stopped in Georgia to visit his ailing mother and was there when the revolt erupted. Among the ambassador's chief military aides, one was dove hunting with a Dominican general and others were attending a conference in Panama that day.

General Rivera Cuesta contended that the plotters were three lieutenant colonels. Reid ordered the general to cancel the commissions of the plotters, then returned to his home after a scheduled visit to another town by helicopter was canceled, allegedly because of "technical difficulties." Rivera Cuesta, with his deputy, Lieutenant Colonel Maximilian Americo Ruiz Batista, confronted the three plotters and informed them that their commissions were terminated. Surprised by this turn of events, the plotters, instead of surrendering, took the initiative and arrested the general and his deputy (who apparently lacked the foresight to have loyal troops standing by). Thus the coup began, presumably two days before they had planned to begin their revolt. This contributed to the confusion that followed.

A varied group of supporters joined the plotters. They included reformists, pro-Bosch constitutionalists, and a mixture of youths, some with communist connections, and some with no political connections but who probably considered the turn of events to be so adventuresome that they did not want to be left out. In the days that followed the military split between those who wanted a new regime and those who didn't. Meanwhile, the calls increased to restore former president Juan Bosch. With the military divided and the rebel side growing in size and diversity of aims, the situation became increasingly chaotic.

About 3 p.m. *Radio Santo Domingo*, the powerful, official government station, announced a national curfew would begin at 6 p.m. A short while later, however, a rebel group, including leaders of Juan Bosch's Dominican Revolutionary Party (PRD), with some soldiers who supported them, took over the station and began broadcasting.

They urged people to go into the streets to celebrate the government's overthrow. Shortly thereafter they controlled four other radio stations. On all of them they demanded the return of Bosch and constitutional government.

Later in the day the pro-government forces recaptured Radio Santo Domingo, so at 8:35 that evening a message by President Reid was broadcast and simultaneously televised. He said the nation was calm and issued an ultimatum for rebel forces to surrender by 5 a.m., promising amnesty and warning that troops loyal to the government would be sent against them if they failed to comply. But as dawn approached there was no sign of any surrender. Sporadic shooting was occurring and a number of policemen were fatally shot. The police became favorite targets of snipers until, fearing for their lives, they disappeared from the streets.

By early morning the rebels had established defenses in various parts of the city, including machine gun emplacements in some key areas of downtown Santo Domingo. Though the situation was confused, it seemed clear to embassy officials that the government's position was rapidly deteriorating. Preparations to evacuate U.S. citizens began. For this purpose units of the U.S. Navy were ordered to the southwest coast of the Dominican Republic, prepared to evacuate up to 1,200 Americans. Later that morning it became clear that the split in the military was such that Reid would not receive the support he needed to put down the revolt. The Dominican military, though split in their loyalties, were not willing to battle each other at this early stage of the crisis.

In the ensuing hours it was impossible to know what would happen next. Mobs roamed the streets of downtown Santo Domingo, looting increased, and rebel soldiers were seen to fire their weapons into the air to attract attention. The U.S. deputy chief of mission, Connett, met with Reid who told him the situation was precarious. He said the communists were taking advantage of the situation while his own military forces were unwilling to act. By 10:30 a.m. of April 25th, barely twenty-four hours since the beginning of the revolt, Reid resigned, possibly in the belief that this would avoid bloodshed. In any event he no longer controlled a viable government. Following his resignation the tanks and armored vehicles of the loyal forces guarding the Palace were destroyed or captured by the anti-government forces, and by 11 a.m.. a group of about fifty rebel officers and men entered the palace. Their leaders were Colonels Giovanni Manuel Gutierrez and Francisco Caamaño Deñó.

Reid was held in custody by the rebels for a short while. Although the rebel officers announced that it was their intention to restore President Bosch to office, officers at the nearby San Isidro Air Base were equally adamant that they would not accept a restoration of the Bosch regime. Although the Dominican armed forces refused to fight each other in defense of the Reid regime, some, apparently, were willing to fight to prevent the return of Bosch. At this point most observers felt that civil war was inevitable. And just as the military had been reluctant to move earlier, Juan Bosch, urged by some of the rebels to return immediately to Santo Domingo (about an hour's flight from Puerto Rico where Bosch was staying), appeared unwilling to do so, at least not immediately. This was probably a wise decision on his part, since no one could have guaranteed his safety if he returned to what was now an increasingly confused, chaotic situation.

Bosch talked by telephone to Jose Rafael Molina Urena, former president of the Chamber of Deputies, and told him to assume the presidency pending Bosch's return. He even indicated that he would return in due course with a committee of PRD leaders who were to fly to Puerto Rico and escort him back to Santo Domingo. This was enough, however, to awaken the anti-Bosch forces in the military. The Air Force under its chief, Emilio de los Santos; General Elias Wessin y Wessin's tank force; and Commodore Francisco J. Rivera Caminero's naval forces all agreed that they would fight the rebel forces.

By Tuesday, April 27th, the embassy advised Washington that the threat to American lives was such that an immediate evacuation should begin. The short-lived Molina Urena government, which had replaced Reid, collapsed. He and some of his aides took refuge in the Colombian Embassy. Law and order in the Dominican capital were now practically non-existent.

American citizens began to arrive at the evacuation site, the Embajador Hotel, in the southwestern suburbs of Santo Domingo, about 6 a.m. As the morning wore on, no one could assure the safety of the evacuees, although the government and the rebels both had agreed earlier that the evacuation could proceed. A polo field near the hotel provided space for the evacuees to congregate.

Radio Santo Domingo, once more in rebel hands, began calling for reprisals and reported that Bonilla Aybar, an anti-Bosch journalist-TV commentator, was at the Embajador Hotel waiting to be evacuated. Shortly following this "news," a number of armed rebels, mostly young civilians, arrived at the hotel and terrorized the waiting Americans— men, women and children. They searched the hotel and when, for some reason, a shot was fired from a balcony, they responded with a burst of submachine gun fire. Later some American reporters would argue that more was made of this incident than what actually occurred.

I talked later with at least one survivor of the incident who told me that at one point some of the armed men forced him and some others to line up against a wall in the hotel courtyard. Since *"a la pared"* (to the wall) is historically a well-known method of eliminating "enemies of the people," he expected to be shot. This did not happen, but some bullets did fly in and around the hotel. Miraculously no one was killed, a fact reporters used later to contend that the situation had been depicted as being much worse than it really was. Yet as heavily armed men who had already fired at least one burst from a submachine gun lined the Americans up against a wall, what were they to think? Eventually the rebel group left the hotel when they did not find Bonilla Aybar, the apparent object of this particular operation. But as John Bartlow Martin wrote about this incident in his book *Overtaken By Events*, "it was a serious rebel mistake, for it indicated to the world that the rebels were irresponsible, law and order had broken down, and the lives of U.S. citizens and other evacuees were gravely endangered."

The ships and helicopters of U.S. Naval Task Force 44.9 began evacuation efforts about 1 p.m. April 27th. Two ships, *Ruchmakin* and *Wood County*, evacuated people from piers at Haina, a town about seven miles west of the capital, while helicopters flew others to the Boxer that was at sea off the coast. By evening 1,176 Americans had been evacuated, mainly businessmen, missionaries, and "non-essential" U.S. government employees and their families.

Two days later, April 29th, the situation in Santo Domingo became even more chaotic and the number of people seeking to leave increased. The number of U.S. military that landed initially to help evacuate Americans also increased. This was followed by a third landing, this time in force as the situation further deteriorated. Some 22,000 U.S. troops were eventually deployed while much of world public opinion, and the American press in particular, questioned why the U.S. had sent its armed forces into the Dominican Republic.

In the meantime the U.S. requested the Organization of American States (OAS) to meet in Washington to discuss the breakdown of authority in the D.R. The Council of the OAS soon adopted resolutions calling for a cease-fire; appealed for the establishment of an International Safety Zone (ISZ); and sent a five-man commission to Santo Domingo. But the U.S. government came under heavy criticism not only for the movement of its troops, but also for not getting the OAS involved in collective action earlier. This latter point may have been fair criticism, but judging by earlier experiences in trying to get the OAS to act, this predominantly Latin American organization would have done little but fiddle while Santo Domingo burned.

A number of books, many articles, and much of the American press criticized the U.S. action at the time and for months thereafter. Yet the goals of the U.S. (as stated by Georgetown University's admittedly conservative Center for Strategic Studies, in its July 1966 study of this event) were all achieved. These were, they said: (1) the protection of American and other foreign lives, (2) the halting of violence, (3) the prevention of a communist seizure of power, and (4) the opening of an option to the Dominican people to choose their leaders in a free election.

I have not dwelled on the various communist and leftist organizations that worked on the rebel side. Yet the three communist parties in the Dominican Republic at the time, while they may not have been in on the takeoff, were there at the landing on the side of the rebels. Furthermore, from the beginning, Cuban radio stations encouraged the revolt.

In any analysis of the Dominican Civil War it should be noted that even before the International Safety Zone was created, the rebellion was confined almost entirely to the downtown areas of Santo Domingo. This was hardly "a massive uprising` on the part of the Dominican people as some journalists claimed.

While Dominicans were killing and wounding each other in the streets of Santo Domingo, U.S. government officials and the media in the city of Washington, long accustomed to focusing on U.S. military involvement in southeast Asia, now turned their attention to the Caribbean. The Marines and the 82nd Airborne Division were engaged in the first U.S. military incursion into a Latin American country in nearly forty years.

As soon as American troops were sent ashore, debate began concerning the wisdom and morality of engaging U.S. armed forces in the Dominican civil war. Criticism rose to high decibels in the nation's media, particularly the press and television; in the Congress; and on the Washington cocktail circuit. As the Caribbean desk officer for USIA, I soon found myself on the State Department's task force that was immediately created for this new crisis.

The Dominican Task Force consisted of Latin American and Dominican experts and specialists. They manned a twenty-four-hour watch in the Operations Center of the Department of State in downtown Washington. Not only did this center provide constant surveillance of the situation as it was developing, but it also served as a ready source of guidance and advice concerning U.S. actions and policies. It enabled American citizens to phone the task force for news about loved ones in the D.R. and their whereabouts if among the evacuees.

I was on duty in the Operations Center when President Johnson appeared on television to announce additional landings of American troops in the Dominican Republic. He notified the American people and the world that he was doing so on the advice of his ambassador in Santo Domingo. (Ambassador Bennett had returned to the embassy Tuesday afternoon, April 27th.) The President said that the embassy had come under sporadic attack from snipers; American lives were in danger; other embassies had asked for help in protecting and evacuating their citizens; and a state of general anarchy now existed in the Dominican capital. But he put all the rationale for ordering the U.S. military intervention on the shoulders of Ambassador Bennett, which I thought, at the time, was most unfair. It was not only Ambassador Bennett who urged military intervention at this time. Almost everyone in the higher echelons of the U.S. government concerned with foreign affairs and aware of what was happening in the D.R. supported the decision to send American troops. What was initially left unsaid in public statements, but which everyone involved knew, was the U.S. fear that a rebel victory would possibly mean a second Cuba. This made the need for providing protection for American citizens no less urgent, but added to the reasoning for the decision to send in American armed forces and in the numbers which were finally utilized.

Most American and other reporters arrived in Santo Domingo on Thursday afternoon, the 29th. It was that afternoon that the second group of U.S. Marines landed, followed at about 2:30 a.m. the next morning by the 82nd Airborne Division which began landing at the San Isidro Air Base. This resulted in many reports being filed by journalists who questioned the U.S. action from the beginning. Some were critical of the number of troops President Johnson ordered sent to the island, contending that 22,000 was "overkill." Perhaps fewer would have sufficed, but to those of us involved in explaining the U.S. actions, second-guessing a military decision appeared to be a very cheap shot. Likewise, criticism of the evacuation of the Americans and the incidents at the Embajador Hotel was made by journalists who were not there at the time. They ignored or failed to inquire about the "wall" incident and the machine gunning which had endangered the lives of the evacuees.

If the U.S. military force had wanted to finish off the rebels who held downtown Santo Domingo, this could have been done quickly, but would have resulted in considerable loss of life. However, this was not the immediate purpose of the U.S. invasion. Rather it was to establish a *cordon sanitaire* to seal off the downtown area held by the rebels. This was quickly accomplished.

U.S. troops soon stood guard along what became known as the International Security Zone (ISZ). The ISZ border faced the rebel zone. Their instructions were to control access in and out of the rebel zone until peaceful negotiations could be arranged among all interested parties, and they were ordered not to fire their weapons unless fired upon. In a hostile environment only a highly disciplined army could be expected to comply with such instructions. The troops of the 82nd Airborne did so admirably, considering the circumstances. Except for the relatively small but important downtown area of Santo Domingo that was held by the rebels (who now called themselves *"Constitutionalistas"* on grounds that Bosch was the constitutionally elected president of the D.R. and they claimed they wanted him back in power), the rest of the country was remarkably peaceful.

An especially active player on the U.S. side who popped in and out of the Operations Center during the days I spent with the Dominican Task Force was Under Secretary of State Thomas C. Mann. He directed the task force in the absence of Assistant Secretary for Inter American Affairs, Robert Vaughn, who was temporarily out of the country. Mann reaffirmed the U.S. concern about a communist takeover of the D.R. when he wrote, in November of that year, "All those in our government who had full access to official information were convinced that the landing of additional troops was necessary in view of the clear and present danger of the forcible seizure of power by the communists."

One evening Charmaine and I had dinner in a Vietnamese restaurant in Bethesda with an old friend and a colleague of his who taught sociology at a local university. It was a stimulating evening as the professor, expressing the typical academic reaction to the U.S. invasion of the D.R., lambasted my views concerning the reasons why the U.S. felt compelled to take the actions it did. Just as the wisdom and morality of U.S. involvement in Vietnam were, at that time (1965), beginning to be heavily debated in the U.S., this sudden new U.S. military action in the Caribbean was seen by some, particularly in academia, as yet another unnecessary and unwarranted imperialistic activity of the U.S. government.

In the first few days of the revolt the embassy came under fire and was defended only by the normal security guard force of nine Marines stationed at the embassy. Whether the chancellery was a target of snipers or was merely hit by stray bullets intended for other targets remains debatable. In those crucial first days, however, when gunfire was taking place near the embassy, a USIA junior officer trainee of USIS Santo Domingo, Al Laun, played a major role in maintaining communication between the U.S. naval force offshore and the embassy. Laun was a "ham" radio operator who soon became the key link between the ambassador in the embassy and the commander of Task Force 44.9.

To communicate with the offshore fleet where the Marines were awaiting word from the embassy as to whether or not they were needed, messages had to be sent from Santo Domingo to Washington and then back to the headquarters of the Commander-in-Chief, Atlantic Forces (COMCINLANT) in Panama, and from there to the fleet. Knowing about Al Laun's hobby as a ham radio operator, the ambassador asked him if, using his ham radio, he could devise a means to communicate with the fleet more directly. Laun believed that he could. He drove his car, in which he had a portable transmitter, onto the front lawn of the embassy, hoping in that way to be able to relay the ambassador's messages. The power was insufficient, however, to reach the fleet. But by borrowing additional equipment that the embassy had and installing it in his car, he eventually succeeded. So for about twenty-four hours, until the Marines had landed and brought with them their own communications equipment, Junior Officer Trainee Al Laun, huddled in the front seat of his car on the front lawn of the embassy, provided the main means of communication between the embassy and U.S. Naval Task Force 44.9!

Another unusual incident concerning communication occurred during those hectic early days of the crisis. Despite the occupation of the downtown area by the rebels who thus controlled the central office of the local telephone company, located in the center of the city, the telephone system remained available for use by the government forces and the foreign embassies. The U.S. Embassy continued to make phone calls to Washington and elsewhere via the central office, knowing full well that the rebels could monitor their conversations.

The leader of the rebel forces (many felt by default as other would-be leaders fell by the wayside) was Colonel Francisco Caamaño Deñó. Col. Caamaño had earlier taken refuge in the embassy of El Salvador but emerged later to become president of the so-called "Constitutional government." On one occasion when President Johnson phoned Ambassador Bennett in Santo Domingo to discuss the situation with him, Col. Caamaño's forces began disrupting the president's conversation with the ambassador. Col. Caamaño came on the line and told Johnson that he had no right to have his troops in

Santo Domingo. Johnson responded with an explosion of expletives and warned Caamaño that if he didn't get off the line and leave the communication between the White House and the embassy open, he would order a bombardment of Caamaño's headquarters. Apparently Caamaño received that message loud and clear. He immediately ceased the interruptions.

While lines were being drawn in Santo Domingo, in Washington American diplomats worked hard to convince the Latin American members of the Organization of American States that U.S. actions in Santo Domingo were designed primarily to save lives and restore peace and order. This argument was supported by reports from a number of foreign embassies in Santo Domingo that they were being invaded. Some were requesting the U.S. to help evacuate their citizens.

On May 1, 1965, the Consultation of Foreign Ministers (CFM) convened in Washington. They formed a special committee to obtain a cease-fire, to reestablish normal conditions in Santo Domingo, and to enable all foreign nationals who wished to be evacuated to leave. The CFM passed a resolution on May 3 making an urgent appeal for aid to the D.R., and on May 6 established the Inter-American Peace Force (IAPF). Fifteen members supported the IAPF; five opposed (Chile, Ecuador, Peru, Mexico, and Uruguay); and Venezuela abstained. By the end of May, five countries—Brazil, Costa Rica, Honduras, Nicaragua, and Paraguay—joined the U.S. in supplying units to make up the IAPF. Once again, as so many times in the past, most Latin American countries preferred to remain on the sidelines, and, once again, Brazil, as in World War II, was in the forefront of Latin American nations willing to cooperate with the U.S.

At the outset public diplomacy would play a key role in getting the world, and particularly the Latin Americans, to concede that the U.S. was acting in good faith and out of necessity (though the term "public diplomacy" was invented only that year and would have to await a decade or more to be more widely known and used). Therefore, while the Washington headquarters of USIA worked overtime in trying to explain the U.S. invasion to foreign audiences, a team of professional USIA Information officers, headed by Associate Director Hewson Ryan, went to Santo Domingo to assist the embassy and the military in responding to queries from the hundreds of foreign correspondents who descended upon the Dominican capital. Ryan's deputy was Darrell Carter, USIA's Assistant Director for Latin America.

The team was kept busy meeting journalists' demands for information. While tending to accept at face value whatever the rebels told them, most correspondents remained highly critical of the Dominican rightists, represented by the majority of the military. Most were also highly suspicious of U.S. motives. The majority of reporters also believed that the U.S. military intervention was wrong and favored the return of constitutional government, which the rebels claimed was the objective of the revolt. These attitudes were reflected in their reporting.

To create the USIA team, officers from various posts in Latin America were either brought to Washington and then sent to the D.R., or sent there directly to augment those sent from Washington. One day I carried out instructions to meet Ben Darling, the USIS Quito press attaché; who was arriving at Dulles airport that afternoon from Ecuador. Darling was a dapper bon vivant who told me upon his arrival at Dulles that he really looked forward to spending a few days or weeks in Washington. Quito, the Ecuadorean capital, he reminded me, was a very quiet place.

"Sorry," I said, "but you're not going to have much time in Washington. I have to take you right now out to Andrews Air Force Base. There's a military plane leaving at 3 p.m. for the D.R. and you have to be on it. They need you down there right away." Darling was crushed. "I expected to be able to buy some things here in Washington before going to the D.R.," he responded. "I hardly brought anything with me other than a toothbrush."

We didn't have time for shopping, however. Andrews is about thirty miles east of Dulles and it was already 1:30 p.m. by the time we cleared customs. We drove off and headed straight for the base, arriving about fifteen minutes before the plane was to leave. It was a Star Jet, capable of reaching Santo Domingo in about four hours. One of the deputy assistant secretaries was making a fast trip to consult with our ambassador and the military had placed this plane at his disposal. With only six or eight seats, Darling was assigned the last seat available. I wished him well as he boarded the plane. I would not see him again until I myself arrived in the Dominican Republic. By then he was a seasoned veteran of the civil war.

On Friday, April 30th, President Johnson again spoke to the American people on television. The President announced that a cease-fire had been agreed upon by the contending Dominican forces but was not being fully respected. In his address he gave the first public indication that "people trained outside the Dominican Republic are seeking to gain control" of the country.

On Saturday, May 1st, the rebels shelled the city's electric plant and ignored the call for a cease-fire in other ways. The embassy recommended that more troops be sent to help enforce the cease-fire. Another Marine battalion and two more battalions of paratroopers were flown in to add to the troops already there.

The OAS sent a peace committee to Santo Domingo. The committee included five Latin American ambassadors and the OAS Secretary General. In the meantime, John Bartlow Martin, a former U.S. ambassador to the D.R. who had arrived in the capital as President Johnson's personal representative, visited Col. Caamaño's headquarters in the Copello building of downtown Santo Domingo. He was accompanied by the Papal Nuncio. Caamaño, who claimed to have 25,000 men under his command, was in no mood to end his bid for taking over the country. In the days that followed the U.S. Marines and the paratroopers completed securing the ISZ and expanded it four blocks east and two blocks north to include several embassies inside the safety zone.

On Monday, May 3rd, the Brazilian ambassador told U.S. officials that all five peace committee members agreed that U.S. military action had saved the D.R. from anarchy and an eventual communist takeover. This strengthened the cooperation of the OAS with the U.S. On Tuesday, May 4th, Caamaño was sworn in by the rebels as the "Constitutional President" of the Republic. The following day a formal cease-fire was negotiated with the rebels, but sporadic fighting continued. By then eight U.S. servicemen had been killed and forty-eight wounded.

On May 5th the Act of Santo Domingo was negotiated. This gave the OAS supervision of the cease-fire. The next day the OAS ministers, meeting in Washington, voted 14 to 5 with one abstention to create an Inter-American Peace Force to restore peace and constitutional government in the D.R. On May 7th the junta, led by Col. Pedro Bartolome Benoit, against whom the rebels were fighting, was replaced by a government of National Reconstruction headed by another military man, General Antonio Imbert Barrera. Imbert wanted to attack the Caamaño forces who continued to ignore the cease-fire but was prevented from doing so because the U.S. forces were now controlling the ISZ which separated the two groups.

Latin American troops soon began arriving. They included a thousand Brazilians and smaller contingents from Paraguay, Honduras, Nicaragua, and Costa Rica. Brazilian General Hugo Panasco Alvim became commander of the newly created Inter-American Peace Force. American paratrooper, General Bruce Palmer, became the deputy commander. To expedite negotiations between the two sides an OAS committee that included U.S. Ambassador Ellsworth Bunker, El Salvador Ambassador Ramón Clairmont Dueñas, and Penna Marinho of Brazil arrived to begin the long struggle to put Humpty Dumpty together again.

While these actions were going on, urgent meetings were being held in Santo Domingo and Washington. In the D.R., the USIA public diplomacy team of about a dozen officers worked diligently with the embassy and the U.S. military to explain to the highly critical foreign correspondents who had flocked to the war scene why the U.S. had taken the action it did.

The USIA team had now been in the D.R. about two weeks under considerable stress, given the hostility of the American journalists in particular who seemed determined to question every American motive and action. This antagonism toward American officials developed because most correspondents held to the opinion that the U.S. should never have intervened militarily. They felt the U.S. was siding with the Dominican military that had long supported the dictator Trujillo (before assassinating him).

The constant concern about possible sniper bullets was also a source of tension, so by early May replacements of some of the USIA team members were planned. The team leader, Hewson Ryan, was needed back in Washington. He returned on a military flight. A few others left to resume their jobs at various posts in Latin America. Ryan's Assistant, Darrell Carter, was named team leader and I was designated to fly to Santo Domingo to be Carter's assistant.

After reading so many cables the past several weeks containing the details about firefights, explosions, and snipers, it was with considerable trepidation that I arrived at the Santo Domingo airport about noon on May 30th. A USIS car and driver drove me to the (now famous) Embajador Hotel, where many journalists and the increasing number of U.S. and other government officials were housed. As we sped down the main road through the International Security Zone I expected to hear shots being fired at any moment, but all was quiet.

Ever since the revolt began, the home of the Public Affairs Officer Malcolm Mclean, whose wife and sons had been evacuated with other American dependents, had been used as the office and headquarters of the USIA Team. This was because the USIS office in Santo Domingo was now in the rebel zone and, therefore, unavailable. Mclean's personal typewriter was one of the few pieces of office equipment initially available to the team, since all the office materials normally used were gathering dust downtown if, in fact, they were not being used by the rebels or had already been destroyed. A few other typewriters had been located and paper had been sent from Washington. Even in wartime nothing happens without paper. But it was the First Psyop Battalion that provided all that was needed when they set up their portable printing presses in an empty lot alongside the Mclean home. Equally important, they provided the USIA team with the same three square meals a day that they provided their own troops, a nice reminder that an army travels on its stomach.

Once U.S. troops were committed, President Johnson assigned overall responsibility for the psychological aspects of the Dominican crisis to the director of USIA, Carl Rowan. He and Deputy Director Donald Wilson led the effort to explain the reasons for the U.S. actions to Latin America and the rest of the world. This involved coordination at the highest levels of government with Department of State, Department of Defense, and White House officials.

With the landing of the first marine on Dominican soil, the job of USIA was clear. The reasons for the landing, as the U.S. saw it, had to be explained both to the Dominicans and the rest of the world, particularly other Latin Americans. As the situation developed, the team of senior officers attached to the Dominican task force in the Operations Center of the Department of State in Washington was available to give prompt policy guidance to USIA's media services.

The USIA's press operation and the VOA went on a twenty-four hour-a-day transmission schedule to Latin America, carrying texts and excerpts of the statements of the President and other senior officials. Meanwhile, pamphlet and leaflet production pertinent to the crisis was initiated in Washington and in the agency's regional service center in Mexico City. The USIA task force sent to Santo Domingo was charged with managing the joint military-civilian information operation in the D.R. Simultaneously, the First Psyop Battalion was flown in from Fort Bragg, North Carolina, with printing presses, mobile radio studios and transmitters, loud-speaker planes and trucks, and all the materials needed to support a psychological warfare operation under combat conditions.

The USIA Task Force was under instructions to establish communications with the Dominican people as rapidly as possible—a formidable task in a city that was dead, as far as most of its normal communications media were concerned. Most of the radio stations, newspapers, and printing facilities were in the rebel-held zone and ceased operating. The few that were operating, especially the symbolically important and powerful *Radio Santo Domingo*, were manned by rebel sympathizers who launched violent, vitriolic attacks against the U.S. as soon as it was clear that the Americans intended to thwart any communist takeover of the D.R.

Five hours after the USIA team reached the embassy, mimeograph machines produced the first copies of a leaflet addressed to the Dominican people stating the reasons for the American military presence. It was distributed by hand. In another two hours, a small printing plant was located in a police substation and pressed into service. By the next morning, 20,000 additional leaflets were dropped from "psy-war" aircraft and distributed by hand throughout the city and the surrounding area.

The following day psy-war printing presses in mobile vans were in operation, producing the first of some two million copies of leaflets, pamphlets, and a tabloid-size two-page newspaper that began to be published every other day in editions averaging 75,000 copies. Originally called *The Voice of the Security Zone* it became *The Voice of the OAS* after the OAS moved in and assumed responsibility for the foreign military presence. Similarly, within twenty-four hours, a burned-out radio station, blasted by explosives, was put back on the air as *The Voice of the Security Zone.* It was manned by USIA and psychological warfare military personnel. Although lacking a crystal needed to transmit, JOT Al Laun's close relationship with local radio station owners enabled one to be found which put the station back on the air. At the same time transmissions of the *VOA* were established in a number of places, including nearby Puerto Rico, from where medium-wave broadcasts could be heard in Santo Domingo.

For the month of May the USIA Task Force ran an intense information program from its headquarters in the home of the public affairs officer. Sporadic sniper fire, combined with torrential rains that continually made communications equipment inoperative, added to the difficulties of the situation. So did the flood of foreign correspondents, not only because of the attitude of many, but also because a number of them had never before been in the D.R. or were not knowledgeable about Latin American affairs. All were frustrated by the difficulties of communicating with their newspapers from that isolated Caribbean island. Also frustrating was the lack of news when there was neither action, nor visible progress, in the stalemate which eventually resulted from the U.S. presence. The correspondents also had their own "war" among themselves, between the "hawks" and the "doves," though the majority were "doves." As a group they were one more unique element in the strange, often confused, melancholic, weird environment I found when I arrived in that embattled, embittered, and divided city.

Within the first week the psy-war operation was more or less stabilized. Four radio transmitters, two of them with five kilowatts of power, were on the air, relaying news and commentary from the *VOA*, staffed and maintained by the First Psychological Warfare Battalion. USIA provided the programming. The PsyOp Battalion, in addition to maintaining the radio network, was operating twelve loudspeaker and pamphlet distribution trucks and two aircraft for leaflet drops and broadcasting to isolated suburbs. Its portable presses were rolling out what was, at the time, the country's leading newspaper, *The Voice of the Security Zone,* edited by a USIA Spanish-speaking media specialist.

That this newspaper met its deadlines is one of the marvels of the war. Very few, if any, of the soldiers who worked as typesetters, make-up men, and printers spoke or read Spanish, and, of course, this, like everything else produced for Dominican audiences, was in Spanish. So one can imagine the painstaking job which fell to the USIA editor, Harry Caicedo, who had to be his own proofreader, among other things.

By the end of May, changing events reduced the need for the large scale, intensive psychological effort initially made by the USIA Task Force and the PsyOp Battalion. The cease-fire brought a temporary stalemate which permitted regular channels of communication to reopen. The OAS began to take over the informational function as part of its operations. This permitted the eventual withdrawal of the Agency's Task Force, as well as the return of the local USIS operation to the control of Malcolm Mclean, the public affairs officer on the scene. Before this happened, however, there were still many loose ends to be tied.

By the time I arrived in Santo Domingo on May 30th there was very little sniper fire during daylight hours. But having followed events here so closely in Washington I was acutely aware of the casualty figures. Yet Santo Domingo was now relatively quiet, except in mid-June. Suddenly the heaviest fighting of the war erupted, though it remained restricted to one area.

One of my major tasks was to accompany an OAS radio specialist on a tour of those parts of the city in which it was more or less safe to travel. We looked for a radio station with the ability, and with the concurrence of its owner, to become *The Voice of the* OAS. Al Laun accompanied us as he knew where the stations were located and also knew their owners. U.S. policy was to get out of the broadcasting and publishing businesses as rapidly as possible by turning over the responsibility for radio programming and newspaper editing to the

OAS, just as the OAS had taken command of the military operations. Both actions would allow the majority of the U.S. military troops and equipment to return home. We soon located a radio station that met our needs, so plans went ahead to close down the U.S. Army's mobile radio operations as soon as the OAS could begin local programming on the new station.

A second task with which I was involved was to find a printing plant in the suburbs where *The Voice of the OAS* newspaper could be printed. We located a small commercial plant which normally printed only advertising signs and packages for food, but it appeared to have the capability for printing a two-page newspaper issued every other day. Within days, *The Voice of the OAS* was being printed there instead of on the mobile presses of the PsyOp Battalion. The Battalion was then able to fold its operation and begin preparations to return most of its staff, and all of its equipment, to Fort Bragg.

The Battalion's liaison officer with the USIA Task Force was Major Richard M. Brown, a tall Tennessean in whose jeep I traversed the ISZ many times. Over six feet tall, he made a good target for snipers. He had, in fact, been shot at at least once when a bullet missed him by half an inch. He had also been caught in the crossfire of a machine gun duel but escaped injury in that incident as well. Both occurrences happened before my arrival, and as things seemed to be quieting down, I tried not to be too concerned about traveling with him in his open jeep as I frequently did. Still, I always thought it somewhat unfair that as we sped through the ISZ to the other side of town he always had his helmet (which went with his uniform) to protect him. I was bareheaded and thus more vulnerable to snipers' bullets.

His driver was the most somber-looking private I have ever seen. With his formidable-looking M-1 slung on the back of his seat for easy accessibility, he always drove relentlessly and for what seemed like an interminable time before reaching any destination. He was all business about which, under the circumstances, I couldn't complain.

One reason we had to spend so much time in that jeep was that we often had to run back and forth from the USIS and PsyOps headquarters to the opposite end of Santo Domingo where the portable studios and transmitters of *The Voice of the Security Zone* radio station were originally located (prior to the OAS takeover). This was about a five-mile drive and meant crossing the Ozama River Bridge. Surprisingly, we could not talk on a regular and dependable basis either by radio or phone with the station's operators, thus had to make frequent personal visits. Communication between Washington and the D.R. was difficult enough at times, but this was often easier than communicating relatively short distances within the country.

As any combat veteran knows, war is a time when waiting takes up much of one's time. The Dominican Civil War was no exception. Nightfall comes quickly in the tropics and when it did, Santo Domingo became, for a while, a hunting ground for snipers. Most of my colleagues on the USIA Task Force made sure that they were back at their hotels before dark, but during these periods, when little could be accomplished, I stayed on at the PAO residence where some of the guys were staying.

About 5 p.m. every day the PsyOps cooks delivered the dinner meal in huge buckets that kept the food warm, placing them in the kitchen where we could help ourselves. Usually those of us still at the "office" would have a few drinks, both before and after dinner. Al Laun, the junior officer trainee who had been so helpful in our communications efforts, was living there and we got to talking about chess one day. He said he'd like to learn, so I taught him the game. Before long, if nothing was planned for the evening, which was usually the case, we would settle in for some after-dinner chess games. Occasionally we'd hear a distant explosion as we sat on the patio moving our chess pieces. Sometimes the phone would ring and someone would call Al to warn him that a sniper had been reported in the area. Often we would hear gunfire, but generally the nights were beginning to quiet down.

I had been provided with a little Volkswagen for transportation. A curfew was in effect from midnight to 5 a.m., so we always had to finish our chess games in time for me to make the ten or fifteen minute run back to the Embajador Hotel before curfew. I generally didn't waste any time once I got rolling, but on the few nights that considerable gunfire had been heard or when a sniper was reported in the vicinity, I drove back to the hotel even faster than usual.

One morning while driving from the hotel to the office I came face to face with a group of lumbering U.S. tanks headed down the road in the opposite direction. As I passed the lead tank, a young Marine who couldn't have been much older than nineteen, if he was that old, was looking out the opening in the front of the vehicle. He had the biggest grin I've ever seen. It was obvious that he and that tank were going home. For him the war was over and he had survived. His joy was written all over his face.

One of the last activities I was involved in before leaving the D.R. was to accompany President Johnson's special representative, Ambassador Ellsworth Bunker, and some of his aides, on an early morning visit to the residence of Hector Garcia Godoy, a neutral businessman and diplomat. Garcia Godoy had agreed to head a provisional government once agreement between the opposing sides could be reached. The plan being developed by the OAS, with U.S. urging and close cooperation, was to establish such a government until elections could be held. Within this framework USIA officials suggested a role for the agency of providing educational materials on democratic voting processes for the D.R.'s forthcoming election. Given the D.R.'s history, these processes were little known and had been little practiced. The U.S. would remain neutral once election campaigns began, but informing Dominican citizens of the meaning and methods of the voting process was considered to be a legitimate way to help develop the sorely needed democratic reforms. My role on the visit to the nominal president was to explain to him some of the ideas USIA had in mind if this issue arose.

On June 20 my turn came to leave the war zone. Never before or since have I been so happy to see my family as when they greeted me upon my arrival at National Airport in Washington. They looked so pleased to see that I had survived safe and sound and, to me, they seemed so happy and healthy, with smiles on their faces a mile wide. I will never forget that scene. Needless to say I was ecstatic to be with my wife and children once again, and to have left that tortured Caribbean country, though I had been in the D.R. barely three weeks.

After weeks of negotiations, agreement was finally reached that on September 3, 1965, the Government of National Reconstruction, headed by General Antonio Imbert Barreras, and the Constiutionalist side, headed by Colonel Francisco Caamaño Deñó, would both be abolished. A Provisional government headed by Hector Garcia-Godoy became the new Dominican government. An institutional act was signed which provided for free elections to be held June 1, 1966, under the watchful eye of OAS observers. The barricades, which separated the rebel zone from the rest of the country, began to be removed, though it was not until October that Santo Domingo was completely reunified. Some months later some of the leaders of both sides, including Col. Caamaño, were sent abroad on assignments designed to remove them from the local scene for awhile. Juan Bosch then returned to run for the presidency once again, as did Joaquin Balaguer, president when Trujillo was assassinated and who had been living since then in exile in New York.

I returned to my duties as Caribbean desk officer and tried to catch up on what was going on in "my other countries." The D.R. continued to take up considerable time, however, especially working with other elements of the agency in developing cartoon booklets, posters, and other information materials designed to educate Dominicans regarding democratic voting procedures. This project was aimed primarily at the large segment of the population that was illiterate. Quickly dubbed the "Get Out the Vote Campaign," it was intended, we often stressed, to show Dominicans why and how to vote but never for whom to vote. The project was considered so successful that it was copied for use in Vietnam, substituting Vietnamese figures for Latin Americans and, of course, the Vietnamese language for Spanish. There is no way of knowing how the large turnout to vote in the D.R. can be attributed to this project, but in Vietnam elections were "overtaken by events" (which, ironically, was the title of John Bartlow Martin's book about the Dominican Republic's civil war).

If Bosch won the election, his poor record as an administrator could not be expected to improve. If Balaguer won the election, though tainted for his association with Trujillo, he was, in the view of most U.S. government observers, a better leader and therefore better for his country. A third candidate, Rafael Bonnelly, was also a former president of the D.R.

Balaguer won the June 1, 1966 election, defeating Bosch and Bonnelly by wide margins. Shortly thereafter the remaining OAS and U.S. armed forces departed. The U.S. continued to provide economic assistance for many years but with mixed results. U.S. officials involved in the crisis at the time strongly believed that the best hope for the D.R.'s future was a political leader like Hector Garcia Godoy, the provisional president. Unfortunately, before Garcia Godoy could become a serious candidate for the presidency, he died of a heart attack. No one else of his stature appeared. By 1990 the election in the D.R. was being fought in a tight battle between two eighty-year-old political Titans—Bosch and Balaguer, the latter already having been president five times!

As the Dominican crisis ceased being front-page news, attention in Washington official circles and in the press focused once again, but with increased intensity, on Vietnam. Just as USIA had played an important role in the U.S. military engagement in the D.R. by working with the military on its public affairs aspects, USIA also was given responsibility by the U.S. president to supervise the information activities of the U.S. government, including those of the military, in South Vietnam. The office in charge of these activities, working out of the U.S. Embassy in Saigon, was known as JUSPAO—the Joint United States Public Affairs Office. A USIA officer was the director and numerous military officers were on his staff.

The demand for more and more USIA officers to be assigned to Vietnam as programs there expanded had reached me once before, but at that time the study of Vietnamese was considered essential. A test of language capability was given candidates for assignment to Vietnam to see how well they might do studying Vietnamese. I must have flunked that exam since I was not among the many that were called. But by 1966, as U.S. involvement in Southeast Asia deepened and expanded, the demand for more personnel had become so great that language testing was no longer required. So once again the long fingers of USIA's bureaucracy reached down and touched your obedient servant.

The new director of USIA's Latin American office, Kermit Brown, called me into his office one day in early 1966 to give me the news.

"Al," he said, "you've been selected to go to Vietnam." Like the good soldier I considered myself to be, I said, "O.K." But then I added, "You know Kerm, I think the agency is stupid to send me to Vietnam. I've never served in Asia, I know nothing about Asian culture or languages, and we're still not out of the woods as far as the Dominican Republic is concerned, where I'm somewhat of an expert. There's also the situation in British Guiana where my knowledge and experience have been helpful in the past and where we still have a situation of special interest to the U.S. So, I'm willing, of course, to go and do my duty as so many others have done and are doing, but I really think it's ridiculous. When do I have to go?"

Brown said he understood my position but we both knew that the demands for more and more agency officers in Vietnam were tremendous. I went home that night and broke the news to Charmaine. In those days families of officers sent to Vietnam could go to Hong Kong or the Philippines where officers assigned to Vietnam could visit them about every six months, or the families could stay in Washington. Charmaine and I spent many hours that night discussing what looked like a fairly grim future while trying to decide which of the alternatives might be best for us. We finally agreed that to uproot our children from the environment they were in under these circumstances would not be the wisest thing to do. So after a sleepless night, I walked into Kerm Brown's office the next morning and told him that our decision was for Charmaine and the children to remain here in Washington when I went to Vietnam.

"Fine," he said. "But you know, Al. I've been thinking about what you said yesterday, and I think you're right. You're really still needed here on the Dominican Republic situation in particular. I'm going to go up and see Carl (Rowan) later this morning and see if we can't keep you here under the circumstances." "Fine," I answered, though

I doubted that USIA Director Rowan would buy the argument for keeping me in Washington.

Later that morning Brown called me into his office. "I've talked with Carl," he said. "You don't have to go." Now it was my turn to smile, feeling somewhat like the Marine I had seen looking out of that lumbering tank in Santo Domingo as he headed for home. Needless to say the news was more than well received when I told Charmaine that evening about Brown's meeting with the USIA Director.

By late 1966 I had been in Washington three years and, counting the year in Pennsylvania, back in the U.S. for more than four years. It was time to go overseas again where Foreign Service officers are supposed to spend most of their careers.

After the election in the D.R. in June, that country was no longer on the front burner. Brown asked me if I would like to be assigned to Montevideo, Uruguay as press attaché. My response was that such an assignment "sounds great." By early 1967 we were getting ready for our move to the small country in the southern cone that was often described, at least in the first half of the twentieth century, as "the Switzerland of South America."

It was now time for us to switch gears and prepare for a new life in Uruguay. Once again we looked forward with great anticipation to the challenges and excitement of a new environment. For the most part, our new overseas experience would bring us much joy and satisfaction. But as 1967 began, and we prepared to depart for Montevideo, neither the Uruguayans nor their American guests could imagine the dark days which were to come. Uruguay's tranquil society would soon be shaken by events adversely affecting most Uruguayans, and some of their foreign guests as well, not least of which were certain members of the American Embassy in the Uruguayan capital.

1.   Nov. 4, 1954. The first director of USIA, Theodore Streibert, administers the oath of office to three members of the second class of USIA's new career Junior Officer Training Program.
(l. to r.) Director Streibert, Weston Olberg, Jerome Bluestein, and Allen Hansen.

2. This is not a used car salesman as the sign might indicate but the author, a new junior officer trainee and vice consul of the American embassy, Caracas, 1955.

3. Mexico City's Diana remains aloof to the busy traffic in the *Glorieta* below her but she fell down July 28th, 1957, during a major earthquake.

4. One result of the July 1957 earthquake (The building was allegedly owned by Mexico's famous comic, Mario "Cantinflas" Moreno.)

5. A typical canal in Georgetown, Guyana.

6. The U.S. Embassy in Madrid, called "the pigeon roost" by some Spaniards because of its architecture.

7. Flamenco fantasy—night life in Madrid.

8.   President Eisenhower (at left) and Generalissimo Franco (3rd from right) discussing U.S.–Spanish relations with aides. (Photo by USIA, courtesy of the National Archives, Photo no. 306PS-D-60-3590)

9. A new twist to an old phrase. Santo Domingo, May 1965.
(Photo by Jack Lantz, USIA, courtesy of the National Archives.)

10. President Lyndon Johnson and Secretary of State Dean Rusk arrive at Punta del Este, Uruguay, on Marine One. They met with all the presidents of the Americas, April 11, 1967. (Photo by Yoichi R. Okamoto, LBJ Library Collection)

11. *Mano a mano* with American movie star Danny Kaye, Montevideo, 1968.

12. When FSO Harry Kendall, former USIA-NASA liaison officer, visited Montevideo on a tour of Latin American with the Apollo 11 moon rock, U.S. Ambassador Charles Adair and Press Attaché Allen Hansen accompanied him to show the rock to the president of Uruguay. (l.to r.) President Pacheco Areco, Hansen, Kendall, and Ambassador Adair.

13.   The USIS American staff gathers for a luncheon meeting at the Costa Brava restaurant, Montevideo, Uruguay, May 23, 1969. (l. to r.) Clark King, Jerry Waters, Bill Lindsey, Anne Gurvin, Al Hansen, Nate Rosenfeld, a visitor, Art Diggle, Susan Strange, and Jake Gillespie.

14. Allen and Charmaine at 12,000 feet. Mt. Illimani (21,190 feet) in the background. Bolivia, 1971

15. A peaceful night in La Paz, Bolivia, 1971. (l. to r.) Annette, Robert, Katherine, Mark, and Alicia.

16.   American Embassy, Islamabad. Aftermath of the Nov. 21, 1979, fire, showing the vault at top, motor pool below. (Photo taken Nov. 23, 1979, by James Thurber, Jr., PAO at the time. He was among those holed up in the vault during the siege.)

17. George Washington's birthday celebration at the U.S. Ambassador's residence, Pakistan's president Mohammad Zia-ul-Haq and the author, Feb. 22, 1982.

18. The author looking into Afghanistan from the lookout of the Kyber Rifles at the Pakistan-Afghanistan border during a visit to the Kyber Rifles by Vice President George H. W. Bush, May, 1984.

19.   Legendary Hollywood star Kirk Douglas breaks nan with Afghan refugees, Peshawar, Pakistan, Thanksgiving Day, 1984. (Photo by Robert Hansen)

7
Murder in Montevideo

"Taking the United States as a model, I wanted the autonomy of the provinces, giving each state its own government, constitution, flag and the right to elect its representatives, its judges and its governors from the citizens native to each state."
—General Jose Gervasio Artigas, leader of the revolution from 1811 to 1820 that brought independence from Spain and Buenos Aires to what is now Uruguay.

"Como el Uruguay no hay" ("There's no place like Uruguay")
—A political slogan of the 1940s.

Uruguay is a small buffer state squeezed between Argentina and Brazil in the southern cone of South America. In February 1967, when the Hansen clan boarded a flight from Washington to Uruguay's capital Montevideo they would have to make four stops en route before reaching their destination. Robert was seven years old; Annette was six; Katherine was three; and Alicia was two. The paperwork alone in checking this entourage in and out of airports and through customs was a major operation.

Adding to the travel time was the somewhat circuitous route required to go from Washington, D.C. to Montevideo, about ten thousand miles to the south. New York was the first stop, where we boarded a PanAm flight to Caracas. Since we were in Venezuela, we took a day's leave en route to our new post in order to visit Charmaine's sister and family. Because airlines seem to prefer sending their planes over the Amazon at night, our flight south from Caracas left at midnight. By 2 a.m. our four children were settled for the night and an hour or so later we began to sleep ourselves, only to be awakened at 4:30 a.m. by the cheery announcement of a stewardess asking if we would like some breakfast as we would be landing in Rio de Janeiro in an hour.

Upon our arrival in Rio we were in a state of exhaustion due to lack of sleep. As we walked out of the plane we were hit by a blast of hot, tropical air. Though it was only 6:30 a.m., we felt like we were entering a hot furnace. This shock was followed by the news that our connecting flight, due to arrive from London about 11 a.m., would be four or five hours late.

As we entered the terminal, more bad news greeted us. Although the old Rio airport had air conditioning, we were told that due to an electrical shortage it was against the law to use it. Despite the heat, we headed for the terminal's only restaurant on the second floor, ignoring the fact that heat rises. We had skipped the breakfast offered in the plane at 4:30 a.m., little realizing that we would regret that decision soon after landing in Rio.

We were hopeful that a good breakfast would lift our spirits, but that hope was short-lived as we observed the unswept, unkempt appearance of the airport's only restaurant. While assuming that the food they served would be prepared with the same lackadaisical attitude that seemed to mark the general appearance of this place, we were by now so hungry we were willing to take our chances. Piles of dirty dishes left over from the night before still sat on many of the tables.

When our breakfast, ordered from a stained, crumbled menu, finally arrived, we discovered that our visions of fresh milk and eggs were only dreams. Both were powdered. The milk tasted like chalk and the eggs like paste. We decided we would have to wait until we boarded the connecting British Airways flight that would take us to Buenos Aires before we could expect to have a decent meal, even though that would be many hours later. Hot, hungry, tired, irritable and sleepy, this may have been the beginning of a great adventure, but at that moment it seemed to us to be the roughest Foreign Service duty we had as yet encountered.

Eventually the British plane arrived and we took off for Buenos Aires. Lunch had already been served so we had to make do with a small snack. After a short stop at Buenos Aires we took off again for the short flight to Montevideo, a mere hundred miles to the east. As we stepped off the plane we were greeted by the public affairs officer, Horace "Tex" Edwards. A highly cultured individual, Edwards was a former teacher whose interests favored the cultural side of USIS programming. We had known him slightly when he was the USIA book officer in Mexico. He welcomed us warmly and accompanied us to the hotel in downtown Montevideo where we would be staying until we found a house. After briefing us on a few essentials he left, knowing full well that what we wanted more than anything else at that moment was a few hours of sleep.

The need to feed our young foursome in restaurants three times a day during the time that we lived in the Victoria Plaza Hotel was a constant challenge. After the first week, the daily ritual of eating in a variety of restaurants ceased to be fun, even for them. We soon learned, however, to love Uruguayan beef, the mainstay of Montevidean menus in a country where the per capita consumption of beef was the highest in the world at the time, amounting to about 456 kilos per capita annually! After what seemed like endless searching for a suitable house to rent, we located one that we liked in the Pocitos section of Montevideo. By that time we had endured hotel living for nearly three months.

The house we moved into was a drab, unimpressive stucco structure when viewed from the outside. However, it boasted a fireplace in the living room that would come in handy on wintry nights. It also had a small garden in the rear and sufficient bedrooms for our growing family. It was only a short block from Pocitos beach, a pleasant place to walk but swimming there was risky. A pipeline of untreated sewage ran out into the bay, ending about a quarter of a mile from the beach where its contents were dumped into the ocean. Sometimes the wind or the currents carried some of it back toward land.

With the major step of finding a permanent place to live accomplished, our new life became much more pleasant. However, by the mid-1960s, Uruguay had fallen on hard times. Long known as the "Switzerland of South America," this description no longer seemed valid. Instead, the country's deteriorating economy and general rundown appearance frequently brought forth comparisons with the drabness of contemporary Eastern European communist countries. But for us, having found a house to call our own, and learning, shortly thereafter, that our furniture and our automobile had arrived at Montevideo's port, we looked forward to a happy and satisfying tour at our new post.

For most of our three and a half years in Montevideo such was the case. While Uruguay suffered many political and economic problems during this period, graceful living was enjoyed by most *Uruguayos* and their foreign guests—until disaster struck in the form of the Tupamaro terrorists.

Uruguay was one of the first countries in the world to initiate state welfarism which it carried to such an extreme that its welfare policies eventually contributed greatly to its undoing. As an example of why welfarism was taking its toll on the government's budget, a fifty-year-old Uruguayan woman on the USIS payroll was still receiving part of her father's pension, a retired Army colonel who had died three decades earlier, because she had never married! As long as she remained unmarried, this pension payment of her long deceased father would continue. The amount wasn't much, but her father had retired nearly half a century earlier and the government was still providing funds from the national treasury in this manner. Such policies contributed to Uruguay's growing economic problems.

Uruguay's political problems were no less severe. The national government was run by a seven-man council, in power for seven years at a time, with each council member taking his turn as president for one year! There were two major political parties, the *Blancos* (whites) and the *Colorados* (reds), as well as a number of minor parties. These minor parties included the traditional communist party and a few other radical parties, all left of the communists.

The communist party's daily newspaper was called *El Popular,* though its circulation figures did not indicate much popularity. However, it was mandatory reading in most government and embassy offices as a window on the thinking of the political left.

Most Uruguayans called the political environment at the time one of *libertinaje,* meaning "license" or "anything goes" rather than "freedom." Often tendentious or completely false articles about the U.S., published in *El Popular* would infuriate U.S. embassy readers, some of whom couldn't understand why the local government permitted such trash to be printed. The reply of most Uruguayans to such concerns was always the same. They usually said, first, except as noted above, "no one reads that paper"; secondly, if they do, they know that anything published there is highly questionable; and, thirdly, "it keeps us informed about what the left is thinking." The latter was probably true, until the Tupamaro terrorists entered the picture.

Uruguay was blessed in a number of ways which prior to World War II, gave the country its reputation as the "South American Switzerland." In comparison with most Latin American countries, some called it "the Great Exception."

Uruguay is almost entirely flat, thus well suited for the cattle industry which thrived to such an extent that eating steak twice and sometimes three times daily was not uncommon. In addition, one of the greatest fishing grounds in the world exists at and near the mouth of the Rio de la Plata, which empties into the Atlantic Ocean at Montevideo. But the Uruguayans generally ignored this rich source of protein, relying instead on the land and their cattle for their main sustenance. They left the abundant schools of fish that thrived along their extensive coastline for other nations to exploit. The one exception to their strange lack of interest in the abundant fruits of the sea in their coastal waters was the delicious *mellejones* (mussels), which most Uruguayans relished. The restaurants in the coastal resort city of Punta del Este were particularly noted for this delicacy.

Uruguay was developed mostly by Europeans, especially Italians, and had few if any indigenous cultures when Europeans first arrived. Being a small country and recognized as a buffer between Argentina and Brazil, the two giants on its borders, there was no need for large military expenditures. The police force was equally diminutive. In 1969, for example, when the Tupamaro terrorists first surfaced, Montevideo, a city of one million inhabitants, had only one patrol car! The police were noted for their horsemanship and were particularly adept at controlling crowds when on horseback. They were clearly ill-prepared to face the growing threat of a clandestine terrorist organization.

In the early to mid-twentieth century, the mild climate, the abundant food supply, and adequate shelter offered few challenges to the average Uruguayan. Living standards and educational levels were high compared to most Latin American countries, but by the early 1960s life was becoming more difficult. For example, because of the high cost of importing vehicles, there were increasing numbers of old cars on Uruguayan roads. While they symbolized the economic recession the country was now experiencing, there were few if any signs of the extreme poverty so evident in many other Latin American nations. Most Uruguayans still ate well, lacked few necessities, and there were always the miles and miles of beautiful beaches to which to escape from their daily concerns. (Only Pocitos, the in-town beach, had the sewage problem.)

The star recreational attraction for many Uruguayans was the beach resort city of Punta del Este, a favorite vacation spot not only for Uruguayans but also for thousands of Argentine tourists. The relatively easy living to which Uruguayans were long accustomed encouraged a complacency and satisfaction with the status quo which made the growth of terrorism in such a society difficult to imagine, let alone combat.

By the mid-sixties, however, Uruguay was beginning to come apart at the seams. In March 1967, shortly after our arrival in Montevideo, a serious drought caused a water shortage. Weeks passed when water was available in Montevideo's homes and offices for only a few hours daily. The water shortage was followed by an electrical shortage. Dining at home by candlelight was romantic but soon ceased being a novelty. And while walking up five flights of stairs at the USIS office when the elevator wasn't working was good exercise, this was not appreciated by everyone.

In May and June, which is autumn in the southern hemisphere, the drought was finally broken. The rains then came in such quantities that rivers ran wild throughout Uruguay's flat terrain. In June when I went on a four-day trip to the Brazilian border to represent the U.S. at the opening of two television stations in interior towns, the rain continued almost constantly. When we tried to return to Montevideo by road we found our way blocked by floodwaters. We left our station wagon with friends and caught the last train out of Artigas in order to get home. A few weeks later we sent someone north to retrieve our vehicle. By then the floods had caused the loss of thousands of head of cattle, seriously disrupting Uruguay's basic food supply.

Meanwhile, in our new home, we ran out of fuel oil, so the house was cold and damp for several days. With the first Middle East oil crisis in full swing, there was talk of a fuel shortage, although this never developed to serious proportions. Our problem was in the local delivery system. After running out of fuel oil a second time we learned to sleep at night with the furnace off in order to conserve fuel and ordered fuel well in advance of when it was needed. We increased the frequency of measuring, with a long stick, the amount of oil remaining in a large underground tank in our backyard.

The floods of May and June were followed by a severe cold wave. It never snows in Montevideo, and seldom reaches freezing temperatures, but that year there was ice on the streets of the capital. The cold affected cattle production some more, causing milk and meat shortages for a short time, followed by a vegetable shortage. By October potatoes were being imported from Poland.

Although Uruguay's educational system was possibly better than that of neighboring Argentina, a government study of Argentina's educational system (by an Argentine newspaper) produced informative figures. Of every 1,000 students initially enrolled in primary schools in Argentina, only 350 completed the courses. Of these, 250 entered secondary school, of which seventy-five graduated; of which sixty began university studies; of which only twelve graduated. The pyramid format of those figures when presented graphically is not surprising, but the high number of dropouts clearly affected that country's social and economic progress. Uruguay, if better, was not much further advanced. The diminishing Uruguayan university budgets and the quality of the education offered in those universities created another drag on economic development. Typical of many Latin American universities, local universities had a number of "professional students" whose purpose for being on campus was not to study, but to play politics. Thus the local universities became important recruiting grounds for the Tupamaro movement.

The school system in Uruguay differs from the U.S. in keeping with the reversed climatic seasons. Classes begin in March and end in December. The summer vacation runs from January through early March. We were faced, therefore, with placing Robert and Annette either a half-year behind or a half-year ahead of the grades that they should have been in if we were back in the states. We opted for the latter, and in Robert's case he adjusted well to the third grade. Although advised by the new American School principal to do the same with Annette, which we did, in later years we realized that this probably added to the struggle she would have with formal education throughout her childhood and adolescence.

A series of articles that appeared in the Argentine newspaper La Prensa in March 1968 puts this small buffer country with its population of about three million in perspective. What is now happening in Uruguay, Ignoto Pastor, an Uruguayan intellectual, wrote, "is but the inexorable result of a policy of socialist control which has been gaining strength since the beginning of the century." He noted that Uruguay was the first country of the western hemisphere to develop its own welfare society with the result, he contended, that her currency depreciated as did her gold reserves. "She reached a world record in the rise of the cost of living and a foreign debt of over 400 million dollars," quite a feat for a country with a population the size of many cities elsewhere in the world.

Contrary to those who saw it as a poor country, Pastor viewed Uruguay as a well endowed one. He pointed out that while Uruguay is only one-fifteenth of the area of Argentina, it is one-third the size of France and six times the area of Belgium. He noted, "eighty-eight per cent of this territory is suitable for agriculture or livestock breeding, has adequate water resources, a temperate climate and sufficient rainfall. There are 140 kilometers of Atlantic coastline perched on a continental shelf which is among the best fishing grounds in the world and 890 kilometers of river borders that are just as plentiful from the point of view of fishing."

In calling Uruguay "a small 'Great Society'" (to use U.S. President Lyndon Johnson's term for his welfare programs), Pastor noted that "for more than fifty years, Uruguay's politics have been dominated by the enunciations of nineteenth-century socialism: the state has to take part in all aspects of the economic life of the country in order to survey, control and protect the individual, and to redress so-called 'social differences.' " Uruguay, he added, has carried through to their conclusion the same ideas that are at the source of President Johnson's policy, albeit under a different name.

Uruguay initiated its welfare state with a pension scheme instituted at the height of the prosperity which followed upon the First World War, in the year 1919. It was based, Pastor noted, on the principle of retirement for absolutely everybody with fifty years of age and thirty years of active service (for men); fifty years of age and twenty-five of work (for women). In the years that followed, "not a single government abstained thereafter from adding to the advantages enjoyed by the pensioners."

How did Uruguay survive the enormous burden of state control and subsidies and in having about 12 percent of its population pensioned while, according to Pastor, only 30 percent made up the active work force? That is, for every 3.3 persons who produced something, there was one who collected without producing anything.

"The mystery" of how the population was able to bear this enormous burden, he noted, was due to three factors: the first is that "Uruguay is free, or nearly free from the weight thrown on military expenditures by other South American countries;" secondly, owing to a persistent lowering of the birth rate, the number of children cared for by adults was greatly reduced; and thirdly, the acceptance on the part of the population of the gradual deterioration of their standard of living, not as regards food, but obvious in clothing, housing, and public services.

Another astute observer of Uruguay's s ills at the time was U.S. Ambassador Robert M. Sayre who, on the eve of his departure after a few years in Uruguay, somewhat courageously presented Uruguayans with an inkling of what he really thought about Uruguayan society. In a talk to Uruguayan Rotarians in October of 1969, he stated that the three most frequent answers he received when discussing Uruguay's economic problems as he traveled throughout the country were (1) "Uruguay is a small country; it is only about 70,000 square miles." (2) "Uruguay has few resources," and, (3) "Uruguay has few markets and its export possibilities are limited."

With these excuses for a deteriorating economic situation in mind, he said, "Every place I have gone in Uruguay I have seen vast agricultural lands, cattle, sheep, occasional forests and orchards of apples and citrus fruit, grazing land, and in the cities, factories. So even though the country is said to be small, I said to myself, it is certainly a fertile country and capable of high production.

"But then I read more about Uruguay and compared it with other countries. I began to realize that Uruguay is not small at all.

"I looked at the list in the World Atlas of the twenty-five largest countries in the world. I noted that many were larger because they had mountains and deserts. But you cannot live in the desert nor can you produce much there or on a rocky mountain top. So I asked myself: If one considers only the land on which people can live and produce, how large is Uruguay?

"I began to see," the ambassador said, "that Uruguay is not a small country—indeed it is one of the largest countries in the world. Uruguay ranks eighth in size in Latin America in the amount of usable land. But there are really only four countries in Latin America that have significantly more arable land than Uruguay: Brazil, Argentina, Mexico, and Peru.

"Of the twenty-five largest countries in the world, only twelve have more usable land than Uruguay. Indeed, in all of Europe there are only three countries that can compare with Uruguay in the amount of usable land: France, Poland, and Spain.

"Taking total (not just arable land) land area into account," he said, "Uruguay is larger than England, Holland, and Belgium combined. Or it is larger than Belgium, Holland, Luxembourg, Denmark, and Switzerland combined. I must tell you quite frankly I no longer believe that Uruguay is a small country. You look very large to any country in Europe, or Central America, or to Israel, for example, which would fit inside your department of Tacuarembo."

The ambassador's unique view of Uruguay received wide attention in the local media. It may have made some Uruguayans view their country somewhat differently than they traditionally did at the time. It is doubtful, however, that his ideas and suggestions expressed in that talk, such as establishment of an export promotion fund and creation of a commission to encourage exports, resulted in the initiation of any concrete actions to stem the increasingly evident deterioration of the Uruguayan economy.

In addition to PAO "Tex" Edwards, other members of the USIS American staff included the Cultural Attaché, Nathan Rosenfeld, with whom Charmaine and I became very close friends. His dry sense of humor often kept us entertained. He had three American assistants: ACAO Shirley Hensch was a middle-aged woman who had considerable experience in cultural affairs as a Department of State officer. ACAO Jake Gillespie was a young man with great potential who was sharp but didn't seem to me as dedicated to his profession as I thought he should be. I was wrong. He went on to become an excellent officer with a distinguished record of service. The third ACAO was Anne Gurvin who was on her first USIA tour. She directed a dynamic, two-story USIS Information Center in downtown Montevideo known as the *Biblioteca Artigas-Washington*[1] which was frequently used by the Uruguayan government, media, and university faculties and students. The center and its theater became one of Uruguay's most active cultural venues. She also traveled to neighboring countries to assist in the development of BNC libraries as a consultant and lecturer. Her friendship with Charmaine and me made her one of a number of "adopted members" of the Hansen family as we became lifelong friends.

I first met Anne some years earlier in Spain. She was a graduate student at the University of Madrid when she visited the cultural section of USIS Madrid to learn more about USIA operations. She claims my enthusiasm in describing USIA activities encouraged her to apply to the Foreign Service. Because of her academic qualifications as well as her fluency in French and Spanish, she was readily accepted and later assigned as the cultural attaché to Stockholm, The Hague, and Lima, Peru.

Two additional USIA officers in Montevideo were Clark King, Director of the BNC, and Bill Lindsey, Director of Courses of the center who later became director when King was transferred. The Americans assigned to USIS Montevideo came and went so often during the three and a half years I spent in Uruguay, including the PAOs, I frequently found myself temporarily acting as the director of USIS while waiting for the newly-assigned PAO to arrive.

As press attaché I had one American assistant, Frank Chiancone. His short stature and his decisive and effective manner of conducting business led me to describe him among friends as "Little Napoleon." He was the only USIA officer I ever encountered who managed to consistently maintain a desk with few papers. How he achieved this, and still completed his numerous tasks effectively and efficiently, which he did, I'll never know.

AIO Chiancone supervised USIS radio and television operations while I ran the press and publications activities. Radio stations proliferated in Uruguay as in almost all Latin American countries, so providing these numerous stations with VOA and locally produced programs was a major USIS activity. Fortunately his local staff included a top-notch Uruguayan employee, Hector Gobi, a veteran of many years as the USIS radio chief. Gobi, a *bon vivant,* thrived on his association with radio station owners and managers throughout the country. He greatly enjoyed the mixture of conducting USIS business with radio personnel in practically every city and town in Uruguay, while socializing with them and other local contacts, many of whom had become good friends of his over the years. Occasionally accompanied by an American officer during his frequent visits to interior radio stations, he amazed all of us by his ability to wine, dine, dance, and whatever until the wee hours of the morning, yet be alert and ready to conduct business with our local contacts virtually at the break of dawn!

Chiancone's other top assistant was Carlos Repeto. Repeto handled contacts and programming with television stations. A young man who was determined that no grass would grow under his feet, he fit very well into the fast, frantic mode of television's *ambiente.* But like most young men in an obvious hurry, he occasionally miscalculated, though never to the extent of causing serious or tragic consequences.

Equally important to USIS' successful electronic programming was a young television producer who worked for USIS under contract for specific projects. For example, utilizing his technical skills and Chiancone's creative abilities, the USIS produced an hour-long special TV program about communist China entitled "The Ant Hill." It was a devastating critique of that country long before President Richard Nixon's historic trip which eventually resulted in the establishment of U.S.-Chinese diplomatic relations. While USIA as a U.S. government agency leant over backwards to be sure that copyrighted materials were protected, "The Ant Hill" did not receive the scrutiny in this respect which would have occurred had it been produced in USIA's Washington studios. And although Chiancone had never before had any experience in television programming, his innate ability and genius for organization, combined with the abilities of Uruguay's talented young, dynamic producer, resulted in an effective, anti-communist program which enjoyed prime-time placement.

Two Uruguayan employees on the USIS staff who were remarkable for their dedication and effectiveness were Nelson Bengochea, responsible for all administrative matters of USIS, and Bonfiglio, the USIS photographer. Bonfiglio was always willing and able, regardless of the time of day or night, to take and develop the many photos USIS needed in the course of conducting its public diplomacy activities. These Uruguayos and their colleagues provided the continuity, the institutional memory, and the knowledge of local customs and traditions which, when shared with the American foreign service officers, greatly helped the latter in adjusting to local conditions and in carrying out their responsibilities.

The USIS press chief was Cazala, a fairly capable fellow but an obvious loner whose not-so-secretive love life was the talk, or the envy, of his Uruguayan co-workers. Like the USIS photographer Bonfiglio, Cazala was, in keeping with local custom, generally known and spoken to only by his last name. This was a peculiar Uruguayan cultural trait that applied to some individuals and not to others. There were also, of course, a number of Uruguayan women on the staff who contributed greatly to USIS efforts, but, except for the chief cultural affairs assistant, Isabel Lussich, most were in subordinate positions.

Tex Edwards and his family left about a year after our arrival in Montevideo. He had two teenaged daughters at the time and never had I witnessed such wailing at a departure as when his two daughters bade goodbye to their many Uruguayan and American teenaged friends at the airport. The extreme emotions of adolescents were clearly evident that day. After a few months Tex was replaced by Irving "Bud" Lewis. Lewis had been the PAO of a Central American country. His assignment to Montevideo was a step-up for him. Unfortunately, he had been diagnosed as suffering from cancer and, while this horrible disease was supposed to have been halted, apparently this was not the case. As time went on he must have become more and more conscious that his time was limited. Although he tried not to show it, he seemed to become increasingly irritated, no doubt the result of the pain he experienced as his illness progressed. I remember one incident in particular that seemed to show how he was being affected by the changes going on in his body.

At the time a number of university students in Montevideo had begun to raise funds by standing on street corners and soliciting money from drivers of cars stopped by traffic lights. Sometimes the students boldly attempted to stop passing cars. If drivers failed to respond positively there was always the danger that the car might be damaged, or worse.

One day I was riding with Lewis who was going to drop me off near my home after leaving the office for the day. We came upon a student group standing in the street. They tried to flag us down. Instead of slowing down, let alone stopping, he hit the gas pedal and headed in their direction, intending, I presume, to narrowly pass by them, which he did. The anger and irritation so evident in his actions I attributed to his illness, but I also became greatly concerned that if his car had hit any of the students, which it nearly did, the consequences would not have been good for him, the American Embassy, or U.S. relations with Uruguay, not to mention the students who might have been killed or injured. Not long afterwards the effects of his illness became fully apparent and he was medivacked to Washington, where some weeks later he died. Once more I was given temporary command of USIS Montevideo until a replacement could arrive.

The new director of USIS Montevideo was Arthur Diggle. Diggle was often described by friends who admired him as "a rough diamond." He had entered USIA as a labor specialist, having had experience in the U.S. labor movement at a time when the agency was placing special emphasis on the role of U.S. labor unions. The importance of the free trade labor movement in raising living standards and improving working conditions was a major USIA theme. He had had two prior USIA assignments; as labor information officer in Mexico, where I had first met him, and then at Rio de Janeiro. This was his first assignment as director of a USIS post.

He and his family, consisting of his lovely Mexican wife and two small children, were warmly welcomed by the USIS staff. It was soon evident, however, that whereas Tex Edwards was strong on the cultural side of USIS activities, caring less about the information side, Art Diggle was at home with information activities. He recognized the value of cultural affairs but the information field was his forte. However, his management style was to often micromanage both entities, which soon grated on the nerves of both Nate Rosenfeld, the CAO, and me. A heart-to-heart talk with him over lunch one day happily resulted in letting both of us and our staffs do what we were fully qualified to do without the PAO feeling compelled to do certain duties normally done by his underlings.

I mentioned how Diggle's wife was a lovely lady. She was also, as I recall, always a stylish dresser. On one occasion she innocently became the main subject of conversation among American Embassy staffers and their families. This came about because a park near the American ambassador's residence had a notorious reputation for being a place to meet ladies of the night.

One afternoon she parked her car near the park and proceeded on foot to the entrance of the ambassador's residence where she had been invited to a tea hosted by the ambassador's wife. Shortly before she reached the entrance to the residence, she was stopped by a policeman who told her she was under arrest! The charge: prostitution! It took awhile before the policeman, who claimed he was just doing his job, became convinced that she was who she said she was, and that she was, in fact, en route to the ambassador's residence to have tea with the ambassador's wife! Strange, sometimes, are the risks faced by Foreign Service families.

Changes also occurred among the officers in the lower ranks during my tour in Montevideo. The day came when the assistant information officer, Frank Chiancone, with whom I had shared many enjoyable work and social activities, was transferred. He was replaced by Gerald Waters, a person with excellent experience in television programming but who maintained a certain degree of aloofness in many of his associations with other people. As far as I was concerned his dedication, hard work, and knowledge, especially in the field of television which was now becoming increasingly important in Uruguay, made up for his somewhat cool personality traits.

By contrast, his wife exuded personality. It was always a joy to be in her company as she sparkled with good humor. Not that she did not have her share of concerns, possibly none more irritating than when the septic tank at her home overflowed and remained unrepaired for what seemed like months on end. On another occasion a fumigator working in her home was overcome by the chemicals he was using and passed out in her bathroom. She rushed him to the hospital single-handedly (as no one else was around at the time) where he died from the fumes he had inhaled. It seemed that there were always minor and major tragedies occurring in and around her, but she always was able to tell about them later in a manner that held everyone's interest, and, when appropriate, with a great sense of humor.

Three junior officer trainees, who came at different times, were also among the Americans on the USIS staff. One left the service shortly thereafter, having discovered at his first overseas post that the Foreign Service was not for him while two went on to highly successful careers.

Another young officer arrived for a short while to fill an assignment as "youth officer." "Youth officers" were a Kennedy-era innovation designed to reach the youth of the world, the next generation of leaders. However, no one knew how they were supposed to do that, including the young man assigned to that job. This latest USIA experiment assumed that it takes "youth" to reach "youth," therefore "youth officers" were assigned to various posts and were free to devise programs which presumably would reach youth, utilizing all available USIS resources. In Uruguay as in most countries, the "youth" USIA had in mind were the university students, especially where, as here, the universities were noted as hotbeds of leftist, anti-U.S. elements.

At many universities in Uruguay and elsewhere in Latin America, especially the large, public universities, the campuses were often not considered safe for U.S. officials to visit. So this young "youth officer," learning public diplomacy for the first time, discussed with his more experienced colleagues ways in which programs might be developed with the university audience in mind. Unfortunately, with so many other USIS priorities, most staffers could devote little time to this goal. As a result he and many other inexperienced "youth officers" floundered about with little direction and few accomplishments to register at the end of their tours. It came as no surprise, therefore, that before long the concept of "youth officers" was abandoned, another experiment which seldom fulfilled its early promise. Public diplomacy, perhaps somewhat like parenthood, tends to be like that.

In April 1967 an event that had never taken place before occurred in the Uruguayan beach resort city of Punta del Este. The presidents of all of the Latin American nations met there with the president of the United States, Lyndon Baines Johnson. That this occurred about two years after the United States had been soundly condemned by many Latin Americans for its invasion of the Dominican Republic made this meeting all the more remarkable.

The American Embassy in Montevideo, including USIS, had long been accustomed to operating as a relatively quiet, distant post, remote from the major problems and foreign policy issues and concerns on which Washington normally focused. The embassy staffers were accustomed to conducting their affairs rather routinely in a generally tranquil environment. Uruguay had no major issues adversely affecting U.S. interests, and the country itself, by most standards, was small and of little strategic, political, or economic importance either to the United States or to international relations. The unprecedented, historic event which was about to occur in Punta del Este, however, required a complete change in the working habits and routines of almost every employee of the U.S. Mission in Montevideo.

The meeting of the presidents was announced a few months before it was to take place. Action plans were immediately formulated by the various embassy elements to support the many requirements that a visit to Uruguay of the U.S. president would necessitate. The logistical support and the need for security measures would have been major undertakings had a presidential visit been planned for Montevideo, where the embassy and USIS offices were located and could be used in providing the many services such a visit entails. However, this visit would not take place in the Uruguayan capital city, but at a resort town about eighty-five miles from Montevideo. And it was not under U.S. or Uruguayan auspices, but under the aegis of the Organization of American States (OAS). These two factors greatly complicated the logistical demands.

Before long a number of advance parties arrived from Washington to check out the environment and to discuss arrangements with regard to housing, meeting places, security efforts, creature comforts, and even the entertainment planned for the U.S. president and his staff. The Secret Service was, of course, primarily concerned about the security of the president. When the advance team of Secret Service agents learned that the OAS planned for the presidents to meet around a large round table located under a giant chandelier, they insisted that other arrangements be made or that the chandelier be removed. The chandelier was removed.

The house in Punta del Este where the president was to stay was referred to as "House No. 1"; the Secretary of State, Dean Rusk, would be quartered in "House No. 2." Other houses were inspected and rented for the staffs accompanying them. With an additional twenty presidents and their entourages planning to attend the conference and the need to provide all manner of support to the conference, there was a mad scramble for available houses. Punta del Este, essentially a beach resort designed for fun and frolic, had never experienced an event of this magnitude. Needless to say, rents skyrocketed.

President Johnson was a tall man who required a large bed if he was to sleep comfortably. To accommodate him in the house selected for the Punta del Este "White House," the walls of the master bedroom were knocked down and the room expanded. A large, oversized bed was then placed in the expanded room. At the same time the room was redecorated, including the installation of new wallpaper with the yellow rose of Texas as its motif, designed to make the president feel at home. At the end of the two-day conference, the U.S. government was committed to return House No. 1 to the exact condition it was in before being occupied by the president. There were those among the embassy staffers who felt strongly that to have made those expensive changes for the alleged comfort of the president for a mere two-night stay was an outrageous use of government funds. Others felt that the expenditure, whatever it was, was not unreasonable given the heavy responsibilities of a U.S. president—anything that eased his burden and provided him with a good night's sleep, it seemed to some, was generally worth the cost.

As the sponsor of the conference, the OAS had the responsibility for providing the conference site where the meetings were to take place. The OAS was also responsible for providing the services that would be needed by the 2,500 media correspondents expected to cover the event.

The major hotel in Punta del Este, a large, sturdy Tudor-style building was selected as the site for the meetings and OAS support activities. Since there was no suitable place in or near the hotel to accommodate the press, a large, temporary building was constructed in record time in the parking area behind the hotel. Built like a huge Quonset hut, it would house working space for the reporters and dozens of telephone and teletype lines to enable them to send out their dispatches. It would also have to offer certain amenities such as bars and restaurants for the working press. Some nails were still being pounded when the conference began, but the building was 99 percent completed and adequately served its purpose.

Like other embassy elements, USIS dropped almost all other activities and concentrated on preparations for the Punta del Este conference. The major responsibility for USIS services which would be needed at this historic meeting fell upon me as the information officer, since the most important USIS role was to provide press coverage for USIA and to assist American correspondents and others in getting the information they needed for their reports. To do this adequately we rented two houses that were side by side and not far from the conference site. One house we designated as the USIS press center, which I would supervise during the conference. The second house was staffed and equipped to support the needs of American and other correspondents, especially our Uruguayan friends, who worked in the television and radio media. This house and its activities would be supervised by AIO Frank Chiancone.

USIA's press veteran Lafe Allen flew in from Washington headquarters to cover the conference for the agency's wireless file. Carl Davis, another Washington official, arrived as the overall coordinator of USIA press and media activities and Harry Caicedo, *VOA* correspondent for Latin America, was also on hand. The PAO from Bolivia, Ned Fogler, arrived to write stories. Office space was provided for them in the two USIS rented houses. In effect, what this conference demanded was the establishment of a temporary branch USIS office in Punta del Este.

The cultural side of USIS was not left out of the conference preparations. ACAO Shirley Hensch was assigned the job of obtaining, on loan, the best paintings available by Uruguayan artists and delivering them to House No. 1 for President Johnson to see if he wished to buy any. Among the artists represented were Enrique Castells Capurro, Uruguay's most famous painter of gaucho scenes, *gauchos* being the Argentine and Uruguayan cowboys who tend the millions of heads of cattle for which the Argentine pampas and the interior of Uruguay are well known.

Castells Capurro had not painted vigorously for some years as he was aging rapidly and suffered from arthritis, but upon learning that President Johnson was to review some Uruguayan paintings, he made a special effort and, within a short time, produced five large paintings of various gaucho scenes. The president, presumably, was already familiar with the work of Castells Capurro, as a large mural of his once adorned a building at the University of Texas. Of the five paintings Shirley Hensch borrowed from Castells Capurro to show the president, the president bought three of them for his Texas ranch.

Punta del Este had been chosen as the site of this historic conference because, among other things, it was on a peninsula, making the control of its physical access fairly easy, an important security consideration. Furthermore, Uruguay was one of the few democracies in Latin America at the time, thus was symbolically well suited to host a conference attended by the U.S. president. Contingency plans, however, included the stationing of an American aircraft carrier offshore just beyond the horizon. The U.S. Navy was prepared, if the need arose, to evacuate President Johnson and his staff by helicopters.

It would be difficult to say what, of lasting value, was accomplished at the meeting of the presidents. It did, however, provide the opportunity for the U.S. president to meet privately, as well as publicly, with all of the Latin American presidents. This, in itself, may have made all the cost and effort that went into the conference worthwhile. For all of us connected with the conference, the days prior to and during the event were exhilarating in comparison with our normal routine in quiet, relatively slow-paced Montevideo. We all felt a sense of sharing in an historic occasion.

I was nearing the midpoint in my career as a public diplomat and yet had much to learn. When my efficiency report was written that year by PAO Tex Edwards, although my single most effective accomplishment in my own view was the success enjoyed in assuring that the public relations support to the president and his staff was fulfilled, he failed to devote a single sentence to the hard work and hours of effort I and my staff devoted to the presidents' meeting. Instead of insisting that he write something about the conference and our public relations efforts in contributing to its success, I accepted the report with an attitude of "Oh well." Others were quick to praise our efforts, but not the PAO. Years later I often thought that I should not have accepted an efficiency report on my activities which ignored a major, historic event with which I was intimately associated. However, I had yet to learn of the value and importance of efficiency reports to one's career in the Foreign Service.

While Montevideo was not a highly sophisticated city it did have a few excellent restaurants, a national symphony orchestra and some theater, and it offered various types of entertainment and recreation that were good for body and soul. There was also, of course, always the possibility of escaping to the booming metropolis of Buenos Aires (B.A.) in neighboring Argentina. B.A. could be reached by ship, plane, or car but we were able to get there only infrequently, particularly since the road system was so underdeveloped that a trip to Argentina's capital by car, though only a hundred miles as the crow flies, meant spending a full day on the road with many detours.

A bridge was being built across the Uruguay River, the major natural obstacle to land travel between Montevideo and B.A. When completed, the trip between the two capitals would be greatly shortened although many Uruguayos seriously believed that construction of the bridge was a mistake. It would enable the Argentine army, they argued, to put its tanks into Montevideo within hours should they ever decide to do so. Others felt this view was nonsense since Uruguay was traditionally a buffer state between Argentina and Brazil. The Brazilians, some argued, would never allow Uruguay to be taken over by the Argentines.

Despite Montevideo's bulging government bureaucracy and the general disintegration of its economy, a few social and recreational outposts, which demonstrated the wealth of a bygone era, were still maintained. For example, one of the choicest pieces of real estate in Montevideo was a golf club with an 18-hole course within ten minutes from the downtown area. Being so convenient, and with diplomats welcomed with diplomatic discounts, for many of us it was the main game in town. It also boasted a first-class restaurant. Given such facilities and convenience it naturally became a leading watering hole for the diplomatic set. There was a second golf club in Montevideo, which was far out of town and more rustic and rundown than the in-town club, yet available for a change of pace and especially popular on weekends.

Just as there were two golf clubs in Montevideo, there were two yacht clubs, both located in Pocitos where we lived. Unlike the in-town golf club, however, these two clubs showed their age and the effects of struggling to survive in a weak economy. Still, they offered their amenities to the dedicated saltwater sportsman, and while there were far fewer diplomats interested in sailing than in golfing, I looked forward to renewing my interest in this sport which I had been unable to do since leaving British Guiana.

In 1969 the new chancery building was completed and USIS, along with other U.S. Embassy offices, moved into the new quarters. The building was designed by the well-known Chinese-American architect, I. M. Pei. Ten years earlier he had submitted what turned out to be the competitive winning design, but a decade had passed before the Congress provided the funds necessary for construction of the new building.

Located at a site on the *Rambla Republica Argentina*, it overlooked the Rio de La Plata. The "Rambla" was a wide avenue that ran along the shore of the river providing easy access to various parts of the city. The new building was attractive and generally practical, a far cry from the offices of the embassy and USIS which had been in old buildings in downtown Montevideo, except for one important element—the new chancery's lack of climate control.

For USIS staffers, being located in the same building as the ambassador and his staff and other mission officials with whom we frequently consulted, instead of seven blocks away, was a great advantage. Furthermore, being in a building that was built to take care of such USIS needs as a radio studio and a photo lab, was also a great asset. Unfortunately, the building's design did not take into account that in a developing country the supply of electricity is not always dependable. By the summer of 1969 periodic electrical shortages in Montevideo were common. Although the building had its own electric generator for emergency purposes, this was insufficient for running the air conditioning system for the long periods that outside electricity was unavailable that year. Had it been possible to open the many large bay windows of the chancery, the breezes blowing off the river could enter and cool the offices. But the windows could not be opened. The architects had made an invalid assumption—that a normal supply of electricity would always be available. So while the new facilities were a great improvement over our old offices, whenever the electricity in our area was shut down because of fuel shortages, a frequent occurrence in the summer, the heat would build up inside the building until it became almost unbearable. As the employees sweltered, many wished they were back in the old rented buildings where they at least worked in relative comfort.

The following year (1970) the Spanish version of a book which had become a best seller in Europe and the U.S., appeared for the first time in Uruguayan bookstores. Entitled *The American Challenge* by the French writer J. J. Servan-Schreiber, it quickly sold out in Montevideo as it had elsewhere, though many Uruguayans who were familiar with the title through reviews and conversation had not actually read it.

The American Challenge presented the U.S. in a highly favorable light, exemplified by one of its chapters entitled "Investment in Man." It also presented strong arguments against the penchant of so many Latin American governments for nationalization; it destroyed Marxist arguments voiced widely and loudly in Uruguay by communist/leftist groups concerning U.S. "ulterior" motives, e.g., "domination," "imperialism"; etc.; and it discussed solutions to social/economic problems which were as valid in Latin America as in Europe.

Recognizing this as something that could enhance U.S. goals, I decided that we should promulgate this book to the greatest extent possible. Its author, being a Frenchman, strengthened its acceptability as an objective analysis of U.S. actions and motives. Furthermore, despite the wide publicity this book received, the local leftist press, including the leading weekly leftist publication *Marcha,* understandably ignored Servan-Schreiber's book in view of its obvious pro-U.S. views.

The first thing we did was to obtain about twenty-five "presentation copies" from our regional book office in Buenos Aires. We sent them to twenty-five leading Uruguayan communicators accompanied by a personal letter from me as the press attaché in which I noted the book's worldwide popularity and interest. I received a number of personal and written expressions of thanks from many of the recipients.

Secondly, we asked USIA to obtain the rights for us to use a synthesis of the book which had appeared in the July 1968 issue of *Harper's* magazine This we used in a monthly Spanish-language publication prepared by USIS Montevideo entitled *Documentos y Referencias* which went to leading governmental and political figures and communicators. We also made copies in English and distributed these to embassy officers for the edification of those not already familiar with *The American Challenge,* enabling them to talk knowingly about the Servan-Schreiber thesis with their Uruguayan contacts.

Thirdly, the local producer of a popular Friday night television talk show, *Conozca Su Derecha* (Know Your Rights), was encouraged to discuss the book on his program. USIS provided presentation copies to the participants, plus copies of the author's synopsis as printed in *Documentos y Referencias.* We also encouraged a number of highly capable, democratically oriented individuals to participate in the TV program.

The interest generated by the TV discussion of this book encouraged the producer of *Conozca Su Derecha* to stay with this theme for five two-hour programs, from March 5th to April 30, 1970. One of these programs, although scheduled for two hours, lasted two and one-half hours because of the heat of the discussion and Uruguay's lax TV time schedules!

The first program consisted of a presentation of the book's theme by Dr. Daniel Ferrer-Lamaisson, a Uruguayan lawyer who was an employee of the Standard Oil Company. Going far beyond a simple presentation of a synopsis of the book, he used charts, well-prepared statistics, and other aids to brilliantly demonstrate why modern American business methods are so successful and should be imitated in Latin America. As for Marxism, he noted that in comparing modern concepts with Marxist ones, the ideas of one man (Marx) in one place (England) more than a hundred years ago have long since proven to be fallacious (as many in the Soviet Union and Eastern Europe were to admit twenty years later).

Only two television programs on this subject were initially scheduled. But because the first two were so popular, the series was expanded to five programs with twelve participants, among them a leading local leftist intellectual who agreed to participate. The participants debated the issues raised by *The American Challenge,* especially as they related to the social/economic problems of Uruguay.

Telephone calls to the station concerning the program were numerous. A bookstore near the university in Montevideo sold fifty copies of the book on the morning after the first program was aired! And there was a run on the book at the Biblioteca Artigas-Washington, the USIS Information Center library in downtown Montevideo.

MARCHA, the weekly leftist publication usually read by most Uruguayan intellectuals, mentioned *The American Challenge* for the first time following its exposure in the television programs. This was done in a long "letter to the editor" which attempted, rather unsuccessfully, to discredit Dr. Ferrer-Lamaisson's presentation on the first program. This was followed by Ferrer-Lamaisson's rebuttal published in the same section of *MARCHA.*

Thus *The American Challenge* was creatively used to advance U.S. foreign policy objectives: advocating a free-market economy and U.S. business methods. This would not have been possible had it not been for the alertness, effectiveness, and capability of USIS Montevideo.

One of the pleasures of working at a USIS post abroad was the opportunity to meet talented and successful visiting Americans from all walks of life, though nothing is as stimulating as meeting American actors and artists of international fame.

In 1969, a great American musician and composer, Duke Ellington, came to Uruguay on a Latin American tour with some members of his band. The tour was sponsored by the U.S. Department of State. This meant that USIS officers overseas were responsible for helping to plan his programs, publicize his visit, provide local logistics, and assist him in each city visited. Ellington was about seventy years old at the time.

One afternoon a group of us were sitting with him in a snack shop near our office where we had gone to take a coffee break and to discuss with him his program for that evening and the next day. Most of us drank coffee but he ordered a coca cola. He then asked for the sugar bowl and proceeded to put spoonful after spoonful of sugar into his drink, stir it, drink a little, then add some more sugar. The sugar must have been the source of his phenomenal energy, though it also allegedly offsets certain narcotic effects.

That evening he was the star attraction at a reception in his honor at the ambassador's residence. Long after the guests had left, he sat down at the piano, about 1 a.m., and started playing. About 2:30 a.m. the ambassador's wife suggested that he might want to call it a night. Most of us who were gathered around the piano could have listened to this great American musician for many more hours, but the Duke graciously got up, thanked the ambassador and his wife for their hospitality, and said his goodbyes. As we were walking down the street with him, ACAO Jake Gillespie who was his "control officer," told him how he wished he could have kept playing the piano and expressed regret that the ambassador's wife had suggested in so many words that it was time to leave. The Duke replied, "Well, I've been thrown out of better places than that."

The well known Hollywood humorist, Danny Kaye, also visited Montevideo that year either on a private visit or in connection with his work with UNICEF. PAO Art Diggle was holding a reception for another American visitor at the time, the sister of Senator Hubert Humphrey. The Senator's sister was a woman who devoted her energies to economic assistance activities as an employee of the Agency for International Development and was second only to her distinguished brother in the ability to talk. After some effort Diggle located Kaye and invited him to the affair that evening. The Hollywood star agreed to attend but only after being told it would be "a small reception."

Looking as if he had just stepped out of a motion picture screen, Danny Kaye was, of course, the main attraction of the evening. But before the evening ended he expressed some annoyance with his host when he realized that Diggle's definition of a "small reception" turned out to be one for about 200 people. As word had spread that afternoon that Danny Kaye would be there, unlike normal diplomatic receptions, no one turned down the invitation to this one.

USIA in the 1960s and 1970s was very much involved in sponsoring, with the Department of State, U.S. music, dance, and theatrical groups on foreign tours, though eventually costs of such large groups increased so much that, as a rule, full U.S. government sponsorship became generally limited to groups sent "behind the Iron Curtain." USIS Montevideo always tried to get USIA Washington to include Montevideo in the itinerary of any performing artist scheduled to visit nearby Buenos Aires. This was sometimes possible but never a sure thing. Uruguay was a low-priority country in the view of those in Washington responsible for cultural programming, given its small size, location, and relative unimportance to U.S. foreign relations.

Another notable U.S. artist who came to Montevideo, though not under USIA sponsorship, was Howard Mitchell, Director of the Washington, D.C. National Symphony Orchestra. He was a guest conductor of the Uruguayan government- sponsored SODRE Orchestra for several weeks each year. USIS cultural attaché Nathan Rosenfeld helped locate living quarters for him and his wife, and during his brief stay, he was a regular invitee to Embassy and USIS receptions. In 1970, as my family and I were about to go on home leave, Rosenfeld arranged for the maestro and Mrs. Mitchell to live in our house while we were on home leave.

USIS activities also brought us into contact from time to time with high government officials from presidents on down, with many Congressmen and, to a lesser degree, Senators, and top-flight foreign correspondents. These meetings with accomplished and distinguished Americans from all walks of life always added spice to our lives in the Foreign Service.

Uruguay in the late 1960s was a country beset by many seemingly unsolvable problems. It was not only the shortages of such things as electricity and potatoes. For example, for four months there were no daily newspapers because the printers were on strike. One simply adjusted to doing without many things usually taken for granted in a normal, peaceful, developed society.

The postal service, essential for any modern society to function efficiently, was one of the most bloated, ineffective government organizations in Uruguay. One could sympathize with the plight of the postal managers and their employees. As living costs rose, salaries in real terms declined, and the postal service, like most Uruguayan government agencies, could not afford to fire anyone because the cost to do so, given the absurd welfare laws of the state, far exceeded the cost of keeping surplus employees on the payroll.

USIS became especially concerned about the postal service when an international agreement between the U.S. and Latin American countries suddenly was ignored by the Uruguayan postal officials. This agreement provided reciprocal host country franking privileges for all official government mail of the signatory nations. However, because the postal system was in such dire straits, someone had decided that one way to raise funds was to abolish the franking privilege of the American Embassy (USIS). Henceforth USIS would have to pay postage for all the invitations to cultural events, magazines, and other materials sent to Uruguayan citizens by mail. This seemed like a good idea to the postal authorities, except that it violated an international treaty that required reciprocal franking privileges for official government mail of countries in North and South America.

Although USIS officers had little personal contact with postal officials heretofore, there was now an urgent reason to call on them. If this problem remained unresolved, USIS publications would not reach their intended audiences, even though the postal service was a haphazard operation at best. If USIS had to begin paying postage, its costs would skyrocket. Retrenchment of our programs would be sure to follow.

The friendship of the postmaster general and his deputy was, for the first time, assiduously cultivated. My administrative assistant and I called on them and were warmly received. Both expressed great friendship and admiration for the United States and were quick to discuss not only their own dilemma with outdated equipment, inefficient employees, and lack of needed funding, but also the problems of handling the voluminous propaganda sent out by the Soviets and other communist embassies in Uruguay. A tour behind the scenes of the main post office facility in Montevideo verified what the post office directors told us. Mail was piled up in what appeared to be a very chaotic fashion, causing us to wonder how anyone in Uruguay ever received a letter. It was obvious that the local postal officials were simply swamped by those factors mentioned earlier. In trying to abolish the franking privilege of the American Embassy they were simply seeking a way to obtain more much needed funding for their postal operations.

We invited both directors of the postal service to embassy and USIS functions whenever feasible, and while the problem was not solved immediately and required the intervention of the Uruguayan Foreign Office, eventually the franking privilege was restored in accordance with the treaty. Like a bad law, however, this was a bad treaty for Uruguay and most other small countries who were in no position to take advantage of utilizing the mail services of other nations on anything like the scale used by the United States. However, *rebus sic stantibus* ("all treaties must be served") prevailed. (The treaty was eventually changed to a more just system.)

If I had any doubts about the efficiency of the Uruguayan mail system before this incident arose, my doubts were confirmed afterwards. Our friendship with the Uruguayan postal officials had so developed that the assistant postmaster sent me a Christmas card that year. It arrived in February.

Charmaine and I considered ourselves among the luckiest and happiest of people, with four healthy youngsters, a profession which I found fascinating, and one which provided us with the means to travel to exotic places while we were still young and energetic enough to put up with occasional hardships. Often in our travels we noted older people, euphemistically now referred to as "seniors," and counted our blessings, for we were seeing parts of the world that many others would not see until their retirement years, if then, and at a time of life when our youth gave us the vigor and stamina to accept the frequent unknown challenges of traveling in strange places.

On May 16, 1969, I rushed Charmaine to the British Hospital, where, a few hours later, she delivered our second son, Mark. He would grow up to be a tall, thin, blue-eyed blond, very much favoring his father's Scandinavian background. But while our family life and my professional career were smoothly and satisfyingly developing, we were not untouched by tragedy.

During our stay in Uruguay I served under three excellent ambassadors. First Henry Hoyt, then Charles Adair, and finally Robert Sayre. Each was a highly regarded professional Foreign Service officer. Montevideo was not the kind of post considered as being a political plum, thus the ambassadorship usually went to the professionals rather than political appointees.

Among the tragedies touching us first was one that occurred on a hot, summer day when the embassy staff had gathered for a picnic. That afternoon I was asked if I wanted to join in a softball game but declined as baseball was never my forte and the heat was oppressive. Ambassador Henry Hoyt, however, perhaps felt he couldn't say no. He went out to the mound and pitched for one of the teams. I went on to other things and about the third inning was attracted by much commotion and shouting. The ambassador had collapsed while on the mound. He was carried over into the shade at the side of a nearby building, apparently suffering from a heart attack. Taken to the British Hospital by a local ambulance, he did not survive.

At his funeral in Montevideo a few days later, the Uruguayan government and public outdid themselves in expressing their grief and in honoring the fallen ambassador with their condolences and military honors befitting a hero. He had won many friends for the United States among the Uruguayans. Many Uruguayans seemed genuinely to have been as shocked, and felt his loss as strongly, as those of us who worked closely with him on an almost daily basis.

A second tragedy that touched us through personal connections occurred about a year later. I was traveling in the interior with the new ambassador and a few of his aides on one of his first orientation trips. We visited an air base where the commandant, a tall, handsome, congenial colonel, held a memorable luncheon in the ambassador's honor. Two weeks later a small group of U.S. Air Force officers flew into Uruguay in a plane that was being shown to various friendly Latin American governments with a view to selling this particular type of plane to them. A demonstration flight was planned for the Uruguayan Air Force, which, as one can imagine, given the size of Uruguay, was not very large. It took place at the air base where we had accompanied the ambassador about a fortnight before.

The flight prepared to take off. The air base commandant was on board, plus about a dozen other officers and men who wanted to see how the aircraft performed. The Uruguayan Air Force was always short on planes and fuel to fly them, so any chance to get airborne was not to be lost.

As the motors were being started, a young cadet came running toward the plane and they let him board, then took off. It was a short flight. Ten minutes in the air, while exercising a special maneuver, the motors faltered, stopped, and the plane crashed. All on board were killed. It was a tragedy shared by the whole country as well as we Americans who had known the base commander and some of his staff, not to mention the loss of the American pilot and his colleagues.

Because the Uruguayan Air Force was so small, the officers and men were like a close-knit family. This not only made the deaths of fourteen of their number a massive loss to that institution, but was also the more painful because most of the men lost were personally known by their colleagues throughout the country.

These tragedies affected the individuals involved and their families, friends, and acquaintances, but the entire Uruguayan society, which continued to suffer from many ills, would soon experience a sad, tragic development that would touch all Uruguayans one way or another, and some foreigners as well. Tremendous frustration at the deteriorating economy and the lack of political will, or simply the inability of the country's leaders to stop that deterioration, increased the despair felt by many Uruguayans with regard to their future.

There were those who believed that all hope for a better and more equitable life in Uruguayan society had disappeared. Destruction of the old society began to be seen by some as a solution to their ills, just as, elsewhere in the world, under similar conditions, some groups turn to violence when hope no longer exists. The unsuspecting citizens of Montevideo would soon experience the nightmarish hell of terrorism on a major scale.

In late 1969 rumors began to circulate about a secretive group of Uruguayans who called themselves the *Tupamaros*. Little was known about them except that they were presumed to consist primarily of leftist university students disenchanted with the way Uruguayan society functioned, or, better said, malfunctioned.

One evening I was having a drink in a downtown bar with a local editor of one of Montevideo's many dailies when he showed me a scribbled note he had received which said, in effect, that the Tupamaros would change Uruguayan society in the near future. He laughed and said, "Who are these people? They must be a bunch of nuts. No one seems to know anything about them." Cazala, the USIS press chief, was with us. He and I nodded our heads. We had heard little about them and could add nothing to the conversation.

Latin America at the time was convulsive. Communist influence seemed to be growing; U.S. "imperialism" was still in the vocabulary of many Latin American leaders; violent revolution was still seen by some as the only solution to the continent's ills; some members of the predominant religion in Latin America, Catholicism, were seeking solutions to social and economic problems at odds with traditional Catholic leaders; and Fidel Castro and Che Guevara were considered by leftist university students in particular as being the role models for the revolutions they felt society needed and which would surely soon develop.

In Bolivia Che Guevara had tried to start the type of revolution some envisioned as needed to bring Latin America out of the decadence, corruption, and unsatisfactory social and economic situations in which many countries found themselves. Guevara ended up, however, for a variety of reasons, being killed by Bolivian army troops in the Bolivian jungle.

The Associated Press bureau chief in Montevideo had gone briefly to Bolivia to cover the story of Che Guevara's demise. It was a grim tale. I saw photos that he showed me that the AP had not used, perhaps because they were too grim, of Bolivian troops, after they had captured him and presumably killed him, trying to boil his body in a large oil drum. However, human bodies are difficult to destroy. The Bolivian solders who tried to burn and boil his body were only partially successful, though his final resting place was a well-kept secret for a long time. The Bolivian government and others interested in Guevara's fate did not want Guevara's gravesite to become a rallying point for leftist revolutionists. As it was, he became their leading martyr.

In this period of Latin America's historical development, communism was still seen by many as the answer to society's woes. For some, violent revolution was also viewed as a necessary first step if society were to change for the better. In this kind of political climate Montevideo became the birthplace of the Tupamaro terrorists, a clandestine organization which would spread havoc among the Uruguayans and adversely affect Americans and other nationalities before being squashed in perhaps as ruthless a manner as the Tupamaros themselves utilized in their determination to destroy the society that had nourished them. Unfortunately, no one to this day has found a way to fight terrorism by means other than those often initiated by the terrorists themselves. It is this requirement, to fight fire with fire as it were, that immediately brings criticism down upon the head of any governing body fighting for its survival against a well-organized, clandestine, determined terrorist organization. The advent of the Tupamaros began a new, violent chapter in modern Uruguayan history.

The Tupamaro terrorists were named after Inca Prince Tupac Ameru who fought against Spanish rule in Peru in the eighteenth century. It is ironic that two centuries later, the organization that undertook urban guerrilla warfare in Uruguay, a country that never had an indigenous Indian population, took its name from an historic Indian figure.

Though little was known about the Tupamaros in the late sixties, they were founded in 1963 as the *Movimiento de Liberacion Nacional* (National Liberation Movement), or MLN. According to Claire Sterling in his 1991 book *The Terror Network: The Secret War of International Terrorism*, "their ranks consisted of teachers, lawyers, doctors, dentists, accountants, bankers, architects, engineers, a model, a radio announcer, and an actress." Not all of these people were among those who, about five years after the creation of the MLN, allegedly to bring about revolutionary change in Uruguay, would pull the triggers and become active terrorists. But all who supported the Tupamaros must share the guilt for the chaos, personal tragedies, and destruction they sowed, whether they became active Tupamaro members because they were true believers; whether they were merely sympathizers who naively thought that this was a means of instigating positive change; or whether they joined just to get their jollies.

In the earlier years, the Tupamaros were not taken seriously by those who knew of some of their activities, though initially most Uruguayans knew nothing of their existence. They fostered a Robin Hood image of themselves by such activities, for example, as hijacking a truck en route to a supermarket and distributing its contents in a poor neighborhood, or robbing a gambling casino and distributing the loot to the presumed needy. In 1969, however, as Sterling notes, the Tupamaro's leader, Raul Sendic, said, "We now have three hundred kilometers of streets and avenues at our disposal to organize guerrilla warfare," which they did. In two years, starting in 1970, to quote Sterling, "they bombed, burned, robbed, kidnapped, and killed with a dazzling display of nerve, skill, discipline, inventiveness, and bravado."

For a variety of reasons I had delayed taking home leave until early 1970. We had been in Uruguay nearly three-and-a-half years by then. Although the social and economic climate continued to deteriorate, and there was more and more talk about the activities of the Tupamaros, we expected to return after our leave for another two-year tour. Uruguay was still a generally pleasant place to be assigned. We, like almost everyone else, could not imagine how drastically conditions would change as the Tupamaros increased their activities. We had reached the point, however, where we rode to and from the office in car pools as a security measure and took other precautions, which, until early 1970, never really seemed necessary. Several leading Uruguayan officials had been kidnapped by the Tupamaros, though most had been released, and few foreigners, if any, had, as yet, been directly affected.

One morning, on our way to work, the road was blocked ahead of us and we had to make a detour. An army general had been killed by machine gun bullets as he rounded a curve while driving to work on the Rambla, the latest victim of the Tupamaros who shot him from a passing car. Had we been a few minutes earlier we might have been rounding the same curve at the same time. Yet these incidents still seemed isolated with little expectation that they would ever affect us directly.

We left Montevideo on home leave in July 1970. As was our custom, we took leave en route to visit Charmaine's relatives in Trinidad and to visit Barbados again. In Miami, a few weeks later, we met Charmaine's cousin at the airport as she was flying back to her home in Amarillo,

Texas after a family visit to Trinidad. When we saw her in Trinidad she had agreed to take care of our youngest son, Mark, now a year old, while Charmaine and I and our other four youngsters planned to tour the U.S. from Florida to Canada towing a "Scamper" behind our rental car. The Scamper, in which the six of us were able to sleep, was loaned to us by a Foreign Service colleague, Doug Zischke. We would retrieve Mark in Texas on our way back to Florida to return the car and the Scamper.

Before picking up the Scamper from Zischke's parents in Fort Myers, Fla., we stayed at the Rodney Motel in Miami Beach. When I phoned USIA headquarters in Washington to let them know of my whereabouts, the Latin American Area Director, Lyle Coppman, had some startling news for me. He told me that he had received a message from the ambassador in Montevideo that my family and I were not to return to Uruguay. He did not say why, but the assumption was that this had something to do with the Tupamaros. I could not believe that, even if this were the case, we would be unable to return to pack our belongings for shipment to a new post. I also thought that, surely, with about six weeks ahead of us for home leave and consultation in Washington, there would be time to work things out. In any event, Coppman informed me that he was planning to send me to Bolivia for my next assignment. This would be my first assignment as a USIS director (PAO), which pleased me. I was not too upset about having to leave Montevideo and felt confident that by the time our home leave ended I would be given permission to return to Uruguay for a few days to supervise the packing of our belongings.

In Washington I spent a few days of consultations in various agency offices but when the question came up with regard to my return to Montevideo to pack our belongings, the ambassador's decision remained firm. I could only surmise that as the highly visible press attaché of the U.S. Embassy who had traveled around the country with three ambassadors with whom I appeared occasionally in press photos, I had possibly been placed on a Tupamaro hit list that had come to someone's attention. It was known that ambassadors were well guarded and therefore not good targets for kidnapping. Members of the ambassador's staff, while not as valued for propaganda purposes, were usually much more vulnerable. Yet, as we were about to head for Canada for a brief visit with a cousin in Toronto, I still expected that in a month's time the situation might change enough to enable us to return to Uruguay briefly for our personal effects.

Charmaine was particularly distraught at the idea of someone else packing our belongings for shipment to Bolivia. In our rush to prepare for our home leave with five children to be concerned about, she had simply shoved anything that couldn't be cleaned or properly stored into the master bedroom which, when we left, had the appearance of a warehouse. The door was locked as everything there was to be undisturbed until our return. The Director of the National Symphony Orchestra in Washington, D.C., Howard Mitchell, was in Uruguay for a few weeks as guest conductor of Uruguay's national symphony orchestra. He and his wife were using our guest room and the rest of the house during our absence and would have left by the time we were expected to return.

While we were in Washington, we were staying at a friend's house in Falls Church, Virginia while the owners were on vacation. From there it was an easy bus ride to USIA headquarters for my consultations and to the State Department medical division for our periodic medical exams.

One morning before going into the office I picked up the morning newspaper. There, on the front page, was a photo of my colleague, Nathan Rosenfeld, the cultural attaché of our embassy in Montevideo! As I read the details of the article under the photo, I realized that the car pool in which I generally rode with Rosenfeld and Gordon Jones, the Commercial Attaché, and sometimes a few others, had been attacked by the Tupamaros.

The normal procedure was for an embassy driver and Jones, who was the first to be picked up, to enter the basement garage of the apartment building where Rosenfeld lived, meet him there and then pick me up a few minutes later in the front of my house, a few blocks away. The morning before Rosenfeld made the front page of *The Washington Post,* the Tupamaros had been laying in wait in the garage when Rosenfeld stepped out of the elevator and walked to the waiting embassy vehicle. As he went to enter the car, one of the terrorists struck him in the head with the butt of a pistol, knocking him to the basement floor. They then grabbed the commercial attaché who was sitting in the back seat of the embassy vehicle, pistol whipped him also, carried him to the back of a pickup truck, wrapped him in a rug which they had ready for that purpose, and drove speedily out of the garage. He was enveloped in the rug in the back of the truck. When Rosenfeld recovered his senses, with the help of the driver he staggered back to his apartment and phoned the embassy to alert them about the attack and the kidnapping.

After going a few blocks the kidnappers came to a red traffic light. Not wanting to attract undue attention, they obeyed the traffic signal. Jones, who had not been knocked out, realized that if he was going to escape he had better do it as soon as possible. Although he could not move very well, bundled as he was in a rug, and could not, of course, see anything, he knew the truck carrying him had stopped for some reason. He made a supreme effort to kick and roll and move until he reached the back of the truck, which was still stopped, fell down onto the pavement behind it, then got to his feet and jumped to where he didn't know. The terrorists, fearing that if they tried to recapture their prey they might get caught, fled as soon as the light turned green. Passersby rushed to Jones' assistance and unrolled the rug. In this unique manner he saved himself from spending weeks or months in captivity or of being murdered. Others were not so fortunate.

The same day that my car pool was attacked the Tupamaros kidnapped Daniel A. Mitrione, a U.S. advisor to the Uruguayan government. Mitrione was assigned by the Agency for International Development (AID) to train the Uruguayan police force in more effective and efficient police administration. Before joining AID he had been the police chief in Richmond, Indiana. His wife and their nine children had been in Uruguay with him for several years. I knew him well from trips we had made around the country with the ambassadors. He always handled security liaison matters with local police forces during those visits while I handled the ambassador's public relations.

With the attack on my car pool and the kidnapping of Dan Mitrione, the Tupamaros were now including U.S. government representatives among their targets. Their rationale for such attacks, presumably, was the assistance the U.S. government was providing the Montevideo police, the military, and various government entities under U.S. economic assistance programs. They probably selected the commercial attaché because he was a young man who drove around town in a red sports car exhibiting, to a certain extent, those Americanisms associated with youth, wealth, and the enjoyment that that combination usually produces. They were, in short, jealous, particularly given their own situation.

Perhaps Jones would not have been targeted had he been a little less visible as an embassy official. As for the kidnapping of Mitrione on the same morning, the Tupamaros let it be known that, according to them, Mitrione had been teaching the local police "North American torture methods." Of course, anyone who has lived in Latin America or knows the history of that region, knows that such methods need not be taught by anyone from outside. The accusation was an excuse. The reality was that although the commercial attaché had escaped with his life, Mitrione was the more important victim of the Tupamaros and although falsely accused, he would not escape.

"At 5:00 a.m. on Monday, August 10, 1970, the body of a stocky, unshaven, fifty-year old man was found in the back seat of a stolen Buick in Montevideo, Uruguay, his blood still dripping through the floor board and running toward the curb. He had been dead for about an hour, shot twice in the head and twice in the body. There were three deep bruises at his left armpit close to a partially healed gunshot wound. His inner arms bore sixteen needle punctures." That is how Ernest W. Lefever, senior scholar at the Brookings Institution who conducted extensive research about the Tupamaros and other terrorist groups, described the scene of that frightful Monday morning when the world learned of Dan Mitrione's fate.

At the time the AID advisor was the fifth kidnap victim of the Tupamaros and their twelfth murder victim, according to Lefever. Lefever noted in his monograph, *Murder in Montevideo: The Dan Mitrione Story*, that Mitrione "had been 'tried' by a Tupamaro 'people's court' and condemned to death for allegedly being a 'CIA agent'; for 'teaching the Uruguayan police advanced torture techniques'; and for 'organizing fascist death squads to kill 'revolutionary leaders.'" None of this was true.

The Mitrione murder marked an acceleration of Tupamaro activities and an expansion of those activities to foreign nationals. During the next two years a Brazilian diplomat was abducted; the British Ambassador, Sir Geoffrey Jackson (who had a reputation for not taking his bodyguards seriously) was kidnapped and spent eight months in a cage six feet long by two feet wide; and numerous Uruguayan officials or former officials lost their liberty, such as the president of the state-owned utilities corporation, Ulysses Pereira Reverbel; the industrial leader Ricardo Ferres; and the former Minister of Agriculture, Carlos Frick Davie. Their victims also included the head of internal security for Punta Carretas prison, where many Tupamaros would eventually reside; a former undersecretary of the interior; two high-ranking police officers; and a naval captain. In addition to kidnapping for which the large ransoms paid in many instances provided them with funds, they invaded and occupied airstrips, police stations, telephone exchanges, and radio stations.

By 1972 what they had achieved was not a revolutionary society, but a reversion to one of the oldest forms of government known to man—a military dictatorship, brought about by the necessity to end the chaos and disintegration of society that the Tupamaros instigated. By the summer of 1970 civil rights were suspended and again in January 1971 as the Tupamaro terror escalated. In mid-1972 the National Assembly declared a "state of internal war," in which, for all practical purposes, the armed forces became the rulers of the country.

By the end of 1972, 2,600 Tupamaros, "real or alleged" according to Claire Sterling, were in prison; forty had died; and their leader, Raul Sendic, had been captured. The legacy of the Tupamaros was a society that was in greater economic and social disarray than when the Tupamaros had begun their frightful games; the loss of freedom for the electorate for the next decade and a half while the country remained under military rule; and the personal tragedies experienced by those who had been killed, maimed, and their lives and those of their families disrupted.

In examining how a relatively small group of misguided individuals could produce the horrors that the Tupamaros wrought, Clair Sterling suggests that they "did not dream it all up out of nowhere." He notes that they had been sending their adherents to Havana for training since 1968, after Raul Sendic met personally with Fidel Castro. A guidebook they used was the *Mini-Manual* published in 1969 by Carlos Marighella. A member of Brazil's pro-Moscow Communist Party for forty years, Marighella was an intimate of Castro and a frequent visitor to Cuba, according to Sterling.

The *Mini-Manual* became well known in Latin America and beyond among those groups looking for lessons in terrorist techniques or for anyone combating terrorism. In forty-eight succinctly written pages Marighella's manual explained why cities are better than rural areas for guerrilla operations; suggested how to drill in urban courtyards; how to blow up bridges and railroad tracks; how to raise money by kidnap ransoms; how to plan the "physical liquidation" of ranking army officers and policemen; how to deal with spies and informers; and other terrorist tidbits. As Sterling noted, "It is also a clinical study of the step-by-step tactics in the strategy of terror whereby the Tupamaros deliberately destroyed democracy in their country."

Though Marighella died before the Tupamaros applied his lessons to Uruguayan society, they were the first to do so outside Brazil. In Brazil, like Uruguay, terrorists provoked the militarists to hold power to combat them much longer than might otherwise have occurred.

Among others who followed the Uruguayan experience were Germans in 1969 who called themselves "the Tupamaros of West Berlin" and the U.S. Weathermen's Bernardine Dohrn bragged about her group's "adaptation to the Tupamaros' classic guerrilla strategy." The original Tupamaros, who were not very original, also maintained ties with such groups as the ETA in Spain, the IRA Provisionals, the German and Italian undergrounds, and Palestinian terrorist organizations, according to Sterling.

Next door in Argentina, the terror of the left led to terror from the right, just as occurred in Uruguay. One of the editors of a Catholic-oriented, conservative newspaper in Montevideo, Edgardo Sajon, whom I had come to know quite well as he was a friendly, personable journalist with strong anti-communist leanings, left Montevideo and took a job a few months later as press secretary to the president of Argentina. He was murdered, presumably, not from the left, but from the right, despite his conservative stance. The May 30, 1985 issue of *The Washington Times* in a story written by Timothy O'Leary and datelined Buenos Aires, begins:

> In September 1978, Carlos Alberto Hours, then a Buenos Aires policeman, was ordered to witness the electrocution of former presidential press secretary Edgardo Sajon on a wet billiard table in a room in the Juan Vucetich school. Mr. Hours said he had been ordered to report to a Lt. Col. Munoz to 'see something' and be taught a 'lesson' for having denounced kidnappings and robberies related to the Argentine military's 'dirty war' against left-wing subversion.

According to O'Leary, " Munoz told Mr. Sajon that he had orders to liquidate him. . . . Sajon was electrocuted on a schoolroom table by attaching cables to the little toe of one foot and his mouth. They put the naked cadaver into a plastic bag and buried it near a tree several meters away from the school." The above was but one of what O'Leary described as "similar bone-chilling accounts of murder, torture, clandestine body dumping and unbridled terror," performed, presumably, this time, by the right rather than the left. Terror begets terror. By the time the Tupamaro phenomenon had passed into history, the military in Uruguay, like those in Argentina, had adopted, apparently, some of the methods the Tupamaros themselves had initiated.

In October 1986, some twenty-three years after the Tupamaros were first organized and some fourteen years after they had been defeated, Raul Sendic, their recognized leader, was interviewed by an Argentine magazine, *El Porteño Cooperativo*. By then the Tupamaros had become a legal political party in Uruguay, which in December 1985 attracted about a thousand people to an open convention. They tried to join the Broad Front, a leftist political coalition that held about 20 percent of the seats in the parliament, but were rejected by the small Christian Democratic Party.

Sendic, then in his sixties, was interviewed in Geneva. He had spent thirteen years in Uruguayan prisons for his Tupamaro activities but had learned little, saying that the Tupamaros remained "undefeated." Citing upheavals in neighboring Brazil, Argentina, and Chile, he claimed all those governments, as well as Uruguay, were *"fascistas"* to which the only answer was the one given by the Tupamaros.

Uruguayan President Julio Maria Sanguinetti presented another view of the Tupamaros when he was quoted by Shirley Christian in the *New York Times* (Nov. 3, 1986) as saying that the Tupamaro phenomenon was an "accident" in Uruguayan life, born of the "radicalization of a typical bourgeois sector—pseudo-intellectual—that one day said let's have a revolution here." After that came the years of repression by military forces unprepared for political warfare.

Just as Raul Sendic, years after the Tupamaro terrorists had been defeated, said that the creation of the Tupamaros was "a reply to fascism," José Mujica Cordano, the secretary general of the new Tupamaro political party, also said, "Our violence was a reply to fascism." Mujica Cordano by then was fifty-two years old, a veteran of fifteen years in prison during four periods, having escaped twice. His last stretch, thirteen years, ended when President Sanguinetti declared an amnesty shortly after his inauguration. For Dan Mitrione and others who were victims of the Tupamaros, there was no amnesty.

In 1967, a leftist Chilean magazine, *Punta Final*, was among the first to publicize the developing Uruguayan organization known as the Tupamaros. The article, focusing on the philosophy of the Tupamaros, said quite amply and clearly that they were nihilists. It stated that they offered no program, nothing positive, nothing constructive; "they claim, in effect, that modern society is so evil only its destruction can save man; after destroying society, they would leave it for someone else to pick up the pieces and figure out how and in what form civilization should be rebuilt. They are like the poor boy who plunged a knife into the heart of a crippled neighborhood playmate and when asked why he did it, responded, 'I wanted to be somebody.' "

To really understand the Tupamaro phenomenon, nothing more clearly explains the philosophy of their members than a small book published in 1951, two decades before the Tupamaros came on the scene. Entitled *The True Believer*, it was written by the American longshoreman philosopher, Eric Hoffer.

Hoffer called the overwhelming number of "True Believers" people who, for one reason or another, feel their own lives are spoiled or wasted. They are frustrated individuals, the disaffected, the failures, the misfits, the outcasts, criminals and "all those who have lost their footing, or never had one, in the ranks of respectable society. They see their lives spoiled beyond remedy and they are ready to waste and wreck both; hence their recklessness and their will to chaos and anarchy. They also crave to dissolve their spoiled, meaningless selves in some soul-stirring spectacular communal undertaking, hence their proclivity for united action."

What Hoffer described as a "True Believer" fit the character of the typical Tupamaro, of which there were many to study as the Uruguayan jails began to fill with them. Since the terrorist temperament is not the sole prerogative of the underprivileged, it was not surprising to find that many fallen Tupamaros were the sons and daughters of middle and upper-class families, including many university students, who joined terrorist cells as the solution to a personal feeling of inadequacy or frustration from causes that had nothing to do with their economic situation.

Among those attracted to the type of terrorism which the Tupamaros offered their adherents, at least three types of persons analyzed in *The True Believers* fit the mold of many Tupamaros: misfits, selfish, and the bored.

Because many Tupamaro joiners were incomplete and insecure persons who could not generate self-assurance out of their own resources, they hung passionately to the Tupamaro cause. In other words, one became a Tupamaro not because of the alleged justice of its alleged cause, but because of one's own desperate need for something to hold on to. This being the case, he or she would never be weaned away by an appeal to reason or moral sense. Similar to Hoffer's "true believer," a Tupamaro was an "anonymous particle with no will or judgment of his own. The result is not only a compact and fearless following but also a homogeneous plastic mass that can be kneaded at will."

Hoffer tried to show that unification intensifies the propensity to hatred and the imitative capacity. He argued that the unified individual is more credulous and obedient, thus the active Tupamaro was more inclined to be so than the potential Tupamaro who was still an autonomous human being.

The Tupamaros were able to hide their identities for as long as they did by maintaining a cell system of operations. Each cell generally had one woman who provided its male members with all their domestic needs, including sex. She cooked, sewed, made love as needed and joined the raiding parties. In late 1970, one such young, misguided girl wrote a letter to her father that was made public in the hope of saving others from a similar fate. The letter revealed the daughter's disenchantment with her life as the female member of a terrorist cell, but, she noted, she would be killed if she tried to escape. She was trapped, and she knew it, although, unlike Raul Sendic, the leader of the Tupamaros, she eventually had second thoughts about her life as a terrorist.

If Hoffer's philosophical view is correct, the root causes of terrorists like the Tupamaros, who were prevalent in various degrees in a number of Latin American countries in the sixties and seventies, stemmed more from personal than social need. This is not to say that the societies that bred them were not suffering from many ills. Certainly Uruguay was a country with many unsolved problems. Nor does this mean that there are not times when revolution is the only avenue open to a downtrodden society. But terrorism of the type instigated by the Tupamaros was not a solution for Uruguay's problems. The emergence of the Tupamaros, while symbolic, perhaps, of the frustrations experienced by many Uruguayans, made a bad situation infinitely worse. Long after the nightmare years of the Tupamaros ended, Uruguayans suffered incalculable damage in lives lost or ruined, and in the brutal punishment that Tupamaro terrorism dealt to the social, economic, and political fabric of Uruguayan society.

When we returned to Florida at the end of our home leave, having picked up our son Mark in Texas, we fully expected that by then the ambassador would allow one of us to return to Montevideo to pack our household effects for shipment to Bolivia. However, the order for my family and me not to return to Uruguay remained firm. We had no choice but to fly to Bolivia for my new assignment.

How our belongings, left behind in Uruguay, were to be packed and shipped to us in La Paz would be determined after we arrived in Bolivia. So once again we left the United States and headed toward a new life. Although we would spend nearly two years in La Paz, which means "peace" in Spanish, Bolivia was not always the peaceful place that the name of its capital would suggest. Adjusting to living conditions two miles above sea level was challenging enough. Learning to live and work in the volatile social and political Bolivian environment of the early 1970s was an added challenge. How we fared in this new life and learned to love our Bolivian friends despite their idiosyncrasies brought on by lack of oxygen and their isolation in a mountainous, landlocked country is the menu for the next "life."

8
Breathless in Bolivia

"This Bolivian Republic has a special enchantment for me. The more I think about the destiny of the country, the more it seems to me a tiny marvel."
—Simon Bolivar

"No one should live above ten thousand feet."
— Al Hansen

Almost the entire USIS staff turned out to greet us when we arrived at the airport which overlooks the city of La Paz at an altitude of 13,500 feet, more than two-and-a half miles above sea level! They brought seven small oxygen tanks with them in case we needed some oxygen while adjusting to the thin air of the *altiplano*, the high plateau of Bolivia and Peru. Leading the group was Kent Herath, the information officer. He had filled in as acting PAO since the departure, a few weeks earlier, of the former PAO, and until my arrival to take up my new duties as director of USIS La Paz.

Charmaine and I experienced a little lightheadedness from the thin air and were exhausted from our travels. We had left Miami early that morning and landed in Quito and Lima before reaching La Paz. The children, however, were unaffected by the altitude. They were more excited about landing in Bolivia than their parents. They were bubbling over with enthusiasm.

After greeting the USIS staff members who met us at the airport, a convoy of vehicles accompanied us down the winding road that leads from the airport to the center of the city, a thousand feet below. The air at the center of downtown La Paz, at 12,500 feet above sea level, is a little more oxygenated than that at the airport, but not much.

The house we would now call home, which was assigned to the

PAO, was another thousand feet down the valley in a section of the city called Obrajes. Most foreigners stationed in La Paz lived another thousand feet farther down the valley, in Calacoto, which, at 10,500 feet, enjoyed slightly more oxygen than those living above them. This is still two miles above sea level. No matter where one went in Bolivia's capital it was impossible to stay within the city limits and get below the two-mile mark.

The first impression one has upon arriving in La Paz is of a very poor, underdeveloped country struggling for its very existence in an environment made hostile to human habitation by the effects of the altitude and the barrenness of the surrounding mountains. At the height at which La Paz is located, trees and shrubbery are actually above the "tree line." For anything to grow it has to be nourished and extremely hardy. Like the people, however, some trees and plants adjusted to the altitude.

The population of La Paz is predominantly Indian, many of whom do not speak Spanish, at least when first arriving in the city from the hinterland. Quechua and Aymara are the two major indigenous languages spoken by Bolivians although Spanish is the official language and is used by the government, in business, and in social intercourse among the upper economic classes.

When entering the city for the first time we were immediately struck by the poverty and backwardness of Bolivia. The shanties that lined the road as it snakes down from the altiplano to the center of the city were mostly one-story, poorly constructed adobe buildings. The people were poorly dressed and physical labor seemed to predominate over all other forms of energy. One was also struck by the novelty of seeing the Indian women, commonly referred to as *cholas*, in their bright, colorful dresses. But most startling and incongruous were the bowler hats (or, if you prefer, derbies) which all of them wore! We were to learn later that among some of the Indians in Bolivia there is a hat for each tribe and each important occasion.

The universality of the derby worn by the Indian women of Bolivia's capital city is one of the things that makes La Paz unique. How this custom began is a subject of much speculation. The favorite explanation is that in the 19th century an English salesman, en route to Chile with an order for bowler hats (popular among the British at that time) stopped off in La Paz. He started selling the derbies and they became so popular he never went on to Chile. The black bowler hat soon became an item of prestige among the Indian women and eventually developed into the universal custom that it is today. Many women added their own creative styles and colors but the black derby remains to this day as popular as ever. This is in addition to the six to 12 flowing skirts the cholas wear, allowing them, when nature calls, to sit on the curb of any street corner and relieve themselves with a certain degree of privacy and decorum.

The legal capital of Bolivia is Sucre, which is today a small town although it was founded in 1538 and was selected as the capital because of its lower altitude and, therefore, its more appealing climate. Only the Supreme Court remains there to this day, all other government offices having long ago been established in La Paz.

Geology and history account for La Paz becoming the actual Bolivian capital. The edge of the altiplano, where La Paz is located, collapsed at some time in the geological past, causing a great, bowl-shaped depression. While the center of the city, at 12,000 feet, is more than a thousand feet below the high Bolivian plain, the earth sinks another two thousand feet down to the neighborhood known as Calacoto. Established ten years after Sucre, La Paz became a staging post on the silver route from Potosi to Lima (now the capital of Peru).

Its silver mines made Potosi, at the height of its mining activities in the seventeenth century, the largest city in South America, boasting a population of 25,000. As the silver moved by mule train across the harsh terrain of the altiplano, La Paz became a welcomed rest stop. Its valley provided some protection from the wind, rain, snow, and frequent hailstorms which sweep the altiplano. Its lower altitude, though not dramatically lower, was also welcomed. So La Paz grew and, relatively speaking, prospered.

When we reached our new home we could not help but be impressed. The front yard was enclosed by tightly spaced shrubbery which reached to a height of about 25 feet, providing complete privacy for the large front lawn. The house was a white, two-story building with a red tile roof. Although the outside walls of the house were actually made of mud, they were reinforced by a thin cement layer on the outside and mahogany wood and other materials inside. Nicely furnished (since one of the "perks" PAOs received was fully furnished lodgings), the house had a family dining room and a formal dining room, two living rooms, a study, and four bedrooms. Behind the house the property extended to the next block. An unused guest house, which we used for storage when our household effects from Uruguay finally arrived; a small house in which our butler, Simón, and his wife and two children lived; a large garden area; a stable (unused), and a water tower took up the extensive property in the rear of the house. We quickly surmised that it was an ideal arrangement for the diplomatic entertaining which would be expected of us and Charmaine looked with delight at the spacious backyard where a garden, if properly attended, could flourish. There was also room near the old stable for raising chickens and perhaps other fowl.

Kent Herath and his wife, Beverly, who accompanied us and showed us our new quarters, briefed us on such essentials as "don't drink the tap water," and "don't plug anything that's 110 volts into a wall socket—all the outlets are 220." They gave us a "welcome kit" containing essential information for new arrivals and left us a few oxygen tanks in case we needed them. Knowing how sleepy we were from the altitude and our journey, they soon departed. The PAO's driver, Victor, would call for me in the morning and take me to the office for my first look at my "empire." Charmaine and I had no difficulty falling asleep as soon as they left, but the children, too excited to nap, explored their new surroundings as soon as their parents dozed off.

The embassy was located in downtown La Paz in a narrow, six-story building. The reception desk, on the second floor, was reached by a wide, cement staircase inside the building. The staircase was gained from an entrance separate from a bank which was on the ground floor. All the floors above the bank were embassy offices.

The flat roof of the building, accessible from the sixth floor, could be patrolled by the Marine guards. During times of crisis, which were rather frequent, they used it as an observation post. It also supported an array of radio antennae needed for communications. Once when the embassy was under attack by a raging mob in the streets below the Marines were falsely accused of firing at the mob from the rooftop. The iron gates which covered the entrance hall on the ground floor held and the mob eventually dispersed. The entrance to the bank was also well protected with iron bars and other security measures which always held firm during rather frequent demonstrations in the streets of La Paz.

The USIS offices had recently moved into a new building about a block away. Renovations were still underway but a large, heavy iron door was already installed at the entrance which could be quickly closed if necessary. There was always the possibility that the same mobs which might attack the embassy as the Bolivian way of expressing anger or disagreement with U.S. policies would also attack the USIS office. The ground floor, a mezzanine area, and the first floor contained the USIS radio, television, and printing operations. The PAO's office, the cultural affairs operations, and the administrative office were on the second floor. The consulate section of the embassy was on the third floor. Because the volatile local political situation was such that an assault against U.S. offices could occur at any time, special security measures were essential.

Each U.S. installation had a room to which, in an emergency, the staff could retreat if the building came under attack and where they could probably hold out until help arrived. This area also provided a possible escape route. At USIS this special security area was the PAO's office, which was large enough to hold the entire staff. It had a special steel door installed at the entrance to the hallway leading to that office and was protected with special screening over the windows, one small section of which could be opened from the inside to permit escape to a nearby roof if necessary. These precautions seemed elaborate, but the threat to the physical security of personnel and the offices was real. Bolivia had a history of getting a new government on the average of every nine months, counting the number of different governments that had run the country from its independence in 1825 until 1970. Most Bolivian governments came into power by military coups, some bloody, some without blood spilled.

Colonel Juan Torres, the incumbent president of Bolivia, was the most recent military dictator to have grabbed power in a coup. What made him exceptional was that his was a leftist regime, supported by communist and other leftist groups, and, therefore, antagonistic toward the U.S. government. Although diplomatic relations were maintained, those relations were greatly strained. President Torres had already demanded that the U.S. Military Advisory Group leave the country. There was a belief that the Agency for International Development might be next to leave, despite its efforts to provide the Torres government with resources and technical assistance for Bolivia's social and economic development. USIS was also believed to be a possible candidate for expulsion. Therefore, in the first USIS country plan for Bolivia written under my direction, I made the number one objective of the new plan a most unique one—to maintain the USIS presence in La Paz! Washington headquarters approved the plan with very few additions or deletions. Our situation was well known and appreciated by our colleagues in Washington, especially those knowledgeable about Latin America in general and Bolivia in particular.

The USIS American staff, in addition to me, consisted of the information officer who was also the press attaché, Kent Herath; an assistant information officer, Howard Lane; and a cultural affairs officer, Andrew Schwartz. There is nothing like a hardship post to bring people together. Our families all became good friends, spurred on not only by the rustic living conditions we faced together but also by the threat to our personal safety. (If housing was fine, such things as having to boil the water with which we brushed our teeth exemplifies how primitive living conditions were in La Paz.)

The concern for the safety of American officials and their families was always present. This was because the Bolivian government was being run by an anti-American leader who could not be trusted to protect Americans from groups or individuals ready to target them as "Yankee imperialists." It was the Yankees, some Bolivians insisted, who were the cause of Bolivia's backwardness. In this respect they were no different from many frustrated third world citizens who blamed their ills on "Uncle Sam," while being first in line if granted a visa to visit or live in the U.S.

One of the arguments to support the view that Bolivia's ills were caused by U.S. policies was the contention that the U.S., as Bolivia's largest market, controlled the price of tin, Bolivia's leading export. Although the world price was controlled by a marketing arrangement determined by an international council in London, the U.S. was usually the scapegoat for any downward trend in the price of tin. If the price of tin fell by a cent or two, the local economy, continually on the edge of bankruptcy, was seriously affected. Thus Bolivian anxiety about the price of its primary export product on world markets was understandable and was always major news in the local media whenever it went up or down, as it often did. Once when the U.S. government planned to unload some of the tin it had stockpiled for emergency purposes in the event of a war, since much more was on hand than was really needed, many Bolivians reacted as if the U.S. had declared war on them. Taking the Bolivian concerns into consideration, arrangements were made to release the surplus more slowly and over a much longer period of time than originally planned, thereby easing the adverse effects on Bolivian tin sales.

The local staff of USIS La Paz, for the most part, was highly qualified. In Bolivia, like most underdeveloped countries where good paying jobs for qualified people are hard to come by, the excellent, guaranteed salaries, interesting work, and the prestige of being connected with the American Embassy attracted some top media professionals to USIS.

Particularly outstanding among the USIS employees was the cultural affairs assistant, Raul Mariaca, who might better described as the post's cultural affairs advisor. He had been the under-secretary of the Ministry of Culture, Information and Tourism in a previous Bolivian government, spoke fluent English, and was a well known local artist. Probably the finest contemporary painter in Bolivia at that time, he was highly esteemed by all of the American USIS officers because of his knowledge and understanding of his own culture and his intellectual and personal traits.

Another outstanding Bolivian employee of USIS was Raul Novilla Alarcon, a young man who had begun to make a name for himself as a television personality. He became very well known locally when he became the USIS producer of a television program entitled "Let's Learn English." A film segment for this series of English language-teaching programs was produced in Washington while the on-camera portion of the series was produced, in this case, in La Paz.

Novilla spoke English fluently, having learned it as an exchange student in the U.S. while in high school. He not only produced the program but acted in it as a professor of English. Although arguments continue to this day as to the value of teaching a language by television, "Let's Learn English" enjoyed great popular success. It encouraged further study of English while expanding viewers' knowledge of American culture. Other Bolivians on the USIS staff who were equally outstanding in their own fields were the motion picture chief, Rafael Flores; the chief of the radio section, Eduardo Medina; the press section chief, Rodolfo Medrano; and the administrative specialist, Armando Orlandini. All were highly dedicated and capable employees.

Prior to my arrival in La Paz the post had had an American administrative officer who handled all of the varied administrative duties required in the post's operations. He had been transferred and there were no plans to replace him as the position, due to the agency's budget cuts, was abolished. (In the early 1970s each new fiscal year brought new cuts in USIA's annual appropriation.) As a result Olandini, under the PAO's direction and with the guidance of the American secretary/administrative assistant who would arrive later, handled all the budget and fiscal matters of USIS La Paz which were formerly handled by an American officer.

The first day in my new job I visited the embassy where Kent Herath introduced me to the key players of the various embassy entities, beginning with Ambassador Ernest Siracusa. A career officer of the State Department, the ambassador quickly gained the admiration and respect of all who came to know him. He was highly professional, yet likable and, as I soon learned, fair-minded in his dealings with his staff. He was certainly no State Department "cookie pusher," for one of his favorite sports was motorcycle riding. He often went riding with members of the local motorcycle club. On one occasion when he, his security guards (who always traveled with him, usually in a jeep that tried to keep up with the motorcycles), and a few fellow cyclists did not return by nightfall from an expedition outside La Paz, there was great concern in the American community that he might have run into foul play. Fortunately it was just a case of bad roads and a swollen river that delayed the return of the group to La Paz until early the following morning.

Walking from USIS to the chancery was not difficult as it was all downhill. Returning to the USIS office was another story. Although only a block away, the cobblestone street that went from the front of the embassy to the street on which USIS was located rose about 400 feet at an angle of four degrees or so. Walking up that hill at 12,400 feet above sea level I had to pause every four to six feet to catch my breath. Although I was able to do much better after my first year of living at that altitude, I was never able to go more than a short distance uphill before having to stop and rest. This was, in a sense, my introduction to "breathless Bolivia." The fact that we walked up and down that hill two to five times daily in order to attend meetings at the embassy, to consult with colleagues, or merely to pick up our classified mail, meant that we became very well acquainted with that hill.

Two Americans who worked for USIS but did not work directly in the USIS office were Ray Burson, director of the Bolivian-American Cultural Center in La Paz and Maynard Clayton, a retired U.S. Navy Chief Petty officer who, as the director of a smaller binational center in Sucre, was beginning his second career. Clayton was a grantee before USIA phased out its grantee program a few years later. The grantees did not enjoy the same benefits as regular Foreign Service employees, which was one reason for changing the old grantee system. Although generally the grantees were recruited and financed by USIA, they signed employment contracts with the binational center boards (made up of Bolivians and Americans) for periods of one or two years. With the number of USIA employees limited by Congress, this was a means of expanding the manpower needs of USIA. It eventually became evident, however, that this two-class system was grossly unfair for the grantees. They shared the same hardships and security problems encountered by FSOs and worked for the same organization but enjoyed far fewer benefits.

As the weeks went by we slowly adapted to living and working more than two miles above sea level. Meanwhile we anxiously awaited the shipment of our household and personal effects from Montevideo. The many cables that went back and forth revealed that cargo shipments from Uruguay to Bolivia were not easy to arrange. Eventually, however, the embassy general services officer in Montevideo arranged to ship our effects by air, shipment by ship to this land-locked country being impractical. But to do so our belongings would have to go by the rather circuitous route of being flown from Uruguay to Panama and from there to Lima, Peru before being sent on to La Paz. This meant they would go from the Atlantic port of Montevideo in the southern cone of South America to the very north of the continent, and then to Lima, Peru on the Pacific Coast in the central part of South America before being transshipped to La Paz. In this round-about journey, they were loaded and unloaded three times.

Since the only cargo flight serving La Paz originated in Peru, the first of two shipments was made in this manner. The items in the first shipment arrived in fairly good condition. Included in it were such things as the steel anchor to my old sailboat, which I had already arranged to sell and for which I had absolutely no use in Bolivia. This and some other items would not have been shipped had we been able to supervise the shipment ourselves. Later we learned that as the bureau from our bedroom was being loaded on a truck for shipment it was accidentally dropped in the street in front of our former residence. A secret compartment in the top opened, spilling all of Charmaine's jewelry located therein into the street! Miraculously most of it survived the voyage.

By the time the second shipment reached Lima the airline that had been the only one to make cargo flights into Bolivia went out of business. This meant that our second shipment of effects, upon their arrival in Lima, could go no farther until the contents of the large crates designed for cargo planes were unloaded and repacked in smaller crates which would fit the baggage compartment of a passenger plane.

At the time that our second shipment was scheduled to arrive in Lima for trans-shipment, the political situation was heating up in Sucre, where one of our four binational centers in Bolivia was located. On two occasions dynamite, which was readily available because of its use in the extensive Bolivian mining operations, was placed at the entrance to the U. S.-Bolivian binational center in that city. The explosions caused damage but no loss of life as once again Bolivian discontent with U.S. policies was expressed in this manner. On both of these occasions BNC Director Maynard Clayton left town for the security of a farm on the outskirts of Sucre owned by one of the Bolivian members of the center's board. After the second explosion our concern for the safety of the director greatly increased.

I kept in close touch with Clayton by phone, suggesting more than once that he leave for his own safety. We would simply close the center I told him, since keeping the Sucre center open was not worth endangering his life. He was very reluctant to do so, but after the second dynamiting he finally agreed. After about ten days in the capital, with little to do, he readily agreed to go to Lima at my request to supervise the transfer of my second household shipment from the large crates to smaller ones. At last the final shipment of our effects arrived on a commercial flight. As the political situation continued to worsen in Bolivia, our cultural programs became more and more restricted. With still nothing to occupy him profitably after his return to La Paz we arranged his transfer back to Washington for reassignment. As for the Sucre BNC, twenty years would pass before USIS support of the reopened Sucre BNC was reinstituted in 1990.

In addition to the binational center in La Paz where about a thousand mostly young Bolivians studied English, and the one in Sucre that was now closed, two other fairly large centers received USIS support. About 500 students studied English at a center in Cochabamba and about 300 at a center in Santa Cruz.

The center in Cochabamba was under the supervision of Guy Gwynne, the branch public affairs officer of USIS Cochabamba. He was a State Department officer serving a tour with USIA. The Santa Cruz center was supervised by William "Jeff" Dieterich, a USIS officer who carried out USIS programs in that tropical city. Located in eastern Bolivia's tropical lowlands, Santa Cruz was at an altitude of about 1500 feet. From La Paz, Cochabamba, Bolivia's second largest city, was 110 miles by air or 180 miles by a torturous mountain road. At an altitude of 8,600 feet, its climate was far superior to that of La Paz and Santa Cruz. Travel time from La Paz by air was one hour, by car, nine hours. A train on a railroad built by the British many years earlier also made a daily trip from La Paz to Cochabamba. This trip took anywhere from seven to fifteen hours, depending on the condition of the train and the tracks which were subject to occasional landslides.

Some months after my arrival in Bolivia, Guy Gwynne finished his tour as director of the Cochabamba center and was transferred. He was not replaced because the USIS Bolivia staff was cut by yet another American position in the new fiscal year. I decided, therefore, that the one American officer stationed outside of La Paz should be in Cochabamba rather than Santa Cruz, a smaller and less important city. Dieterich was thus transferred from Santa Cruz to Cochabamba to run the larger center. He continued to supervise the Santa Cruz BNC by periodic visits.

Of the four centers, the one in La Paz normally received my greatest attention. Then in October 1970 it required the attention of the ambassador as well. It suddenly became a cause célèbre.

Located in a large two-story house in downtown La Paz, about a quarter of a mile from the embassy and USIS offices, the La Paz Center was broken into on the night of October 7 by a group of leftist labor union members supported by some leftist university students who shared their anti-U.S. feelings. Accusing the Center's administrators of "polluting the minds" of Bolivian youth, they occupied the building and declared that this American-sponsored institution could no longer operate in La Paz. After announcing that they had taken the center over and were closing it to the public, they initially occupied it only in the daytime. They soon announced that they planned to donate the building to the local government for use as a public primary school.

Despite the U.S. ambassador's strong complaints to the Foreign Ministry about the center's usurpation, the Torres government, which depended on the support of the leftist labor unions and student leaders for its existence, refused to take any action against the usurpers. Furthermore, Bolivian government officials argued that since the center was a Bolivian institution (run by a Board of Directors made up of Bolivians and Americans, most of them being private citizens), it was not U.S. government property. They rationalized that the takeover was, therefore, a tolerable situation that the Bolivian Government would resolve in its own cool time.

When it soon became apparent that the Bolivian government would not take any action to restore the building to its rightful owners, the director of the center, Ray Burson, entered the building on a dark night a few days later and, aided by some of his Bolivian staffers, removed hundreds of books from the center's library as well as other equipment and some furniture, all of which was then stored elsewhere for safe-keeping. After discovering the following morning what happened, the labor leaders placed guards in the building at night as well as during the day to assure that it would not be reentered.

More than three months passed with no progress being made toward regaining use of the building. The center had been the home of an active, vibrant cultural institution serving Bolivian and U.S. interests. Now the frustrations Burson and I experienced with this situation increased with each passing day. And since we drove past the front of the center daily on our way to work we were constantly reminded of the Bolivian government's failure to take any action against the usurpers.

One day after having lunch together downtown and discussing our favorite subject—the status of the La Paz BNC—Burson and I walked by the center and, on the spur of the moment, attempted to walk into the building. We were immediately stopped by one of the labor types, probably a miner who was assigned guard duty that day by his labor union. This formidable, heavy set, tough and rough-looking individual placed his forearm between himself and the entrance door, blocking our way. As we tried to enter the building we brushed up against his solid, muscle-rippling arm that he refused to move. Holding that position for a few moments, we looked him in the eye, saw that our bold effort would not succeed, and backed away.

"We merely wanted to see how things are here," I said. He said nothing, just shook his head and stood his ground. Only then did we realize what a foolish thing we had done. We could have been taken hostage, although hostage taking was not yet the common phenomenon it was to become in later years. We might also have been physically injured or abused. The combination of frustration after three months of living in the same city, where one of our major USIS resources had been illegally and unjustly taken from us, and the impatience that seems always to be accentuated with the lack of oxygen, contributed, I suspect, to our actions which were as unsuccessful as they were foolish.

After four months had passed Burson and I decided on a new ploy. We invited two of the labor leaders to have dinner with us at the "Dragon," a popular Chinese restaurant that we frequented a few blocks from the center. We thought that if we could talk with them in a relaxed atmosphere we might be able to arrange a peaceful negotiation and settlement whereby we would be able to get back into the binational center business.

Burson and I arrived at the Dragon shortly before six p.m. and checked out the private dining room we had reserved. We had no way of knowing whether our guests would really accept our invitation and by 6:15 p.m. began to think that our ploy would probably come to naught. But then three men appeared, two of whom turned out to be the ones we had invited. The third one was a colleague they had brought along as reinforcement.

The dinner proceeded with considerable strain. Over desert and coffee I reached into my pocket and pulled out some cigars. Burson and I were to laugh at this later when he accused me of acting like a true capitalist. The labor leaders took the cigars but they all said that they would smoke them later.

After discussing the purposes of the center and describing how it was helping Bolivian youths to learn a foreign language; that it was merely an educational institution that served the needs of the community and, therefore, was a nonpolitical entity that did not justify their actions, they said they would think about this but could offer no ready solution at this time. We shook hands all around and they departed, never to be heard from again.

Three more months went by and we still had not regained possession of the center. In the meantime, the sign in front of the building identifying it as the Centro Boliviano-Americano was scratched out. Crudely painted letters appeared on various parts of the building that said "U M S A." This stood for Universidad Mayor de San Andres, the leading (and only) university in La Paz. The takeover of the center was fully supported by the leftist student organizations of the university. The crude lettering of "U M S A" on the doors, windows, and sides of the building was intended to demonstrate the students' solidarity with the unionists.

At one point during the stalemate we produced and distributed thousands of leaflets, the centerfold of which displayed photos on one side of the center swarming with Bolivian students of English who attended the BNC when it operated normally, and, on the other, recent photos of the building defaced with "U M S A" signs. The caption of the photos read "Yesterday and Today."

The cover of the leaflet, in large letters, said EL CENTRO BOLIVIANO-AMERICANO. There followed an explanation of how the center was "an institution founded May 2, 1946, for the purpose of cultural interchange between Bolivia and the United States and to increase the mutual understanding of both peoples and their respective languages, contributing thereby to improved international comprehension in the hemisphere.

"The teaching of the English language is the major activity of the Center. Many Bolivian students and professionals have been able to continue post-graduate courses abroad thanks to the courses given at the C.B.A. Until now more than 25,000 Bolivian citizens have passed through the classrooms of the Institute."

The back cover stated: "Who is responsible for the sacking of the Center, for destroying the source of income for 36 Bolivian employees, and the fact that more than 1,000 students can not continue their studies in EL CENTRO BOLIVIANO-AMERICANO?"

This and other actions we took had little or no effect on the usurpers. Looking back one can understand why. At the time, however, we felt we had to do something. Political considerations overrode all others as the occupation dragged on. The president of the center's board of directors who was a well-known Bolivian lawyer, while sympathetic to the need to regain the building, knew his countrymen and his society too well to do more than stand by, knowing full well that eventually there would be a change of government, and then a change in the wind which would bring the Bolivian ship of state back to a more even keel, at least for awhile. When that happened he believed the center would be returned to its rightful owners, though in what condition would remain to be seen. Another active board member, Bolivia's most distinguished contemporary musician and composer, Raul Barrigan, shared our frustration but likewise knew that, in time, the pendulum would swing in our direction.

During the many months that the center was occupied, and thus out of business, our other programs continued, though not at full speed. In May of that year, long before the center was occupied, we held an exhibit on space achievements at which a piece of the moon rock was the central attraction. Some 70,000 Bolivians attended the exhibit. But as the political situation heated up, as evidenced by the taking of the center and other anti-American activities, this kind of exhibit could not be held. Nevertheless, we continued to maintain about forty exchanges annually among Bolivian and American students, scholars, and specialists; to loan fifty to seventy-five films per week to schools and other groups in La Paz; and to continue to place news and feature articles in some of the country's thirteen dailies.

Other USIS activities continued as best they could. It was strange, however, to visit the Ministry of Education and observe USIS furniture that had been removed from the binational center and transferred to a government ministry. When a new government came in, as surely it would, we would have no qualms about demanding that the furniture taken from the center either be returned to the center, or compensation for it paid to the institute.

As the months went by the political and social situation in Bolivia under the Torres regime disintegrated further. There were rumors about planned coups against the government but so far they were only rumors. Precautions among embassy personnel to avoid incidents increased. For example, when Victor drove me to the office in the morning and back home in the evening I insisted that he take a different route every day. However, from my neighborhood in Obrajes there were only two roads that we could take to get to the downtown area where the embassy and USIS were located. Thus there were parts of our journey where the choice was not as varied as we would have liked. We also varied our departures and arrivals by anywhere from ten to thirty minutes in order not to provide a set schedule for possible terrorists.

As the political situation deteriorated, the embassy became more and more concerned about the possibility of an attack by leftist groups who viewed the U.S. as the chief cause of Bolivia's woes. At one country team meeting the discussion centered on whether using banana oil or some other product, poured on the wide concrete stairs which led to the second floor entrance to the embassy, would be effective in deterring mobs bent on entering and destroying the chancery if the embassy were attacked.

Our binational center in Sucre had now been closed for months following its occupation by student extremists. Our small center in the mining town of Oruro was completely sacked. In any event we had planned to close it, but had not anticipated such an efficient termination. Everything in that center was looted and every window broken, most from the inside. The center in Cochabamba was also attacked and looted, although the employees managed to save the building by fighting off the looters after they had destroyed three classrooms. In Santa Cruz the BNC and USIS office were also sacked. And in the small town of Trinidad, where USIS had a local representative, vandals destroyed his one-room office.

A special concern was felt for the American Cooperative School. Most of the children of Americans who lived in La Paz attended this school that had mostly American teachers. Courses were taught in English along the lines of regular American schools. Many of the students were from missionary families who lived in La Paz. The best hospital in the country, for example, was known as the Clinica Americana. Located in the Obrajes section of the city, it was run by Seventh Day Adventists. While the American Cooperative School was rustic by U.S. standards and always in need of additional funding despite a substantial State Department grant, the American community was thankful that it was available. Most parents with children in the school took an active role in supporting it. The school always had a waiting list of Bolivian students whose parents wanted them to get an American-style education prior to attending a university in the U.S. when the time came or to perfect their knowledge of English.

The American Cooperative School was located in Calacoto, the valley farthest from the downtown area. Special efforts were taken to protect the students, teachers, and administrative personnel of the school as well as the school itself. Fortunately it never became a target during this unstable period. One advantage was its relatively isolated location. Another was that it was far removed from the volatile San Andres University where leftist students were known to plot their "fun and games" that often included marches, demonstrations, and violent acts.

In the Hansen family both Robert and Annette, our two oldest children, attended the American School. We had decided to send

Katherine and Alicia, both of whom had attended Spanish-speaking schools in Uruguay, to Saint Andrews, a Bolivian Catholic school, in order that they might continue to improve their Spanish language ability. As a result, in later years both were quite at home with the Spanish language.

The deteriorating security situation increased the hardships we all experienced in the isolation of La Paz. In more peaceful times excursions could be made outside the city on weekends, which provided considerable recreation and entertainment. But with growing concern about anti-Americanism which could lead to the kidnapping of Americans or other terrorist acts, we had to be even more circumspect than normal in planning our activities. This meant that excursions to places of interest outside the city had to be curtailed and activities inside the city always had to take the potential security threat into consideration.

Two additional USIS American employees were added to my staff in La Paz shortly after my arrival. The first of these was a junior officer trainee whom we shall call Bill (not his real name). Originally sent to Sucre to manage the binational center there until the new director for the center arrived, he was there for three months and then returned to La Paz to continue his training. When he left La Paz he was assigned to an isolated post, a questionable assignment as he could have benefited from more training.

Another American staffer, Margrett Buchholz, arrived in La Paz after I did. She was the new administrative assistant, the title given former American secretaries who had proven that they were capable of handling much greater responsibilities than those normally required of secretaries. An intelligent, mature, personable young woman, she soon endeared herself to all of her USIS colleagues, both Americans and Bolivians. As the PAO's assistant who also performed secretarial duties, she was highly professional, efficient, easy to get along with, and dependable; in short, my right arm.

Some time after our first JOT left to start his first assignment as a full-fledged USIS officer, Fred Emmert, a JOT from the latest class, joined us. Another bachelor, his legacy became somewhat different from that of his predecessor. He rapidly learned the business of public diplomacy and soon was making a solid contribution to USIS programming in La Paz. Part of his legacy, however, was that of breaker of female hearts.

Good looking and personable, he did not go unnoticed by the eligible young Bolivian lasses who held prestigious (by local standards) jobs in the U.S. Embassy. One young lady in particular, renowned locally for her attractive appearance, was quite taken by Emmert, and he by her. Romance blossomed and shortly before his tour was concluded bets were being placed by American and Bolivian staffers alike that Cupid would pierce his heart and he would marry the lovely Bolivian lass with whom his name became more and more linked. Alas, that was not to be. He escaped, leaving behind, we presume, a saddened soul (who probably went on to marry a wealthy Bolivian and lived just as happily ever after). After his training he was transferred to Mexico where rumors reaching the altiplano were that he came even closer to marriage with one of the Mexican beauties of the embassy staff in Mexico City. Whether or not the rumors were true, he once more escaped matrimony. On his third tour with the Foreign Service he was finally captured and went on to what we can only presume was a happy wedded life and certainly a successful career in the foreign service.

The political situation in Bolivia continued to deteriorate. Evacuation plans were reviewed in the event that embassy personnel, their families, and other Americans living in La Paz had to be evacuated. Since most American families lived in the lower sections of the city (Obrajes and Calacoto), and since there were only two main roads from these areas which led to the main highway to the airport, the Americans were in a difficult position if their evacuation became necessary. They would also have to take that highway to arrive on the altiplano where dirt roads led to other parts of Bolivia and eventually to neighboring countries. (There was one paved road on the high Bolivian plateau, constructed with the assistance of the U.S. government, but it led to Oruro, a mining community known for its volatile, anti-American sentiments.) Escape in the opposite direction, to the Yungas, a tropical jungle far below the city and reached only by a harrowing mountain road, would mean going to a dead end.

If fighting broke out between two opposing military forces, or if the government's security forces disintegrated and mob rule took over the city, the evacuation of Americans might be required if lives were to be saved. Either scenario was considered a real possibility as lawlessness within the city was increasing. Sporadic gunfire was now heard almost nightly in the downtown areas and dynamite explosions occurred from time to time as buildings, and occasionally people, were blown up .

In most countries help from outside in the form of helicopters, conventional aircraft, or military assistance of some type can be called upon to evacuate Americans if necessary. In La Paz there was only one airport, reached only by traveling on the one narrow, winding road that connected La Paz to the altiplano. If any help were to come from abroad, evacuees would in all probability have to safely reach the airport.

There was an unpaved road which skirted the city which might be used. It ran from what was known as "the Valley of the Moon" (a moonscape plateau a short distance from Calacoto), past the La Paz golf course (the highest in the world), and up into the mountains by which one could, if the road was not impassable from swollen streams and landslides, reach a part of the city which was accessible to the main road to the airport. The Americans living in Obrajes and Calacoto were informed where to gather for a convoy to take that route if it appeared that the two main roads through the center of La Paz were blocked or were too dangerous to transit.

During this time the dependents of American Embassy staffers were instructed to stay at home and not to travel around the city unless absolutely necessary. The embassy and USIS continued to function but with security precautions implemented to the highest degree. Outside doors were kept closed and visitors had to identify themselves before being admitted. Some mornings we would find bullet holes in the USIS building and, occasionally, spent bullets. They probably had been intended for other targets and had ricocheted into our building, though we could never be sure.

A few months earlier, as the occupation of the La Paz binational center dragged on, I recommended that its director, Ray Burson, be transferred as he was becoming, understandably, more and more frustrated, unable to work under the circumstances. In a normal situation we would have welcomed his assistance in USIS cultural programming but these programs, though still functioning somewhat, were doing so in low gear due to the general social unrest the country was experiencing. Shortly thereafter he was assigned to take over the center in peaceful San Jose, Costa Rica, a country known for its tranquility. After his arrival there he wrote to his old buddies in La Paz that it felt so strange to walk in downtown San Jose and not have to be concerned about the possibility of dynamite explosions or flying bullets.

Knowing that the day would eventually arrive that we would settle the BNC issue, Darrell Schmidt, a replacement for Burson, arrived in La Paz some time later. One evening he was visiting JOT Fred Emmert. Emmert lived on the top floor of an eight-story apartment complex across the street from the main building of San Andres University. The two young men heard a commotion outside at street level. They opened a window and peered out. A bullet whizzed by, about a foot from Schmidt's head, and implanted itself in the window frame. Quickly pulling their heads inside and closing the window, Emmert, if he kept his cool, probably said to Schmidt, "Welcome to La Paz"—and poured two double Scotches.

In August of 1971 rumors persisted that Bolivia was soon to experience another of its not uncommon military coups. For days the split in the Bolivian armed faces between those who supported the leftist Torres regime, which had grabbed power less than a year before, and those who were more conservative and felt the country was veering much too far to the left, became the main topic of conversation on the diplomatic circuit. Most felt it was just a matter of time before Torres would be overthrown. He had no solutions to Bolivia's social and economic problems, which were getting worse with each passing day.

On August 19th, the day of decision arrived. The "conservatives," led by Air Force Colonel Hugo Banzer, sent an ultimatum to General Torres to abandon the presidential palace and turn the government over to Banzer or risk a bloody battle. Torres was reluctant to give in so easily and decided to resist.

The Banzer forces were holed up in a military garrison on the west side of the city. They fired some artillery shells in the direction of the presidential palace and received some fire back from forces loyal to President Torres. I was at home that day with my family as all embassy personnel, with the exception of a very few who were needed at the embassy, had been instructed to remain in their homes until further notice.

Later in the morning, a typical bright sunny day in La Paz at that time of year, we heard the artillery fire and the sounds of machine guns echoing down the valley. Charmaine and I climbed onto the roof of our house to see if we could see from there what was happening about two miles from us in the center of town. It was then that a lone Bolivian Air Force plane, which had been circling the city, suddenly dove out of the bright blue sky as if it were making a bombing run on the San Andres University, where so many university students were supporters of the Torres government. From our vantage point we could see the small plane heading directly for the large ten-story university building. It was a one-engine, propeller-driven Mustang trainer. Painted on its fuselage behind the propeller and clearly visible when it flew over our neighborhood were shark teeth, a seemingly incongruous decoration for the air force of a land-locked country. (The Bolivian Air Force was known to have only three or four planes.) It pulled up just short of striking the building and veered off to the left.

But no bombs fell. Instead we heard the "rat-tat-tat" of machine gun fire. It had strafed the building.

Fred Emmert, at home in his apartment, heard the sound of machine gun bullets hitting the university building across the street. He was talking with Don Mathes, the information officer of USIS Lima who was visiting him, when the attack began. They both dove for the floor. The noise of the machine gun was quickly followed by the roar of the plane gaining altitude above Emmert's building, as well as the sound of bullets piercing the roof. As Emmert's apartment was on the top floor a few bullets lodged in the ceiling of his living room. Both men were unscathed, but now Emmert had something else to relate about his experiences as a JOT in Bolivia.

The revolt continued for five days. Pitched battles were fought between opposing military sides in the Miraflores and Sopaocachi residential areas and around the university, near the homes of some members of the embassy as well as the building where JOT Emmert lived. Considerable fighting also occurred for a few days in the Calacoto suburb where the majority of Americans lived. In addition to organized battles and indiscriminate fighting in different parts of the city, we were concerned about guerrilla-type activity conducted by armed civilian bands. These groups, representing both sides of the civil war, wandered about the city and suburbs looking for the enemy. When they couldn't find the enemy they looked for trouble. They were a constant threat to foreigners as well as Bolivians.

Some months after the five-day war ended, Ambassador Siracusa recommended to his superiors in Washington that the U.S. Mission be given a Meritorious Honor Award in recognition of the performance of its personnel during this trying period. The award was duly approved and signed by the Assistant Secretary of State for Inter-American Affairs. In advocating such an award, the ambassador wrote:

> I view the period of fighting as a culmination of almost a year of living under constant threat and an undue barrage of hate-America propaganda. During this period Americans were subjected to acts of terrorism such as bombs and personal threats. Some were publicly charged by the Minister of Interior with conspiring against the government and subjected to official harassment. They bore these trying times, including the vicious lies against them singly and together, in a magnificent way without losing their dignity or high morale, thereby demonstrating on an almost daily basis that they had the fiber to turn in a superior performance even when the stakes came to

be raised to a life and death situation.... My recommendation for this award, therefore, while based primarily on the performance of all our people during the recent fighting, takes into account the equally superior performance of their daily tasks during the last ten months leading up to the revolution.

At the height of the Torres administration the sole purpose of the regime was to stay in power, which it did for awhile, mainly by doing the bidding of the extreme left. It was during this period that an Oxford historian, Professor Alistair Horne, came through La Paz on a visit to Latin America. He called on me in my office and we had lunch together. Upon his return to England he published a book about his trip, entitled *Small Earthquake in Chile* (Viking, 1973). Although Chile under Allende was his main interest, in Chapter 12, entitled "In Bolivia, a Fire Is Nothing," he depicts the situation he found in Bolivia and describes me as being "rather lugubrious." Perhaps I was, for at that time I had the unenviable record of having lost five binational centers—Sucre, Oruro, La Paz, Santa Cruz and Cochabamba, and our representative's office in Trinidad—and all this at a time when the budget for USIS operations was being cut by 17 percent! He wrote:

> Since the Torres 'October Revolution' the Yanqui community in Bolivia has been living in a state of semi-siege. The anti-American outbreaks then were of quite extraordinary violence. Embassy offices were broken into and smashed. One of the principal targets was the USIS-run Centro Boliviano-Americano, operated by thirty USIS employees (sic) where some thousand Bolivian students study English. The doors were dynamited (a favorite and easily obtainable weapon among the Bolivian miners), and all the furniture and books pillaged. The seized Center continues to be used as a 'workers' meeting place'—despite three separate representations made to the Foreign Ministry by the U.S. ambassador. The Center in Oruro was also dynamited, and every single object inside it pillaged. The sack of the U.S. Centers was largely carried out by the students; as the rather lugubrious USIS chief in La Paz remarked to me: 'It used to be deliberate policy to place the Centers as near the universities as possible in South America—now we are making a hundred-and-eighty-degree turn, and removing them as far away as we can!' His own office, on an upper floor out of range of stones, was protected behind sliding steel doors, with an armed guard and wire-netting over

the windows. In the prevailing mood, U.S. diplomats have abandoned carrying C.D. plates on their cars, and the Clinica Americana has changed its name to *Clinica Metodista,* in fact, anything to avoid blazoning the pejorative word 'American'.

Also during the Torres heyday, while "American" was a "pejorative" word, as Professor Horne noted, the Soviet Union and "Russian" were "in words," at least in pro-government quarters. La Paz became flooded with visiting Soviet delegations. Rumor had it that the Soviets were financing the Bolivian revolution with U.S. dollars. At this time the Cubans were also considered by pro-government groups and individuals as representing the wave of the future.

During this period the U.S. and Soviet governments were once again moving toward a period of detente although detente did not really begin until the first Nixon-Brezhnev summit meeting of 1972. Thus it was that a visiting Soviet official and the Soviet Embassy press attaché, a young man who introduced himself as "Smirnoff," called at my office to become acquainted and exchange views. They invited me to a luncheon at the press attaché's "home" the following week. This was such a rare invitation I readily accepted.

The luncheon was notable for several reasons. The assistant military attaché of the Soviet Embassy, a Lt. Col., tried to ply me and two other American luncheon guests with vodka. He himself acted as if he had had a few too many. I was suffering from a slight headache when I arrived at the luncheon so vodka was the last thing I wanted. But I would have refrained, or at least been restrained, from drinking much vodka in any event. The two other Americans at the luncheon were the embassy political officer, Perry Shankle, and an American priest assigned to a local parish.

Russian Foreign Service personnel at that time apparently performed many of their own household chores. With the probable exception of ambassadors and KGB heads, many apparently did their own cooking and gardening. On this occasion Mrs. Smirnoff cooked the meal and served it. She did not join us at the table, either because it was not customary to do so or because she was too busy cooking and serving the food.

I was, at first, struck by the austerity of this Soviet home. Except for a few mirrors there was absolutely nothing on the walls that might reveal the personalities of the occupants. This was in such marked contrast, I thought, to the homes of American Foreign Service personnel who always decorate their homes with art, sculpture, and "collectibles" from their various postings. I learned later that the press attaché and his wife probably did not actually reside in that house but lived in much smaller quarters on the embassy compound. Such houses were rented for use only for such occasions as the luncheon I attended. They were probably also bugged, possibly by both the KGB and the CIA.

Although I planned to reciprocate Smirnoff's hospitality, events began to move so fast in La Paz that I was unable to do so. With the change of government following the five-day war, "Russian" replaced "American" as the pejorative name among many Bolivians. Eventually the public learned from the new government that there were more than a hundred Soviet officials in La Paz. What that high number of individuals was doing in a country where the Soviets had no "Peace Corps," "AID program," etc. was a question one could only surmise. More than seventy-five members of the Soviet Mission to La Paz were asked to leave shortly after the new government came into power, including my new acquaintance, Smirnoff. (Some years later I finally was able to reciprocate his hospitality by inviting him to our home in Peru. He showed up in that country while I was assigned there. By then he said he was no longer a Soviet Embassy official but had become the correspondent for Moscow's *New Times.* He was, therefore, allegedly independent of the Soviet government, though he unquestionably remained a Soviet official.)

My only other association with the Soviets in Bolivia was to observe a group of them one day at a bullfight in the small, rustic ring where the *corrida de toros* was held in La Paz. As was always the case whenever one saw the Soviets in downtown areas of La Paz, they traveled in groups of two or more. To have seen a Soviet official walking alone in the street would have been as rare as breathing too much oxygen in La Paz.

The first time we went to a bullfight in La Paz we were surprised to learn that eight bulls were on the program. The normal number at most bullfights is six. Then we learned why. The bulls are brought to the Bolivian capital from Peru where they are raised at lower altitudes. The first announcement at the ring that day was that the first fight was canceled. The bull had died. Apparently the altitude was too much for him.

Some Soviet Embassy staff members attended the bull fights one day in a group of about twenty strong. They clung together like quail in cold rain. They were rugged-looking types—no "cookie pushers" there. One could only wonder whether they were the ones who did the gardening and other chores; whether they were the security forces; or miners sent because of the presumed rapport they would have with the miners of Bolivia. They looked well fed and of such stocky build that they reminded one of prizefighters and wrestlers. Whatever their true profession, some were surely among the more than seventy-five Soviets that were declared personas nongrata when the new Bolivian regime came to power.

The overthrow of the Torres regime was bloody. An estimated 200 people, mostly military, were killed and over 500 wounded. But with the new government of General Hugo Banzar, the near-anarchy that existed before the war came to an end, to the general relief of most Bolivians. Like people everywhere, the majority simply wanted to live in peace and be able to plan for tomorrow.

Ideologically, the new government represented a 180-degree turn from the old government. Because of this, and the fame the CIA had gained for allegedly overturning governments (far beyond its proven capability in my view), Lewis Duigud of the *Washington Post* charged that the U.S. government was involved in the overthrow of General Torres. This may or may not have been, but in a country that had 180 changes of government during about 150 years of independence (or on average a new government every nine months), there is reason to believe that the Bolivian military was simply following an old tradition with little need of help from the outside.

After the new government came into power and it became fairly safe for Americans to walk the streets of La Paz and other Bolivian cities once again, one of the first things that we in USIS did was to try to get the binational cultural centers (BNCs) back into operation. We had spent many hours seeking to resolve the problem caused by the occupation of the La Paz BNC and to recover the Santa Cruz and Cochabamba centers. The Torres regime, uninterested as it was in anything except remaining in power, had been completely uncooperative. Under the new government we expected to be able to recover the buildings and once again support the BNC operations. The two centers in the interior were quickly recovered due to the cooperation of sympathetic local authorities. What happened with the center in La Paz was a different story.

The labor union and student occupiers of the La Paz center eventually turned the building over to the Ministry of Education, which is one reason why we found some of the furniture from the center in the offices of that ministry. While still under the Torres regime, the building was used by the ministry as a public elementary school.

To return the building at this stage to its rightful owners created a delicate problem since it would mean closing a Bolivian public school that had few if any choices as to where to move, and one which was occupying a building superior to most Bolivian schools. The diplomatic solution seemed to be to let the school now functioning in the center's building continue to do so and for the new government to compensate the binational center board by purchasing the building from them. With the funds received from the new government the board could re-establish the center in another building.

This seemed like an excellent solution, especially since the U.S. government was particularly anxious to remove this irritant from its relations with the new regime. Until this situation was resolved, normal relations between our two countries was hindered. There was only one hitch. The new government claimed its treasury had been so seriously depleted by the Torres regime it could not come up with the approximately $40,000 that most agreed was a fair price for the building. (General Torres was said to have absconded with considerable amounts of the national treasury and was living in luxury in Buenos Aires.)

American bureaucrats are not well known for their sleight-of-hand tricks, but eventually someone devised a solution to this nagging problem. The new Bolivian government had been granted AID funds for primary education programs. Arrangements were made to use part of these funds for the purchase of the La Paz BNC building for use (as it already was being used) as a primary school. Although the government bureaucracies did not move as fast as we would have liked, the BNC Board eventually received a check from the Bolivian government for $40,000 for the purchase of the BNC building. The search for a new site for the La Paz BNC could now begin in earnest.

With this major problem resolved Charmaine and I decided to take some "R & R" (Rest and Recreation) leave to which, after what we had been through, we felt fully entitled. "R & R" is a benefit granted Foreign Service personnel at hardship posts. At the time it provided transportation (usually air fare) for employees and their families to return to the U.S. once during a two-year tour of duty abroad.

We arrived in Miami in June 1971, determined to spend some time at the Rodney Motel at Miami Beach. The Rodney by then had become a favorite hangout of a number of American staffers assigned to the U.S. Embassy in La Paz. The DCM's wife found it so pleasant she stayed there a month one time, rather than put up with the unpleasantries of La Paz. Several other embassy colleagues found the relatively inexpensive Rodney, with its kitchenettes, two swimming pools, and access to the beach, a good place to recover from the traumas experienced in Bolivia.

USIA Washington officials were beginning to have second thoughts about supporting binational centers in Bolivia, and especially in La Paz where the situation had only recently been resolved. Partially because of this, but also for other reasons, after arriving in Miami I phoned Lyle Copmann, the assistant director of USIA for Latin America. He urged me to interrupt my vacation and come to Washington for a few days. He said he would like a firsthand view of the current Bolivian situation and was sure others would also. He then proceeded to arrange travel orders for me to fly to Washington for a few days of consultation.

My visit to USIA headquarters proved fruitful. I was able not only to provide him as well as a number of other headquarters officials with a firsthand view of current USIS La Paz operations and the situation in general in Bolivia, but probably my most valuable discussion was held with the deputy director of the agency, Henry Loomis. Loomis was among those top USIA officials who questioned putting any additional resources into Bolivian binational centers following the disastrous looting and takeovers we had experienced the year before.

Based on my hastily written notes after that meeting with Loomis, held June 23, 1971, I noted that he agreed that we could go ahead and reopen the La Paz BNC "if we wanted to use the post's limited funds. But," he said, "if more funding is needed it becomes a different ballgame." He indicated that if we had only "a 50-50 chance" of getting hit again by armed mobs, he would opt for not opening, but if we had a "90-10 chance" of succeeding, O.K. "But if we open and get hit again, then they have another victory," he added. In short, if it appeared that the centers would be attacked again, he would opt for not reopening the center. "However," he concluded, "the decision is up to you, so long as GOE is used." (GOE, "going operating expenses." are funds controlled by the PAO for the post's operating expenses.)

On other subjects I expressed concern that "the White House doesn't seem to realize that Bolivia could be a second Cuba in Latin America. This would be bad politically for the administration. Our 'friends' don't want to pay the high costs of a second Cuba, but if handed the country on a silver platter, wouldn't they take it? Why not?" For this reason, among others, I argued, we should be willing to put a minimum amount of funds into maintaining our (USIS) presence there.

Loomis had recently sent a taped message to all field posts expressing his views as the deputy director of the agency. I told him I thought that was a good idea; that it was helpful to get the deputy director's thoughts on a variety of subjects of professional interest, but that on the last tape "you talked too long."

On the subject of "national development," a theme USIA was pursuing, I told him we in the field were unclear as to what exactly that term means. I agreed that basically "How to do it" is the job of AID. When political content is involved, USIS should be involved. But if the U.S. Mission has, for example, ten objectives in a given country, and USIS programs can advance only two or three, we should not waste time on the others.

All too quickly my trip to Washington and our vacation in Miami Beach ended and we were back in La Paz. It was a more peaceful La Paz than the one we had experienced during most of 1970 and for this we were thankful. A few weeks after my return I received a glimpse of the questionable efficiency of the State Department pouch services in those days. On July 12th I received a letter from area director Copmann in Washington dated June 29. It had taken only two weeks to reach me, much faster transit time than a letter I had written to him. His letter read in part:

Dear Al:
On June 28 at 3 P.M., your letter of May 10 reached my desk. How's that for lousy service?

Even in the darkest days of the Torres regime USIS was able to place some things in the local press. We also maintained good relations and placed considerable materials with local radio stations, and occasionally were able to get USIS programs on the local television station. With the new government, however, we had virtually blanket access to all local media for USIS materials. The new media environment made the demand for our programs greater than the supply, a complete reversal from the year before.

A new site for the La Paz binational center was located. The entire second floor of a commercial building in downtown La Paz was rented. The new BNC Director, Darrell Schmidt, was kept busy urging the workmen to expedite the completion of the alterations needed for the new BNC library, an exhibit and concert hall, and classrooms. When the center opened a few months later nearly a thousand students enrolled to study English. Cultural programming got underway once again and the library became as popular as ever, despite having far fewer books since so many had been destroyed or stolen during the occupation of the old center. It was the only library in the capital where books could be checked out and taken home.

Bolivia's only television station at the time was the government-run La Paz station. An earlier administration had the station built by an outside contractor in a way that could possibly happen only in Bolivia. The TV tower, understandably, was on the altiplano overlooking the city. From this high point the signal could reach most of the populated areas of La Paz and also some of the small communities on the high plateau. But the contractor also built the studios on the same location, which meant that all the personnel who ran the station always had to make the hour-long trek from the city to the altiplano. There were times when the single road to reach there was blocked due to accidents or other causes, in which case the trip was much longer than an hour. Eventually a studio was built in the center of the city and the transmissions sent by microwave from the downtown studio to the transmitting tower. The amount of time the production staff and the technicians saved in not having to go up the hill for their telecasts was tremendous.

The new studio was located a few blocks from the presidential palace. The president could now talk on television to the Pazeños much more easily and frequently. Visiting VIPs and others also were saved the two-hour round trip from town when participating in telecasts. "Remotes" were as yet unheard of, so interviews were generally conducted in the studio of the station.

When possibilities arose of developing television stations in the other two major population centers of the country, Cochabamba and Santa Cruz, various earlier regimes, as well as the Banzer government, expressed little or no interest. They seemed to assume that construction of interior stations would create competition with the government line on various issues. But they could hold progress back for only so long. When television finally came to those two cities some years later, the government initially controlled them as they did the station in La Paz.

With the virtual carte blanche we enjoyed for USIS programming under the new government, our programs were suddenly limited only by the availability of funds and our own creativeness. Remembering the success we had in Uruguay with Servan-Schreiber's book, *The American Challenge* (which so brilliantly praises American business methods and crucifies Marxist economics), I decided to introduce it to Bolivian audiences since it was practically unknown in this country.

The first thing we did was to encourage a leading local book importer to order several hundred copies by guaranteeing that USIS would purchase any copies, at cost, which remained after six months. (We bought very few as he nearly sold out all he had imported.) We then obtained the rights to publish Serban-Schreiber's own synopsis of his book as a USIS pamphlet. The first printing of 5,000 was so popular we printed a second edition of 3,000 copies. This stimulated sales as well as requests among key contacts for presentation copies. (The Army General Staff, for example, received USIS-supplied copies from the embassy's military attaché who noticed during one of his visits that the one copy they had was thumb-marked and worn from use by the members of the General Staff.) As in Uruguay, because of USIS efforts, the book became a best seller.

About this time another interesting book, also written by a Frenchman, appeared on the world scene. Entitled *Without Marx or Jesus*, by Jean-François Revel, its subtitle was "The New American Revolution Has Begun." Months after its publication in Spanish it was no better known in Bolivia than *The American Challenge* had been before USIS began its multimedia publicity campaign. Revel's book also praised private investment and democratic freedoms as enjoyed in the United States and contended that they provide the only way to go for economic and social growth. In many ways it was far ahead of its time. The world had to wait about twenty years before the evidence of this thesis became obvious in the late 1980s with the disintegration of the communist system in Eastern Europe and the Soviet Union, and the growth of democratic governments in Latin America. In a chapter entitled "The Information Revolution," Revel described the great effect communications in the modern world was having, and would increasingly have, on governments throughout the world.

Having by now had the experience in Uruguay and Bolivia of how media and other programs can spur interest in a good book, USIS made another special effort with the Revel volume, getting it discussed on local television and stimulating sales in a number of other ways. It was another successful campaign in a communications environment that, like the local government, had changed from being so opposed to our views, to welcoming them. Our report to Washington describing what we had done in Bolivia with the Revel book as an "evidence of effectiveness" so impressed headquarters that it was distributed in its entirety to every USIS post in the world (USIS LA PAZ Field Message No. 31, May 4, 1972). We were cited as an example of "what a post can accomplish in promoting a book important to the achievement of Agency objectives."

It was during this period that the editor of a conservative (by Bolivian standards) La Paz daily newspaper, with whom I had become a fairly good friend during one of the more troublesome periods of Bolivia's modern history, interrupted his newspaper career to become an advisor to the new foreign minister. Since the Foreign Office was but a few blocks away, he would pop into my office quite often to exchange views. Among other things, he kept me informed of the status of the campaign to declare *personas non grata* some of the more than one hundred Soviet officials who had entered Bolivia during the Torres administration. These exchanges were highly useful to me and the embassy in interpreting the interactions taking place within the new government.

In February 1971, six months after the change in government, Ambassador Siracusa asked me to write the first draft of a speech he intended to make in which he wanted to present American ideas on economic and social development. These were, in my view, just what Servan-Schreiber and Revel had written about. I undertook this task with enthusiasm, often speculating, as I and others who lived or had lived in developing countries often did, as to why the societies in such countries couldn't move forward faster.

That evening, after work, alone in my study, I composed some of my thoughts on this subject. It was a subject I had thought about many times as I served in country after country where the problem of economic development was obvious. When I retired that night about 3 a.m., I felt that I had captured my thoughts in a successful way. The following day at the office, after reviewing, editing, and sharpening some of the ideas, my draft was typed and sent to the ambassador for his review. As he did not have much opportunity for formal speechmaking given Bolivia's political *ambiente* in recent years, and since this was the first time I had been asked to draft a speech for the Ambassador, I was not familiar with his style and penchants. I had no way of knowing if he would find my draft helpful or not.

The speech, as finally presented, included most of the ideas I had presented in my draft. However, no doubt press attaché Kent Herath and the embassy economics counselor, Gordon Daniels, felt the same way as they also submitted drafts of their ideas and we were probably all on the same wavelength.

Entitled "Times of Change," the ambassador's speech was very well received. It was pertinent to Bolivia's needs and was given front-page treatment in all Bolivian dailies. One of the leading dailies in La Paz, *El Nacional*, published the full text. USIS also published it as a pamphlet and distributed 5,000 copies. But perhaps what most pleased all of us involved was a short note the ambassador received from President Nixon which congratulated him and his staff on the speech for its content. Such a note from an incumbent U.S. president was possibly unprecedented. Syndicated columnist Georgie Ann Geyer, a Latin American specialist who later moved on to global concerns, also found this particular speech interesting enough to quote parts of it in one of her columns some days later.

As 1971 marched on the BNCs were operating again and USIS was back in the cultural programming business. Life In Bolivia was returning to as close to normal as life there ever is.

With the changed political climate the foreign community in La Paz was once more able to move outside La Paz and official travel was again possible. Once we drove to Cochabamba and Santa Cruz and once went to Cochabamba by train. Once was enough in both instances. Plane trips were, of course, easier and faster.

The Bolivian airline, which had a monopoly on in-country flights, was *Lloyd Aero Bolviano*, usually referred to as "LAB." LAB flew old twin-engine DC-3s which were the workhorses of World War II. A quarter of a century later they were still flying daily within Bolivia. If you planned to fly from the Bolivian capital to almost anywhere else in the country you would probably have to board one of these old workhorses. LAB also had some old Fokkers that carried fewer passengers but were able to land in towns smaller than Cochabamba and Santa Cruz, some of which had dirt runways. Fortunately they were quite dependable and LAB had a good safety record.

Despite their record I always found it rather exciting to fly into Cochabamba on a LAB flight. The airport is 8,400 feet above sea level and is surrounded by higher mountains that the pilot has to fly over and maneuver around before coming into the valley where Bolivia's second largest city is located. (Its population was about 150,000 at the time.) Approaching the airport we seemed to skim the tops of those mountains so closely that one could look down and count the rocks and pebbles below. We always seemed to be no more than a hundred feet above the surrounding mountain peaks before dropping into the valley.

One day at a country team meeting at the embassy in La Paz, it was time for the AID Director, Ed Coy, to say whatever was on his mind of interest to the rest of us. What he told us that day was very interesting. He said that the Bolivian government had just learned that LAB's DC-3s, which they had been flying for years, weighed a thousand pounds more than they thought they did. A thousand pounds, or half a ton, might not make too much difference, but we all knew that the Bolivians always loaded their planes to the hilt, especially on the La Paz-Cochabamba-Santa Cruz run. We also knew that even at Cochabamba, which is a mile below the La Paz airport but still a mile-and-a-half above sea level, the air is still quite thin and planes operate differently than at sea level. Knowing how LAB pilots skimmed Cochabamba's neighboring peaks as close as they did, we could only hope that they would no longer overload their planes.

The Bolivian roads and railroads were something else. The railroads were built by the British, some in the last century. The Bolivians nationalized the railroads many years ago and at one point had to ask the British to come back and maintain them as they were disintegrating under Bolivian management. This is another example of American longshoreman philosopher Eric Hoffer's observation that one of the biggest problems in underdeveloped countries is maintenance.

The only paved road in the La Paz area outside the city and beyond the airport was a road built with U.S. government assistance. It was completed during our tour. For the first time one was able to drive across the altiplano with considerable speed and comfort. The newly paved road ran from La Paz to the mining town of Oruro, 140 miles to the south. Founded in 1601, Oruro was a mining center for tin, silver, and wolfram. The Siglo XX Mine (Twentieth Century Mine—a misnomer if there ever was one), Bolivia's largest, is located in Catavi, about a four-hour drive from Oruro. This was where two USIS officers, Tom Martin and Mike Kristula, some years before my time, made world headlines by being held as hostages by some rebellious miners. They were later freed unharmed.

When USIS officer Jeff Dieterich was transferred from Santa Cruz to Cochabamba to run our operations there, we reluctantly left the Santa Cruz binational center to fend for itself. But one day, back in La Paz, I asked Raul Mariaca, our cultural affairs assistant, about his family. He answered by confiding in me that his wife, who was pregnant at the time, was hemorrhaging. The doctor had advised her, he told me, to get out of the altitude for a while or she would be in danger of losing her baby. I immediately thought, "Why not send Raul to Santa Cruz as our representative there and director of the BNC, in which case his family could accompany him and his wife, perhaps, would recover her health?" (Santa Cruz is only about 1500 feet above sea level.) It was the PAO's prerogative to assign in-country personnel wherever needed. Mariaca was enthused about the idea. He performed magnificently for the year or so he was there before returning to the staff in La Paz. When he and his family returned they brought with them a fine new baby boy.

After awakening abruptly from a deep sleep in the early morning hours of July 1, 1972, I went into the study, turned on the light, sat down at my desk, and began writing about the effects of altitude on me and my friends, living as we were, two miles above sea level.

I had been planning to write such an article for some time and had begun some research on it, but since I generally sleep well beyond 7 a.m. it was rather unusual for me to awaken in this fashion at an early hour. However, this is not an uncommon occurrence for many people living at high altitudes.

"One of the physical effects of 'Soroche' (altitude illness)" I wrote, "is that one can be in a sound sleep for several hours when the level of oxygen in the room relative to the body's needs is such that suddenly you find yourself gasping for air. This 'gasping' usually results in one of two things—either the individual goes off into dreamland, the low oxygen content of the air possibly stimulating the unconscious and the wild dreams so common to visitors to the highlands, or the individual immediately awakens, as I did on this occasion." Of course, after I had awakened, that which had a high priority in my mind at the time came to the fore, which was to write something about what every American in La Paz was always chatting about, the effects of altitude.

Like most foreigners who came to live and work in Bolivia, I often felt the effects of high altitude, both mentally and physically. Seldom were thoughts about these effects far from our minds. I was, however, among the few who decided to investigate this subject in some depth. I began my research by discussing altitude sickness with the embassy medical doctor, Dr. Dwight Babcock. He was most cooperative and let me review his library on high-altitude illnesses. I also sought other sources, all of which were quite limited. Only after leaving Bolivia and spending more than a year of sea-level living was I able to complete the task I began that July morning in 1972.

On November 12, 1973, in Washington, D.C., my short paper on the physical and mental effects of altitude, based on my research and personal experiences in La Paz, was completed. Entitled *No One Should Live Above Ten Thousand Feet*, I began by quoting paragraph 6-5, General Flight Rules (2 Aug. 71) of the United States Air Force Manual 60-16:

> All occupants aboard Air Force aircraft will use supplemental oxygen on flights in which the cabin altitude exceeds 10,000 feet.

In addition, I cited paragraph 6-5a of the same publication:

> On unpressurized aircraft the pilot at the controls will use supplemental oxygen above 10,000 feet. If supplemental oxygen is not available to other occupants, flight between 10,000 and 13,000 feet must not be longer than three hours and flight above 13,000 feet is not authorized.

These regulations applied, of course, to the unpressurized cabins that were common in those days. I reminded readers that I didn't say that people "couldn't;" I said "shouldn't" live above 10,000 feet. The document ran to twelve pages, single space, and became known as "The Hansen Report" when it was used on one occasion to defend the special hardship allowance granted U.S. Foreign Service employees stationed in La Paz. The section that follows highlights some of my observations and conclusions on this subject.

There are only three places in the world where people customarily live above ten thousand feet: the Andes in South America, the High Rockies in the western part of the United States, and the Himalayas in Southeast Asia. The person who reminded me of this, who was almost eighty years old at the time and on a visit to La Paz (which, at 12,500 feet, is the highest capital in the world), was the inimitable news commentator and explorer who became a household word in the 1930s and 40s, Lowell Thomas, Sr. Having been raised in the Colorado Rockies, he was unaffected by the altitude in La Paz which frequently affects so many others.

One of the most visible signs of the effects of altitude, which was noticeable among my colleagues and me when living in La Paz, was the ease with which one became irritable in an environment where oxygen is at a premium. Hardly a day passed when I was not consciously irritated at something or somebody. This was not due, in my view, simply to cultural differences or the isolation of La Paz, both of which are capable of causing problems of adjustment leading to irritability.

The "irritability factor" can be devastating if not understood. How one discharges his frustrations and anger becomes an important problem for everyone, but especially for diplomats who are always expected to "keep their cool." It requires astute handling of the effects of the dearth of oxygen in relations with family, friends, and all with whom one comes in contact. In short, the *altitude* can very seriously affect one's *attitude*.

In the early 1970s, studies of altitude illness did not have a high priority in the scientific community. Furthermore, most research involved short periods of time and produced mixed results—some persons experience high blood pressure from the altitude, some low; some experience wakefulness, others experience somnolence, etc. Yet there was general agreement, even then, that acute mountain illness, known in Bolivia as "soroche" and by other names elsewhere, affects some persons more than others. It affects different people differently, and in differing degrees, and some, not at all.

A classic study of altitude illness was conducted in India in 1963. Almost 2,000 soldiers of the Indian army were quickly moved from the lowlands of India to the highlands of the Indo-Chinese border because of a conflict between China and India at the time. Dr. Inder Singh and his associates studied how acute mountain illness affected these men. They found that in 840 *untreated* cases, the symptoms were, in order of frequency: headache, nausea, loss of appetite, breathlessness, insomnia, muscular weakness, fullness or pain in the chest, giddiness, vomiting, disinclination to work, thirst, indigestion, flatulence, constipation, tachycardia, palpitation, hysterical outbursts or other disorders of behavior, lack of concentration, mental impairment or confusion, fever, pain in the legs, cough, edema of the legs and feet, hallucinations, diarrhea, difficulty in micturition, epistaxis, pain in the abdomen, elevated blood pressure (above 160 systolic, 100 diastolic), low blood pressure (below 110 systolic, 75 diastolic), blackouts, hemoptysis, incoherent speech, lack of response to questions, sudden collapse in bed during sleep, visual disturbances, stupor, seizures, coma, and paralysis. The treated cases were, of course, more serious than these relatively minor discomforts, with the exception of the latter-mentioned effects.

There is general agreement that some individuals are prone to the "delayed" or chronic type of altitude illness. This chronic "soroche" can affect even those who enable their bodies to adjust more gradually to the reduced oxygen levels of high altitudes, either through gradual movement into the altitude, which helps considerably if feasible, or those who wisely abstain from alcohol, cigarettes, heavy meals, and exercise their first few days in the highlands. Yet there are those who argue that chronic mountain illness simply doesn't exist. Symptoms attributed to "chronic altitude illness" are really caused, they contend, by more traditional factors. Whether *hypoxia* i.e., insufficient oxygen to vital organs, is primary or secondary to another organ problem is the main thrust of the differing views. Despite this etiological argument, the end result in both cases is hypoxia and decreasing human function in all areas.

Historically the major concern of the medical profession has been the cardiac-vascular and respiratory systems, both of which are affected by the amount of available oxygen. The Department of State, for example, in the 1970s was conducting what it called a "high altitude test" for persons slated to serve at high-altitude posts. The test consisted solely of checking lung capacity and an electrocardiogram. This was added to the standard physical examination for employees assigned to La Paz and other high altitude posts.

Any individual with a borderline physical or mental problem would have greater difficulty in adapting to the altitude than individuals without such problems. A high altitude environment could be expected to accelerate the deterioration of an organic or nervous condition to the point where persons with such conditions might have to leave the altitude or suffer dire consequences. In short, anyone who is a borderline case with respect to any physical or mental problem could normally expect such a condition to worsen at high altitudes.

In Dr. Singh's study of the Indian army incident, he classified the effects of acute mountain illness, for the purpose of numerical scoring, as follows:

> *Cerebral* (headache, giddiness, dizziness, etc.)
> *Gastrointestinal* (anoxia, nausea, vomiting, abdominal pain, etc.)
> *Pulmonary* (undue dyspnea i.e. shortness of breath at rest and during exertion, excessive cough, etc.)
> *Psychosomatic* (insomnia or restlessness) General (tiredness, weakness, body aches, etc.)

Dr. Singh found that the normal duration of incapacitating illness was between two to five days, although in some cases complete recovery occurred only after a long time. He noted that the cerebral blood flow increased 40 percent within twelve to thirty-six hours after arrival in the mountains and approached normal values by the fifth day. Only nine soldiers of the 1,925 who were studied failed to acclimatize in six months and were considered unfit for duties at high altitudes. This is a clear indication that the vast majority of persons adapt to their new environment following an initial period of discomfort. However, the question of physical capability and mental alertness after ostensible adaptation to the altitude remains.

The most common and persistent symptom among the Indian troops as they shuttled from sea level to Himalayan altitudes in the neighborhood of 18,000 feet was headache. During exertion hysterical outbursts and other disorders of behavior occurred and there were seventeen cases of blurring of vision and engorgement of retinal veins. Among other symptoms was breathlessness which increased when lying down. During sleep, breathing had a tendency to become irregular or, as it is known medically, Cheyne-Stokes in type, and patients affected, according to Dr. Singh, often woke up suddenly with a feeling of suffocation. In addition to breathlessness, they often complained of fullness, discomfort, or pain in the chest.

What causes acute mountain illness? There seems to be general agreement that the decrease in barometric pressure at high altitudes is of little or no significance. It is the concomitant diminished quantity of oxygen per unit volume in the inspired air that brings about "soroche." Individual susceptibility is impossible to predict though it is doubtful that anyone would entirely escape after reaching an altitude of 16,000 feet above sea level. From 18,000 to 25,000 feet unconsciousness occurs in most persons unless there is an oxygen supply available. Each individual probably has his particular threshold altitude.

The major causative factor of acute mountain illness is *hypoxia,* which, as noted earlier, is insufficient oxygen to such vital organs as the brain, pulmonary arteries, etc. The symptoms mentioned earlier are a consequence of hypoxia. In normal adjustment to altitude, which, fortunately, is the experience of the vast majority of visitors to the highlands, respiration becomes deeper and slightly more rapid in order to permit normal oxygenation of the blood. Breathlessness during exertion occurs much more quickly than at sea level, but this is normal. As respiration is deeper, more carbon dioxide is eliminated from the body and a temporary state of alkalosis is present for the first few days after arriving in the highlands. Usually no symptoms are visible and the kidneys excrete an extra amount of sodium bicarbonate to correct this situation. In a week or two the blood returns to a normal degree of acid-base equilibrium.

The symptoms of headache, loss of appetite, weakness, fatigue, shortness of breath after easy exertion, and disturbed, restless sleep, while common, are not particularly harmful and represent the adjustment of the central control of respiration to the high altitude. These symptoms generally disappear, as noted earlier, in less than five days and more often in the first few days. They rarely occur below 9,000 feet. It is at ten thousand feet and above where they can be most expected, which makes life in La Paz more of a potential problem for visiting lowlanders than any other capital city in the world, since all other capitals enjoy altitudes of less than 10,000 feet.

Since it is the oxygen deficiency in the vital and special centers of the body that causes *mal de montagnes,* hearing, vision, and reaction time are often disturbed and delayed, and all of the principal physiological adjustments are directed toward the preservation of oxygen tension in the region of the cells above some critical value. In severe cases the pulse rate is increased and the patient becomes cyanotic (bluish in color). If relief is not given, the patient becomes unconscious, cardio-respiratory failure rapidly follows, and the victim expires, as some mountain climbing expeditions have regrettably experienced. But it is worth stressing that fortunately, cases of this severity are rare, particularly where oxygen supplies are readily available.

The normal occurrence is that the body generally adapts to the situation using mechanisms of acclimatization to the hypoxia it experiences. These mechanisms of the body can be separated into those involving the struggle for oxygen and those involving adaptation to hypoxia. The struggle occurs at the organ level by hyperventilation, increased blood flow, polycythemia, change in the activity of the blood enzymes, and the acid-base response. At the tissue level there are increases in myoglobin and change in enzyme activity, and there are also changes in the brain function.

According to my research, hyperventilation occurs in order to bring more oxygen into the body. The cardiovascular system adjusts to the new situation. The blood supply begins to increase almost immediately, so that within three to four weeks the lowlandsman has increased the quantity of blood in his body by one third, or about two pints. With the lowered oxygen pressure, the bone marrow produces more red blood cells enabling additional oxygen to be carried by the blood and this process is completed in from four to six weeks. When a person returns to sea level the process is reversed and a normal sea level state is attained within one or two weeks. It is the respiratory system, however, which reacts first to the lack of oxygen and is manifested by greater respiratory minute volume mediated by the cardiac and aoristic bodies. This sets in motion the secondary responses in properties of the blood as mentioned above.

In one experiment conducted at 14,250 feet it was shown that there was a decrease in oxygen saturation during sleep to a value characteristic of an altitude of close to 16,000 feet. However, it was noted that this may be of less importance than the fact that during sleep, whether at high altitude or at sea level, there is a decreased response to CO_2. According to one study, the decrease in oxygen saturation might explain the difficult first nights often experienced by the newcomer to high altitudes. The effects experienced include nightmares, sleeplessness, and the morning headache that tends to wear off during the day.

The above is a medically sound explanation of the abundant, seemingly endless dreams that persist when living at high altitude for months or years. My own theory is that some of those weird dreams of the type I and others experienced when living for a few years in La Paz are due as much to stomach gas as to anything else. A gas bubble in the intestine is small at sea level. At ten thousand feet it can be three times sea-level size (because of the reduced air pressure). This causes not only greater pain and discomfort and, occasionally, embarrassment, but, when occurring at night, can cause the same kind of unique dreams which sometimes occur at sea level following a heavy, late-night meal. In any event, problems involving the excretory system can occur due to the disturbance of acid-base balance brought about by increased pulmonary ventilation. At the same time, the lack of oxygen reduces the tone and mobility of the stomach, whether empty or full. One study showed that emptying a person's stomach is appreciably prolonged at 10,000 feet. While difficulty in sleeping during the first few days in the altitude can be caused by faulty respiratory regulation prior to the body's adjustment to its new environment, it can also be caused simply by cold feet. This comes about sometimes as a result of a reduced amount of blood to the extremities.

An interesting sidelight about acute mountain illness is that children and adults in excellent physical condition are more likely candidates for soroche than individuals who are not in top physical form. This is because the organ systems overreact to the stimulus of hypoxia. The elderly and less robust individuals do not have the ability to react as strongly as those in top physical shape.

All the symptoms associated with acute mountain illness and which are generally short-lived can and do return to haunt those individuals who, for physical or mental reasons, cannot adjust to high altitudes. When this occurs this condition is described as delayed or chronic mountain llness.

Shortly before our arrival in La Paz, a family from the U.S. found that while the mother and father were able to adjust easily to the altitude, their four-year-old child was somnolent and uncomfortable almost from the moment they arrived in Bolivia. After a few weeks the family visited the Chilean seaport of Arica where they stayed about one week. In Arica the child quickly recovered and remained healthy. While returning to La Paz by train, his somnolence returned upon reaching an altitude of about 9,500 feet. The family, in agreement with the embassy medical doctor, decided that there was no recourse but to abandon La Paz and return to sea level since this youngster could not adapt to the high altitude. He would never be able to lead a normal life in La Paz.

In another case a middle-aged man assigned to the embassy in La Paz who found himself working in a high-altitude environment for the first time was forgetful, nervous, and generally inefficient. He was a heavy cigarette smoker, which probably contributed to his inability to adapt to the altitude. Smoking causes the inhalation of carbon monoxide that combines with the hemoglobin in the blood, further reducing the amount of oxygen that can be transported by the red blood cells. This effect at sea level, where the amount of arterial oxygen is high, is not particularly important for healthy individuals. In a borderline oxygen-level situation, however, such as that found at 10,000 feet and above, carbon monoxide uses about 5 percent of the blood volume in moderate and heavy smokers, making this factor extremely important. When transferred to another embassy at a lower altitude, his normal efficiency returned.

A cigarette smoked at 10,000 feet can be the straw that breaks the camel's back. One morning in my office I was smoking a cigarette (as I did rather frequently in those days) when, having finished about half of the cigarette, I suddenly found myself extremely light-headed and weak, so much so that I felt compelled to open the windows for more air, stretched out on the couch in my office, and though greatly embarrassed at my situation, called my secretary and asked her to phone the embassy medical unit and request an oxygen tank. I had in mind one of the small green oxygen tanks we commonly took with us to the airport when welcoming first-time visitors to La Paz. But about ten minutes later the embassy nurse appeared lugging a three-foot tank that she had heroically carried up the block-long hill from the embassy building to the USIS building, then up three flights of stairs to my office. By the time she arrived I was feeling much better but took a few whiffs of oxygen so her trip wouldn't be wasted. A complete medical exam shortly thereafter could determine no physical problem and I never experienced a similar situation during the rest of the time that I was in La Paz. After this incident I tried to smoke less but with only partial success until many months later when other factors reinforced my efforts to quit smoking.

This incident, and similar ones which occurred to others which I witnessed from time to time while in Bolivia, were not caused by chronic mountain illness. But where an individual continues to suffer a number of such incidents, chronic mountain illness is probably the cause.

Symptoms of chronic mountain illness may be similar to other diseases. However, those who contend it is a disease in its own right agree that it can develop insidiously and that prolonged oxygen deficiency is the probable cause. Dull headache, shortness of breath after moderate or even slight exertion, diminution or loss of appetite, nausea, gaseous indigestion, and disordered bowel function are some of the more common symptoms. Furthermore, the patient is irritable and unable to work or carry on normal functions without assistance.

If the symptoms become steadily worse and cannot be controlled, the individual must return to sea level or at least to a lower altitude where normal functioning generally quickly returns. Whether hypoxia is primary or secondary to another organ problem, and whether chronic mountain illness per se actually exists or not, makes little difference to the person affected. The cure remains that of returning as soon as possible to a more oxygenated environment.

To fully appreciate the challenges faced by anyone born and raised at or near sea-level who must live and work for a period of time at altitudes above 10,000 feet, a few comments about the mental effects of living and working in high altitudes are in order. I have already discussed "irritability," but there are others.

More research has been done on the physical aspects than the mental aspects of altitude illness, probably because the physical aspects are easier to observe. I submit, however, based on my research and experience, that the mental effects of altitude are just as prevalent and, possibly, more widespread. Although difficult to prove, some of the effects of altitude, such as irritability, may well have been a contributory cause to Bolivia's volatile history—a history that, at least until the early 1970s, was marked by governments being overthrown on an average of every nine months.

Forgetfulness is one common characteristic brought about by lack of oxygen. This trait was particularly noticeable in La Paz during my stay there because it was so universal. Forgetting names, dates, places, etc. occurred far too frequently, among all age groups, to be attributable to such popular beliefs as "growing old." Supporting the thesis that altitude affects memory is the theory that the elderly are generally less alert than younger persons because their brain cells receive less oxygen. Research by various investigators has determined that brain cells deprived of normal amounts of oxygen do not perform efficiently, resulting in a diminution of intellectual and reasoning powers. Conversely, when increased oxygen is delivered to the brain, mental alertness improves.

Clinical psychologists in studies at the Veterans Administration Hospital in Buffalo, New York, have demonstrated that when they administered pure oxygen to senile patients placed in a pressurized chamber, the patients' scores on standard memory tests improved as much as 25 percent following two pure-oxygen treatments daily for fifteen days. In another study conducted by Dr. Herbert A. DeVries at the Gerontology Center of the University of Southern California, DeVries and his colleagues concluded that mental processes can be significantly improved by a program of regular exercise which increases oxygen transport to the brain through natural processes.

On more than one occasion when the USIS driver drove me to the office I feared we were about to collide with another vehicle. I would feel compelled to shout in alarm, "Victor, Victor! *Cuidado!*" (Careful!) I believe my warnings resulted not solely because I am at times a "back seat driver," but because my reaction time was quicker than Victor's. Why was his reaction slower, if indeed it was? I suspect the reason may well have been due to the smaller quantity of oxygen he had been breathing all of his life in La Paz and environs. Never before, or since, have I been so conscious of such a slow reaction time by a driver of a vehicle.

The human body, in most important aspects, adapts in the course of a lifetime to the unique oxygen requirements of high altitude living just as the short-range visitor to the altitude generally adapts. In one study autopsies were made on thirty-six persons, most of whom had died in accidents and all of whom had lived above 12,000 feet. The autopsies revealed exceptionally large lungs and heart organs. The liver, spleen, kidneys, testicles, ovaries, muscle fibers taken from the biceps, the brain and suprarenal glands were found to differ little, if any, from sea-level inhabitants. The conclusion was that blood and lungs, the major organs involved with oxygen, are the organs most affected by altitude. The enlarged lungs and heart organs seem to compensate sufficiently for the lowered oxygen content of rarefied mountain air, but given the evidence available of other effects of altitude, full compensation is doubtful.

Some years ago a group of international alpinists set out to climb Mount Everest. They had to abandon the attempt not because of the difficulties of the climb, bad weather, or the usual reasons, but because they discovered that they could not agree on essential decisions once they were high in the Himalayas. They became so argumentative they were forced to cancel the expedition. Once again, the altitude, apparently, had claimed some victims—mentally.

In 1923 members of an expedition to the high Andes reported to the Peru High Altitude Committee that the effect of the altitude on the mental processes were insidious but, eventually, quite apparent. They noted that although short and precise exercises did not exhibit any pronounced change in the nervous and reflex capacity of the members of the party, prolonged concentration gave evidence of lowered control. Whereas at sea level certain members of the group would use a Haldane gas analysis apparatus or other similar technique for days without a mistake, hardly a day passed at Cerro de Pasco in the high Peruvian Andes without once or more frequently having to take the apparatus apart for cleaning because of a foolish mistake or manipulation.

Similar errors were evident in the arithmetic calculations of the group. Frequently simple sums had to be gone over repeatedly before the person was satisfied with respect to accuracy, according to the report. Similar conditions pertained when the slide rule and logarithms were used.

Although the group worked long hours they noted that the amount of work accomplished in a day was sometimes disappointing. They concluded that this was due to the conspicuous mental and physical fatigue that gradually developed as the day wore on, resulting inevitably in slowness and clumsiness. Nor was the effect of prolonged and steady work confined only to the members of the expedition. Men who had lived at Cerro de Pasco for years without any symptoms of acute "soroche" informed them that the best results were obtained by short periods of work with long rests between. This was particularly true for those whose occupation was mental, such as accountants, draftsmen, etc.

There are other disadvantages to "high living" which are not related to lack of oxygen. These include the question of the effect of radiation on the human body. This is a phenomenon against which astronauts take such elaborate precautions, as do we earthlings when it comes to X-rays and the sun's rays.

A person living at sea level receives an annual dosage of natural radiation from his surroundings of about forty millirems (the unit used as a measure of biological effect of absorbed radiation). A person living at 5,000 feet is exposed to about ninety-two millirems annually. Natural solar radiation increases about one millirem for each one hundred feet of elevation. While there is probably no radiation danger from the sun to the occasional visitor who spends relatively short periods of time at 10,000 feet and beyond, radiation at that altitude results in a substantial increase during the course of one's lifetime. While this may not be significant, no one would want to go out of their way to seek greater exposure to radiation except for specified medical reasons.

One noticeable effect of radiation at high altitudes can be observed in the eyes of Andean Indians. The area of their eyes that is exposed to the sunlight is brown as a result of radiation i.e., one sees not the "white" of their eyes but the brown of their eyes. This is, allegedly, not due to racial differences but is caused by radiation from the sun at high altitudes.

I had not thought about my boyhood and about growing up in New Jersey for a long time until a visitor unexpectedly arrived in La Paz, a city where visitors were generally as scarce as rain in the dry season. He suddenly reminded me of my boyhood days.

From Madrid to Montevideo, meeting famous and accomplished folk like Helen Hayes, Albert Knopf, Danny Kaye, and Duke Ellington, to name a few, who came in and out of a Foreign Service officer's life abroad, was fairly common. But no known giants of American life had as yet landed in Bolivia during our tour here, and none anywhere ever stirred my memories the way this visitor did.

Back in the early thirties in Metuchen, N.J., our family—consisting of my parents, my brother and me—gathered for dinner almost every evening at the kitchen table. We seldom ate in the dining room of our small house except on special occasions when we had company. Dinner was almost always at 6 p.m. sharp. We were usually still sitting at the table when my dad turned on the radio for the evening news broadcast that began at 6:45 p.m. on Station WJZ New York. The newscast was presented in that familiar, distinct, and entertaining voice of the man who always ended his broadcast with, "So long, until tomorrow." I refer, of course, to the most famous newscaster in the business at the time, Lowell Thomas. His name was a household word in the U.S. in the 1930s and 1940s and well beyond, not only because of his daily radio broadcasts but also because of his exploits as an explorer, writer, lecturer, and motion picture producer.

The radio in our kitchen was a small, dark brown table model that was kept at the corner of the kitchen counter that my father had built, back against the wall. I can visualize it even now as I write this, nearly forty years later, just as I can remember so vividly Lowell Thomas's daily broadcasts which we and millions of other Americans depended upon as a major source of news. Those broadcasts were as much a part of my daily living as eating dinner, since the only time we failed to listen to Lowell Thomas was when we weren't home for dinner, a very rare event in those days. But in La Paz in the early 1970s, when these thoughts came to me, reminiscences of this type were rare. Not only were the problems of daily living in the altitude enough to keep one's mind on current survival rather than ruminations about the past, but the political and social turmoil during the past year, prior to Thomas's visit to La Paz, demanded considerable concentration.

What stimulated this reminiscence was a telegram from the PAO in Asuncion, Paraguay. It stated that Lowell Thomas, his wife, and his secretary would be arriving in La Paz the next day. The cable suggested that USIS extend appropriate courtesies. The telegram wasn't clear as to whether this was Lowell Thomas, Sr. or his son who had become governor of Alaska, but might now be out of office. My first thought was that the telegram must be referring to the latter.

To my knowledge Lowell Thomas, Sr. had not been heard from for years and was now quite elderly. Since I was uncertain which of the Thomas' was headed our way, and since visitors were such a rarity in La Paz, I decided to make the trip to the airport myself to greet the visitors rather than send one of my staffers. If it were the senior Thomas who I would be meeting, his advanced age might cause him to have breathing problems in the altitude. I made certain, therefore, that we would have an oxygen tank available.

Our visitor was, indeed, the senior Lowell Thomas, then seventy-nine years old. He was completely unaffected by the altitude, yet I was glad we brought the tank with us because his wife found the oxygen most welcome. Perhaps, I thought, her stamina had not been fortified by earlier expeditions to high places like Tibet and Afghanistan as was the case with the old explorer. Later I learned that she was suffering from a long-term illness that would, a few years later, be fatal.

Lowell Thomas, despite his age, was easily recognizable to anyone who had seen any of his motion picture travelogues or his Cinerama production, "The Seven Wonders of the World." When he spoke, in that marvelously distinct, carefully cadenced voice of his, I could have closed my eyes and easily imagined that I was back home in Metuchen and the year was 1935 or thereabouts. In tone and cadence there had been no change in all those years. His wife was obviously not too well but trouper that she was, did not complain. His secretary, Electra Nicks, was a pleasant, middle-aged widow with grown sons. Her duties included being nurse and helpmate to the aging, ailing Mrs. Thomas. I met them at planeside and escorted them into the terminal building.

We cleared the airport after the usual delays and headed down from the altiplano into the sides of the bowl which holds La Paz. The visitors, somewhat to my surprise, were as awed at the sight of La Paz in its bowl, as seen from the narrow road that winds down around the crater that holds this unique city, as they were at the colorful Indian women, the cholas in their bowler hats. I asked Thomas if, given all his travels, he found Bolivia particularly unique. He said he did, despite his worldwide travels.

He said he was fascinated by the similarity in the racial features of the Bolivian Indians and the Tibetans he had known. He remarked that because of these similarities, "There must surely be a relationship between these two peoples." When he left La Paz a few days later he again commented about how the two peoples struck him as looking so much alike.

"The Tibetans," he added, "seemed to be a more alert people."

This comment was based on his admittedly superficial observation of the Bolivian Indians. If true, which is debatable, nutrition and a much longer Tibetan history might be the causes of differences among two peoples living in very similar isolated, mountainous environments.

This was Thomas's first time in Bolivia. For a few moments we had a play on words. I mentioned how the llama, which inhabits the Bolivian highlands, is used for meat though primarily for its fur and as a pack animal, since the meat is tough and stringy. He said that in Tibet the llama is unknown (not so the lama—a priest of Lamaism, or Buddhism as practiced in Tibet and Mongolia), whereas the yak is a common animal. Yak meat is excellent, he added. I said perhaps the yak should be imported into Bolivia, a country that still doesn't grow enough to feed itself. And, I added, "There is a Yak (capital "Y") about to come here later this month." I was referring to the Russian short-range jet that the Soviet Union was demonstrating in various South American capitals with the hope of building a Yak market in this part of the world.

We arrived at the Hotel Crillon about 5 p.m. I checked at the desk to see if the reservation, which had been made by the Thomases by cable, had been received. It hadn't. We were told that the hotel was full. "But this is the famous American radio commentator, Lowell Thomas!" I said. "Surely you don't want to turn him away."

The clerk looked at me rather dubiously. "Who?" he asked.

"Lowell Thomas! You know, for decades he's been the most famous radio commentator in the United States."

The clerk still didn't react the way I thought he should, but he eventually became convinced that Lowell Thomas was someone important enough to be paid special attention. After a little more discussion he finally decided he could accommodate him and his party.

After getting them settled in their rooms they expressed their appreciation for our attentions and said they would retire early. I invited them to lunch with us the next day (a Saturday) as we were planning to go to our favorite outdoor restaurant in Achocalla, a beautiful green valley about a forty minute drive from La Paz. Although they didn't join us at lunch they readily accepted an invitation to cocktails at our home that evening.

About 6:30 p.m. the next day I called for the Thomases and Mrs. Nicks at the hotel and drove them to our house in Obrajes. I had managed, on short notice, to invite a few people who, I thought, would enjoy meeting Lowell Thomas. The group included Amadee Landry, USAID educational officer and his wife; Kent Herath, the USIS information officer, his wife and oldest daughter; Ingrid Schwartz, the wife of the USIS cultural attaché (who was in Washington, D.C. on a business trip); Seldon Rodman, author of many books including histories of the Dominican Republic and Peru, who was visiting La Paz and had earlier expressed a desire to meet Lowell Thomas; Rodman's friend, Kent Stacy, a Britisher with AID; and our house guest, Frank Gomez, the USIA Washington desk officer for Bolivia. Gomez was on an official visit to La Paz. Charmaine, unfortunately, could not join us as she was suffering from a temporary stomach ailment.

During the first fifteen or twenty minutes after the arrival of the Thomases there was the usual cocktail chatter. But once the initial formalities were over we all settled around the guest of honor and he began to spin his tales. He mentioned how Eric Savereid, Ed Murrow, and other former newsmen of the World War II and post-WWII era had all succeeded him; that when he began his newscasts in the twenties and thirties, long before television made its appearance, there were no newscasts on radio. He said that when he started he used to take the news from the newspapers, using his own style and treatment (which was what most radio stations in Bolivia in the early 1970s were doing). Later, he said, he started taking news from the Associated Press and UPI but always quoted them as his sources. Then this became a problem. "After a while," he said, "AP told me to go ahead and use their news but 'don't quote us as the newspapers are beginning to complain.'"

He told of the time he went to Tibet as the first American correspondent ever to enter that little-known land. On one of the mountain passes, when leaving Tibet, he fell off his horse, breaking his hip and leg in eight places. For twenty days he had to be carried by stretcher to get out of the country. "Through the grapevine," he said, "word reached the outside world about my mishap. The U.S. Air Force planned to send in a helicopter to rescue me but it soon became apparent that no helicopter then flying could operate at the altitude common to Tibet, so there was nothing to do but to come out as I had gone in, on horseback."

He credited his son Lowell Jr. with saving his life, "and in recognition of this I insisted that he write the book that I had planned to write on Forbidden Tibet. It later became a best seller." Two days later, as we were awaiting the arrival of his plane for Lima, Peru, he told me that he had written fifty-two books to date and was currently deep into his memoirs. He added that his publisher, Doubleday, had encouraged him as far back as 1926 to write his memoirs.

"You have to be circumspect when you write about yourself," he said. "When you write about others, that's not the case, so I've always shied away from writing my memoirs. But now I think I'm ready to write my own history. As a matter of fact, I've finished about 40,000 words so far, and am up to 1932."

As we sat listening to Lowell Thomas, my daughters Alicia (7), Katherine (8), and Annette (10) passed hors d'oeuvres before saying goodnight to our guests. As Annette kissed me goodnight she whispered in my ear, "Is he the only one who is allowed to talk?" Frank Gomez later described the evening as a lecture for which one would willingly have paid to listen to any time, anywhere.

Seldon Rodman asked Thomas if he thought that T. E. Lawrence, the famed desert fighter, had really been a homosexual. Thomas had been the only American correspondent to travel with Lawrence in Arabia. In 1924, Thomas gained his initial fame with the publication of his book *With Lawrence in Arabia*, as well as his well-attended lectures in New York and London about Lawrence's Arabian escapades.

"I don't believe so," Thomas answered curtly. "After all, he traveled all over England on his motorcycle with Lady Astor."

"That's not convincing," Rodman retorted, and added, "I wrote a book on Lawrence myself, long after yours, and I have my doubts." Thomas was not disposed to discuss it further.

The following evening the subject of Lawrence came up again while visiting Ambassador Siracusa's home. In another long, fascinating monologue Thomas said that the popular Hollywood film, "Lawrence of Arabia," was "a phony. His life wasn't at all as it was depicted in that film."

We were enthralled as we listened to Thomas discuss a few of his many experiences and some of his philosophical observations based on a unique, amazingly active life that spanned close to eighty years. His mind was still clear as a bell. He retained the ability to capture his audience, a trait that had made him a millionaire on the lecture circuit in the U.S. and Canada, as well as a household word in broadcasting for at least three decades. As far as I was concerned the evening could have continued indefinitely. But as the clock neared nine he indicated it was time for his wife to retire. Reluctantly on our part, they said their good-byes and I drove them back to the hotel.

As we parted he said he had decided that his wife was holding up all right in the altitude so they planned to go to the altiplano the next day, Sunday, to take a look at famed Lake Titicaca. He wondered, he said, what was meant by the claim that Titicaca was "the highest navigable lake in the world," since Lake Victoria in Africa "is certainly a candidate for that title." I said I presume that Lake Titicaca garners the title because it has a large steamboat that crosses the lake from Bolivia to Peru. (Later I checked my Atlas. Lake Titicaca at 12,506 feet, is definitely the champ; Lake Victoria's altitude is only 3,720 feet!)

The next afternoon I received a phone call from Thomas. He said they had been to the lake in the morning, that all went well, that it was a beautiful sight to see and he was glad that he had not missed seeing such a famed body of water while visiting La Paz. He enquired about Charmaine who had been ill the night before and wondered if we hadn't eaten lunch yet if we could join them. I told him Charmaine was still not up to par and we had already eaten but I was available if he wanted to see more of the city that afternoon. He replied that he would like to see the La Paz Golf Club since Jim Cagle, the manager of the hotel where he was staying and an ardent golfer, had told him about "the highest golf course in the world." We arranged for me to pick him up about 4 p.m.

I left home about quarter to four and started up the hill toward town but ran into a traffic jam well before reaching the downtown area. The traffic tie-up was caused by a car that was burning on the side of the narrow road, just below the horseshoe curve where the Presidential Guard, known as the *Batallón Colorado* (the Red Battalion), had its headquarters. Any visitor to La Paz could not but be aware of that turn in the road because it was always guarded by at least two soldiers armed with machine guns. Invariably their guns were aimed at passing motorists, for reasons best known to the Bolivian Army. We always drove past those armed guards with some trepidation for fear one of them might have a slippery trigger finger, though to my knowledge no innocent motorists were ever shot. Since it was the easiest way to get to the center of town we frequently went that way.

I made a quick U-turn before cars coming up the hill behind me bottled me in and went back down the hill. A few minutes later I was able to turn left on the only other road that led from the valley, where my home was, to the city. This was the road to a residential area known as Miraflores. I thought I could get to the Hotel Crillon by going cross-town after getting through Miraflores. Unfortunately, I had not reckoned with the fact that carnival was being celebrated in La Paz that day. Traffic in the whole city experienced delays because of parades and demonstrations. I found that I had to go to the opposite side of town, following the northern edge of the bowl, before finally being able to cross over to the southern edge in order to drop down into the bowl. This way I would reach the hotel from behind. When I reached one of the few gas stations in La Paz (seven in all) I decided to phone the hotel so that Thomas would know my predicament and would not have to stand in the lobby an hour or more as I suspected he was now doing.

The gas station had a telephone, but no telephone book, so I called home. My son Robert was there and gave me the number of the hotel. I then called the hotel and asked them to page Lowell Thomas in the lobby. Sure enough he was there and quickly came to the phone. I explained my plight and suggested that he might want to go to his room as I didn't known how long it would take before I arrived, but would call him from the lobby when I did. I also told him that I had talked with the ambassador, who had been out of town the day before, and the ambassador had invited him for a drink at his home when we returned from the golf course. He readily accepted and after phoning the ambassador to confirm acceptance of his invitation, I resumed my wanderings trying to circumvent the center of La Paz and get to the hotel by the quickest and shortest route.

I continued skirting the center of town, following the curvature of the basin in which La Paz nestles, seeing parts of the city that I had never seen before. Besides the parades, carnival in Bolivia is a time when youngsters throw water by the bucketful and water-filled balloons at any moving object or person. Sometimes they simply use a hose. Prudence requires that any motorist driving in the city during the three days of carnival must keep the windows of his car tightly closed or be in danger of getting soaked. The water is thrown in good fun. It is a far more satisfactory sport than the bullets and bombs Bolivians had thrown at each other during the volatile political atmosphere prior to the latest revolution.

I finally arrived at the hotel. Thomas was in the lobby. It would have been impossible to miss him, not only because his face is so well known but because he was wearing a bright red Scotch-plaid shirt that could have been spotted a mile away, particularly in the clear, thin air of La Paz. We set off immediately and headed down the hill, past the Batallón Colorado and their omnipresent machine guns and past the sad sight of the burned-out car that had now been pushed to the side of the road. We entered Calacoto, often referred to as "gringolandia" because so many foreigners lived in this residential area of La Paz.

About five roads led out of the Bolivian capital. Most had military check points on the outskirts of the city. An exception was the road to the airport where the military post was much farther out on the altiplano, well beyond the airport. Depending on which turn one takes, that road eventually reaches Argentina, Paraguay, Peru, or Chile. The other four roads peter out somewhere within the vastness of Bolivia.

The road to the golf club normally is one of two roads where one is never stopped, but for the first time since my arrival in Bolivia, a barrier was down across the road and a policeman stopped us. He asked to see our credentials. A few days earlier the Minister of Interior had announced that a plot to assassinate the president had been uncovered. This was the reason, I presume, for the extra precautions. I showed the policeman my driver's license, told him I was with the American embassy and that we were just going to the golf club, and we were allowed to proceed.

Upon leaving the check point the dusty dirt road crosses a bridge under which flows the sewage of La Paz. Fortunately it is distilled somewhat by the time it reaches this bridge by the inflow of two small streams which, at Calacoto, join the open river that flows through the center of La Paz and serves as the city's garbage disposal and sewage system. The beneficent rays of the sun, which so forcefully fall on Bolivia at this altitude, also help distill the open sewage system of La Paz. The road then climbs up towards the Valley of the Moon which is reached after passing through two dirt tunnels.

The landscape of the Valley of the Moon is a unique and striking bit of real estate in this unique and striking country. It is a weathered, rocky, dirt area of small peaks and valleys with little vegetation except a few cacti. Weird-looking rock and dirt formations are sculptured by wind and water erosion into grotesque forms. They make it appear as similar to any moonscape as one can imagine. Even world traveler Lowell Thomas was impressed.

At the fork in the road near the top of the plateau the left fork leads to a longer valley off to the southwest, about ten miles distant, where the road fizzles out at a small Indian village. We took the right fork that leads to the golf club. A few hundred yards down this road a column of dirt about twenty feet high with a large rock balanced on top stands out like a giant phallic symbol overlooking this grotesque landscape. The column is close to the road and the rock seems to lean toward the center of the road.

"Why don't they knock that down," Thomas commented, "before that rock falls down on somebody." I didn't reply. In a country where the paved road from Cochabamba to Santa Cruz, the two leading cities in Bolivia after La Paz, was left to disintegrate for eighteen years without any serious maintenance, and where the runways at the airports in those same two towns are left untouched until it becomes necessary to repair them or planes cannot land, I knew of no one who would come along and eliminate that rock hazard. Some day, perhaps, it will fall down from its own weight, possibly on a passing motorist.

There is one more challenge to be met before arriving at the clubhouse of the world's highest golf course. After passing through the Valley of the Moon the road runs down into a riverbed that is crossed by a narrow wooden bridge. It then climbs through a sharp, narrow, one-lane passage with several sharp curves and where dirt cliffs hem you in on both sides. Only by blowing your horn are you able to warn any cars coming from the opposite direction that you are there. Once through this channel of dirt you reach not only the world's highest golf course, but one of the most striking panoramic views available anywhere.

The view from there presents the dry river bed nearby that we had crossed; the long valley behind the Valley of the Moon when looking in another direction; the stark, dirt hills on the other side of the course; the lip of the altiplano in the distance, with the green valley of Achocalla just below it; and the backside of a peculiar rock and dirt formation to the south that is known locally as "Devil's tooth." Devil's tooth got its name because from central La Paz, far above it, it appears on the southern horizon like a giant tooth with a cavity that needs filling.

The clubhouse was a new cement structure, still unfinished but tastefully designed in a modern motif. An outdoor heated swimming pool was nearby. With the surrounding green grass of the golf course and the fantastic view, this was a pleasant place to be on a sunny afternoon.

A heavy rainstorm was approaching from the southwest with a rainbow in front of it, but the sky over the golf course was still bright blue. As we walked into the clubhouse looking for Jim Cagle, first one and then another man came out and walked past us, each with a smile on his face and the polished eyes of one who has consumed considerable quantities of alcohol.

When we opened the door to the main hall of the clubhouse we came upon a three-piece band that was blasting away in loud tones. A carnival fiesta was grinding to a halt in the late afternoon. Apparently most of the partygoers had gone as only a few people were left. Jim Cagle, whom we expected to meet, was nowhere in sight and no one knew where he was.

We walked out to the patio and down to the tenth tee, a par-3 hole 189 yards long. The chief obstacle for this hole was a gully about fifty yards or more deep, a real challenge if you top your drive. Thomas was delighted with the course. Golf, along with skiing, were among his major recreations, he said. He told me he had designed two golf courses. His secretary later said that his home in Pawling, New York, is surrounded by a golf course, probably one of the two he designed.

On our way back to town we stopped briefly at my house to see how Charmaine was doing. She was feeling better and was glad to meet Lowell Thomas as she had been too ill the night before to join us. Thomas had said to me sometime during the day that we were to be complimented on the behavior of our children, which "must be due to your wife." He was absolutely right on that.

We reached Ambassador Siracusa's house about 6:30 p.m., and after the introductions settled down in the ambassador's comfortable living room for a few drinks and another marvelous monologue from that well-known, well-traveled man. His audience this time was, besides the ambassador and me, Gordon Daniels, the economics counselor of the embassy, his three daughters, and a friend.

At the ambassador's that Sunday evening Lowell Thomas started talking about a man who, he said, was very short, maybe no more than five feet three, but who, when he was in college in California, gained a reputation as an excellent pugilist. He was a lightweight, of course, but since he won every fight in his class, the boxing coach matched him against the school's middleweight champion who lasted only about two minutes of the first round before being knocked out. So the coach tried his heavyweight against the lightweight, and the same thing happened.

"'Now I know you're a lightweight,' the coach told him, 'but you're the best we've got to fight in the state championships next week, so I'm going to put you in against a heavyweight.'

"When the state championship bout took place, this five-foot-three lightweight came out and the heavyweight from the other school, who was to box him, turned out to be a strapping six-feet fellow who looked as big and as strong as an ox. The crowd thought that putting that little man in the ring with a big man was a joke and that the main bout was to take place afterwards. The big boxer also took it as a joke and slapped the little guy playfully with his gloves. But the fight went on and when it was over, the little lightweight won.

"Following this victory he thought seriously about becoming a professional boxer but the girl he met in school and fell in love with, and later married, didn't like that idea and talked him out of it. He became a test pilot for the Curtis Company and flew their famed Curtis-Hawk fighter around the world." (At this point Thomas suggested that we try to find out who it was that he was talking about.)

"Some time after Charles Lindbergh flew the Atlantic the Curtis Company hired Lindbergh. Lindbergh and this other man became the company's two top pilots. Just as the *Spirit of St. Louis* is in the

Smithsonian, so is the Curtis-Hawk plane that this fellow flew around the world.

"Prior to World War II," Thomas continued, "the Germans were trying to sell the Chileans some planes. They sent one of their fighter pilot aces to Santiago to demonstrate their plane. At the same time the Curtis Company sent this man who flew down in his Curtis-Hawk fighter to demonstrate its capabilities. A few days before the demonstration of the two competing planes, a party was going on in the hotel where the pilots were staying and after a number of drinks everyone was asked to do his bit—whether it was singing, dancing, or what have you. When it came his turn, he got up on the windowsill of the hotel room and started to do a tumbling act that he had learned in college. He fell off the sill and broke both of his legs.

"They took him to the hospital and he was there for several weeks. The German pilot let it be known that he thought his competitor was stalling—that he was taking a lot more time than was necessary to get back into business. So the German decided he would demonstrate his plane without waiting any longer and took off to show the Chilean military what his plane could do.

"Unknown to anyone except the American's mechanic, when he heard that the German pilot was going to go ahead with his demonstration he had his mechanic gather up some corsets, took out the herringbone stays in them, and with them fashioned splints on both legs from his hips to his ankles. His mechanic then carried him out of the hospital to the flying field where he had had his plane especially prepared so that he could pilot it with the splints on. He took off and started a mock dogfight with the German ace, coming so close that finally the German landed and complained bitterly to the Chileans that what had happened was unfair. On examining the German's plane there were some holes in the fabric where the German fighter had been scraped by the American plane. As a result of the American's acrobatics his unhealed legs broke again and when reset they were wrongly set, so that his legs stuck out rather than in when they finally healed.

"During World War II he was considered to be too old to fly but President Roosevelt called him in and said he wanted him to handle an extremely important project. Even if he couldn't fly, the president wanted him to supervise the project. As it turned out, he not only supervised it, but was the lead pilot on the mission.

"His plane took off from the aircraft carrier *Hornet* with fifteen other B-25 bombers. One of the officers on the *Hornet* looked at his watch some time later and said, 'Well, the Colonel is just entering

Japanese waters.'

"A short while later he looked at his watch again and said, 'Well, he must have just released his bomb.' Some time later he again looked at his watch and remarked, 'Well, General Doolittle has just landed in China.' He was talking, of course, about Jimmy Doolittle who was the leader of the first U.S. bomber raid of the Japanese mainland in April 1942, just four months after the Japanese sneak attack on Pearl Harbor."

The ambassador asked Thomas if he wasn't concerned about coming to La Paz, of all places, since his wife was not in the best of health.

"We've both been born and raised in Colorado," Thomas answered, "so we don't get concerned about the effects of altitude as others might." He went on to say that his wife was a wonderful woman with whom age is catching up. "You should have seen her when she was younger. I suppose we didn't have to come to South America but I thought it would do her good to get out of the house for a while." His secretary told me later that Lowell Thomas believed that his wife, who had been going downhill for some years, would do much better traveling and seeing new things than if she stayed at home. She died a few years after this visit to South America and Thomas, who was by then in his early eighties, married his secretary (who had been a widow for some years) an appropriate time later. Thomas died August 29, 1981, at age eighty-nine.

We asked him about his son, Lowell Thomas, Jr. He said he had never tried to direct his son as to what he should be or do though they did manage to get together every so often, as they did, he said, on the trip to Tibet. "He now lives in Alaska and I suspect the reason he does is that that is as far away as he can get from me and still be on American soil. He is the State Republican Chairman and is involved in politics, something I never got into."

He talked about his father, a surgeon in the mining town in Colorado where he grew up. He said his father had wide-ranging interests, from astronomy to botany, and would have made a great professor. "But he stayed with medicine, and years later when I made a donation to the American University in Beirut, I endowed a chair in his name, anonymously, of course, though I'm sure my father suspected that it was my doing and I insisted as part of the agreement that he be the first to fill the chair. Although, as I said, I'm sure he suspected it was my doing all along, but he never knew for sure until just before his death.

"My father once said to me," Thomas commented, "that there are three things we do a lot of all our lives—eating, sleeping and talking.

He had a theory that we pay far too little attention to the third thing, talking, and sometimes not enough to the first two. But, he contended, if one would learn to be a good public speaker, then instead of becoming friends with only a few people as we go through life, we could become friends with a great many people because more people would know us. So whenever I would say anything wrong he would correct me and worked at making me a good public speaker. Though I hated him for it at the time, especially in a small mining town where physical feats were more admired, I later came to appreciate what he had done for me.

"Once, after I had become fairly well known," he continued, "I was invited back to my old home town to speak to the graduating class. I flew into town in a small plane and we flew over the high school. I dropped some leaflets in the schoolyard that said I was happy to return to the school which I had flunked out of many years before.

"I don't say this in a boasting manner," he said, "but a year after I was out of high school I had earned a million dollars by speaking." His father's advice had been well taken.

"Once when I was on a speaking tour of Canada, I was in Nova Scotia when I was talking with a farmer. I always enjoyed talking with everyone I met from every walk of life. This farmer was raising foxes and appeared to be very successful at it, so I said, 'Why don't you try raising them in the United States with the market that is there?' He said he had that in mind, but never was able to interest anyone. 'Well,' I said, 'if you will send me a man who knows the business I'll provide the land and maybe a little more.' So he sent me a man who came with his wife and daughter. His daughter is my secretary who is traveling with us now (Mrs. Nicks)."

We asked him how the fox fur business went.

"Well, I didn't lose a great deal. But I thought I'd be smart and eliminate the middle man, so I tried to deal with the big department stores directly, like Macy's, but I soon found out that they just took what the middleman would otherwise have taken, so we finally gave up."

I asked him, "What ever happened to Cinerama?" Cinerama was a unique, three-dimensional motion picture system that was widely publicized in the 1960s and shown in New York, Washington, D.C. and a few other places for a brief period of time, in theaters especially adapted for Cinerama.

"Cinerama was a great thing," he said. "But the process was sold to some people who only wanted to make a fast buck, without the talent, and so it died."

He then recalled how he was selected to be a member of the U.S. delegation attending the coronation of the Nepalese king. It was bound to be a unique and colorful affair that he wanted to film in Cinerama. But filming in Cinerama is not like ordinary filming, he noted, since you have to carry extra cameras and tons of equipment.

"In those days the world's largest airplane was the Globemaster, so I went to the Secretary of the Air Force and asked if he would ship my equipment there in a Globemaster. He said it was all right with him but I would have to sell the idea to the Chief of Staff and several others. He promised to get them all together.

"Now I reasoned that if I was going to have to sell this idea to the Air Force I had better come up with something which would make it of interest to them. So when they were all together and I was making my pitch, I said the story I planned to do was about an Air Force pilot who had just completed his first tour of duty and was debating whether to reenlist or to make religion his profession. But before he makes this big decision, he decides to go to the Far East and live with Buddhist monks for a year. Of course, after the year was up, he opts for the Air Force. Needless to say, they gave me the use of the Globemaster.

"The Globemaster was too big to land in Nepal, so with Nehru's cooperation we landed in New Delhi and from there the Nepalese made a number of flights to Katmandu to bring in my camera crews and our equipment."

Thomas was now getting warmed up and could probably have gone on with his tales all night, but he believed it was time to go so the ambassador walked with us to the car and I drove him back to his hotel. His wife and secretary were waiting for us in the lobby. It was about 8:30 p.m. His wife and secretary had had dinner but Thomas and I hadn't so I joined them in the Crillon dining room. On the way upstairs we ran into Jim Cagle and told him that we had visited the golf club that afternoon but were sorry we missed him. He joined us later for a short while in the dining room where he said he wanted to make Lowell Thomas an honorary member of the highest golf club in the world, which seemed to please the old adventurer. Cagle was to get the certificate to me and I would send it to Thomas, which I did a few weeks later.

The next day the Thomases left for Peru where they planned to visit Cuzco and the famous Machu Picchu ruins. They had provided us with a most entertaining weekend, aside from stimulating memories of my boyhood. When they left the next day I was tempted to say, "So long, until tomorrow."

In April 1972, with a relatively quiet period in Bolivia, Charmaine and I decided to take a vacation by driving across the altiplano to Cuzco, Peru, the home of the Inca Empire, and visit famed Machu Picchu. We were able to leave our four youngest children in the care of our maids and friends and took our oldest son, Robert, with us. CAO Andy Schwartz and his wife, Ingrid, joined us in a second jeep with their sons, Eric and Michael. Information officer Kent Herath supervised USIS activities during our absence.

In Cuzco, Pisac, and Machu Picchu we saw the remnants left behind by the Empire of the Sun. We could now more fully appreciate the achievements of the Incas at the height of their glory. One could not help but wonder, however, when, if ever, the Andean Indians would awaken from the sleep into which their culture had sunk following the fall of the Inca Empire. If they are ever to recover from the blow their society received when Pizarro put their man-god Atahualpa to death in 1532, they will have to change their current ways and enter the modern world of trade, commerce, and technology. Yet, as this is being written, the distance between them and the modern world grows ever greater. While their culture stagnates, or disintegrates, and slowly disappears, modern dynamic societies, for better or worse, marked by change, move further and further beyond them.

Within two weeks after returning to Bolivia I became ill. At first Dr. Dwight Babcock, the embassy physician, diagnosed my illness as typhoid fever but it soon became apparent that I was suffering from hepatitis. Symptoms of both are similar in the initial stages.

I had a high fever for five days, my blood count was initially more than 2,000 above normal, and the yellow count of my blood test was at nine (where one is normal). For nearly four weeks I was confined to lying down at home most of the time. Recovery from this ailment, like most illnesses experienced in the altitude, was slow and not at all certain. I was certain, however, that the lunch at a hotel on the shores of Lake Titicaca, on the last day of our trip to Peru, was where I picked up the germs that "done me in."

Because of my illness I asked Washington headquarters to assist the post for a few weeks by sending another officer to La Paz for temporary duty. The reply initially was negative. They informed me that there was no one available who could be spared. However, a few days later the area director, Lyle Copmann, phoned and said that they could send a JOT who was currently in training in Quito, Ecuador to help us for a few weeks if we wanted him to come. This was not what I had in mind but even a JOT could help. Within a week our new JOT, Michael Stevens, arrived. He learned quickly, showed good judgment and maturity in adapting to La Paz, and was a great asset to USIS. By the time he left a few weeks later he had gained the respect and admiration of all of his USIS colleagues, both Americans and Bolivians.

As I slowly recovered I was able to accomplish more and more chores from my "sick room," the study of our home. This became my office and sleeping quarters for about a month. It became routine to have my administrative assistant, Margrett Buchholz, visit me each morning with the mail and cables. She would return to the office with the memos and messages I had drafted the day before. By keeping in close contact with the office by telephone and holding frequent conversations, either by phone or personally, particularly with the IO and the CAO, I managed to supervise USIS operations without too much difficulty while lying on my back in my study. Eventually the day came when I could begin to move around a little and, though somewhat thin and weak from my ordeal, was able gradually to increase the amount of time I spent at the office.

I did not quite complete my two-year assignment to Bolivia. As a result of my weakened condition from my bout with hepatitis, I was happy to be reassigned to Washington shortly before our planned two-year tour ended. My Washington assignment would be as policy officer for the Latin American area in the office of the assistant director of USIA for Latin America. Having now lived in four Latin American countries as well as British Guiana in South America, and as a mid-career officer, well experienced in the ways of USIA, I looked forward to my new assignment where I expected to put my knowledge and experience to good use.

My recovery from hepatitis would continue to be slow but eventually complete. By the time we would again leave Washington, nearly four years later, my family and I would be ready, willing, and even anxious to begin another "life," this time in Peru.

9
Peruvian Panorama

"Peru is not one country, but many countries."
—Mario Vargas Llosa, Peruvian novelist

In 1972, my new assignment to Washington as the USIA policy officer for Latin America promised to be an interesting experience as well as highly rewarding professionally. That promise was fulfilled. I soon became involved with most of the major U.S. concerns with respect to Latin America, particularly those U.S. objectives to which USIA's public diplomacy resources could contribute. What one cannot escape from in Washington is the bureaucracy. It permeates all actions of government at all levels, restricting creativity. At times it is a wonder how anything is ever accomplished by the U.S. government. Yet, things do get done.

After my bout with hepatitis, my health gradually returned, although not until I put behind me a good year of abstinence from alcohol. Before going fully "on the wagon," my liver painfully reminded me that it had been through a rough time in the mountains of Bolivia.

As the policy officer in the office of the assistant director of USIA for Latin America, the traditional aspects of U.S. foreign policy toward Latin America were daily items of interest. U.S. encouragement of free market systems and trade; support for democratic societies and institutions; and regional and global cooperation among nations were among the major emphases of USIA programs in Latin America. There were three unique fields, however, which were not traditional policy concerns that drew my special interest. I viewed these fields as being important phenomena in the modern world that could and should be addressed by public diplomacy strategies. I also knew it would be necessary to sell the importance of the contribution USIA could make in these fields to those agency officers who were strict traditionalists.

These relatively new U.S. foreign policies were (1) the fostering of population planning as an important aspect of economic development; (2) efforts to disrupt illicit narcotics trafficking in which Latin America had become a major player; and (3) combating terrorism, which also had become a major problem in a number of Latin American countries. All of these issues adversely affected U.S. interests. While at this writing they seem to be quite natural U.S. policy concerns, in the early 1970s many in the State Department and USIA considered them as being in the bailiwick of other agencies and departments.

One of the most astute persons in the overall policy office of USIA at the time was Mildred Marcy, a woman who was quick to recognize the important role of family planning in economic and social development long before many others did. This aspect of development had first become public policy of the Agency for International Development during the administration of President Lyndon Johnson. He was the first U.S. president to declare that the U.S. government would support family planning in developing countries as a part of economic assistance programs.

The criticism from religious and conservative groups that followed this declaration was substantial. This issue still has its critics, although there is now wide acceptance of population programs. In the early 1970s, when such programs were but a few years old, adverse opinion about such efforts by the U.S. government existed within USIA as it did in the general population. Mildred Marcy was in the vanguard of those who recognized the importance of this issue and the contribution U.S. public diplomacy could make to foster knowledge about the "population crisis" of developing societies. In me she found a supportive soul.

The two largest countries in Latin America, Brazil and Mexico, were among those in greatest need to adopt policies that would help lower their population growth as a spur to economic growth. The majority of the citizens of both of these countries was Catholic in their religious outlook and thus held traditional Roman Catholic views concerning population planning. Anyone who dared suggest that family planning was a means to help solve their economic and social problems, especially if the use of contraceptives was mentioned as the means for reducing population growth, could expect to be criticized by those holding traditional Catholic views. In that context it was understandable that when I, in my capacity as USIA's policy officer for Latin America, suggested to the PAOs in Mexico and Brazil that they might include references to family planning in their programs, their negative replies to the area office were loud and clear.

I felt that they missed the boat. I was not suggesting that USIS conduct seminars on population planning, but take a much more subtle approach—the inclusion of information about the negative effects of overpopulation on economic/social development. This point could be made, when appropriate, in USIS publications, USIS-sponsored seminars, and other USIS activities. But as the PAOs in those countries were presumed to be the most knowledgeable about what they should and should not undertake in their programming, they had the final word. This was an agency policy I fully agreed with, yet I remained with the opinion that they could easily have introduced this subject in support of U.S. policy in subtle ways without adverse effect. In later years this is, in fact, what occurred.

The second non-traditional foreign policy issue in Latin America that greatly concerned me was illicit drug trafficking. I believed USIA could and should devote some of its resources to support U.S. efforts to curtail this dangerous, illicit trade. Latin America was not only the main source of a growing U.S. market in cocaine, but shipments of marijuana and heroin from Latin American countries were entering the U.S. in increasing amounts. When I and only a few others initially raised this issue with our colleagues in Washington, the response often was that this issue was "not our business." Some contended that the problem had to be handled by the Drug Enforcement Agency (DEA). This reluctance and failure to see a USIA role was similar to those who had argued earlier that population control was AID's concern, not ours.

How wrong these traditionalists were is evident by the high priority given to this issue by USIA and other U.S. government agencies during the following two decades, a priority concern that continues to this day. As the drug culture grew to epidemic proportions in the U.S. in the years that followed, more and more persons realized that to combat this societal disease, more than police action was necessary. Any hope of successfully combating illicit drug trafficking requires educational, treatment, and rehabilitation activities as well as police action. As a growing U.S. concern with definite foreign policy implications, this subject deserved USIA public diplomacy support, which it received only grudgingly at first. Not until the 1980s did an awakened USIA hierarchy give it the priority it deserved.

One of the activities in this field that a few others and I encouraged was the first ever USIA anti-narcotics film. Because of growing interest in this subject, independent filmmakers were producing numerous new anti-narcotics films. But as one wit noted, "some of these films are worse than the drugs themselves."

We reviewed a number of commercially produced films searching for something usable in USIA overseas programming, however, none seemed to convey the message I believed was most important for USIA overseas audiences. In an era when most Latin Americans contended that the narcotics problem was a problem for the U.S. (the major market) and of little concern to them, I wanted to convey the message that any society that became involved in illicit drug trafficking could not remain immune from it. None of the films we reviewed carried that message. It was a message that those societies eventually learned the hard way, as country after country suffered the same fate as the U.S., especially Colombia and Peru, the Latin American countries most involved in illicit narcotics trafficking at the time.

The USIA film that was eventually made was entitled *The Trip*. Produced by USIA film producer Ashley Hawken using Colombia as a model, it depicted the various ramifications resulting from illicit narcotics trafficking in that country; how the local society became affected, particularly the youth; and how the struggle against the illicit use of narcotics should involve not only police action but education, treatment, and rehabilitation. Hawken recognized my contribution to the film's production by crediting me as a "technical adviser" in the credits, much to my surprise and delight. *The Trip* was broadcast on television, held private showings throughout Latin America, and was still being used more than five years later. Unfortunately, despite the need for updated sequels as the problem of illicit drug trafficking and use worsened, no other film like it was ever produced, partly because USIA switched gears to television production. With the emphasis now on TV, the agency's interest in producing similar anti-narcotics films ended.

Another growing phenomenon in Latin America was the use of terrorism as a political weapon. Having witnessed the drastic results of the growth of the Tupamaro terrorists in Uruguay, I viewed terrorism at the time, as some others certainly did, as a menace that would increasingly and adversely affect U.S. interests in Latin America and elsewhere. Therefore, I felt, that like population planning and illicit drug trafficking, terrorism should also be a subject to be treated in USIA programs. However, once again, a non-traditional foreign policy issue was met by many agency colleagues as something that should not concern USIA. Some of those who thought enough about it at the time to express an opinion doubted that little, if anything, could be done by the government's public diplomacy agency to combat this problem. I did not share this view.

What the three non-traditional foreign policy issues mentioned above had in common was, I believed, that U.S. interests regarding these activities could all be advanced by public diplomacy activities. I felt that given our resources and cultural and media experience, programs designed to garner support of foreign audiences for family planning, or to encourage opposition to illicit narcotics trafficking and terrorist activities, could be developed by USIA. I felt that such programs could be effective if included among USIA priorities in selected countries.

Some Department of State officials were also becoming increasingly concerned about the growing terrorist threat to U.S. personnel and interests. A special office to pay greater attention to this phenomenon was established in the State Department. They called this office the "Office of Terrorism," a misnomer in my view. I always referred to it as the "Office of Anti-terrorism." It took a number of years before someone, who must have shared my qualms, had the name of that office changed. It became known later as the "Office of Counter Terrorism."

Anti-terrorism was of little interest to the office of policy and plans of USIA at that time. This was the office responsible for overall agency policies. Thus when that office received an invitation for a USIA representative to join an inter-agency committee formed to discuss what the U.S. government might do to combat terrorist activities affecting the U.S., and could not readily find anyone who had thought much about this subject, my name was mentioned. Joseph Hanson of that office asked me if I would be willing to represent our agency on that committee, an assignment I willingly accepted. The committee consisted of a person from the State Department's office of terrorism, a person from the Central Intelligence Agency (where records of global terrorist events were meticulously kept), a psychiatrist from the State Department's medical unit, and me as the USIA representative.

As hostage taking was relatively new to modern America, those dealing in foreign affairs had to learn how to handle hostage situations. One of the lessons learned was the need to allow freed hostages time to obtain a more balanced view of their freedom. If press contacts were granted immediately upon their release, their euphoric feelings at being freed were immediately relayed to the world press. This often resulted in kind words being expressed by freed hostages about the terrorists who had freed them, yet terrorists who had committed the crime of kidnapping and worse hardly deserved praise for releasing their prisoners. Nor did they deserve publicity for their causes. With experience this kind of free, positive publicity for terrorist causes was generally avoided. There was also the need to alert former hostages to avoid public statements that would endanger the lives of those still held captive. This and other aspects of the terrorist phenomenon were why a psychiatrist was an important member of this committee.

This special committee met a number of times during my tenure as policy officer for Latin America. During that time I developed a paper that spelled out what I thought the USIA role in supporting U.S. anti-terrorist activities against U.S. interests should be. As an introduction I noted that by March of 1975, in Latin America alone during the prior six years, terrorists killed or kidnapped twenty-eight foreign diplomats, thirteen of whom were Americans. The time had come, I contended, to devise new means of meeting this threat.

Since the goal of terrorism committed for political purposes is generally initiated with the idea of attracting the widest possible attention to a specific group or cause, I argued that the mass communications media often become, unwillingly or not, allies of political terrorists. They frequently carry the messages which the perpetrators of terrorist acts wish to bring to public attention. Because modern communications technology allows an instant, global reach, terrorists were now gaining the capability of capturing far greater attention than ever before.

"Because of the role assigned to the mass communications media in the plans of most political terrorists," I wrote, "any U.S. response to terrorist activities abroad which affects U.S. personnel or interests should include participation of the Foreign Service organization which has the most experience in global, regional, and (foreign) national mass communications media. That agency is, of course, USIA."

I discussed two separate though related USIA programs designed to support U.S. anti-terrorist policies: an ongoing information program to discredit terrorism as a political weapon, and a specific-incident type of information program to be implemented using predetermined guidelines whenever U.S. personnel anywhere in the world were victims of terrorist attacks.

"The main thrust of an ongoing anti-terrorist information program should be the dissemination of information about the psychology and philosophy of terrorist groups—information which discredits terrorism as a political weapon. These materials should be general in the sense that they would not, as a rule, specifically mention contemporary groups." I provided a number of examples of such materials, ranging from Eric Hoffer's *The True Believer* to *The Eric Fromm Theory of Aggression*. I suggested that a second category of information, utilizing all of the agency's resources (press, radio, television, books and other publications, etc.) should deal with specific foreign policy objectives relating to such things as extradition treaties, hijacking treaties, etc., all intended for highly selective audiences. A third category would be stories and articles dealing with specific historic incidents where it could be shown that terrorist activities failed to bring about the intended changes or, like the activities of the Tupamaros in Uruguay, brought about the opposite of what was alleged to be their goal.

On the specific-incident information program I envisaged, I urged that USIA, to use Ed Murrow's famous expression, should be in on the "takeoff" of the U.S. response to a terrorist incident involving U.S. overseas officials, "since the agency's worldwide and local information dissemination capability is an important resource for dealing with such incidents." Among several suggestions was that a USIA officer should immediately be assigned to any Department of State task force formed following such an incident, preferably the person normally assigned to anti-terrorist programming in the agency's office of policy and plans, and additional personnel as needed from the pertinent geographic area office.

"If the situation warrants," I noted, "as it did in the case of Public Affairs Officer Barbara Hutchison (kidnapped September 24, 1974, in the Dominican Republic), a USIA officer familiar with the local environment should be sent immediately to the post where the incident occurred to act as the embassy's spokesman if sufficient USIS personnel are not available at the location of the incident." And finally, I noted that agency press and radio services should be considered as counter-weapons available for use against the terrorists, "within the limitations imposed by normal agency standards of truth and credibility."

Eventually USIA distributed a document known as an "Infoguide" to all USIS posts alerting them to the agency's concern about terrorism and how USIA might support the U.S. government's anti-terrorism policies. Little more was done. The committee met less and less frequently, perhaps because it had served its purpose. What could be done was slowly becoming institutionalized in the various agencies, though certainly the problem of terrorism persisted and actually increased.

When the committee on terrorism first met, terrorism as an international activity was a relatively new but growing phenomenon. Today, long after that committee ceased to exist, far more effort has been put into anti-terrorist activities by the U.S. government than could possibly have been imagined at that time.

In 1976 we left our home in McLean, Virginia, and drove to Miami, Florida, to deliver our car to a pier there for shipment to Lima. We caught a flight to Peru, my new overseas assignment. As usual, I had mixed feelings. My job in Washington had been interesting the past few years, and as our family grew, there were many delightful times.

Our flight to Lima on Braniff Airlines was uneventful. We were met by the cultural attaché, Frank Florey, and his wife, Adela. We had met them in Washington a few months earlier as Florey had received notice of his assignment to Peru shortly before I did. They had only been in Lima a few weeks when we arrived. During the next four years he would be the one I usually entrusted with the supervision of USIS whenever I was absent, and Charmaine and Adela Florey became the best of friends. Eventually, both became the only women wood carving students of Peru's leading woodcarver, Julio Cesar, a master craftsman of an art that was rapidly disappearing in Peru. They also worked together in many voluntary welfare efforts on behalf of poor Peruvians. In May, 1980, on the recommendation of the American Women's Club of Lima, they were cited for their joint efforts and awarded a Department of State "Tribute of Appreciation" for outstanding service to the community.

Lima is on the coast but in the center of a desert that extends far to the north and south of the city. The Rimac River flows into the Pacific Ocean at Lima, and heavy mist from the sea during the winter months makes the Peruvian capital a giant oasis.

The Andean mountains rise sharply from the coastal plain some thirty miles inland from Lima. They act as a barrier to the winds that sweep in from the Pacific Ocean. From Peru, the Pacific stretches thousands of miles west until reaching Tahiti. Because of the mountain barrier, inversion of the air is frequent. During the long winter months the city is enshrouded in dark, low-lying clouds as fog banks roll in off the Pacific and the inverted air keeps them from dispersing. For weeks on end Lima remains damp and gray, yet never reaches the point where rain falls. One of the first things a visitor to the Peruvian capital learns is that rain never falls in Lima.

Added to the overcast of low-hanging clouds, which keeps the sun from shining for most of the winter, is the pollution of the city. The gray, polluted air gave Lima's winters a generally depressing environment all winter long. Yet if one leaves Lima and drives north or south for twenty or thirty minutes, the desert is reached where the sun shines brightly. Those who can escape the city on weekends do so. After even a week of the *garua*, the name given to Lima's normal winter mist, sunshine is a marvelous tonic.

The drive from the airport to the San Isidro neighborhood where the PAO's house was located took us from one side of the city to the other and directly through the center of town. Our initial view of Lima was even more depressing than the climatic conditions because so many areas, especially near the airport, seemed so unkempt. Garbage and trash were visible in numerous places. Many of the homes of the lower economic classes were little more than shacks. Some of the areas we passed were the *pueblos jovenes* (young towns) we had heard about, where private or government-owned land had simply been taken over by squatters. The hundreds of shacks that were now the squatters' homes lacked water and sewage facilities. And as in any inflation-ridden society, a circumstance in which Peru at the time excelled, we also saw many more permanent homes that were partially constructed. With inflation raging, the value of Peruvian money was becoming less and less while buildings appreciated in value; thus the effort to put money into buildings was apparent.

Initial impressions are usually the strongest. Ironic in this case, however, was the fact that this initial, negative impression about Lima would be completely reversed. We soon discovered that life in Lima for the Hansens would, in most aspects, turn out to be a marvelous, positive experience. This contrast, between our first impression upon setting foot in Peru, and the life style and positive professional and family experiences that we would enjoy in Lima during the next four years, was remarkable.

Jack Gallagher was the PAO I was replacing. He had completed his tour of duty a month or so earlier. The house the Gallagher family had lived in had been the PAO's residence for many years. Located in San Isidro, a fashionable neighborhood on the south side of the city, not far from the ocean, convenient to the embassy and bordering the most chic neighborhood of Lima, Miraflores, it was an ideal location. The house itself was old and would have served well for a couple without children. The garden in particular was nicely designed for outdoor entertaining, surrounded by hedges that soared thirty feet into the air. With our five children, however, we found the quarters cramped and wondered how Gallagher and his wife had survived there since he had more children in his family than we did! We determined that we should try to obtain other quarters, if possible, and thus began a search for more suitable housing.

Our initial efforts to find a suitable house were unsuccessful. We wanted a house roomy enough for the seven of us to live in relative comfort; that would enable us to entertain Peruvian contacts in suitable fashion as was expected of us; and was relatively convenient to the embassy.

We found Lima to be full of big, old houses in certain neighborhoods and large, newly constructed homes in areas on the outskirts of the city, where transportation would be a problem. We saw some suitable houses located in new neighborhoods, but the dust raised by neighboring construction projects or unfinished streets dampened any enthusiasm we might have had for a particular house. We found one house in Miraflores that we liked, in a nice neighborhood on a wide, tree-shaded street with a large backyard garden ideal for outdoor entertaining. But when we became serious with the owners about renting their home they had a change of plans, or heart, and decided not to rent it to us.

As the months passed we were nearly resigned to giving up the search and adjusting to crowded quarters in the old PAO house when we heard about a house that might be available only two blocks away. This house was not much to look at from the outside. It was a large, rectangular structure and stretched the length of at least two normal houses. Once inside, however, we realized that it would be great to live here yet we doubted that satisfactory arrangements could be made to do so. The house had much more space than we really needed.

After taking the grand tour of this rather large house that promised to be excellent for entertaining, we at first thought that surely it would be out of reach for the restricted amount of rent that the U.S. government would pay for the PAO's residence. However, the owners, a retired American public health officer and his Chilean wife, were anxious to rent their house to Americans in order to obtain U.S. currency. When they learned that it was possible for the U.S. government to pay at least a part of the rent in U.S. dollars, they became as interested in renting the house to us as we were in renting it.

We arranged for a meeting with the owners and the administrative officer of the embassy, Sam Lupo. Lupo would negotiate a new lease for USIS if it met U.S. standards and was within the price range allowed for the PAO's residence. When the owners learned that in addition to dollar payments the U.S. government would be willing to pay a year's rent in advance (if a long-term lease were signed without any increases during the period covered), we were well on our way to getting a new home. When Lupo offered a choice of $1,000 U.S. per month for a long-term lease or a higher amount in Peruvian pesos, the owners quickly accepted the former. (With the frequency of Peruvian currency devaluations, the rent in U.S. dollars, while maintained at the same amount for four years, increased dramatically when converted to Peruvian soles.)

With the hunt for housing now ended and all five of our children enrolled in the Franklin D. Roosevelt School in Lima, an American school financially supported by the State Department, I could now focus my full attention on USIS programming.

Peru has always been a fascinating country. Many factors make this so—its diverse pre-Inca civilizations dating back to 2500 BC (such as the Chimu, the Chancay, the Mochica and the Chavin) that left behind thousands of relics which to this day continue to be discovered periodically; its legacy of the Inca dynasty; and the Spanish conquest of the country by Francisco Pizarro followed by the long Spanish rule thereafter. The Nazca lines in the desert of central Peru, never satisfactorily explained, add to the country's mysteries. Peru's geography is equally fascinating, a combination of high Andean mountains with tropical forests on the eastern slopes and deserts on the western side, plus a long expanse of Pacific Ocean shoreline. These factors give Peru a historical record and a contemporary setting that is as fascinating as it is challenging for the outside visitor to comprehend.

Many countries can be described as "more than one country," but Peru is particularly prone to this description. As Peruvian writer Mario Vargas Llosa once wrote, "We are not one country but many countries." Presumably he was referring to the differences between the inhabitants of urbanized Peru seeking to join the modern world; the Peru of the rural, mountainous, traditional Indian cultures; the Peru of the jungles where some Indian tribes live as they did centuries ago; and that of the dry, coastal areas. Even in the cities there are those Peruvians who own such houses as the one we had just moved into, compared with those who live so differently as squatters in the pueblos jovenes.

When we arrived in Peru, natives were still reeling from the negative effects of the government's takeover by the latest military dictator to have grabbed power, General Juan Velasco Alvarado. On Oct. 3, 1968, he had ousted democratically elected President Fernando Belaunde. The Velasco regime was one of many experienced by Peruvians over the years that came to power by a military coup.

Velasco's rule ended in 1975, about a year before we arrived. He was a poorly educated, left-leaning, anti-American type whose main interest, like so many of that ilk, seemed only to maintain power. The result was a disaster for the country, both economically and politically. He nationalized industries and heavily subsidized basic goods to gain the support of the masses. These actions put the government further and further into debt and adversely affected productivity. By this and other actions he alienated the U.S., other western nations, and international lenders whose economic and financial assistance would have been helpful. One of his infamous claims to fame occurred when he urinated in public as an expression of his *machismo* (manliness)!

When Velasco was eventually replaced by more traditional military officers, General Hernando Morales Bermudez became the president of a new junta. The military leaders had finally concluded that their latest experiment in governing was not working well so their new leader, General Morales Bermudez, switched the gears of the government. He promised that free elections would be held by 1980, an implicit admission that military rule had been unsuccessful. He also began talks with the Americans and others about economic assistance as well as compensation for foreign entities in Peru that had been nationalized by Velasco without compensation to the owners. U.S. law required this latter situation to be resolved before there could be any increase in U.S. economic assistance.

After much stalling on the part of the Peruvians, Secretary of State Henry Kissinger sent the State Department's counselor to Lima to negotiate a settlement of major U.S. copper interests that had been nationalized. With this issue settled, and with a U.S. desire to see Peru return to a democratic form of government, U.S.-Peruvian relations were at a turning point. Aside from wanting to aid Peruvian social/economic development by providing increased economic assistance to Peru, a major U.S. objective was to encourage the new leaders to abide by their decision to hold free elections. This was an objective to which USIS contributed substantially during the following years.

As the political climate changed, most of the Peruvian media became much more friendly toward Americans and things American. Under Velasco, the press had criticized the U.S. at every opportunity and usually rejected most USIS press materials. This changed when General Morales Bermudez became president. Most remarkable was the change that occurred with the television stations. They moved from not accepting hardly anything from USIS to practically providing carte blanche admittance of USIS programs! What a nice time for me to have arrived in Peru, I thought. The doors to the Peruvian media, so long closed to USIS under the Velasco regime, were now opening.

The American staff of USIS Lima was a mixture of highly experienced professionals and newcomers to public diplomacy. They were to achieve much as a group, though one in particular would create unimaginable problems. I have always believed that the most important aspect of a manager's responsibilities is to maintain the kind of relationship with subordinates whereby, if they are happy in their work, an attitude to which a supervisor can contribute substantially, they will be as productive and efficient as possible. In this one case, however, my efforts to stimulate productivity came to naught.

The cultural attaché and most senior person on my staff was Frank Florey. He was a dedicated and experienced professional. I could always rely on him to make the right decisions and to responsibly and adequately supervise the USIS operation whenever I was absent.

Florey had a tendency at times, however, to fire off letters or memos which called a spade a spade if he thought someone deserved to be told the naked truth. As I was ultimately responsible for all official correspondence originated by USIS Lima, on more than one occasion I considered it prudent to put a letter or memo he had written into a drawer until the next day, letting him and it cool off. The next day I would ask him if he wouldn't mind revising it slightly to present his view a little more diplomatically. He was always responsive to these suggestions. A tall man who sometimes sported a handlebar mustache, he resembled Theodore Roosevelt. This added to his aura as a decisive individual.

Florey had two American assistants. One was Christopher Paddack, a highly educated academician who was new to the Foreign Service but dedicated and anxious to perform his best in his new profession. He was close to reaching the seven-year period in which he had to produce a thesis to obtain a doctorate or lose the opportunity after completing all the other requirements. Both Florey and I encouraged him to "go for it," which he did with our blessings and a little extra time off to complete writing it. He did what was expected, took leave to defend his thesis, and was awarded the doctorate.

The second assistant cultural attaché we shall call "Jane" (not her real name). Jane arrived in Lima after her JOT tour in Spain. She had already gained a reputation for being very independent minded. A tall, black woman whose height attracted the attention of everyone with whom she came in contact, and who claimed to have a law degree, had caught the attention of her USIS colleagues at other posts because of an incident alleged to have occurred in downtown Madrid. Wearing shorts or miniskirts in traditional Spain, even in the Spanish capital some two to three decades ago, was rare. In her case this was possibly the stimulant that caused a Spaniard to pinch her while she was walking in a crowded street in downtown Madrid. She responded by striking the aggressor a blow he must have felt. What happened then is not too clear to those, like myself, who heard this tale repeated third hand a number of times. Suffice it to say that the police became involved; the embassy became involved; and, if she had had her way, the Spanish courts would have become involved, though for what useful purpose only she seemed to know.

Information Officer Gerald Waters headed the information section of USIS. He had been my assistant in Uruguay. He was an experienced professional for whom work was his forte. Divorce had ended his marriage to his first wife whom Charmaine and I had known and who had been a favorite of ours in Montevideo. He was now married to a younger Venezuelan woman he had met while stationed in Caracas and they had one child, a daughter. I knew from my earlier experience working with him that he was highly dedicated and competent in his field. When Waters' tour ended he was replaced by another seasoned information officer, Joseph Marek, a competent officer who was an equally strong asset to the USIS staff.

Waters had two American assistants, Donald Hamilton and Perla Manapol. Hamilton was capable but much younger and less experienced. Although he did not overly impress me at the time, he would go on in his career to become PAO in El Salvador; would be the spokesman for the White House czar of drug programming for a while; twenty years later would return to Lima as the PAO; and eventually would become director of the American Republics area of USIA, the supervisor of all Latin American USIS posts.

Perla Manapol, Waters' other assistant information officer, was born in the Philippines, married an American, and maintained a Filipino philosophy that clashed somewhat with the straitlaced bureaucratic regulations of the U.S. Foreign Service. Her marriage also ended in divorce, so she arrived at the post with her three children and her elderly mother. A fantastic tennis and squash player, she eventually would represent Peru in international tournaments because of her membership in a Peruvian tennis club.

Manapol was a remarkable sportswoman. I had met her in Washington briefly after she and I learned that we were both being assigned to Lima. She appeared in my office one day in as casual an outfit as one could imagine, as if she had just stepped off the tennis court. I was taken aback as I was accustomed to more formal attire at the office. Since this was the way she apparently almost always dressed, I took the liberty of telling the area personal officer, also a woman, to have a "woman to woman" talk with Manapol before she left for Lima concerning what most of us considered proper office attire for Foreign Service officers. She promised me she would. I think it had a positive effect.

The USIS administrative officer had been a binational center director prior to this assignment and was really not cut out for this particular position. His heart simply wasn't in it or, perhaps, I expected too much. In any event when he left on an onward assignment and was replaced by Vance Pace, I could not have been more lucky. Pace was knowledgeable, sharp, and willing to do all that had to be done in the various activities required in administering a rather complex operation. I recommended him by the end of his tour for a globally competitive award as "Administrator of the Year." Much to his surprise and delight, though in competition with administrative officers worldwide, he received the award. His ability in providing general services and handling budgetary and financial matters efficiently was phenomenal. He and his family were Mormons whose ideals permeated all of his activities.

Jane was eventually replaced by David Evans, a black officer who handled the educational exchange activities of the post and worked diligently and satisfactorily. Evans went on to successful positions elsewhere, including Moscow.

I recall one heart-to-heart talk I had with him in my office. For some reason I was concerned about something which led him to say to me, in effect, that every action undertaken with respect to his activities he viewed as being white against black. I was flabbergasted at this assertion. I replied that, from my perspective, I surely did not consider race every time I spoke to him or took an action affecting him, and, I said, I thought that was the case with many if not most whites. He disagreed completely. He said I couldn't possibly understand, and perhaps he was right. However, I added, that if he goes through life, as he seemed to be doing at the time, believing that every little single action affecting him has racial undertones, then I really feel sorry for him. He may not remember that conversation, but I never forgot it. In any event, he was a good officer and deserved the promotions and, I hope, good assignments that should have come his way in the future. Both in his case and that of Perla Manapol, their adult attitudes were so visibly a reflection of the environments in which they had been born and raised, as is no doubt true of all of us.

The final American staff member of USIS Lima, but by no means the least important, was the American secretary. She was the PAO's secretary and handled classified materials for all of the American officers.

When I arrived in Lima the American secretary's position was vacant. The first person to fill that position after my arrival was Elizabeth Lording who would soon reach her sixtieth birthday. (At the time forced retirement was required for any Foreign Service employee reaching the age of 60 and still on active duty, although appeals could be made for short extensions.) Although I appealed to Washington to allow her to stay on a few months longer after reaching retirement age, which I believe could have been arranged (especially since she was in the midst of having extensive dental work performed by a Peruvian dentist at the time), we received a negative reply to my request. She was ordered to return to Washington for immediate retirement. Because of her age, the wisecracking Peruvian press chief of USIS, who worked directly for Jerry Waters, said to me the day after she first arrived in Lima, "Did your wife pick your secretary?". Her age notwithstanding, her experience and competence fully satisfied the requirements of her position.

Elizabeth Lording, forced to return to the U.S. and retire after celebrating her sixtieth birthday, was replaced by Gisela Elliston. My new American secretary was top notch — fast, efficient, and personable. A tall woman of German origin, she had been married to an American soldier after World War II. They had one daughter. She had been divorced and was now married to a retired USIA officer, some years her senior, but they seemed good for each other. Unfortunately, one evening at a USIS sponsored concert a year or so after their arrival in Peru, her husband, Tom Elliston, suffered a heart attack and died in the hospital that evening. The post lost a good friend, not to mention the tragedy for his wife and stepdaughter.

My next secretary after Elliston's transfer was Lee Harmon, a black woman who was highly efficient, seemed to enjoy Foreign Service life, and appeared not to be weighed down with any chips on her shoulders. She easily picked up where the others left off. The fact that I also had a Peruvian secretary reporting directly to me helped with regard to the workload. It was important, of course, that good communication and cooperation existed between the two.

Only one American on the USIS staff was not stationed in Lima. Ronald Reafs was the director of the binational center (BNC) in Arequipa, the largest and most important city in southern Peru. Reafs lived in that isolated interior city with his wife and infant daughter. Both he and his wife were experiencing living and working abroad for the first time. To be so isolated, with little experience in overseas living and with USIS Lima being unwilling or unable to give him the support he felt he deserved, they found adjustment to life in Arequipa difficult. After completing his tour he left the Foreign Service but worked in Washington for USIA until his retirement. His replacement,

Kyra Eberle, a single, dynamic woman who thrived on the kind of challenge that directing the BNC in Arequipa afforded, soon captured both Lima's and Washington's attention and admiration. Under her direction the center enjoyed highly successful academic, cultural, and building programs.

The first houseguest in the "Hansen Mansion" was Bob Chatten, the Area Director from Washington--my immediate superior. Upon his return to Washington he wrote:

> I was most honored to be the first guest and to be there for the first party in your *elegantisimo* quarters. I know you are pleased to be free at long last from concerns about house, secretary and car and to be able to focus your attention away from those housekeeping considerations...and get back to program and management.

The senior Peruvian staff at USIS Lima was also a mixture of some highly qualified professionals and a few who had passed their prime.

The most senior Peruvian employee was Francisco Pardo de Zela. He was chief of the radio section that maintained extensive relations with radio stations throughout the country. This USIS program was the one least affected by the anti-American climate generated in Peru during the Velasco era. Radio has always seemed to be less political and less affected by government controls in most countries. This is probably because, unlike the press, it is instantaneous and doesn't leave a visible record to be mulled over and criticized to the extent that press articles permit.

Although he had been with USIS for many years and was now a senior USIS employee, Pardo de Zela had a unique background. In his younger years he had been in the Peruvian army and was an exchange student at a Chilean military academy. His roommate at the time was now the President of Chile, General Augusto Pinochet. Pinochet became president of that country in a bloody coup in 1973. Pardo de Zela visited Chile one weekend a few years before my arrival in Lima while he was on vacation and the president laid out the red carpet for him. However, Pardo was definitely not in tune with his former roommate who, by then, had the reputation of being a ruthless dictator. It was the first time they had seen each other in more than twenty years.

Fernando Cervantes was the press chief. A good writer with excellent contacts within the fourth estate, intelligent and *vivo* (to use a good Spanish term), he was like many of his counterparts at other USIS posts — a great asset to USIS. But when he tried on behalf of his brother to get a U.S. visa under questionable circumstances (a Peruvian who was not, apparently, fully qualified — his brother had emigrated to the U.S.), the consul general, a woman who was a dedicated, no-nonsense, by the book consular officer, insisted that I fire him. I argued that this would be too great a loss to USIS. She reluctantly agreed not to press me further on the issue. Some consul generals later he was able to realize his own dream of emigrating with his family to the U.S., something he might have been able to do earlier had this incident not occurred. He became a member of the Latin American Branch of the *Voice of America* where his many talents could be utilized. Nevertheless, I suspect that the consul general had good reason at the time to be upset in this case. In those days Peru was said to lead the world in visa fraud cases.

Another section chief supervised the motion picture service of USIS. He was much admired for his hard work and diligence until a visit to USIS one day by a man who brought us evidence that this individual was selling some of our motion picture projectors for personal profit. We probably should have fired him without compensation. Instead, taking his wife and five children into consideration, we allowed him to resign.

Among the Peruvian employees of USIS, the most senior position held by a woman was in the cultural section. Jackie Portal had been with USIS as long as anyone could remember. Her age had begun to take its toll on her health so she was frequently absent. There had been suggestions that perhaps it was time for her to retire, but her corporate memory was tremendous as were the contacts she had with local cultural leaders. And so she stayed on and contributed to USIS cultural programs with her knowledge and experience for many more years.

Another important Peruvian employee was Max Nicolini. He handled administrative and financial matters, often working alone and at other times being the chief assistant to American executive officers assigned to the post. Dedicated and hard working, he could always be relied upon to contribute to the solution of almost any administrative problem that arose.

USIS activities were conducted with the disadvantage of not having the staff under one roof. The offices of the PAO and the CAO and their immediate staffs were located in the chancery. The USIS radio section was located in the basement of the embassy, as was a small auditorium usable for cultural events. The remainder of USIS operations were carried out at the USIS annex, an old building located three blocks away. There the administrative officer and the information officer supervised their respective activities, while a librarian and an assistant ran a special USIS reference library for media and professional contacts. These operations had been located in a building much closer to the embassy, but after a recent earthquake the building suffered irreparable damage and was condemned, requiring a change in location.

When I first arrived in Peru, Robert Dean was the U.S. Ambassador. He had experienced the anti-American period of the Velasco era. Being an athletic type, he fully supported a USIS plan to bring an American coach to Peru at the request of the Peruvian women's national basketball team. At a time when the Peruvian media had been unreceptive to USIS programming, sports programming was one area in which the post could operate and enjoy the friendship and admiration of Peruvians despite the Velasco regime's negative views of things American. Furthermore, sports crossed all fields and included the high and the low of Peruvian society.

The American coach brought to Peru under a contract with USIS turned out to be so good that the Peruvian team, under his direction, won the women's basketball championship at the Pan American Games the following year. Some of us who might not have normally been inclined to attend a woman's basketball game, did so a number of times in order to cheer on the team being coached by a USIS-sponsored American. With the changed political climate and consequent easy placement of USIS materials in the local media, as well as acceptability once more of USIS programs by local cultural organizations, the sports program became less important to USIS objectives.

The deputy chief of mission, the ambassador's alter ego, was Lyle Lane, a career professional who had the respect of all who knew him. A gentle man, he was highly competent and a pleasure to work with. He was my main embassy contact. Eighteen months later he was transferred and became the first person to head the U.S. Interests Section in Havana, Cuba. This was at a time when many thought there would be reconciliation between Cuba and the U.S. However, this was not to be, so Lane never became an ambassador, the natural desire of most DCMs. He was replaced by Ernest Preeg with whom I would work during the remainder of my Peruvian tour.

Other State Department officials came and went during the four years I was in Peru. With most of them USIS enjoyed excellent professional and personal relations. The country team meetings, held at least weekly, kept the heads of the various agencies and departments of the U.S. mission fairly well informed of activities in other sections that might affect their own operations..

Shortly after my arrival in Lima I realized that in order to brief visitors about USIS operations in Peru, a series of briefing charts would be helpful. With charts I could quickly and easily present the overall view of the local environment and demonstrate how USIS operates in that environment. After writing the "script" I hired an artist from the binational center to artistically produce a series of flip charts. They enabled me to give visiting fireman a quick, succinct view of our operations and the challenges we faced.

Beginning with the physical and psychological environment (a country of 500,000 square miles, two-thirds living outside the money economy, the principal languages in the mountainous regions being Aymara and Quechua, etc.), I noted that 50 percent of Peruvians live on the coast, less than 50 percent in the mountain regions, and only 5 percent in the tropical jungle. Lima, with four million inhabitants, is the focus of wealth and political authority; the nerve center of trade and finance; and the cultural center of Peru. Until 1968, a small upper class controlled the wealth of the country along with the military and the Roman Catholic hierarchy. Since 1968 there has been an emerging elite of military officers of middle-class origin.

Two leading social concepts permeate Peruvian society: The importance of the family and the importance of the individual. Regarding the former, family loyalty and solidarity is an overriding social obligation, thus there is a long tradition of nepotism in social, business, and governmental matters. As to the individual, individuality is a basic theme in the psychological make-up of most Peruvians. They have great sensitivity to praise, slight, or insult. I noted that such things as one way street signs, no smoking signs, and traffic lights were often viewed as challenges to one's individuality and, therefore, frequently ignored. Although these are typical traits in all Spanish-oriented cultures, after some months in Peru I firmly believed the Peruvians were even more sensitive in this regard than Spaniards, i.e., they were *más papa que el papa* (more like the Pope than the Pope)!

The educational system of Peru, so important with respect to USIS informational and cultural programs, boasted thirty-three universities, of which seven were in Lima. This included the oldest university in the Western Hemisphere, the University of San Marcos, with a student population of about 20,000. The overall student population in 1975 (the most recent figures available at the time) was typical for a developing country: primary students, 2.7 million (of which 75 percent do not go on to secondary school); secondary school, 680,000; and university level, 185,000.

A sweeping reform of the Peruvian educational system took place with the enactment of the University Reform Legislation of 1969. The new law ended the "Tercio," a system whereby one-third of the members of the autonomous university councils were students. It established the *Consejo Nacional de La Universidad Peruana* (National Council of Peruvian Universities (CONUP)), consisting of rectors and professors but no students. This was a sharp departure from Peruvian tradition whereby students had a strong voice in administering the universities. The new law also emphasized technical and scientific studies as being necessary for economic development.

A major interest of USIS was the communications systems of the host country. In Peru in the mid-1970s, the effects of a 1971 law whereby the revolutionary government of Velasco extended government controls to all media, were still being felt. The new law brought government news and views to an unprecedented number of Peruvians.

Radio is the main source of news and entertainment for people in a country where the illiteracy rate is high and where television is not yet firmly established. There were, at the time, 222 radio stations in Peru. They operated under the 1971 law that gave the government the right to purchase 25 percent of any station and to exercise veto power on all programming!

There were three leading television stations in Lima. Under the 1971 law, the government owned 51 percent of two channels and 100 percent of the third channel. *Telecentro*, two-thirds of which was owned by the government, produced all of the programming for the first two channels. In addition there were twenty-one TV stations in the provinces, all of only local significance.

In a decree July 26, 1974, the Peruvian government expropriated all daily newspapers of national circulation and ordered that they be turned over to different social and economic sectors by July 1975. This was the most radical and unique action instigated by Velasco's revolutionary government. The six sectors chosen, by who knows what means, and the daily newspapers taken over by these sectors were:

Sector	Newspaper
1. PROFESSIONAL	*El Correo*
2. PEASANT	*El Comercio*
3. EDUCATION	*Expreso*
4. LABOR	*La Prensa*
5. GOVERNMENT	*La Cronica*
6. CULTURAL	*OJO*

In practice, although newspapers were assigned sectors, the government maintained control through government-appointed directors. By 1976 the sectorized press was being studied by a government-appointed commission. This ridiculous system would eventually be abolished and control of the newspapers returned to their rightful owners.

When the "sectorized press" came into being the third world rhetoric in the press became extensive and shrill. This changed some months after Velasco left office and Bermudez became president of Peru. The changed climate meant that the U.S. was no longer vilified daily; about thirty leftist foreign journalists were deported; and USIS press placement increased dramatically.

In July 1976, only one serious periodical, *7 DIAS (7 Days)*, was being published. The others, known collectively as the "independent press," were closed when a national state of emergency was declared at that time. This occurred after considerable criticism of the government's handling of economic and financial affairs by these publications.

To assure all the controls described above were maintained, the government had a large organization called the central office of information. It was reported to have 5,000 employees whose only job was to keep the media in line!

To operate USIS programs in the above environment, USIS had a staff of eight American officers and about thirty Peruvians. The operating budget was $450,000, plus support provided by Washington and American salaries, all of which totaled about one million dollars. The objectives of USIS Lima, as spelled out in my briefing charts were:

(1) *Explain/promote U.S. Lat. Am. Policy* (Panama Canal, Cuba, anti-narcotics, human rights, anti-terrorism, etc.)

(2) *Explain/promote U.S. Economic Policies* (U.S. Trade Act, private foreign investment, nationalization policy, export promotion, etc.

(3) *Demonstrate U.S. political/social institutions are retaining their vitality.*

(4) *Increase awareness of U.S. as a cultural leader.*

(5) *Demonstrate U.S. willingness to share science & technology with the developing world.*

The above objectives were in addition to advising the ambassador and the country team on public affairs matters and acting as spokesman for the embassy.

Some forty to forty-five grants annually for educational and cultural exchanges were awarded under the educational exchange programs of USIS. USIS also supported numerous cultural programs such as visits to Peru in the late 1970s by the Preservation Hall Jazz group and musicians of the Julliard School of Music, among many others. A major cultural asset for USIS was the major binational cultural centers in four Peruvian cities and smaller centers in four other towns. Other USIS cultural activities included a book program and a reference service that operated out of the USIS Annex, plus various exhibits presented periodically.

Press and publications, such as the USIA magazines *Facetas*, *Horizontes*, and *Perspectivas Economicas*, and a commercial bulletin were increasingly being distributed. Other information activities included three locally produced radio programs and features used by fifty-eight radio stations. As the political climate changed, the number of stations using USIS programs increased as did the placement of news clips, films, and features on television stations. Our film and videotape lending service for selected audiences also expanded dramatically as the Peruvian government, under President Morales Bermudez, turned away from Velazquez's earlier anti-American policies.

I usually ended my spiel at those briefings by saying that, "to summarize, eight Americans and thirty Peruvians carry out a $450,000 informational /cultural program to explain and promote U.S. political/economic policies, to demonstrate U.S. political, social, and cultural vitality, and U.S. willingness to share its technology with the developing world. This is done through a variety of informational/cultural programs as we have seen."

Probably the most distinguished audience of one I ever had in presenting the USIS role in Peru was U.S. Congressman Dante Fascell. He was, at the time, on the Foreign Affairs committee of the House of Representatives and later became the committee chairman. He was the rare congressman who expressed genuine interest in USIS programs in the field during a visit to Peru. Generally admired and respected for his savvy on international affairs, he had a long history of interest in, and appreciation for, the role of public diplomacy in U.S. foreign policy.

A major activity of USIS Lima, similar to most Latin American posts, was supporting the binational cultural centers. The BNCs that existed in the capital and in a number of other Peruvian cities and towns were varied in the size of their student body, physical plant, and the degree of cultural programming they sponsored. Each also had unique problems and challenges.

The most important center was in Lima. Some five thousand students studied English in downtown Lima and at the center's branch in residential Miraflores. During the Velasco era the number of students attending English language classes was somewhat less, but while regular USIS programs were forced to retrench or were abolished, the Lima BNC and other Peruvian-American cultural centers continued to function.

The Lima center occupied a four-story building in downtown Lima that it owned. In addition to many classrooms, it had a large auditorium, a large exhibit area, a library, and a cafeteria. About a fifth of its total student body attended English language classes at its branch center in the Lima suburb of Miraflores. The branch center was housed in a beautiful old mansion that the BNC also owned.

For many years the Lima Center was supervised by an American USIS officer. During the Velasco years, however, many labor disputes arose, some instigated, possibly, by agents provocateurs sympathetic to or paid by Velasco supporters or a foreign government. In any event, in those years the director of the center had to spend more and more time on labor-management relations. The time came for the American USIS officer to bow out, and a Peruvian director who would be in a better position to deal with Peruvian labor issues was named. Also, USIA was moving in the direction of phasing out American directors of binational centers throughout Latin America. By replacing American directors with local directors, USIA could cut its costs for BNC programs. Furthermore, USIS officers who had been administrating centers often became available for other activities.

The Lima center, like others in the hemisphere, was, from to time, threatened with bombings by terrorist elements. Despite the threats and occasional fireworks at the entrance to the center, it continued to serve thousands of mostly young Peruvians who were anxious to study English and learn more about the U.S. The majority was motivated to study English as a means to a better job or to prepare themselves for attendance at a U.S. university.

A board of directors was in charge of the Lima center, half of whom were Peruvians and half were Americans. The Peruvians were well-known, successful businessmen, professionals, or educators. The Americans were mostly businessmen resident in Peru. When I arrived and learned that both the cultural attaché and I, as the PAO, were on the board and required to attend periodic board meetings, I soon arranged for CAO Frank Florey to be the sole USIS representative. This indicated no lack of interest on my part, but I considered it a better use of manpower to have only one USIS officer attend these meetings.

Faced with the need to replace the American director of BNC Lima who had already departed when I arrived in Peru, I arranged to hire a former USIS officer, Conrad Sponholtz. He had written to us that he was available and would come to Peru if offered that position. He arrived and supervised the center and its activities quite well, I thought, for a year or so. But with increasing expressions of the Peruvian members of the board to have a Peruvian director, and given the situation described earlier, Sponholtz left. The BNC's chief accountant, who had held that position for as long as anyone could remember, took over as the first Peruvian director. Much controversy swirled about him as the Board favored the hiring of a prestigious cultural type if they could find one who was willing to be the new director. What was really needed, however, was a good business manager. As a result, the new director carried out his duties with no serious complaints as far as USIS was concerned. A few years later his successor, also a self-made manager rather than a cultural type, performed well enough to remain in that position for many years.

The second largest BNC was in Arequipa, an isolated but dynamic city in southern Peru. This cultural center, housed in a historic building, had strong support from local businessmen who were sympathetic to the U.S. Many had ties with the U.S. and saw the value of young Arequipeños learning English. They finally obtained, with some help from USIS, the necessary funds to expand their physical plant dramatically. Other smaller centers were located in the cities and towns of Trujillo, Chiclayo, and Piura in the north; Huancayo in central Peru, and Cuzco and Ica in the south. Americans who were hired locally ran the centers in Trujillo, Chiclayo, and Cuzco. These centers received grants from USIS to help pay the salaries of their directors.

As PAO Lima I became more knowledgeable about the BNCs and their programs than at any time in my career. I soon gained a new appreciation for their value in teaching English to thousands of youthful Latin Americans and in bringing to future leaders greater knowledge about Americans and American society, knowledge that would increase their future understanding of U.S. policies and actions.

While some USIA officials still did not view the centers as being especially important to USIS objectives, at USIS Lima we recognized how they had proven their worth during Velasco's anti-American stint. At a time when many other USIS programs were sharply curtailed, their value to U.S. interests was clearly evident. Therefore, I made sure that during my stewardship of Peruvian USIS activities, USIS would support the BNCs to the fullest extent possible. Later I would say that, if I achieved anything for the U.S. during my four years in Lima, perhaps the most important achievement was to help the cultural centers, with USIS support, to grow and flourish.

The elderly Peruvian lawyer who served intermittently as president or vice president of the BNC Lima Board of Directors for many years, and who was a hail fellow, was eventually replaced by a younger businessman, German Kruger. When Kruger took over as president my professional relationship with the BNC's president became one of personal friendship. We enjoyed great rapport and while we usually discussed much serious business about the USIS-BNC relationship, we shared many laughs together. When USIS Lima obtained a financial grant from USIA Washington to construct twenty-two new classrooms and a modern auditorium for the Miraflores branch center, Kruger and I met many days over lunch to iron out problems and move the construction along. We became good friends in the process.

Lima was noted for its many fine restaurants and for its most famous drink, the *pisco sour*, a delicious cocktail that is without equal in that part of the world. Though the pisco sour is the national drink of Peru, it was allegedly invented by an American who lived in Lima. He substituted pisco (a brandy which comes from cactus) for bourbon, which is used in a whisky sour. The result is a pisco sour — tasty and potent. It tends to make any business luncheon a happy affair.

At the binational center in Arequipa the local businessmen who served on the board of directors were anxious to expand the size of their center to enable more students to study English. I requested a construction grant from USIA to help finance the expansion program and Washington responded with a $50,000 grant. This was added to funds borrowed from a local bank by the BNC board. Under the dynamic leadership of FSO Kyra Eberle, who replaced Riefs when he was transferred, the construction of new classrooms and a small theater and exhibition area was completed in record time.

The BNC in Trujillo was another center in need of assistance. When I first visited Trujillo, a relatively small provincial city north of Lima, the center was renting rooms in a municipal building. The classrooms were small and crowded and the building dirty, decrepit, and poorly maintained.

The center owned some land in the suburbs where a foundation for a new building had been started some years earlier, but construction was stalled because of lack of funds. I tried to convince my colleagues in Washington that the current center's poor physical condition was a disgrace and that this reflected badly on the U.S. I suggested that a grant be provided to complete a new building but my request was turned down. I was grateful for the agency grants given to the Lima and Arequipa BNCs, but soon realized we could expect no help from Washington for the Trujillo BNC. Trujillo was just too small and unimportant to warrant Washington's attention.

I discussed this situation with colleagues in the Agency for International Development (AID) in Lima whom, I knew, were supporting numerous economic and social welfare projects in Trujillo. I asked them if they could use their influence to help the Trujillo BNC board obtain a loan from a Peruvian bank. Much to my surprise and delight, with AID's encouragement, the BNC was granted a loan from a local bank. It was sufficient to construct a new three-story building on the land the center owned. The new building was completed in short order. After moving into the new structure, which provided housing on the third floor for the locally hired American director, his wife and small child, as well as an auditorium and exhibit area, the number of students studying English soared from about 350 to more than a thousand. With that many students paying tuition, the center easily met the payments of the construction loan.

A USIS officer no longer ran the center in Cuzco, which we had visited some years before during our trip to that city from Bolivia. A locally hired American director, Don Smith, was now in charge. He ran the center fairly well in the few years he was in Cuzco until he left and a Peruvian director was appointed.

Cuzco, at an altitude of 11,500 feet, is not the kind of place one associates with swimming as a sport. However, it had, in fact, at least one private swimming pool, located at the home of a wealthy Chinese businessman. I would never have known about that pool had I not received an urgent phone call one morning from Cuzco. At a pool party the day before, Smith jumped over some bushes near the pool, landed on a wet surface, somehow slid and managed to hit the corner of the pool between his legs. Not only was this a painful experience but he soon discovered he could no longer urinate. Despite this, the local doctor had recommended that he drink fluids! He began to doubt the doctor's qualifications. When he phoned me about what had occurred, and knowing how primitive conditions were in Cuzco, my reaction was immediate.

"Catch the next plane out," I told him. "We'll meet you at the airport and get you into a hospital here."

When he arrived at the Lima airport he was wrapped in a blanket and looked pale and forlorn. We met him at planeside, bundled him into a wheelchair, and rushed him to a nearby hospital where we had learned about a highly reputable urologist who was available to examine him. Unfortunate as the incident was, Smith was very fortunate to survive intact. After a few weeks of hospitalization he was able to return to Cuzco. We later learned that he and his Peruvian wife decided to split. I could only wonder if the pool incident was a contributing factor.

Peru is earthquake country. The Andes, an extension of the mountain chain known as the Rockies in the U.S., covers the central part of Peru roughly paralleling its coastline for more than a thousand miles. Geologically speaking it is a new mountain with high peaks not yet worn down by wind and water. For centuries periodic earthquakes have destroyed homes and killed people in mountain villages, either by striking them down in their homes and on the streets of their villages, or causing mud slides that envelop their communities, burying them under tons of mud and boulders.

One of the major tragedies of this type occurred May 31, 1970, when 70,000 Peruvians died during a major earthquake. The side of Huascaran, a 20,000 feet high mountain peak, was shaken loose by a quake, causing a giant landslide that swept over towns and villages in its path. Six years later we visited the site where the town of Yungay once stood.

Yungay is about 300 miles from Lima and had a population of about 30,000 when the earthquake struck. Most of the inhabitants were buried beneath tons of debris. Little evidence remains to indicate that a bustling town had once been at the spot we visited, but there are signs still visible that indicate the depth of the tragedy Yungay suffered.

About a dozen feet of the highest portion of a church steeple still points skyward from what is now the valley floor. The church and the base of the steeple were buried with the rest of the town and its inhabitants. A short distance from the steeple the remains of an old bus, which was caught in the deluge of giant boulders, trees and flotsam of the mudslide, lays twisted and torn asunder. Nearby, protruding from what had been the town square, were the top ten feet of four royal palm trees.

About a thousand yards to the west the rounded top of a small hill broke the surface of the now-hardened soil. That hill had been the town cemetery. Now the whole town was a cemetery. There were also many grave markers at various points above the buried houses, placed by friends and relatives to indicate where their loved ones had been buried alive.

One of the members of Lima's BNC Board was in Yungay the day of the quake. He told of standing in the street near the cemetery that day when, following the rumble of the quake and the shaking of the earth, he looked up at the peak above the town and saw part of the mountain break away. He realized what was about to happen and rushed with his friends to the high ground of the cemetery, followed by some of the local residents. Shortly thereafter, as the mudslide enveloped the city and lapped at the sides of the hill where they had sought safety, they helped pull others from the mud. One woman collapsed from the exertion of running up the hill ahead of the slide, and as the mud and debris covered her legs, he managed to grab her arms and pull her up out of the swirling mass of mud and stones.

The Yungay tragedy occurred when General Juan Velazco Alvarado was still president of Peru. His friendship with the Soviet Union inspired the Soviet authorities to send Soviet aircraft with food, medical supplies, and temporary shelters for the survivors, despite Peru's great distance from the Soviet Union. This was compared by many Peruvians with what they saw as more limited assistance forthcoming initially from the U.S., although President Nixon sent his wife, Pat Nixon, to Peru to view the damage and express U.S. concern for what was then Peru's latest tragedy. U.S. economic assistance to Peru, under the Alliance for Progress, was ongoing, but humanitarian aid was increased to help alleviate the new situation. However, it was the orange-colored huts brought in by the Soviets that caught the attention of most Peruvians. Even six years later when we visited Yungay, whenever the earthquake was mentioned, comparisons were invariably made about how the two superpowers responded to this particular Peruvian tragedy. Some of the orange huts of the Soviets were still being used and the general belief among Peruvians, as expressed at times at cocktail parties in Lima, was that the Soviets had done much more to help Peru in this instance than the Americans.

Lima was generally spared the terrible effects of the many quakes the country as a whole experienced, but not entirely. It received its share of quakes although most were relatively innocuous. Whenever the chandeliers shook and windows rattled in our home we would often soon hear the eerie sound of a shock wave rumbling toward us and then fade away after passing, sometimes as we sat down for lunch or dinner. If the quake was a small one and we were attending a cocktail party or similar noisy event, the minor quakes were seldom noticed. Sometimes we would only know that one had passed recently because we would suddenly notice that all of the pictures on the walls of our home or office had been shaken askew.

Our visit to the site of Yungay's tragedy some six years after its occurrence, while dramatic in our memories, was incidental to the main purpose of our visit to that region. We specifically went there to visit an archeological site in the mountains nearby where one of the earliest inhabitants of Peru, members of the Chavin culture, had left their mark. This pre-Inca culture, believed to have originated between 1500 and 1300 B.C., survived until about 300 B.C.

As we entered the remains of a Chavin underground ruin built possibly as much as three thousand years earlier, we should have been awe-struck. As it was, we were becoming immune to such experiences, for Peru abounds in so many pre-Columbian archeological sites they are almost common place. Even more common is the pre-Columbian pottery, known as *huacos,* which has been unearthed, particularly in recent centuries. Despite years of looting and shipment abroad of these unique historic artifacts, huge public and private collections of huacos can be found throughout the country, revealing, as they do, what little is known about the pre-Inca cultures of Peru. To this day gravesites, where so many huacos were buried with their owners, are still being discovered.

When the Spaniards arrived in Peru in 1532, they found that the various Indian cultures that had preceded them had developed roads, ingenious irrigation systems in the dry coastal valleys, terraces in the mountains for their agricultural production, elaborate textiles, and exquisite gold-smithing which heightened Spanish interest in finding the fabled El Dorado. During the following centuries, great quantities of meticulously crafted vessels were unearthed. These vessels, or huacos, were made from clay. In cultures with no written language the potters were the ones who recorded for posterity the appearance of these early peoples and the way they lived. Thousands of huacos were shipped out of Peru and became part of museum and private collections worldwide. Eventually Peruvian laws and international agreements, sponsored by the United Nations, were made to prohibit the looting of such national treasures and their shipment abroad.

Early Peruvian history, particularly the period from 2500 B.C. to the Spanish conquest in 1532, is recorded in these huacos that have been discovered at thousands of grave sites. The dry desert climate of large regions of Peru have preserved many of them throughout the intervening centuries. Despite the looting of the past five centuries, many can still be seen in Peruvian museums and in Peruvian private collections.

Once during a visit to Truijllo where I was accompanying U. S. ambassador Harry Shlaudeman to the inauguration of the new binational center building in that city, our Peruvian host proudly showed us his private collection of more than 500 huacos. One was especially memorable. It showed figures in various poses that appeared to be suffering from "Hansen's Disease," or leprosy as it is more widely known. (Named after A. Hansen, the Norwegian physician who discovered its causative bacterium). What made this particular piece unique, according to our host, is that leprosy was believed to be non-existent in the Western hemisphere at the time the Spaniards conquered Cuzco, seat of the Inca Empire. Yet this particular piece of pottery, produced long before the Spanish conquest, seemed to indicate, he said, that leprosy did in fact exist in the Americas before the arrival of the Spaniards. (However, a Venezuelan medical scientist with whom I later discussed this, contended that the huaco in question depicted a disease known as leishmaniasis, not leprosy. Leishmaniasis resembles those of lepromatous leprosy in the skin, he said). Who was right? Probably the medical scientist.

One of the more exotic pottery collections in Peru was in one of Lima's museums where thousands of huacos were on display. One room was dedicated to erotic themes of the potters. Signs outside the entrance to that section declared that children were not allowed to enter, certainly an enticement for older children. (The museum had only a small staff of two persons who were engaged in a variety of activities other than guard duty.) This particular exhibit of pre-Inca cultures, cultures in which the Sun God was the top deity, seemed to clearly demonstrate that there's nothing new under the sun, at least in that field.

We had expected our house in Lima to serve my professional needs as the Director of USIS in addition to being our family home. It met these needs admirably.

One of our most memorable evenings was the night we invited about eighty people to a concert in the large foyer of our home. Samuel Theviu, a violinist and former concertmaster for the Cleveland Symphony Orchestra, was in Lima on a Senior Fulbright Scholarship. Under USIS auspices he performed a series of smashingly successful full-house concerts for violin and piano in Lima and other Peruvian cities. He also occasionally directed Peru's National Symphony Orchestra, thus became well known in the capital's music circles. All of us at USIS came to admire and respect him and his wife during their approximately three-month stay in Lima. On the evening he performed at the Hansen residence, our large foyer with its marble floors, low ceiling, and gathering of people seated in a semi-circle around our piano provided just the right acoustical environment for the occasion.

It was a splendid evening for all concerned, but, perhaps, even more so, for Sam Theviu. It was his seventieth birthday.

Our unique home was ideal for entertaining professional contacts, one example being on the occasion, described below, shortly after the arrival of the new U.S. Ambassador who replaced Robert Dean — Ambassador Harry Shlaudeman. Shlaudeman's arrival was preceded by considerable publicity in the leftist press that repeatedly alleged that he was "the head of the CIA in Latin America."

After the ambassador's arrival in Peru and at Press Attaché Jerry Water's suggestion, I strongly recommended to the ambassador that we hold a press conference in which he could meet this ridiculous charge head on and, hopefully, put an end to it. As a career Foreign Service officer who had earlier been the deputy chief of mission in Santiago de Chile and, most recently, ambassador to Venezuela, this accusation was simply silly. Yet in the Peruvian context there were some who would believe it, or wanted to believe it.

The ambassador agreed to hold a press conference that, we decided, would be in an informal setting in my home. We invited the leading editors of all of the Lima newspapers as well as major foreign correspondents assigned to Peru. Following the formal question and answer session we served refreshments, which gave the editors and correspondents an opportunity to talk informally with the new ambassador. The conference not only resulted in much favorable publicity for him but also, as intended, killed the rumor that he was a CIA official. The editors were delighted to meet him for the first time and to have the opportunity to talk with him informally so soon after his arrival in Peru.

Ambassador Harry Shlaudeman, a career Foreign Service officer as noted earlier, was one of the most intelligent, savvy diplomats sent abroad by the U.S. I first met him in the mid-sixties when he was the desk officer for the Dominican Republic at the Department of State. That was when, as the USIA Caribbean desk officer, the D.R. took up so much of my time and where I spent three weeks in that country during the civil war there. He had come a long way since then, and still had much of his career ahead of him. He later became assistant secretary of state for Inter-American Affairs and filled other notable assignments, including assistant to former Secretary of State Henry Kissinger when the Kissinger commission on Central America was formed. He later became the head of that commission. His wife was a "down to earth" woman whom we much admired. The professionalism of Harry Shlaudeman and the charm and friendliness of his wife made working with this new team an enjoyable experience for most of us. This is not to say that all was always peaches and cream. But to work with and for a chief of mission as articulate, experienced, knowledgeable, and fair as Ambassador Shlaudeman made for excellent working conditions for most embassy staffers.

The cooperation USIS was able to obtain with violinist Samuel Theviu and other visiting American performing artists was in no small measure due to the energy and dedication of Assistant Cultural Attaché Chris Paddack. Paddack was a pianist himself, much attuned to the musical world (no pun intended). He helped arrange Theviu's stunningly successful performances. He also contributed to the successful USIS programming of such groups as the Alvin Ailey Dance Group, Alvin Nicholai, Jennifer Muller and the Works, the Roger Wagner Chorale, the New York Kammermusiker, the Portland Quartet, the Preservation Hall Jazz Band, and the Charlie Byrd Trio.

One evening the Hansen family had dinner at home with the noted sculptor Felix de Weldon. His best-known work is probably the Marine Corps Memorial that depicts the raising of the flag by Marines at Iwo Jima during World War II, located across the Potomac River from Washington, D.C.

De Weldon was in Lima by chance. He had gone to Quito, Ecuador, under USIA auspices to inaugurate a statue he had made for the Ecuadorean government and to lecture. However, to abide by the rules USIA had set for itself in sponsoring such visits, a second country had to be included in his itinerary to make the trip more cost-effective. USIS Lima had been urged by Washington officials to program him in neighboring Peru. We were reluctant to do so since we already had what we considered to be a full plate of cultural activities. Furthermore, the suggestion was made with little advance notice, leaving us insufficient time to make arrangements that would guarantee a successful program. With little choice in the matter, we reluctantly agreed to arrange a lecture by him at one of the local cultural organizations.

The subject of sculpturing being in itself somewhat esoteric; de Weldon being little known in Peru; and having insufficient time to build interest in a lecture of this type, we were convinced that this would not be one of our more successful cultural events. We surmised correctly. The one lecture for which we programmed him, while interesting, was poorly attended for reasons mentioned above. Being unable due to time considerations and other commitments of the cultural staff to arrange anything else, and thinking it inappropriate for this elderly gentleman to dine alone after flying from Quito to Lima to participate in a USIS program, I asked him if he wished to take "pot luck" with my family at home. He expressed enthusiasm for the idea. Following his lecture we proceeded in my car to my home, but first drove Cultural Affairs Assistant Jackie Portal to a downtown area where she was late to an appointment following de Weldon's lecture. De Weldon was seated beside me and Jackie Portal was in the back seat when we were stopped in heavy traffic in one of Lima's narrow downtown streets. The window on the driver's side was open. While holding the steering wheel in both hands, I turned to say something to Jackie when I felt a light tap on my right hand. My immediate reaction was to lift my hand from the steering wheel. In the time that it took me to turn around, I saw an arm extending through the open window on the driver's side, the hand of which, in that instant, grabbed the wrist watch I always wear on my right wrist, slipped it off my arm and withdrew it through the open window. The theft of my watch had happened so suddenly I was flabbergasted! This type of crime was well known to all Lima residents, but this was the first time I joined the list of victims. There was little we could do because the culprit easily made his escape through the crowd. When the traffic began to move again, we dropped Jackie off on a nearby corner and drove home. I was determined in the future to keep my window closed when driving downtown.

The "pot luck" dinner with sculptor de Weldon proved enjoyable for my family and, I hope, for him. Among his many entertaining stories he told us about a mammoth project he was working on to build a gigantic statue of Hercules on the island of Rhodes. At the time the idea was in the planning stage. I was somewhat amused when he reached into his jacket pocket and pulled out a small stack of autographed post cards of his most famous work, the Iwo Jima Memorial. He then proceeded to hand one card to each of our children.

In 1990 de Weldon was eighty-three years old. With 2,000 other public sculptures in addition to the Iwo Jima Memorial, the *Washington Post* called him "something of a national monument himself." In Washington, D.C. alone he has thirty works ranging in size from the equestrian statue of Simon Bolívar near the Pan American Union to a marble copy of Michelangelo's "Pieta" at St. Matthew's Cathedral.

An immigrant from Austria, he was an aviation combat artist in the U.S. Navy during World War II when he saw a wire service photo by Joe Rosenthal of AP. It showed American Marines raising the flag over Mount Suribachi on Iwo Jima. He was so impressed by the photo he immediately started making a model, which would eventually become the model for the now well-known Marine Corps War Memorial in Washington, D.C. Once again, our life in the Foreign Service had brought us into contact with someone whom, in the normal course of events, we would probably never have met.

Shortly after Ambassador Shlaudeman arrived as chief of mission, a new deputy chief of mission arrived to replace DCM Lyle Lane, the latter having been slated to head the new U.S. interests section in Havana, Cuba. Lane was well liked, highly professional, and easy to work with. He would be a difficult man to replace under any circumstances. A highly experienced Foreign Service officer, he had come up through the ranks and knew the intricacies of administering a multi-faceted mission like the embassy in Lima.

In addition to normal embassy functions of political and economic reporting, the Agency for International Development conducted major programs in Peru. The Drug Enforcement Agency was also involved in major activities aimed at cutting the flow of illicit cocaine from Peru to American markets. The Central Intelligence Agency was busy monitoring Soviet and Cuban activities that had long been encouraged by some elements of Peruvian society, especially the recent Velasco government. In addition, the embassy was still working on the resolution of major problems caused by the nationalization of U.S.-owned entities by the Velasco regime. Other activities of importance included an export promotion program, run by a dynamic commercial attaché, Bob Kohn, and the Mission's belief that U.S. interests were served by encouraging Peru's military leaders not to waiver from their professed plan to return their country to an elected government. And finally, there were the cultural and information programs of USIS. The deputy chief of mission oversaw all of these activities. Acting for the ambassador, he could exercise veto power over any action taken by any U.S. government entity in Peru.

The position of DCM at U.S. overseas missions is usually a very demanding job. This was particularly true in Peru at the time, since Peruvians were making the transition from more than a decade of an anti-American, leftist military dictatorship to a democratic, freely elected government.

The new deputy chief of mission was a scholar who had written several books on economic subjects and, prior to this assignment, had served abroad relatively briefly in a specialized position. As DCM he not only acted as the ambassador's alter ego, but was responsible for writing efficiency reports of the heads of the various U.S. government agencies and departments operating in Peru, like USIS. These reports were in addition to those written by Washington officials to whom I and other heads of agencies also reported. At times Washington supervisors had their own ideas about what their respective representatives in Peru should be doing, how they should be doing it, and why. Some differences of opinion were, therefore, occasionally bound to arise between the DCM's views and those emanating from Washington.

Neither the new ambassador nor his DCM seemed to understand, or at least appreciate, the role of USIS as I saw it. They both seemed to think that USIS Peruvian contacts, and the PAO's contacts in particular, should include more contacts in the political field. Although we never directly discussed this point, I believe they both felt that I was not the political animal that they thought the PAO should be. Perhaps I should have told them I was a firm believer in Aristotle's comment that "without an understanding of politics, all of man's other works stand in danger of being destroyed." The fact was, however, that with them and the political section of the embassy focusing their attention, as they should, on the politicos, I strongly believed that USIS officers, myself included, should focus on relationships with cultural, educational, and media leaders of the community. These leaders were often as influential as the politicos. By cultivating such friendships, U.S. interests were advanced in many of the diverse fields wherein these interests lay. The former ambassador, Robert Dean, clearly saw this when USIS supported a sports program at a time when most U.S.-sponsored programs were declared non grata under the Velasco regime. I particularly viewed the binational center program, for example, as an extremely important, worthwhile, nonpolitical program. With our new building program we eventually reached 36,000 Peruvians who were studying English under that program annually, all of whom were learning to view the U.S. favorably at the same time. Some were destined to become future leaders of their country.

After the ambassador and the DCM, the third most important State Department official in a U.S. Embassy as regards professional relationships with the PAO, is the administrative officer. This is because the "admin officer" controls the administrative functions of the embassy, much of which affects USIS operations. The general services officer, also an important State Department colleague, reports to the admin officer. Office space, warehousing arrangements, car pools and other transportation needs, certain supplies, logistical support, and housing are among the in-house activities controlled by the admin officer or members of his staff.

Three different individuals filled the admin officer's position during my four years in Peru. The first one we met was a friendly, helpful man who had only one weakness—he seemed never to say "no," but we did not always get what we asked for. The second person was Sam Lupo, the one who negotiated the rental arrangements for the new PAO residence. He eventually became a consul general and, later, ambassador, a position for which he was eminently qualified. The third person was a type who believed in following the letter of the law, down to dotting each "i." He was sincere in carrying out his duties but was difficult to deal with at times. A major bureaucratic battle developed between him and me when he wanted larger sections of USIS to be moved out of the chancery, where we maintained considerable space, than I thought wise or prudent to give up. If his original plan had been carried out, my office and immediate supporting staff would have been removed far from the ambassador, the DCM, and other section chiefs with whom I frequently consulted. Eventually we were able to compromise with a minimum of disruption to USIS operations, but not until we had engaged in considerable bureaucratic infighting. My office and the major cultural activities of USIS remained in the embassy while some administrative and specialized activities were transferred to the USIS Annex three blocks from the chancery.

There were other embassy stalwarts with whom I, as PAO, considered it essential to maintain good professional relations because they could help assure successful USIS programs. These included the consul general, who often cooperated with us in expediting visa applications for newspaper editors and other important USIS contacts planning to visit the U.S.; the personnel officer, who handled personnel administration for most of the agencies attached to the embassy; and the budget and fiscal officer, whose office handled our pay records. On program matters the head of the Drug Enforcement Agency and the head of the Agency for International Development were often consulted on information matters affecting their agencies. I and other USIS officers worked closely with them on many matters of mutual interest.

On April 1, 1978, President Jimmy Carter incorporated State Department educational and cultural exchange programs into USIA. These programs had always been managed overseas by USIS officers but administered in Washington by the State Department. Now they became a 100 percent USIA activity. At the same time, the name of USIA was changed to International Communication Agency (ICA).

I shared with many other Foreign Service officers a critical view of the name change since "ICA" could be easily confused with "CIA." (One day at the Hansen's dinner table, for example, when a guest asked our children who their father worked for, our youngest child quickly responded, "the CIA," to which I immediately responded, "No! No! No!"). I also believed that to leave the "U.S." identification out of the title was a mistake. Equally important, to forsake nearly a quarter of a century of building up the respect and admiration for the term "USIS" (the well-known acronym of USIA's overseas offices which stood for U.S. information Service) was foolish. USIS was known and respected by many of the world's scholars, students, and community leaders who had benefited from USIS libraries and other programs identified with USIS. Four years later, on August 24, 1982, President Ronald Reagan let USIA be USIA by returning the U.S. government's public diplomacy agency to its original name. During the four years when the agency was known as ICA, some posts continued to use USIS while others substituted the term "USICA." Now they were all, once again, known as USIS posts.

The visit to Peru in 1976 of "the First Lady of Plains," Rosalynn Carter, five months after Jimmy Carter's inauguration as President of the U.S., was an event which demanded the time and energies of almost all sections of the U.S. mission. Only if the president himself had planned to land in Lima might the effort to assure a smooth visit been more complicated.

USIS had a major role in the planning and execution of her public affairs activities while in Peru. This role involved publicizing the visit, the arrangement of press conferences, background briefings, and logistical support for the local media. USIS also provided working space, typewriters, and communication facilities for the twenty-seven members of the U.S. press who accompanied her on the Air Force Boeing 707 in which she and her entourage traveled.

There were nineteen in her entourage, including national security council advisor for Latin America, Robert Pastor; the assistant secretary of state for Latin America, Terry Todman; several other State Department officials; Gay Vance, the wife of the secretary of state; a nurse; her secretary; her press secretary; and Secret Service agents.

The visit of a First Lady traveling officially as the president's personal representative with the intention of discussing U.S. policy with government leaders was historically unique. As soon as her trip to Latin America to meet with the presidents of seven countries was announced, it became the subject of considerable criticism by the naysayers in both the U.S. and Latin America. How could the wife of the U.S. president expect to discuss with the presidents of these countries the serious problems and issues affecting their relations with the U.S.? One European diplomat was quoted in *U.S. News and World Report* as saying: "I don't think any Latin American statesman will take her seriously, even if she is the wife of the President of the United States."

Some members of Congress, including Congressman Dante Fascell, also opposed the trip. In her autobiography Mrs. Carter noted that when Representative Fascell walked into one of her briefing sessions prior to the trip, he said bluntly, "The Latinos are macho and they hate gringos and women. What else do you want to know?" So although she prepared herself on the major issues and concerns of the countries she would visit, she must have felt some trepidation at the start of her precedent breaking voyage.

On May 30, 1976, she left Washington for Jamaica, Costa Rica, Ecuador, Peru, Brazil, Colombia, and Venezuela, which she would visit in that order. Her visits to Jamaica and Costa Rica proved she would be taken seriously and the visit with Ecuadorean leaders went well. As she wrote later in her autobiographical book, *First Lady From Plains*:

> Though by now the leaders of the countries were taking me seriously and the questions about my credentials were diminishing, one critical U.S. reporter persisted as I was leaving Ecuador, "You have neither been elected by the American people nor confirmed by the Senate to discuss foreign policy with foreign heads of state," he said. "Do you consider this trip an appropriate exercise of your position?" I tried to have patience, but considering the many important issues he should have addressed, this time I'm afraid I snapped at him. "I am the person closest to the President of the United States, and if I can explain his policies and let the people of Latin America know of his great interest and friendship, I intend to do so!"

If anything, that assertion of the value of pillow talk strengthened her resolve to prove the naysayers wrong, which she did. She spent five days in Peru which included a rest stop at La Granja de Azul, a small resort just outside Lima that provided a relaxing atmosphere and was ideal in other ways for a stopover in the middle of her taxing trip. Built like a Spanish village, it had housing facilities of different types for about 150 people; recreational facilities that included two large swimming pools and a number of smaller ones at individual cottages; and dining facilities of various types. La Granja de Azul was isolated and could assure privacy for the First Lady and her entourage. Dependable phone lines had to be installed in this distant suburb of Lima, both for official business and for the media, but all was ready in time for the visit and no serious problems in communication emerged. In addition to the USIS press center at the Sheraton Hotel in downtown

Lima, we established one at La Granja de Azul shortly before and during the time that Mrs. Carter was there.

From the moment she stepped off the plane in Lima until she left, the First Lady favorably impressed all who came in contact with her. She was knowledgeable about the host country and its people and the issues affecting the relations between Peru and the U.S. From President Francisco Morales Bermudez and Ambassador Harry Shlaudeman on down, all Peruvians and embassy staffers who came in contact with her were enchanted with her graciousness and ability to articulate U.S. policies and concerns. By the time she left Peru more than one embassy staffer remarked, "Now we know how Jimmy Carter got to be president." As with all of the presidents she met, after some possibly initial doubts on their part, Peruvian President Morales Bermudez took her seriously and welcomed the opportunity to talk to the person closest to the president of the U.S.

In Ecuador she learned that Ecuadorian officials were fearful that Peru was planning a military attack on the hundredth anniversary of the War of the Pacific, a year away. (Patrol skirmishes were almost routine, and now oil had been discovered in Ecuador near the Peruvian border, increasing the plausibility that Peru might take such action). The U.S. was concerned about Peru's arms purchases from the Soviet Union, while Peru worried about Chile's intentions vís a vís Peru in the south. Morales Bermudez argued, according to what the First Lady later wrote, that he needed a strong national defense system and that Peru was buying Russian arms only because the U.S. would not sell him any. These were plausible arguments.

During the stopover at La Granja de Azul Gay Vance, the wife of the Secretary of State, celebrated her birthday. Mrs. Carter invited all of the embassy staffers who were there in support of her visit and the traveling media to a birthday party for Mrs. Vance. It provided the opportunity for many of the staffers to exchange views with the First Lady in an informal setting.

Retired USIA Foreign Service officer Tom Elliston, whose wife was the USIS American secretary, was temporarily hired by USIS during those two hectic weeks during and prior to the visit. His extensive experience in dealing with the press on numerous occasions when on active duty was put to good use. When the visit was over, he was moved to write to his former friend and colleague, USIA Director Reinhardt, that Mrs. Carter's visit had been "an exhilarating experience" for him working with USIS Lima and its professional staff. Later on, of course, I told him that flattery would get him everywhere.

President Morales Bermudez confided to Mrs. Carter, according to her 1984 book, that he was going to establish democracy in Peru and give up his power. At the same time she promised that she would come back to Peru for the inauguration of the newly elected president. In the summer of 1980 she returned to attend the inauguration of the first freely elected president of Peru in a dozen years, President Fernando Belaunde Terry. Ironically, he was the same man who had been president when ousted by a military coup twelve years earlier.

Highly qualified professionals on my staff like information officer Gerald Waters and Peruvian Press Chief Fernando Cervantes, plus the hard work and dedication of all of the USIS staff, had made the contribution of USIS to Mrs. Carter's visit not only efficient and effective but enjoyable as well.

After home leave during which we crossed the U.S. by train, visiting friends and historical sights en route, we again settled down to life in Peru, which was now even more enjoyable than the first two years had been. We really felt at home here now, enjoyed the company of American and Peruvian friends, and knew where and how to get things done which comes with experience. We continued to visit various parts of the country whenever possible, saw our young children grow and develop satisfactorily, and all in all these were good years for the Hansen's. Work at USIS continued to be interesting and, as usual, no two days were alike.

The Peruvian government planned to hold elections and return to civil government in 1980. We gave high priority in USIS information and educational exchange programs to U.S. policies that supported political freedom and economic development. We had been doing this the past two years but now intensified our efforts in this direction. At the same time anti-narcotics efforts had become a major new U.S. government program for which there was a definite role for USIS. This soon became a major USIS theme. Particularly important were our efforts to try to change the attitude of many Peruvians. High government officials, for example, contended initially that the narcotics problem was "a U.S. problem," not a Peruvian problem, since the U.S. was the main market for the cocaine that was exported from Peru.

It took time and effort to convince Peruvian authorities that the negative effects of illicit drug trafficking were as drastic for Peru as they were for the U.S. Eventually most agreed, though the problem persists to this day. In 1991, for example, Peru received a ninety million dollar grant from the U.S. to combat the illicit narcotics trade. By then, as U.S. government officials had reluctantly predicted years earlier, Peruvian youth had become as susceptible to drug use as American and European youth.

While everyone in USIA seemed to agree that the Country Plan document, which spelled out the goals of a USIS post was necessary, in 1979 Agency officials were still toying with its format. Each year efforts would be made to "simplify" the Plan. Some of these efforts did anything but. Nevertheless, knowing the need to keep the varied informational and cultural capabilities of USIS posts under some kind of controlled direction, most Foreign Service officers accepted the challenge and tried to develop the annual goals in as meaningful a manner as possible.

Goals were developed at the post and had to have the ambassador's approval, meaning, usually, the approval of the deputy chief of mission who usually handled this chore. Once over that hurdle, the goals were submitted to Washington where the area office and the policy office either accepted them as submitted, which was rare, or edited, refined, and made suggestions for changes in the initial draft.

In November 1979, our Country Plan ran into problems when the DCM's views differed from those of USIA Washington and, in certain aspects, my own. Despite considerable correspondence between Washington and the post, we had reached a point where I decided that if those in Washington wanted to have the last word, I would accept it. This did not set well with the new area director, Victor Olason, who informed me "since I didn't want to make any more changes, they would make them." He added, "There is no requirement that the goals you agree with and those which you have with the embassy be identical."

The DCM must have been as tired of going back and forth on language as I was, so after being presented with Washington's latest, he said "fine with me." He said he was puzzled, however, as to how USIS would operate with two different sets of goals and objectives — one for USIA and the other for the ambassador. I do not recall what I responded, but perhaps the PAO is the only person in the world who can serve two masters! Most of the time they do, and I did, with little difficulty, though that was not necessarily the case this time.

By June 1980 our four-year tour in Peru was rapidly coming to an end. Since, as a PAO, I served two masters, two efficiency reports on my performance were written annually, one by the Area Director in Washington and one by the DCM, representing the ambassador. When the draft of the final report to be written about me by the DCM was given to me a few months before my actual departure from Lima, I took issue with it.

I knew the DCM and I had occasional misunderstandings. We viewed USIS operations from different angles, but I never expected the kind of Officer Evaluation Report (OER) he wrote about me that June, a few months before the end of my Peruvian tour. After mulling over the report the evening after receiving the draft, and remembering how I had missed an opportunity to change an OER written about me following the presidents' meeting in Punta del Este years before (when the rating officer ignored that major event), I made an appointment to see him the following morning, presented my views as to the number of ways the varied activities of USIS Lima during the past year had furthered U.S. interests and our foreign policies through our press, radio, and TV programming and our substantial educational and cultural exchanges. He rewrote the report much more to my liking, and which was, in my view, a much fairer view of my administration during this time.

USIA operated under a personnel system called "Open Assignments," which gave FSOs an opportunity to indicate their preferences as to where they would like to be assigned. In some instances individual preferences coincided with Agency needs. In such cases the individuals concerned should have been delighted, and probably were. Prior to my impending transfer I had not exercised this option, being delighted with the jobs that had been offered to me. Now, for the first time, I would test the system. As my departure date from Lima was just around the corner, I followed up correspondence I had earlier with the director of Foreign Service Personnel about my next assignment.

CAO Frank Florey, who had arrived in Peru about the same time I did, was also completing his tour of duty. I thought he had performed in a superb manner, contributing greatly to the successes enjoyed by USIS Lima, and thus merited another challenging and interesting assignment. In various messages to the Agency over a period of about eight months, he listed, under the "Open Assignments" program, twenty-two positions for which he was, in my opinion, qualified to fill and which were becoming vacant at the time of his transfer from Peru. These positions were on almost every continent in the world. Unfortunately, perhaps like me, he had no godfather in Washington. He was offered only one position—that of cultural affairs officer at a branch USIS post in Karachi, Pakistan. Not only had he not applied for that position, but it was presented to him practically on the eve of his scheduled departure from Peru. While professionally going from a countrywide CAO to a CAO at a branch post was viewed by some as a step down, he accepted it, for whatever reasons, despite my urging that he explore other possibilities. Perhaps he was fed up with a system that theoretically takes the individual's preferences into consideration, but in his case, failed to accept any one of twenty-two suggestions.

Strangely enough, although I had made fewer suggestions, I also was slated to go to Pakistan on my next assignment. In looking back I admit to being naive in requesting some of the jobs I requested as they were jobs slated for career officers with much more political clout than I had. Nevertheless, when the only offer to be made to me from headquarters was as deputy public affairs officer in Islamabad, Pakistan, I indicated my reservations based on my interest in other areas, my lack of Asian experience, and the question of what school and medical facilities would be available for our three children who were still at home, ages ten, fifteen, and sixteen.

The only knowledge I had of Pakistan was from press reports which caught the world's attention when the U.S. embassy and USIS centers in Pakistan were burned by rioting mobs two years earlier. All these factors combined to make me reluctant to grab the ring the powers in Washington were offering me. More than a year would pass before the dust settled with regard to my next assignment. Because no other foreign positions were offered, and because of my expressed reluctance to accept the Pakistan job, I received "loose pack" orders to report to Washington at the end of my tour. "Loose packing" meant that our household effects would be held in Peru until my final destination was determined.

By July my replacement, William Lenderking, was named. He was scheduled to arrive the end of August or in September. Since we were assigned to Washington where we would have to find schools for our children and housing (since our home there was rented and we expected another overseas assignment shortly), it seemed imperative that we arrive before school began in September. We had heard so much overseas about the disintegration of the public school system in the U.S. in the late seventies, particularly the drug and discipline problems, that we decided, if at all possible, to put our children in private schools upon our return to the U.S. They had, after all, been educated in essentially private schools overseas. We believed the cultural shock of reentering American society in the volatile late seventies would be challenge enough for them. With this in mind, Charmaine left Peru with the children in July. They visited her relatives in Trinidad and then stayed with her sister in Barbados where I would join them in August for a week's vacation before returning to the U.S.

Rosalynn Carter was scheduled to return to Peru for the inauguration of President Fernando Belaunde, the first freely elected president of Peru in sixteen years. During her first visit to Peru she had promised to return for his inauguration if he won the election, which he did as expected, and if the military government abided by its promise to respect the election.

Belaunde's inauguration was the culmination of a process that the U.S. government fully supported—the ending of more than a dozen years of military dictatorship, which began when Belaunde, the elected president at that time, was overthrown in a coup d'etat. It was important for me to remain at my post until Mrs. Carter's brief visit to the inauguration ceremonies was completed because it would require the usual USIS public relations planning and support. Following her visit in August there was really no reason why I would have to remain at the post since another experienced officer, USIS executive officer Vance Pace, was fully capable of holding down the fort for the few weeks until the new PAO arrived. I particularly wanted to be able to get my family settled in Washington and my children's schooling arranged by early September. I also felt that a week's vacation on our favorite island of Barbados, where I was scheduled to meet them, would recharge my batteries after our hectic departure from Peru.

Departures from Foreign Service posts are almost always hectic. This one was especially so as not only had the four years we spent here been so pleasant for us, having enjoyed the friendship of many Peruvians and others, but it was the longest time we had spent in any one place in my whole Foreign Service career. Thus the parting was indeed sweet sorrow.

Mrs. Carter's visit went off without a hitch. She left the same impression of a charming, intelligent, articulate lady among all who came in contact with her that she had left during her first visit to Peru. When she flew off from Lima's Jorge Chavez International Airport to return to the U.S. I went home to pack my bags. I felt my job in Peru had been accomplished. It was time for me to leave and join my family.

Many times during our years in Peru we were told, "You should have been here in the good old days." That was hard for us to imagine, for how could life for a diplomatic family in Peru be more pleasant than it was for us? Nearly a decade later, the contrast between the Peruvian paradise we knew and Peru during the late 80s was startling.

As the 1990s began, Peru's political, social and economic systems were in deep trouble. Poverty had expanded; the country was debt-ridden; the hope for an oil bonanza had faded; illicit drug trafficking was entrenched; and terrorism had adversely affected thousands of Peruvian citizens and many foreigners. Compared to this scenario, our years in Peru were "the good old days."

By 1992 Peruvians were worse off than they had been a decade earlier. Their social and economic conditions had deteriorated. Although Peruvian citizens enjoyed greater freedom than when ruled by military dictatorships, Peru remained, like so many other countries in the Third World, an example of a country that was basically wealthy but so poorly organized that its wealth was dissipated in ways that favored a minority at the expense of the majority. The economy was in deep trouble and a terrible terrorism stalked the land, led by a shadowy group who called themselves *El Sendero Luminoso* (The Shining Path).

The Shining Path was one of the most peculiar terrorist groups in the world. Highly secretive, its members were allegedly dedicated to Maoist philosophy at a time when Mao was long since gone. Most of the rest of the world, including the Soviet Union and Eastern Europe, have eschewed communism, which, in earlier days, encouraged and supported many leftist terrorist groups in developing countries. Yet the Shining Path, which began as an offshoot from Peruvian communist party members and sympathizers, stuck with Mao. Like the Tupamaro terrorists of Uruguay and others of that ilk, most were in it for escapism, the excitement, and the feeling of belonging.

"The total collapse of the state" was the alleged ultimate goal of *Sendero Luminoso* according to most authorities who studied the organization's development. But by 1993 their leader was in jail and *Sendero Luminoso* was weakening. By mid-1994 there were increasing indications that their heyday had passed. In 1996, a startling incident occurred which may have been their swan song. About a dozen of their members attacked the Japanese Embassy in Lima and held many hostages for several months. When the Peruvian military dramatically retook the embassy, all the terrorists who participated in that caper were killed as they tried to defend their positions. With the demise of terrorist activity and other factors that brought greater stability to Peruvian society, the Peruvian economy surged forward.

In the sea of misfortunes that befell Peru in the 1980s, one thesis stood out as a road map for a way to bring greater peace and prosperity to Peruvian society. That thesis, developed by Peruvian economist Hernando deSoto and his *Instituto de Libertad y Democracia* (Institute of Liberty and Democracy) was called *El Otro Sendero* (The Other Path—an obvious counter to the Shining Path). Hernando deSoto's study of Peru's economic and social conditions in the mid-1980s was published in a book of the same title. It received global attention and was translated into numerous languages. While citing the problems of Peru, its formulae are applicable to most developing countries and for this reason attracted the wide attention which it received.

DeSoto compared Peruvian society in the 1980s with mercantilism as practiced in Europe in the 15th to 19th centuries, an original and innovative idea. Mercantilism was the doctrine that arose with the decline of feudalism. It contended that the economic welfare of the state could only be secured by government regulation of a national character. DeSoto's main point, however, as true of Europe of earlier centuries as of 20th century Peru, was that a small minority who controlled the economy profited while the vast majority, in the case of Europe, the serfs, and in the case of Peru, the landless peasants, were kept out of the money economy. Special privileges for the privileged prevailed in mercantilist Europe, as they did in Peru in the late seventies.

DeSoto's thesis, spelled out in great, practical detail, was to change the rules. A free market economy is necessary, he contended, to enable the thousands of small businesses operating outside the government's warped and biased legal system to function legally; they accounted for two thirds of the Peruvian economy when his book was written! Equally important, he said, is a democratic political system that would replace the administrative dictums of Peruvian presidents by laws freely debated and publicized prior to enactment by the legislature. The traditional Peruvian government practice at the time was for the president to impose administrative decrees, with no prior public discussion in most cases, at the rate of about thirty per day!

In using the example of mercantilist Europe as being replicated by modern Peru, he warned that unless Peruvian leaders take action the European experience could also take place in Peru. Mercantilism collapsed between the end of the nineteenth and the beginning of the twentieth century, "when the contradictions of a system that was incapable of governing a more complex and urbanized society reached their peak," he argued. "As formal businesses were gradually stifled by taxes and regulations and informals openly defied the law and voiced dissatisfaction at being pushed to the margins, the stage was set for collapse." The "informals," he refers to, like their Peruvian counterparts who accounted for two-thirds of the economic activity of Peru at the time, are individuals operating outside government rules and regulations. And he went on to say:

> Those European mercantilist countries which made the
> transition from bad to good laws (granting political, social and

economic freedoms) gradually calmed down and were able to prosper. ... Countries which resisted change and insisted on preserving their mercantilist institutions were unable to adjust their legal systems to reality and continued to oppose their people's needs and aspirations. Almost all of these countries underwent violent revolutions.

DeSoto noted that among the different scenarios generated by the failure of mercantilism there were two kinds of situations: peaceful and violent. "England is an example of the first. Examples of the second are France, which ultimately established a system of democracy and widespread entrepreneurship; Spain, which alternated between institutional repression and attempts at liberalization and maintained a semi-mercantilist system for a considerable number of years; and Russia, where repression and confrontation ultimately led to a totalitarian system." In short, he warned that Peru, finding itself in a similar situation, could go either way depending on what it now does. The violence route was being sought by the Shining Path terrorists. He concluded: "The trait common to all was the wide gap between the countries' legal institutions and their economic and social life."

In December 1990 Peru's most famous novelist, Mario Vargas Llosa, long noted for his political commentary, wrote an article in Harper's Magazine in which he discussed one of Peru's major dilemmas ever since the Spanish conquest of that country—the fact that two cultures exist in Peru and have existed now for nearly five centuries—one that is today Western and modern, the other that continues to be aboriginal and archaic. One culture, he states, "is separated from the other because of exploitation and discrimination that the former exercises over the latter." He caused considerable controversy when, after describing the two cultures and noting "apartheid prevails" in Peru today, he wrote:

> Important as integration is, the obstacle to achieving it lies in the huge economic gap between the two communities. Indian peasants live in such a primitive way that communication is practically impossible. ... The price they pay for integration is high—renunciation of their culture, their language, their beliefs, their traditions and customs, and the adoption of the culture of their ancient masters. After one generation those who emigrate to the cities become mestizos. They are no longer Indians. Perhaps there is no realistic way to integrate our societies other than by asking the Indians to pay the price. ... If forced to choose between the preservation of Indian cultures

and their complete assimilation, with great sadness I would choose modernization of the Indian population, because there are priorities; and the first priority is, of course, to fight hunger and misery.

By the mid to late 1990s Peru was returning to being the peaceful and, for many, wonderful land that we "gringos' enjoyed so much when we were guests in that fascinating country in the years 1976 to 1980.

10
Passage to Pakistan

"Islamabad is half the size of Arlington Cemetery, and twice as dead."
—Comment by a Western diplomat

"Thanks for sharing the fun, the hustle, the bustle, the sound, the fury, the excitement and occasionally the frustrations of working for USIS."
—Mujtaba, senior Pakistani employee upon his retirement.

Our return to Washington in September 1980 was full of challenges. I wanted to find an agency assignment that would be good for my career and satisfactory for the needs of my family; we had to find a place to live since our house in McLean was rented; and we had to find good schools for three of our children. With these uncertainties and concern about placing our children in the Washington area public school system, we planned to place Katherine and Alicia in a private boarding school. The local public schools at that time had gained a reputation for decreased quality of education, increased drug use, and disciplinary problems. Furthermore, we thought that if we received another overseas assignment within a matter of months while they were in a boarding school, they could complete the school year and join us later.

Katherine was a senior in high school and Alicia was entering the tenth grade. At one private school in Virginia, the director would accept Alicia but not Katherine because newcomers to the school could not be seniors. When we decided to enroll both in the O'Connell High School, a Catholic school in nearby Arlington where they would live at home, the situation was reversed. The principal said she would accept Katherine since the senior class was small, but could not accept Alicia because all tenth grade slots were filled! Not wanting to send the two sisters to separate schools, we were betwixt and between as to what to do.

After finding a house in McLean that we could rent for a year, with a diplomatic clause in the lease to allow us to leave if I received transfer orders to an overseas post, we renewed our efforts to get our girls into the Arlington school. We went back to talk to the nun who was the director of the school, and we prayed. After telling her of our dilemma, and, perhaps, because she considered their excellent academic records and unique background of living in other cultures, she relented and allowed both of them to enroll. Whether it was our prayers, the possibility that some other students dropped out, or her empathy with our situation that changed her mind we'll never know. Mark was enrolled in the fifth grade of St. John's Elementary School in McLean, a few blocks from where we lived.

Initially we searched for a furnished house to rent, believing our stay in Washington would be short. We found one in Arlington, but as the time approached to sign the lease, the owner had second thoughts and changed her mind. As a consequence, we rented an unfurnished house in McLean.

Moving into an unfurnished house had its own set of problems. We had some of our household effects in storage in Washington and these helped us in setting up housekeeping. Much of our household effects, however, were in storage in Peru, where they would remain until a determination was made as to my next overseas assignment. We would not see these things until more than a year later when we reached Pakistan and moved into our "permanent" quarters. Meanwhile, we lived a somewhat stoic existence in a house with only part of our household effects and with other things that we borrowed or bought. It was a far cry from the comfort and convenience of the "Hansen Mansion" in Lima, but we were happy to have our children enrolled in school and to be back in McLean, a suburb with which we were familiar and was convenient for going in and out of Washington.

Having more or less settled in a rented house a few months after being back in the D.C. area, and having enrolled our three children in satisfactory schools, I turned my attention to seeking a suitable overseas assignment. I still believed our stay in Washington this time would be relatively short, but it turned out to be somewhat longer than anticipated. Our final destination would remind me of that old saying, "the more things change, the more they stay the same." The only overseas post offered to me was the same one offered when I was in Lima—Islamabad.

When I reported for duty after home leave I was not warmly welcomed by the Office of Foreign Service Personnel at headquarters. I think the personnel people believed I should have accepted the assignment to Islamabad while still in Peru. They offered me nothing else that fall, contending that all other positions for which I might be considered, given my background and experience, were already filled or wouldn't open until the following year. As to a Washington assignment, they were unprepared to offer me a definitive slot as I was part of the problem the personnel division constantly faced: what to do with employees who are essentially qualified for overseas assignments but who must spend a few years every so often in Washington. Part of the rationale for periodic Washington assignments was that this would enable FSOs to maintain their roots with their own culture.

I was not the first Foreign Service officer to return home and to find myself "walking the halls." The bureaucrats in the personnel division had enough problems in moving people back and forth throughout the world without having someone fight the system. In not readily accepting the assignment to Pakistan when offered just before I was about to leave Lima, I became persona non grata as far as the bureau of personnel was concerned.

Darrell Carter, a former director of USIA's Latin American office, was the acting director of the Office of Public Liaison at the time. This was the office that dealt with the American public and the press and also served as the Congressional Liaison office. As the area director he was my boss when I was the director of USIS La Paz. He was also my supervisor when I was the policy officer for Latin America, and during the civil war in the Dominican Republic, I was his deputy on the USIA task force in that country. Now he "took me in from the cold" by offering me a job in the Office of Public Liaison which I readily accepted. We agreed that it would be a temporary position until I was assigned to a regular slot in Washington or overseas.

The director of USIA at the time was John Reinhardt. The late 1970s and early 1980s was a period when USIA budgets suffered continuing reductions. Reinhardt and his top aides were looking for ways to encourage the Congress to hold the line on USIA budgets and increase, if possible, USIA resources. There was a general feeling within the agency that the budget knife was now cutting deep into the bone.

Someone came up with the idea that if key senators and congressmen, particularly those on the committees responsible for USIA appropriations, could be convinced of the importance of the agency's activities in fostering the goals of U.S. foreign policy, the agency might fare better in its annual appropriations. One idea that was explored, and with which I became involved in the research aspect, was to ascertain which organizations and institutions in the home territory of those key congressmen might become powerful proponents of more adequate appropriations for carrying on the work of the agency if fully informed regarding the important work of USIA. The scheme was developed close to the chest, as there was always the possibility that it might be interpreted as going against the ironclad rule that USIA was not permitted "to propagandize its own people." But whether this effort would have had any effect will never be known because it never really got off the ground. Before initiating this project, Director Reinhardt left and was replaced by Charles Wick.

Wick was a close friend of Ronald Reagan, the U.S. president who was sometimes called "The Great Communicator." With Reagan as a friend of the new USIA director and sympathetic to the goals of USIA, the agency's financial fortunes were reversed. For some years following Reagan's inauguration, the trend of USIA budgets was no longer downward. On the contrary, the agency's financial resources increased dramatically for a number of years. President Reagan was a Cold War warrior who believed that USIA programs were an important U.S. asset in that era and should be used. And use them he did.

During my brief tour in the Office of Public Liaison, I was not overworked. Research on the project to influence key congressmen did not fill my day. I had time to reflect and to research other matters of interest, so I began to explore some of the issues that had been subjects of concern or controversy among agency officers for some time. For example, what was the real meaning of the term "public diplomacy?" Different people had different ideas. What should be the agency's goals? Were its programs really effective? Was "propaganda" really a bad term to describe the agency's activities? For once in my career the demands of my job were such that there was considerable time for reflection on such matters.

I wrote a number of papers on various subjects related to the goals of USIA and how those goals are carried out. My initial thought was that perhaps some of these papers could be used for discussing these subjects in talks or in print. For example, others and I had long thought that USIA's in-house organ, USIA WORLD, should discuss serious subjects concerning the work of the agency. Unfortunately, for whatever reasons, it remained a bland, generally non-controversial publication about the agency's personnel and those programs and events considered to be especially effective.

Controversy about the agency's varied activities, of which there was always an adequate supply, was seldom discussed except in informal talk among the professionals or in formal discussions by committees. Although any two Foreign Service officers would often disagree about how any one program or event might be most effectively conducted for USIA purposes, there were few forums outside the two avenues mentioned where such disagreements could be argued on their merits. As I ruminated about the agency's various programs and activities and put some of my thoughts on paper, a spark struck my consciousness. What if I had the time and energy to incorporate some of these ideas into the pages of a book?

Some months later, although I was appreciative of Darrell Carter's kindness in arranging a slot for me in his office, I felt that my wheels were spinning and I was going nowhere. The chances of an overseas assignment any time soon were diminishing. Therefore I was pleased when given the assignment of chief of the Latin American branch in the Office of Research. I had always valued research as a basic tool for policy makers, so I welcomed the opportunity to make use of my knowledge of Latin America that was based on my work in four Latin American countries.

As with many agency activities, I found there were aspects in the research field with which I could not agree with my superiors. For example, I thought that the decision of USIA Director Reinhardt to abolish all research that sought to determine the effectiveness of USIA programs was wrong. Apparently he saw this as a way to cut costs. I saw it as an important activity of the Office of Research, which should not be abolished. In my view, if USIA did not examine the effectiveness of its own programs with an eye to eliminating those of little value, and strengthening those that proved to be effective, no one else would. The Office of Research had done this for years and admittedly had a spotty record, yet I believed many of their projects were worthwhile. Director Reinhardt, however, ordered such research terminated, with the exception of research designed to determine the effectiveness of VOA broadcasts, mainly through listnership polls. (Although my views were shared by many others in the Office of Research, I was in no position to influence the director's decision. In later years, however, the agency returned to this traditional type of research).

Having abolished studies to determine the effectiveness of agency programs (except for *VOA*), the Office of Research was left to conduct and/or contract research, the results of which would show trends, traits, and tendencies of various foreign audiences on subjects of interest to the U.S. government. Some excellent, helpful information developed from such projects, but Foreign Service officers and agency administrators often found the results reached them far too late to serve their purposes.

The Office of Research was one of the most meticulous developers of reports of any office in the agency. Because its reports passed through so many internal reviews and each reviewer had his or her own idea about how a thought should be expressed, they moved through the bureaucracy at a snail's pace, more often than not leaving the office in what the final signer thought was a "more perfect state." For this reason the reports often arrived at the desk of the end-users too late to be useful. While not always the case, this happened frequently enough that most Foreign Service officers in the front lines seldom bothered to call on the Office of Research because of its reputation of providing "too little, too late."

In the field, and in certain positions in Washington, we often saw CIA or military intelligence reports which were equally of little value, but for a different reason. Many were unevaluated "raw intelligence" reports that, although timely, were often suspect with regard to reliability. The final reports issued by the Office of Research, usually from polls and surveys or other overt sources, frequently went to the other extreme because of the meticulousness of the many bureaucrats who had a hand in their development.

The branch that I now supervised in the Office of Research was a small operation. My staff consisted of two researchers and a secretary. Both researchers had doctorates in sociology. One was a veteran USIA employee who was also vice president of the agency's government employees' union (AFGE Local 1812). He had agency authorization to spend part of the working day, which he did, on union affairs. His first love was the union and he later became its full-time president. Like the younger of the two sociologists, he was a former university professor with experience in Latin American affairs. Aware that they might be among those who chafed at the idea of a Foreign Service officer being given a supervisory position to which they, as civil servant employees, were not considered eligible despite their qualifications, (since certain jobs were reserved for Foreign Service officers), I met this challenge head on. I let them know that I respected their expertise in the methodology of accepted social science research practices. At the same time I indicated that I considered my contribution to the current studies, and those to be initiated, would be my views concerning the topics covered based on my practical Latin American experience. We soon discovered that under these guidelines, we enjoyed working as a team.

Once again, however, as when I was assigned to the Office of Public Liaison, I found that my workday was not filled to the brim. I had time to ruminate. I returned to what I considered the broader issues and concerns of the agency's activities. I collected data, read reports, and conducted my own research into those areas which held my interest. This in no way interfered with carrying out the responsibilities of my new position, for in truth, those responsibilities were not that demanding. In time, my individual essays on various facets of the agency's operations and the data I accumulated grew considerably. I now thought more seriously than ever about writing a book to present my views about how USIA conducts its multivaried activities, and how and why, in my opinion, the agency might be more effective.

A second house we bought in McLean in May 1981 was not far from the house we were renting. We moved in the following month. About that same time I was once again offered the job of deputy public affairs officer in Pakistan. This was the only overseas job offered to me. If accepted, I would be expected to leave as soon as possible since the position was vacant. Although I was still not enthused about a tour in Pakistan, Charmaine thought it would be a great assignment and, as usual, she was right. I insisted that, before leaving, I should at least be able to attend a week-long course on Southeast Asia which the Foreign Service Institute sponsored periodically, since I knew so little about that part of the world. This was arranged and we began to prepare for our departure.

A few weeks after moving into our new home, we spent the weekend at our vacation condo at Bryce Mountain in Virginia, thinking this would be our last opportunity to relax at Bryce Resort before going overseas. We arrived home that Sunday afternoon. Charmaine started to get out of the car but could not put her left foot on the ground. Her knee was locked in a bent position! No matter what she did, her knee remained frozen in the position it was in when sitting in the car. This strange happening was beyond our comprehension.

The following morning she was examined by an orthopedic surgeon. After the examination and reviewing x-rays, he said the cartilage was frozen and an operation was needed to remove it. He said physical therapy would be required for some months after the operation, but in due course she should be able to regain the normal use of her knee. We felt we had no choice but to proceed with the doctor's recommendation. Surgery was scheduled a few weeks later at Arlington General Hospital.

After leaving Charmaine in the hospital the evening before the operation was to take place, I returned home, depressed and concerned. That night was a sleepless one for me. I kept thinking, "What if she is never able to walk again? Why didn't we get a second opinion? Should we really have arranged this? Did we do the right thing?" I suppose I did get a few hours of sleep that night, but it was with great trepidation that I returned to the hospital in the morning to see Charmaine before she was wheeled into the operating room. She kept up her usual cheerfulness and courage, exuding a calmness that helped ease my anxiety.

A few hours later, when the operation had been completed, the doctor told me that all went well and that she would regain the full use of her knee in a few months. She left the hospital a few days later. Shortly thereafter she began physical therapy sessions that eventually brought about her full recovery. Under the circumstances our departure for Pakistan was delayed. She slowly recuperated during the summer months and our new departure date was set for early September, right after Labor Day.

By the time we were ready to leave for Islamabad, my idea of writing a book about USIA was developed to where I now had an outline of the chapters I hoped to write and drafts of the first two chapters. Among other things I planned to include the ideas presented in a paper I wrote in 1976 while attending a nine-week seminar on communications theory and methodology as applicable to USIA. The seminar was held at the School of International Service of American University in Washington. At the conclusion of the seminar, I wrote a lengthy monograph entitled "Whither USIA?." In it I argued that USIA, using modern communications technology, particularly satellite communications and computerized databanks in the U.S., should cooperate with the Agency for International Development in its social and economic development programs in developing countries. These programs, I argued, greatly served U.S. interests. In late July I sent copies of the first two chapters I had drafted and the outline of the forthcoming chapters to two potential publishers.

We had our household effects packed by the end of August and they were now, along with the items we had left in Peru, presumably en route to Pakistan. We were told not to ship anything of high personal value, such as paintings, because hardly two years had passed since the U.S. Embassy in Islamabad and some USIS offices in other areas of Pakistan had been attacked by violent mobs as an expression of disagreement with alleged U.S. actions. We had little choice, however, but to do so since our paintings and other personal items were with our effects in Peru.

With our household effects packed and shipped, we arranged to spend our last week in Washington in a hotel. On the last afternoon that we were in our house about to leave for the hotel, the phone rang. It was Betsy Brown, an editor with Praeger Publishers in New York. She told me that their editorial board had met and that they were excited about the outline I had sent to them for the book I planned to write about USIA. She said that if I agreed, she would send me a contract for the book to be published when I finished writing it. The timing could not have been better. A few more hours and she would have missed me. Since I had completed considerable research on the book I hoped to write and planned to take my notes with me to Pakistan, I was elated.

The few final days before our departure to the land where our "ninth life" would begin were as hectic as always on such occasions. This would be our last overseas assignment with USIA, though hardly the least exciting.

To reach Islamabad from Washington, D.C., one has to fly nearly halfway around the globe. For this reason, U.S. government travel regulations permit a rest stop for those on official travel. We chose London as our rest stop, even though this would leave us with two-thirds of the distance to be traveled still ahead of us. We had enjoyed the British capital so much during our initial visit a few years earlier that we looked forward to returning, even for the short, two-day layover.

Gone were the days when we were a traveling family of seven. With Robert and Katherine in college, and Annette married and on her own, we were now only a family of four. We were sure that Alicia and Mark would enjoy the many sights of London with its bobbies, double-decker buses, and such places as bustling Piccadilly Square just as much as we did. We introduced them to the Tower of London and were able to view the city from a boat on the Thames, which for them were great adventures.

When we had disembarked from our PanAm flight at Heathrow Airport, we decided we would check some of our luggage and retrieve it when we returned to the airport to continue our journey. Although Heathrow is one of the largest airports in the world, we were surprised to learn that there was only one place for passengers in transit to check their baggage, and then only between the hours of 6:30 a.m. to 10 p.m. Luckily we had arrived about 7 a.m. But there were only three men to handle the checking in and out of the large amounts of luggage of numerous transient passengers, many of whom, like us, did not want to bring all their baggage into the city. All of this voluminous luggage had to be personally lifted, stowed, and retrieved by these three men, a system which hardly lent itself to speed and efficiency. We spent at least an hour in line awaiting our turn. Behind us, in our slow moving line, a frustrated American tourist remarked, to no one in particular, "No wonder the island is sinking."

I should have known better than to have asked an acquaintance about hotel accommodations in London, and then to have taken his advice without checking on costs. He was a person who frequently visited the British capital when alone on business, so he mentioned a hotel not far from the U.S. embassy. We learned upon our arrival that it was a luxury hotel in the heart of London. Naturally it charged appropriate rates for what was offered. It was far more hotel than what we needed for a brief two day stay with two children. As life goes on, we still learn from experience. On this occasion I learned to undertake a little more research before making reservations, as all we wanted for those two days in London was a place to sleep. As it was, we didn't really get much of that. There was so much to see and do in so short a time.

On our second day in London, our sleep was disturbed by the phone ringing in our room at 5 a.m. It was the wake-up call we had requested. We were scheduled to fly out of Heathrow on the next leg of our flight at 8:30 a.m. After hurrying to the airport and retrieving our luggage, we learned that the flight from New York, which was to take us to Frankfurt, Germany, where we would change planes, had been diverted from Heathrow to Birmingham because of fog earlier that morning. Our plane finally arrived at Heathrow about noon and by 1:30 p.m. we were airborne.

In Frankfurt we were rushed to a waiting plane and took off for Karachi, Pakistan's largest city and its major port, located on the Arabian Sea. En route to Karachi we made a brief stop at Abu Dhabi in the United Arab Emirates where we entered a sterile, super modern, round airport terminal building. A somewhat incongruous structure, it was surrounded by the desert sands of this sparsely populated desert kingdom. There was nothing else in sight. This was in sharp contrast to the well-worn terminal building we later entered at the Karachi airport. Even at 4:30 a.m. when we arrived in Pakistan, September 4, 1981, the Karachi airport bustled with activity.

The American government sought to assure added income for the various American airline companies by its Fly America Act. This required that travelers flying at U.S. government expense fly on American carriers whenever possible. The Pakistani government, on the other hand, made sure that its government-owned Pakistan International Airlines, with very few exceptions, was the only airline to fly into Pakistan's twin cities of Islamabad and Rawalpindi. For this reason almost all American official travelers arriving from overseas had to change planes in Karachi for the final leg of a trip to Islamabad or Rawalpindi.

We were glad to be able to stop off in Karachi, not only to break up the long flight to Islamabad, but because we would have the opportunity to visit our old friends from Peru, Frank and Adela Florey, who now lived there. Frank was assigned as the cultural attaché of the branch USIS post in Karachi. The brief stopover also would be a good introduction to Pakistan.

Several other flights had arrived about the same time as ours, so the Pakistani check-in system through customs and immigration, not overly efficient at best, moved the voluminous recent arrivals through long lines at a snail's pace. Our family huddled together and tried to remain patient and undisturbed, though tired from the long flight from Frankfurt and suffering jet lag. Alicia, at age sixteen with light blonde hair, stood out among so many dark-skinned, dark-haired individuals, all looking so strange to us at first sight.

Most of the Pakistani men were wearing the traditional loose fitting clothing of Pakistan known as the *shalwar khameez*. This type of clothing is also worn by women, although as in any public place in Pakistan, the men far outnumbered the women. We did not find out until later that one of the men touched Alicia on her backside several times as we stood in line awaiting our turn. Had we known this at the time we might have caused an international incident in the first few moments of our arrival in Pakistan. Understandably, Alicia was terribly upset to be welcomed to Pakistan in such a manner.

Our friend and colleague Frank Florey, undaunted by the early hour of our arrival, met us as we emerged from the customs area. We were happy to see him as we were being besieged by taxi drivers and sundry others who wanted us to buy something or exchange currency. Frank was able to send them away and the USIS car and driver took us to his home. We stayed with the Florey's for five days, which included the weekend, and slept most of that day and a good part of the following day, victims of jet lag. The time difference between Washington and Karachi is nine hours. Even with the two-day layover in London this switch in hours was a jolt to our systems. We were more accustomed to traveling north and south than east and west. When I awoke that first day in Karachi, I was ready for breakfast and it was dinnertime.

A sprawling, unkempt, extremely hot city, Karachi had grown in the last decade to upwards of five million. Window air conditioners in the homes of foreigners whirr constantly to combat the intense heat.

The heat then seems to strike so much harder outside.

On Karachi streets dress is informal. The shalwar khameez is worn by the majority of the local population but western style clothes are also seen. Some women wear veils (though not as many as in Pakistani villages), rickshaws are motorized, and various panoramic scenes are painted in brilliant colors on the many trucks and buses that are outnumbered only by the rickshaws. Camels and oxen also plod along the busy streets of Karachi, as do water buffalo. Suddenly, we realized that we are, for the first time in our lives, in exotic Asia!

One of the oldest cities of South Asia is Hyderabad, about 125 miles north of Karachi. On our third day as guests of the Florey's we drove there on a dangerous, two-lane, bustling highway. Our route took us past ancient mausoleums of former rulers of the Indian subcontinent. Upon our arrival in Hyderabad we visited a branch USIS post run by a Pakistani employee. After lunch in a restaurant darkened at mid-day by heavy curtains to keep out the heat, we returned to Karachi by the Hyderabad-Karachi "Super Highway." This is a three-lane road that seemed to be more dangerous to drive on than the two-lane Karachi-Hyderabad road. This was because drivers from both directions on the three-lane road acted like the middle lane was only for them, not to mention the cattle and camels who shared the road.

On September 9th we boarded a Pakistan International Airlines plane for the final leg of our flight to Islamabad. PAO Jim Thurber met us at the airport and escorted us to the Holiday Inn in Islamabad. We spent the next ten days there before moving into our temporary quarters, a house vacated by the former information officer. Soon, what seemed so strange and mysterious to us, in comparison with the cultures we had known in Latin America and in our own country, would become familiar. It would take longer, however, for us to really feel at home here when compared with our experiences in previous overseas assignments.

Our "temporary quarters" were to be temporary for eight long months! It took that long to find what we considered to be an adequate, comfortable home in which we could carry out our professional entertainment duties in a manner we considered appropriate. Perhaps we were too demanding, but if we hadn't been our tour probably would have been much less satisfying.

In an Islamic society where there are restrictions on western ways at every turn, there were only about two or three adequate restaurants in the city that met our standards. Every other kind of entertainment was extremely limited, thus our home was more than ever our castle and our place to entertain friends and professional contacts. We looked at many houses and spent considerable time and effort in our search for "permanent quarters" before settling in for what was left of our three-year tour.

In keeping with local custom (and because many modern conveniences were non-existent in Islamabad), we needed to hire a number of servants to care for our needs and those of the house we lived in, whether temporary or not. So we hired a cook-bearer, a *dhobi* (laundryman), a *mali* (gardener), and a sweeper. The *chowkidar* (night watchman) was always provided by the embassy. Later, rather than a cook-bearer, we would periodically have a cook and a bearer. The bearer was responsible for all of the housework except the cleaning of the kitchen. (In this male-dominated society, all of our employees were men. The one exception was the sweeper who was assigned to sweep the driveways and sidewalks, and was paid very little. This led our daughter Annette to write to us, in one of her rare letters, that she thought it was hilarious that in Pakistan we had "male maids"!) The sweepers were Christian women, considered by the predominantly Islamic Pakistanis as being at the lowest class of their hierarchal society. Although possibly not as low as the untouchables in India's Hindu societies, the similarity exists.

The inefficiency of many of these employees was extraordinary. As a result, they would come and go with some frequency. The exception was our cook-bearer. He seemed so energetic and willing to please that we were greatly impressed by him for a number of months. For one thing he spoke English quite well, while most of the others only did haltingly. This greatly increased his value and importance to us. He was also the only one who lived on the premises in the servants' quarters. Unfortunately, one day when repairs were being made to his living quarters, we learned that he had stolen numerous bottles of Scotch and other items from our liquor locker. He had more of my liquor supply in his room than I had in my liquor locker. With this discovery we felt compelled to fire him. Despite our warnings, he was hired shortly thereafter by a married couple who were teachers at the International School. Before long they also suffered losses and again he was fired.

Because most of my career was spent in Latin America where language was usually not a barrier for most Foreign Service personnel, we were accustomed to finding our own housing when arriving in a new country. In Islamabad we experienced a system whereby the embassy obtained and assigned housing to all newly arrived families. A housing committee with representatives of the various agencies at the U.S. Mission was in charge of assigning selected houses to new arrivals. In making the assignments, consideration was given to the employee's rank, family size, representational duties, and, to a lesser extent, personal preferences.

I was not the only one with difficulties in finding suitable housing according to what I believed were my needs, but perhaps my case was one of the most frustrating for the individuals involved. Had we simply been able to unpack our things and stay in the house we were temporarily occupying, that would have been fine. Unfortunately, the Pakistani landlord of our temporary quarters was trying to regain the property and wanted us to move out as soon as possible. During this eight-month period, houses we found to be suitable were unavailable for one reason or another. Other houses that the embassy committee urged us to take had major problems from our viewpoint.

The minutes of the housing board meeting of May 27th show that DPAO Hansen was finally assigned to house #6, 19th St., LF-6/2, which at that time was occupied by the Rattray family. Alex Rattray was the economics counselor who had just been assigned to Karachi as the consul general and would shortly leave for that southern Pakistani city. Six weeks later we were able to move in and unpack our things that had arrived from Washington and Lima. It was nice to be finally settled in a "permanent" home.

Aside from the embassy's involvement in providing housing, the housing situation for diplomats in Islamabad was further complicated by a Pakistan government regulation. Foreign Ministry approval was required before any foreign diplomat could move into a house in Pakistan's new capital city.

Another unique feature of the housing situation in Islamabad was that the Embassy General Services Office (GSO) paid all rental, utility, maintenance, and repair costs of the houses where its American employees lived. The only cost to the employee was the telephone expense. Although many new houses were being built in Islamabad, a planned city that was only about twenty years old at the time, the influx of personnel assigned to the various embassies greatly increased the demand for suitable housing.

Foreign interest in Pakistan grew in the early 1980s because of the Soviet invasion of neighboring Afghanistan and the growing illicit heroin trade in Pakistan. This trade was increasingly detrimental to the U.S. and Europe and was growing extremely serious for Pakistan as well. Furthermore, the demand for housing was also increased by the loss of the American Embassy along with the apartments in the embassy compound that had been burned and destroyed by raging mobs only two years prior to our arrival. Of course my problem in getting settled in adequate housing paled in comparison to what my compatriots had to face in Islamabad two years earlier.

Less than two years prior to our arrival in Islamabad in September, 1981, many Pakistanis had been greatly influenced by the tirades of Ayatollah Ruholiah Khomeini of neighboring Iran. The U.S. Embassy in Tehran, which had been stormed by Iranian mobs in 1979, held forty-nine U.S. hostages while crowds outside chanted "Death to (U.S. President) Carter!" Iranian broadcasters declared that, for Muslims, "The U.S. is Enemy No. 1 of Humanity." Khomeini's speeches, which resounded throughout the Islamic world, were full of such phrases as "America—the Mother of Corruption," "It is a struggle between Islam and the infidels," and "We will close these spy nests." On November 21, 1979, Pakistani mobs attacked one of those so-called "spy nests," the American Embassy in Islamabad. An American marine and a U.S. army warrant officer, two Pakistani embassy clerks, and two rioters died in the seven-hour assault on the embassy and other buildings in the embassy compound.

While the embassy in Islamabad was being attacked there were also large anti-American demonstrations in the streets of Karachi, Lahore, and Rawalpindi. Only in Karachi did the local authorities act efficiently to save the American consulate and the USIS library from destruction. The American cultural centers in Lahore and Rawalpindi were burned and gutted.

The spark that set off the demonstrations were false radio reports reaching Pakistan to the effect that the Americans were responsible for seizing the Saudi Arabian "Sacred Mosque of Mecca" and taking a number of hostages. This was on the last day before the Islamic New Year. Why Americans would be involved in such an undertaking was not considered. In fact, a mysterious band of Muslim fanatics were responsible for this incident, and although government officials in Riyadh shortly thereafter claimed complete control of the mosque, a week later some invaders were still holding out. They were eventually killed or captured by the Saudi armed forces. This occurred, however, only after the violent anti-Western and anti-U.S. reaction of the Pakistani mobs had been spent.

By the early 1980s the Soviet Union had become the chief arms supplier of neighboring India. Communist sympathizers in India were enjoying a heyday. On more than one occasion communist-controlled media had been the source of disinformation about the United States government and its policies. Whether the particular Indian radio broadcast that triggered the mobs to take decisive actions against

American installations in Pakistan was made by Indian communist sympathizers or instigated by the KGB using assets in India is not generally known. However, the false accusations seem to have been carefully planned because attacks on U.S. property were coordinated in four Pakistani cities at the same time.

The mob attacking the embassy in Islamabad began by throwing bricks and setting cars on fire. Later shots were fired. The crowd was estimated to be about 10,000, many of them students who had been bussed in from a nearby university. The surge through the gates and over the walls of the embassy compound began about 1 p.m. An hour later the police arrived to find themselves far outnumbered.

According to the December 3, 1979, *Time Magazine* report, the Pakistani military arrived two hours later, and then merely stayed to one side. This was after President Carter, informed of the attack, telephoned Pakistani President Zia ul-Haq and told him that the safety of Americans was Zia's responsibility. Zia, in office by then for two and a half years after engineering a coup d'état that ousted the elected Bhutto government, was possibly unable initially, and later, unwilling to use force against the mob.

No major military force was stationed in Islamabad. Troops had to be brought in from neighboring Rawalpindi and nearby military posts. And, as many Pakistanis still questioned Zia's rule, he presumably did not want to cause more anti-government feeling by using troops against his own citizens. Some also felt he was piqued at the U.S. for various reasons and therefore did not act quickly and forcefully enough. (In studying reports of this incident before I went to Pakistan, and in talking with many knowledgeable individuals after arriving in Islamabad, I concluded that Zia purposely dragged his feet but did not expect the demonstration to become as serious and tragic as it did. Furthermore, at the time his armed forces were too distant from Islamabad to take immediate action. When we arrived in the new capital city, it was much more heavily patrolled than it had been during the storming of the embassy.) What probably Zia did not know was that as parts of the embassy burned, some ninety employees were trapped in the embassy vault. As the attackers smashed their way into the embassy, some yelled "Kill the American dogs!" When this happened the marine guards moved everyone up to the third floor and covered the retreat with tear gas. The thick walls and the steel security doors of the vault saved them. When the heat became too great, however, they had to flee through an escape hatch in the roof, not knowing if snipers were there to pick them off as they emerged. One marine had already been shot and killed.

Time Magazine's New Delhi Bureau Chief Marcia Gauger, who had been in the Embassy when it was attacked, was in the vault with the embassy employees. In the December 3rd, 1979, issue of *Time*, she wrote:

> At 5:30 came a frightening call from the back of the room: "Fire in the vault!" Amazingly, no one panicked. One official carried the fire extinguisher over to where the carpet had begun to burn. Two blasts put out the flames.
>
> The steel shell of the vault was now so hot from the fires raging below that the tiles laid over it were beginning to crack and buckle. We were all drenched in sweat. We were breathing through wet paper towels, very slowly and shallowly, trying to save oxygen. The smoke was getting heavy, making it hard to breathe. It was doubtful we could have lasted another 30 minutes in the vault. Dave Fields (the administrative counselor) asked: "Are there some senior Pakistanis who would like to establish contact with the dissidents on the roof?" There were a number of volunteers.
>
> "We will see if it's clear on the roof and we will go out very slowly, very orderly," said Fields. "I will say who goes."
>
> Finally it was the Marines who led the way up the stairs to the hatch. The first Marine opened the hatch and stuck his head out into the darkness. He had no way of knowing what might be waiting for him out there on the roof. It had gotten quiet; the shooting had stopped, the hammering and pounding had stopped. But it could well have been a trap. We didn't know. The only thing we had going for us was the darkness itself, and I guess the fires too. That must have been what drove the rioters away.
>
> When we finally reached safety, Ambassador Hummel praised us for 'having done more for ourselves than I could get the government of Pakistan to do.' He was absolutely right. I don't care what President Carter says. I don't care what Secretary Vance says. We came out all by ourselves. It was our Marine guards who saved us. Nobody else.

Ambassador Arthur Hummel was in his residence located a short distance from the chancery in a corner of the embassy compound. Miraculously, the mobs did not go to the residence, concentrating their efforts instead on the embassy building and the nearby housing and utility buildings.

While the embassy was under attack another group of rioters went to the American School, known as the International School of Islamabad. School was in session. Only through the heroic efforts of a retired Pakistani colonel, whose children were in the school and who stood up to the mob that was ready to storm and destroy that building also, was the crowd turned away. Through this heroic action, the school and its students and teachers escaped injury or worse, and the school building was saved.

All dependents and unessential American personnel were evacuated as soon as possible following the embassy's destruction, some 400 men, women and children in all.

Nearly two years after the destruction of the embassy compound the chancery, the embassy apartments, and other buildings were being rebuilt. In the meantime the Department of State had taken over a large, seven story building which formerly housed all of the AID activities, forcing AID to move many of its offices to other smaller buildings around town. The ambassador's office, the political, economic, and other sections of the embassy, and the consulate operated from those temporary quarters. The General Services Office, which had the formidable job of providing maintenance for all the non-AID offices of the U.S. government in the Pakistani capital and the housing of all U.S. government employees except those with AID, was relocated in a large house on the other side of the city.

USIS was assigned a large residential home that had been converted to office space while awaiting the completion of the new American Center in Islamabad. The new center, when completed, would contain the USIS offices as well as the USIS library and areas for cultural activities that were formerly conducted in the burned-out center in neighboring Rawalpindi. A large house next to the temporary USIS office was used as the temporary American Club, a great convenience to the USIS American staff since we were able to entertain some visitors there as well as enjoy lunch or coffee breaks a minute or two away from our desks. (The building housing the club on the embassy compound had been destroyed in the 1979 incident.) Because the club served alcoholic beverages, it was against embassy policy to invite Pakistanis to events held there since to do so could result in the embassy being accused of trying to mislead Muslims by offering them alcoholic beverages. This was one of the unique rules to which we had to adhere in this Islamic society or pay the consequences.

Many Muslims drank but the usual manner in which Muslim professional contacts were entertained at our homes was for bartenders to serve drinks from bar-like tables set in the corner of a room or on patios. Thus whenever Pakistanis were present at official parties or receptions in American homes, guests generally would have to approach the tables and ask for drinks themselves. In this way, the theory was, Muslims who are forbidden by their religion to drink alcoholic beverages, took the action to get an alcoholic drink themselves and we could not be accused of "forcing them" to drink. Because fundamentalist Islamic rules are so strict and so different from Western customs in many ways, and especially because the Zia ul-Haq regime was attempting to reinstitute all kinds of fundamentalist Islamic customs to garner support for itself from Islamic fundamentalist leaders, we westerners, as representatives of the U.S. government, were very sensitive to Islamic mores.

Because of the Soviet invasion of neighboring Afghanistan and the growing illicit narcotics trafficking conducted in Pakistan, the USAID program was the third largest in the world, following Israel and Egypt. The U.S. military assistance program was also large and included delivery of substantial numbers of F-16 fighter aircraft, by then considered the world's most efficient military aircraft. The Pakistan military forces had an excellent reputation with regard to their fighting ability. Their F-16 pilots, trained in Texas, were no exception. The F-16 became the best-known symbol of U.S. support for Pakistan. It was common knowledge that the Pakistan government sympathized with their fellow Muslims, the *Mujaheddin*, the Afghans who fought against the Soviet invaders and the Soviet-supported government in Kabul, Afghanistan's capital. It was also an open secret that the Mujaheddin was being provided with arms by the Americans and others, and that the flow of arms was being supervised by the Pakistan military.

Millions of Afghan refugees who had fled from their country now lived in Pakistan. While many lived in isolated refugee camps, others began competing for jobs which created tension among some Pakistanis. The influx of refugees also brought many bilateral and multilateral economic assistance programs into Pakistan, as well as a number of private, usually church-run organizations that provided assistance, especially food and medicines.

Peshawar, a frontier-like town at the foot of the Khyber Pass and located about thirty-five miles from the border with Afghanistan, became a haven for war refugees. The horrors of war were clearly evident in the hospitals and clinics of Peshawar, where Afghan men, women, and children were treated, many of whom were horribly scarred or missing limbs as a result of being caught in the fighting or from stepping on land mines. Many of the men vowed to return to the fighting for their homeland as soon as they could. Some arrived in Peshawar merely to rest and regain strength before returning to the battlefields.

It was within this environment that we arrived in September 1981. It was an environment where anti-Western attitudes were prevalent among some segments of the society; where strict fundamentalist Islamic laws were being reinstituted; where the Afghan-Soviet war cast a shadow over Pakistan, flooding the country with millions of Afghan refugees; and where international heroin trafficking was growing, as well as a heroin epidemic within Pakistan. In this complex situation, most official U.S. government business was being conducted in temporary, makeshift offices in Pakistan's new, unfinished capital city.

The entrance to the ground floor of the USIS building served as the reception area. The rear office was the information section while the sun porch in the front was used by the regional librarian who advised and assisted USIS library operations in Pakistan and about seven other Middle Eastern countries. Upstairs, the country public affairs officer, Jim Thurber, used the master bedroom as his office. As his deputy, my office was a former front bedroom. The executive officer worked from a side room and a converted hallway while the cultural affairs section utilized two former bedrooms in the back of the building.

When I first arrived USIS was getting its first Wang computers. For many visitors to USIS these were the first computers they had ever seen. I had a little experience with Wang computers used for word processing and record keeping both in Washington and at USIS Lima, a pilot post for the installation overseas of Wang computers. With this minimal experience I supervised the establishment of the system in USIS Islamabad.

The Wang organization's representative in Islamabad was a Pakistani engineer named Amanullah Khan who taught computer science at a local university. He had just started his own computer business and thus was delighted to work with us in installing our new system that he would then be able to demonstrate to potential customers. He was easy to work with and highly adept at solving all the installation problems we encountered in getting the system up and running.

The initial installation was a challenge since the electrical system of the house in which we operated was designed for a one-family home while the electrical needs of the USIS office, with our electric typewriters, copiers, etc., were much greater, especially after installing the Wang system. Fortunately, he was as anxious as we were to get our new Wang system operating. He wanted to be able to show a working system to local bankers and others, most of whom knew very little about the marvels of the computer age. The only other U.S. government office using the Wang system in Islamabad was the CIA, and their system was not, of course, visible to potential buyers. After our system was installed the major chore of training our staff to use it began. By the time I ended my tour in Pakistan we didn't know how we had survived so long without it. Months later the embassy installed its system. During this period AID in Islamabad worked primarily with Apple personal computers.

Two USIS Teletype machines were installed in a shack in the backyard of the house we called our office. This was where we received the news and information sent out daily by the agency from Washington in what we always referred to as "the wireless file" because originally this file arrived via radio Teletype. By 1981 it was sent via satellite to many posts.

Our daily "wireless file" was picked up by satellite in Karachi and then sent by landline or microwave to Islamabad where we received it via a local telephone line. This latter segment of its transmission often caused omissions in the transmission because of faulty connections, so we sometimes had to guess about missing letters or words. If we weren't sure we sometimes would not use a particular article in our press releases for fear of using a wrong word. If we considered the information important enough we could cable Washington for a direct telegraphic copy to assure accuracy. Eventually the file was tied into our Wang system and sent out of Washington by computer, resulting in considerable savings to the agency over the years. Furthermore, we could receive perfect copy. Any errors in the text were made in Washington and not by us in retyping. In this and other ways Pakistan was entering the twentieth century, but in many ways, such as Zia ul-Haq's efforts to force his citizens to return to fundamentalist Islamic customs, the country was mired in tradition and, if anything, was going backwards. At the time I wondered how this vast society, already beset with a multitude of problems, would fare in a world where so many other countries were entering the modern era of expanding technology and political freedom.

Pakistan's population in 1981 was estimated to be about eighty-one million. General Mohammed Zia ul-Haq was not only the president, but also held the title of "Chief Martial Law Administrator." Keeping martial law in effect since his takeover of the government made the country easier to rule. And to emphasize that Pakistanis were Muslims

(97 percent were estimated to be nominally practicing Muslims), the official name of the country is "Islamic Republic of Pakistan."

Although English is spoken by almost all well-educated Pakistanis, the national language of the country is Urdu. Yet Urdu, which is also the official language of three of the four provinces of Pakistan, is not spoken by everyone. The large province of Sind, where the country's largest city, Karachi, is located, considers Sindhi its official language. Nearly 60 percent of all Pakistanis speak Punjabi while Pushto, Baluchi, and other regional languages are predominant in certain areas.

The overall literacy rate for the country as a whole in the early 1980s was only about 25 percent, with females accounting for only 12 percent! The overall literacy rate was higher in urban areas, being 42 percent compared to 15 percent for rural areas. But despite these depressing figures, the Pakistani government attempted for a while in 1982 to ban the teaching of English in Pakistani schools. Urdu was to become the universal language of the country. This attempt, like many others by the government, to dictate cultural, religious, and social activities countrywide, eventually fell into disuse. To most westerners and many educated Pakistanis, it made little sense to downplay a global language like English that opened doors to modern trade, technology, and other cultures, and to try to instill Urdu as the leading language of a heterogeneous society where, for many Pakistanis, Urdu was as foreign as any foreign language.

Like all military dictatorships, the government controlled radio and television broadcasting. The government-owned Pakistan Broadcasting Corporation was the only organization authorized to operate radio stations in Pakistan. Small wonder that the short-wave broadcasts of the *BBC*, *VOA*, and other foreign broadcasters were highly popular among many Pakistanis.

The Pakistan Television Corporation, a semi-autonomous entity, was supervised by the Ministry of information and Broadcasting. Its programs, many in English, had to comply with both Pakistani political views and Islamic standards. As for the movie houses, all films shown in Pakistan had to be cleared by the Central Board of Film Censors. Kisses on the silver screen and, of course, anything beyond a kiss, were cut, making, at times, for some choppy movies by the time they reached local theaters. Most newspapers were privately owned but heavily censored. Most were published in Urdu and a few in English.

The Pakistan I knew was about the size of California. It became a separate Muslim nation on August 14, 1947, when the Indian subcontinent was partitioned by the British, who granted independence to the two countries following World War II. Some six million Muslims fled to Pakistan and about as many Hindus and Sikhs fled from what is now Pakistan to India, one of the largest population transfers in history and marked by horrendous communal rioting and bloodshed.

Aside from a habitual historic antagonism between the Muslims and the Hindus, a new major irritant was created between these two major religious groups at the time of the independence of the two countries. The Indian sate of Kashmir was left undecided as to which country it would become a part of. Although ruled by a Hindu maharaja, Kashmir had an overwhelmingly Muslim population.

The maharajah hesitated in deciding whether Kashmir should belong to India or Pakistan. Shortly after the partition, some of his Muslim subjects, aided by tribesmen from Pakistan, revolted in favor of joining Pakistan. In return for military aid the maharaja offered his state to India. Indian troops took the eastern section, including its capital Srinigar. The western half came under the control of Pakistan.

Despite involvement of the United Nations in attempts to end skirmishes of the disputed area between Indian and Pakistani troops, war broke out between the two countries in September 1965. The UN was able to bring about a cease-fire three weeks later, but the Kashmir problem remains unresolved at this writing.

Until 1971, what is today known as Pakistan was called West Pakistan, which was united with East Pakistan, now known as Bangladesh. With India separating the two Pakistans geographically, differences between the Muslims in the East and those in the West came to a head with the outbreak of war between Pakistan and India in that year. East Pakistan became Bangladesh.

In addition to the loss of the eastern areas, Pakistan suffered a devastating military defeat to India, which took some 91,000 Pakistani prisoners of war. Not until 1974 were somewhat normal relations restored, but the Kashmir problem remained. The fact that the Indians, who maintained a strong military relationship with the Soviet Union, saw the Soviet invasion of Afghanistan (where a pro-Soviet regime had been established) in a different light from the Pakistanis, added to the difficulty of rapprochement between India and Pakistan.

For Pakistanis, Afghanistan was viewed as a fellow Muslim nation. The Soviet presence there threatened the tranquility of Pakistan. In fact, Soviet planes occasionally bombed frontier towns of Pakistan as the Soviets fought with the Mujaheddin who were battling the invaders and the Soviet-supported Afghan government. The world knew that the Pakistan government provided support to the Mujaheddin and that the latter used Pakistan as a "safe area." Because of this and other factors, India and Pakistan, while sharing a long, common border, continued to remain at odds.

Jim Thurber was the country public affairs officer in Islamabad when I arrived to serve as his deputy. The position of deputy had been vacant for well over a year, ever since it was first offered to me in 1980 while getting ready to leave Peru. By September 1981, Thurber's replacement had been named and he was getting ready to leave. He had been among the ninety people trapped in the vault in 1979 when the embassy was attacked and burned, and since his family had left Pakistan at that time, he was more than ready to leave.

Thurber's replacement was Marilyn Johnson. Her last assignment was ambassador to Togo, a small West African country squeezed between Ghana, the Upper Volta, and Dahomey. Because she was the only female U.S. ambassador in Africa at the time, some Foreign Service types referred to her, when she was assigned there, as the State Department's women's representative in Africa, reflecting, perhaps, how women were discriminated against in the U.S. Foreign Service. This situation would change considerably in later years, although some would still argue, not enough.

Few USIA officers ever became ambassadors. Those few that did were exceptional, and they generally rose to that level after being a PAO in a large country. Even more rare was someone who becomes an ambassador then reverts to being a PAO, as did Marilyn Johnson. Aside from being exceptional in this way, this former naval officer was exceptional in that she traveled with an invalid sister, Persis Johnson, who, in her own right, was as remarkable and courageous as Marilyn.

Persis Johnson was bedridden and traveled and entertained using a wheel chair. The two sisters worked as a team in hosting dinners and lunches for professional contacts at their home. Although this is always a part of a USIS officer's responsibility in maintaining friendships with the host country's movers and shakers, Persis undoubtedly contributed to the success of these social/business affairs. This greatly enhanced Marilyn Johnson's professional capabilities in her position as counselor of embassy for public affairs in Islamabad, a job in which she had to entertain frequently as Director of one of the largest USIS posts in the world. (In terms of number of employees and number of branch posts, USIS Islamabad was the sixth largest post in the world.)

With Jim Thurber ready to leave Pakistan in October, word came from Washington that Marilyn Johnson, scheduled to arrive shortly thereafter, would like to delay her arrival until January because of a complicated family situation. The question was whether I would be willing and able to hold the fort from the time of Thurber's departure until her arrival in January. I welcomed the opportunity to be the acting PAO. Thurber departed on schedule and in early 1982, Johnson arrived as planned.

Five USIS posts were larger than Pakistan in terms of the number of personnel and branch posts—Brazil, West Germany, Japan, India, and Italy. USIS Mexico was about the equivalent size. There had been, until recently, sixteen American and 131 Pakistani USIS positions in Pakistan. A budget cut had reduced the number of Pakistani employees to 104. That initially seemed to me to be a high number, but as one might expect in any large organization, while some Pakistanis were outstanding in their knowledge, experience, and efficiency, some were average. The efficiency of the average employee was, in a few cases, less than average.

Three additional USIA employees were stationed in Pakistan who did not report directly to USIS Islamabad—a regional secretary, a regional library consultant, and a VOA radio-monitoring officer. A regional management consultant had also been stationed in Karachi but had left prior to my arrival and was not replaced. Later a VOA correspondent would be assigned to Pakistan, and, on two occasions, the post would welcome a junior officer trainee. A major reason for stationing regional employees in Pakistan, all of whom traveled through the Middle East to assist smaller posts during periodic visits, was because the U.S. government had millions of dollars worth of surplus Pakistani rupees. These funds, accumulated over the years from U.S. economic and military assistance programs, could only be spent in Pakistan.

Operating out of temporary quarters in Islamabad, the PAO supervised branch posts in Karachi and Lahore and a small operation in Peshawar, all with branch PAOs. Paul Rappaport was the branch PAO in Karachi where the USIS library and USIS offices were in the same building as the American consulate. Three American officers were on his staff, including my old colleague, Frank Florey. At the branch post in Lahore, where construction was being completed on the completely renovated American Center that had been heavily damaged in the November 1979 riots, the BPAO was Sherman Ross. He had two American assistants and about the same number of Pakistani employees as USIS Karachi. The third post, Peshawar, was small but important. The BPAO was Douglas Davidson. He had four Pakistani employees on his staff. In addition, USIS officers cooperated with and provided backup support to the Pakistan American Cultural Center in Karachi and English teaching centers in Hyderabad, Peshawar, and Quetta.

Most of the information and cultural/educational programs found at any USIS post were among the various activities conducted by USIS Islamabad. The American Centers in Karachi and Lahore with their libraries, film, and eventually, video programs, were major operations, well attended and respected by many Pakistanis even though they had been attacked by dissident elements a few years earlier. Work was progressing on the new American Center in Islamabad but many problems had to be solved before that center became functional.

The information officer in Islamabad was Don Jones, aka Don Juan because of his uncanny ability, and consequent reputation, for attracting women. His chief Pakistani employee was Hamid Alvi, an experienced, middle-aged journalist and writer who contributed greatly to the success of the information program. Jones gave him free reign and he never misused it. Like so many of his counterparts at other USIS posts, Alvi was an invaluable employee because of his knowledge of his own society, his professional contacts, and his journalistic skills.

One evening at the American Club, Jones (who had become rather vocal after a few drinks) told some out-of-town American visitors that the forthcoming visit to Pakistan of the U.S. attorney general was a typical political boondoggle at taxpayers' expense and ought not to occur. It happened that the visitors were members of the attorney general's advance party. They took issue with Jones and news of the incident reached the ambassador, PAO Johnson, and me as Jones' immediate superior and the one required to write his OER (Officer's Efficiency Report). Under pressure to take the incident into consideration in his OER, I did, much to his chagrin. After reading my draft and discussing it with me, he convinced me that I was overly harsh in my comments and I, in effect, "raised his grades." After completing his tour in Pakistan he went on to become the director of USIA's Press Center in Los Angeles, a marvelous job where he was his own boss and part of his duties involved him in the glamour of Hollywood.

The cultural affairs officer was Robert Jones (no relation). A former professor of political science, he was fairly new to USIA as it was his second career, but he was not new to Pakistan. He had served in Lahore some years earlier where he and his family had greatly enjoyed the experience, so he and his wife, Rosemary, being familiar with Pakistanis and their ways, were very much at home in Islamabad.

His forte was an ability to quickly gain rapport with people. He, his wife, and Charmaine and I became close friends and enjoyed many travels and many laughs together. Like us, they had five children, but their children were all grown and no longer lived with them.

The American Center director was Dean Brown. Frustrated for many months because the center he was to direct was still being built, most of his time was spent in planning and preparing for the big move into the new center. Although he developed some highly successful alternative cultural programs in the interim, when delay followed delay in completion of the new center, and his frustration with the slow pace of construction became almost unbearable, he suggested that Don Jones' old residence be converted to a temporary library and cultural center so more cultural programming could take place until the new Center became available. (Jones had been transferred and his replacement located elsewhere.) Marilyn Johnson welcomed the idea and the temporary center soon opened. The temporary cultural center enjoyed notable success especially since, aside from the French Institute, there was little in the way of cultural activities to be found in Islamabad, a city still under construction in many aspects and which was Islamic to the core.

Dean Brown's wife, Mary, was the embassy nurse. As such she knew everyone's secrets I suppose. Her husband seemed always to be so serious and absorbed in his work, but she was jolly and was almost always smiling. One of the most remarkable things about this couple was that they traveled frequently by air and had perfected a system whereby whatever they needed for a week or more of vacation was carried in two small carry-on bags. In this way they were able to go around the world with no additional baggage to bog them down. They said it enabled them to always leave the airport right after landing. How they were able to do that remains their secret. I wish I knew. This could never happen in my family.

Because USIA saw an opportunity to capitalize on the traditional interest of many people of the Indian sub-continent in expanding their knowledge of English, an English-teaching officer was assigned to USIS Islamabad. David Queen, who replaced Dean Finney shortly after our arrival in Islamabad, filled that position and assisted local institutions and the binational centers in different ways. Ironically he arrived at the post at a time when President Zia ul-Haq was demanding that English teaching be abolished in Pakistan's schools. The president wanted Urdu installed in all schools as the official language of the country. This policy, like a number of others pushed by the regime but not strongly enforced, as noted earlier, fell into disuse, but not before adversely affecting many programs. Queen's wife was Vietnamese, another example of the international character of the U.S. Foreign Service.

Annica Reddish was the executive officer. She was a petite Swedish woman who had become an American citizen and was now widowed. In my opinion the PAO was overly demanding of her. The post was still recovering from the tragic events of 1979, and was also engaged in major building projects in Islamabad and Lahore. Her duties involved providing general administrative services and supervising financial, budgetary, and personnel records for USIS Islamabad and backup support for USIS Peshawar. Despite these heavy responsibilities, she was assigned to that job when still a relatively junior officer (Class 5), although she was later promoted to Class 4. After completing her tour her replacement was Bruce Kreutzer, a counselor in the senior Foreign Service (like myself at the time)—five grades above Reddish's personal grade when she was initially assigned to that position! This indicated to me, at least, that her personal classification was far below what it should have been considering the duties she was given.

The USIS secretary, Lucy Gibb, was a talented, middle-aged woman who, like Robert and Rosemary Jones, was very much at home in Pakistan having lived there for many years. Like Jim Thurber, she also was a veteran from the vault and felt that that incident was an anomaly, so she continued to feel comfortable living in Islamabad. Her job gave her the freedom she needed to pursue her love of painting, with which she was quite accomplished. The Pakistanis and others bought so much of her artwork that she could hardly keep up with the demand. When her tour as the USIS American secretary in Islamabad ended, she switched jobs with the regional secretary in Karachi but managed to keep her home base in Islamabad. She was replaced by Liz Cemal, the former regional secretary who had been living in Karachi. Her husband was from Turkey where they had met and married. He soon obtained a job at the embassy motor pool, probably through the good offices of Marilyn Johnson, who wanted her secretary's husband busy and happy for the morale of all concerned. Like most USIS American secretaries, Liz Cemal played a vital role in whatever success USIS Islamabad enjoyed.

Dean Philpott, a USIA architect, was assigned to Islamabad where he was charged with supervising the construction of the new American Center. He was his own boss in many ways, having no obligation to keep USIS Islamabad informed of his activities since he reported directly to agency headquarters more than ten thousand miles away in Washington. He had already been in Islamabad for many months when I arrived. It soon became apparent to me that he had strong differences of opinion with PAO Jim Thurber regarding the Center's design, its construction, and his dealings with local contractors. I myself thought it rather strange to have the architect who designed the building in residence, for surely he would want to change his mind on a number of things as the building took shape, and I believe that is what happened.

There were other problems in the Center's construction, many of which I later became intimately involved with. When Philpott finally left, I became the person most directly responsible for supervising construction, given my vast experience in this field! I pleaded with Washington headquarters innumerable times to send an engineer to Islamabad, if only for a visit, to advise us and consult with the various parties involved in the construction, but to no avail. This situation was partially caused by the ambivalence held by some Washington officials as to whether or not the center should really be completed given Pakistan's track record with regard to U.S.-Pakistan relations.

One other USIA employee, Tobie Huston, called Islamabad his home at the time we arrived. He was a quiet man who liked social events like I like to go shopping, which means avoiding them like the plague. He was a Voice of America monitor. The Russian service of the *VOA*, which was beamed to the southern Soviet provinces, could be heard in Pakistan, as could the Pushto, Urdu, and English services which had expanded because of the Soviet invasion of Afghanistan. Huston's job, which he carried out with the help of one Pakistani employee, was to report on the technical quality of VOA's reception in order to fine-tune broadcast antennas. His wife was Czechoslovakian. Our not-so-little USIA community in Islamabad in those days was clearly international, considering the different nationalities of the various families. But what might one expect when young bachelors are sent abroad at a marriageable age? Perhaps Foreign Service families are an expression of the American melting pot. Huston eventually was transferred during my tour and was replaced by John Winfree, a down-to-earth man who sometimes came on rather strongly. He and his wife (who was German) and daughter had lived most recently in Hong Kong for five years. They did not relish having been sent to the "boonies," which was how they felt about Islamabad.

Among the outstanding veteran Pakistani employees in Islamabad were Hamid Alvi of the press section; Syed Mujtaba Ahmed, senior cultural affairs specialist; Hasan, chief of the radio and television section; and Neelofar Mahmood, the only woman of the 104 Pakistani employees of USIS in this Islamic country!

Pakistanis may not have had much freedom under the various military dictatorships that often ruled them, but they were free to do whatever they wished with their own names. Whether one wanted to use a first name as his or her common identity, or a last name, or both names, or several names, was up to the individual. Thus Syed Mujtaba Ahmed was addressed by everyone as "Mujtaba" as this was, presumably, his preference while Hasan gave no one a choice—it was the only name he generally used, although he might, if pushed, write "H.H. Hasan."

Mujtaba was one of the few remaining USIS employees who had joined USIS nearly three decades earlier, when information/cultural activities were still a part of the Department of State and when Karachi was the capital of Pakistan. When he retired in March 1985, he reminisced in a letter to his colleagues:

> I can recollect the birth of USIS in May 1948, its functioning in a roadside shop turned into office, with just three of us, David Newsom, Mauji and myself. A couple of junky typewriters, motion picture projectors, record players, transformers, etc. were all that we had. They bore the insights of the Office of War information, New Delhi, signifying the war-torn world we had left behind in an effort to establish justice and peace for mankind." (PAO David Newsom later became Undersecretary of State and retired in 1983).

Mujtaba's letter reminded his colleagues that Pakistan had become an integral component of Secretary of State Dulles' policy of containment of the USSR and that, in 1959, the Pakistan-American Cultural Center was founded in Karachi. He also noted that the burning of the U.S. Embassy in 1979 (when he also was in the group of ninety trapped in the vault of the burning building) was not the first anti-U.S. violence in Pakistan.

"As a result of massive US arms aid to India in 1962 and the postponement of aid to a Pakistan Consortium meeting in Paris in the fall of 1964," he wrote, "a wave of agitations and demonstrations against the United States started throughout the country. The Karachi American Center library and the offices of the U.S. Educational Foundation were burnt to ashes. It was the worst period of the Pakistan-American relationship and correspondingly very hard for Pakistani nationals working for the U.S. Mission."

He recalled how he was among the first group of Pakistani employees asked to move to Rawalpindi following the establishment of the new national capital of Islamabad. Shortly thereafter a budget cut occurred and five branch USIS centers, three in East Pakistan plus Quetta and Murree, were closed, as were numerous programs.

He lamented the eight years it took to build the new American Center in Islamabad "nearly one-third of the time the Taj Majal was completed in the second quarter of the seventeenth century." And he ended his farewell letter to friends and colleagues by thanking them for sharing with him "the fun, the hustle bustle, the sound, the fury, excitement, and occasionally frustrations" of working for USIS.

Hasan, who ran the radio and television section of USIS Islamabad, was a workaholic, extremely dedicated to his work and his family. It was always a pleasure working with him, as he was a person full of good programming ideas and ready and willing to put them into practice. He was selected for a job with the *Voice of America* in Washington that he accepted but with mixed feelings, as he was concerned about bringing his family to Washington, D.C. and exposing his young daughters to western ways. We knew we would miss him at USIS but encouraged him to undertake the new assignment. His contract was for three years and he could have stayed on indefinitely but he soon realized that his young daughters, who were in their early teens, would soon become so Americanized in the U.S. that they would never again be happy living in Pakistan's Islamic society with all its restrictions and taboos. To avoid this, after his initial contract ended, he decided to return to Islamabad. *VOA's* loss was USIS's gain, as he returned to his old job with the same vigor and dynamism as before.

Neelofar Mahmood, the only woman on the USIS local staff, was young, attractive, and intelligent. She worked as a librarian with other staff members who were preparing books and equipment for the day when the American Center in Islamabad would finally open. However, with the installation of the Wang computers in USIS, she seemed to be the best person available to supervise that new activity. With training provided to her both in Islamabad and at USIA headquarters in Washington, she soon became knowledgeable and efficient in the Wang way of doing things.

There was one other Pakistani employee whose presence in USIS was always evident, not just because he was a large man who was always ready and willing to assist in whatever was needed, but because he had a way about him of making his presence felt. His full name was Masoodur Rahman Khan, but he went by the name of Masood. Having been with USIS more than fifteen years when I first arrived in Pakistan, he had held various jobs over the years. But in the aftermath of the 1979 incident, the reorganization of USIS and the loss of many programs left him, while still as dedicated as ever, lacking a specialty in any of the programs that remained. He was assigned to supervise the distribution unit that included the motor pool of USIS, which he did almost too well. As a strict disciplinarian, he tended to make big issues of what his superiors felt were of little importance. This soon brought him into conflict with the more libertine drivers of the car pool and sometimes others. Yet he was one of the few Pakistanis who invited the American staff to his home in Rawalpindi. On those occasions he and his wife would provide an extensive spread of various foods, and, invariably, I would sometimes be sick the next day. But he meant well, was helpful on many occasions, always ready and willing to assist when assistance was needed. On a few occasions when someone was stranded because of a vehicle breakdown in the hinterlands, he would make sure that someone, either he himself or someone he could trust, would come to the rescue.

Most of the Pakistani nationals employed by USIS were generally no different from many USIS foreign nationals the world over—loyal friends of the Americans with whom they worked, dedicated to USIS objectives, and willing even, if need be, to put their lives on the line when the going got rough.

It is impossible to understand the people of Pakistan without some inkling of the importance of Islam to Pakistanis. Islam is not only a religion, but a way of life. The study of Islam fills libraries and consumes lifetimes, so the brief comments that follow are but a cursory view of a complicated subject.

Doctrinaire Muslim beliefs concentrate on the Middle Eastern tradition of Islam, which began with the ministry of its prophet Mohammad who lived in the early seventh century at Makkah (now Mecca) and later at Madinah in Arabia. Prior to his ministry a religion was practiced there which was centered in the *Ka'abah,* a large stone and mortar structure where a special ceremony was held annually and where a number of good and evil spirits were worshiped. Islam incorporated the Ka'abah into its ceremonies by making it the site of a required pilgrimage and incorporated the concept of spirits (*jinn*). It did not, however, define their relationship to human affairs.

Muslims believe that the teachings of Mohammed came to him by a revelation from Allah, the Arabic name for God, over a twenty-year period. These revelations have been preserved in written form in the *Qur'an* (Koran). A second scripture consists of the sayings and actions of Muhammad as recorded by others which Muslim scholars have analyzed and categorized, giving greater credence to some of these writings than to others, although all have been used to formulate human affairs.

Muslims consider Mohammad as the last of a long line of prophets who brought scripture to mankind. He taught that the Christians and the Jews were to be accorded respect and tolerance since they were earlier recipients of the same divine message. Adam, Abraham, Moses, David, and Jesus were cited by Mohammad as major prophets while maintaining that the *Taurah* (Torah), *Zebur* (Psalms), and *Indji* (New Testament) were all earlier versions of the Qur'an and which had been corrupted by their followers.

Although refined by later Muslim scholars, Muhammad emphasized the six articles of faith: belief in only one God, belief in the holy books, belief in angels, belief in prophets, belief in the day of judgment, and belief in predeterminism. Also evolved from Mohammad's teaching are the five pillars of Islam: "There is no God but God and Mohammad is his Messenger;" performance of prayers five times daily (*salat*); fasting during the month of Ramadan; giving the poor tax (*zakat*); and undertaking a pilgrimage to Mecca once during a lifetime (*haji*). Important obligations of Muslims include dietary laws, particularly abstinence from pork and alcohol, and standards of dress to cover the body.

The importance of community (*ummah*) was also emphasized in Muhammad's teachings as Muslims were considered as being a super-tribe that was more important than the nation-state. The community has obligations, notably the communal prayer held on midday Fridays, as well as the *jihad* (holy war) and a general admonition to promote good and banish evil. The communal prayer always provides an audience for a sermon (*khutbah*) given by a prominent Muslim. In modern times this has provided a political platform on many occasions. Only after the death of Mohammad did many of these customs become doctrinaire.

In response to challenges by conquering groups and because of a dispute over leadership in the Muslim community, Islam underwent a three-way split. The *Sunni* (path or way) came to accept scripture as the cornerstone of the culture, believing that rational thought could develop religion and its role in society. The Sunni eventually dominated the Muslim world and today is predominant in South and Southeast Asia.

The *Shiah* (party or sect) sometimes called the *shiite* movement, regard the scripture as a mystical document and believe that man's mind is a tool to be used to discover the true nature of things as distinct from their apparent nature. These are subgroups but most Shiah's are located in Iran, southern Arabia and North Africa. The third group, the *khariji* ("those who go out") resisted the influence of other cultures and interpreted the early teachings of Muhammad literally. Although no longer found in South or Southeast Asia, they influenced both of the major sects particularly in their militant views.

The Shiah and the Sunni are the two major branches of Muslims, comprising about 85 percent of the total. Although Pakistanis are predominantly Sunni's (Shiite's make up only about 10 percent of the population) individual Shiah's have played important roles in Pakistan's history. For example, Mohammad Ali Jinnah, the leader of Pakistan's independence movement and the nation's first Governor-General, was a Shiite Muslim.

The Sunni interpret Muslim law as based on the teachings and practices of Mohammed and observed by orthodox Muslims. Sunnites approve the historical order of the first four caliphs as the rightful line of succession to Mohammad and accept the *Sunna* as the authoritative supplement to the Koran. The Shiite's consider Ali, Mohammad's son-in-law and the fourth of the caliphs, as the first imam and the rightful successor of Mohammad. Shiite's do not accept the Sunna as authoritative.

Among doctrinaire Muslims, the concept of a functioning Muslim law is the *shariah*. Muslims frequently refer to shariah either as an aspiration or as a reference to Muslim obligations in general. It is in the matter of interpretation of Muslim law that problems arise between traditionalists and modernists. The militant form of doctrinaire Islam stresses the importance of imposing the shariah on society and to do this some traditionalists advocate, if necessary, varying degrees of Jihad. While militant Islam does not always insist on an open break with established governments, one can easily see the problems that can arise, and, in fact, have arisen, in Pakistan and elsewhere.

Pakistan also has a relatively small group of doctrinaire Muslims who consider themselves mystics (*sufis*). Strongest during the tenth to fifteenth centuries, the modernists and many traditionalists today are anti-sufi and downgrade their importance because of their own faith in Muslim law. Islamic scholars also identify "indigenous Islam," influenced by local cultures, and "secular Islam," strongly influenced by western cultures, as having their own idiosyncrasies. Thus like communism or Catholicism, Islam is not universally practiced the same way in all places, not even within the Islamic Republic of Pakistan.

Muslims in Pakistan, as elsewhere, traditionally pray five times a day: at sunset, night, dawn, noon and afternoon. The prayer times are sounded in mosques all over the country, many using loudspeakers to call the faithful to prayer. When we first arrived in Islamabad the loudspeakers from nearby mosques would awaken us at early morning hours, but after a while we became accustomed to them as people do who live near railroads and seldom hear the trains passing in the night.

There is a strict ritual before each prayer. If it is Friday, you roll up your prayer rug and take it to the nearest mosque. On other days you pray wherever you are, using your rug to kneel on as you face Mecca.

In traditional practices your body must be purified by washing the hands from the wrist down, gargling and spitting to cleanse the mouth, washing the face and the lower arms up to the elbows, moistening part of the head, combing the hair with water, and finally washing both feet up to the ankles. All this is repeated three times in strict order and always starting with the right side.

If a man touches a dog or a woman, goes to the bathroom, or passes wind, he must repeat the ritual cleansing. Before entering a mosque shoes must be removed, and once inside, all must be careful not to touch any person or object. Fellow worshipers are greeted as one often greets friends and acquaintances when meeting anywhere, by saying *As Salaam alaikum* (Peace be with you), and one responds with *Alaikum salaam* (And peace be with you).

Most Westerners brought up in traditions where the individual is largely responsible for determining his or her own actions find Pakistani society, which is so accustomed to authoritarianism in its political, social, and religious life, rather dull and certainly unique. They especially find the treatment of women and animals in this culture a far cry from their own experience. But as Professor William Griffith of M.I.T. once said when talking about the Islamic resurgence in Iran in the 1960s, "Fundamentalist Islam was the nemesis of the Shah of Iran—we must not forget that it is primarily a reaction against the western style of modernization." That same reaction against western ways was evident in Pakistan and occasionally, as it did in 1979, explodes into violent action against a major symbol of western culture, the U.S. embassy.

When General Zia ul-Haq came to power he welcomed the support of the *maulanas*, the local Islamic leaders, most of whom favored the strict puritanical Islam of Saudi Arabia. Fundamentalist Muslim laws, some of which had fallen into disuse, were now enforced. Those who suffered the most by this return to fundamentalism were women. For example, the evidence presented by a woman in court, according to the new government, should, as in the Middle Ages, have only half the legal weight of a man's testimony. In cases of rape there had to be four male eyewitnesses to "penetration" for the woman's word to be taken seriously. And at one stage the president ordered that Pakistani women should be withdrawn from international athletic competition because men might see their legs.

On one occasion, the day before the International School of Islamabad i.e. the American School, was to have its senior prom at the Holiday Inn in Islamabad, dancing in public was decreed by the Zia regime to be unlawful. (The surprised school authorities and the students were able, through much effort and perspiration, to prepare the school's gymnasium for the event.) Such rules were minor irritants compared to what the country was losing by having 50 percent of its population sidetracked and unable to contribute to many of the problems Pakistan faced then, and still does.

In July of 1984 the Pakistani press, both the English and Urdu dailies, discussed the growing trend of harassment of women by men in public places. Such men were referred to as "Eve teasers." As an example of the heights reached regarding the role of women in Pakistan, the following letter to the editor, under the title "Corporal punishment for eve-teasers" (sic), was published in the July 27, 1984 edition of a Pakistani newspaper published in English in Peshawar, the *Khyber Mail*:

Sir. Through your newspaper I venture to put forth my viewpoint in connection with recent amendment in the Penal Codes of the country ... (The amendment in question) pertains to the Molestation of Womenfolk in public. The punishment prescribed now is indeed compatible with the gravity of the crime. But I personally view this action as an incomplete one unless further measures are adopted by not only discouraging the criminals by a deterrent punishment but also eradicating some social evils which are presently in vogue in the society. I therefore, in a very humble way recommend to the Islamic government to further strengthen good intentions by the following acts:

(a) To remove all lady TV announcers and news casters from their jobs and instead decent gentlemen be appointed for the purpose.

(b) All TV and radio dramas in which lady actresses are required should be banned and this job should also be assigned to men who can be dressed like women for the purpose. It may be mentioned that all plays/dramas staged in the ancient Shakespearean Theaters were done through the male participants.

(c) All types *of* Meena Bazaars and ladies shows which in fact are more of a fashion display and beauty competitions rather than genuine charitable and social welfare activities should be banned.

(d) Ladies fully loaded with make-up and transparent clothes and a blaze of scents and perfumes following them should be prevented/stopped from coming into the markets. In case of real needs, the women folk can come out properly dressed and clad in 'burqas' in the company of their 'Mehrams" as is laid down principle of Islam.

(e) It may further be mentioned that presently in the films and TV studio, make-up to the ladies is done by a male specialist particularly appointed for the purpose. This is an anti-Islamic practice.

(f) Imparting of military training and reviewing of parades by males in girls schools and colleges should totally be discontinued forthwith.

(g) Hand shake of ladies with gents is an unIslamic act.

(h) No TV and Press coverage (taking photographs and pictures) of the functions exclusive of the women in chardiwari should be allowed.

(i) It has also been witnessed that on the occasion of the visits of the foreign dignitaries young girls from schools and colleges are made to stand in line and under directions of the high ups showering flower petals on foreigners. This is not at all in conformity with the Islamic character of the state.

(j) Luncheons and dinners in connection with the visits of the foreign dignitaries in which young ladies of higher social status are made to sit in the middle of the gentlemen by intervals. This is a highly objectionable act from the view point of Islamic tenets and injunctions. If ladies accompanying the foreign dignitaries are to be entertained, then separate arrangements in separate enclosures should be made.

(k) Pakistani leaders while on their visits abroad should be discouraged and refrained from taking their wives or any fair sex on their tour abroad.

There is no gainsaying the fact that the above mentioned evil practices provide great temptations for sex-crime and it would be quite unfair and looking to only one side of the picture if we remain satisfied with the promulgation of corporal punishments without undertaking measures to reform society.

Yours etc.;

B.M. Kahn
Civil Secretariat
Peshawar

The above article is obviously *not* a reflection of the beliefs of many Pakistanis, but an example of how extreme views can develop in a restrictive society. One is reminded of how strict a drill sergeant can be compared with a General in a highly disciplined military unit.

In many of the rural areas of Pakistan women remain separated and secluded in what is known as *purdah*. This is not an Islamic dictum but a custom observed for centuries that has the force of Islamic law among many Muslim fundamentalists. In traditional families the women must wear a veil in public. The most conservative families require the women to wear *burqas,* a tent-like apparel which covers the whole body from head to foot and which contains small slits in the face covering to enable them to see. What they see is certainly a man's world. In such families women and girls after the age of puberty stay in the home most of the time and are generally seen only by immediate family members.

In 1989 the World Bank published a study, undertaken in cooperation with the Pakistan government, entitled "Women in Pakistan, An Economic and Social Strategy." It concluded, "a major obstacle to Pakistan's transformation into a dynamic, middle-income economy is underinvestment in its people, particularly women. Development is held back—and the gains of growth are not widely shared—if half the population cannot participate effectively either as contributors or as beneficiaries." The report said that the role of women in Pakistan is complex; that in many social contexts they are accorded esteem and importance, but that on most counts their status is among the lowest in the world, including the rest of South Asia. The study suggested ways to increase the participation of women as providers and beneficiaries in education, family planning, and health services. It recommended several approaches to improve women's access to extension, credit, new technology, inputs, markets and formal sector employment which would raise their productivity and hence their contribution to economic development and family welfare.

Given the dictums of Islamic rules and regulations as practiced in Pakistan, can the changes recommended in the World Bank study ever take place? In Western Europe, medievalism was toppled during the two or three centuries of the Renaissance and the Reformation. As Freeland Abbott points out in his 1968 book *Islam and Pakistan,* the new social emphases that emerged by the end of the eighteenth century in Europe "made their way during the nineteenth and twentieth centuries to every corner of the world." Historians called that process "the Europeanization of the world."

In the twentieth century many people called the modernization process "the Americanization of the world." Abbott suggests that not until people began to talk and read and ponder did the Reformation in Europe catch fire. Nearly forty years ago when writing *Islam and Pakistan* the author remained somewhat pessimistic about whether or not change of this nature could or would take place in Pakistan. Although some change was taking place (men change even if systems remain static), as long as literacy rates remain as low as they are it is difficult to be optimistic about Pakistan's future. As late as 1985, the World Bank report noted, Pakistan's female primary school enrollment ratio was 32 percent, among the ten lowest in the world. Women had lower survival rates than men, the female to male ratio being 0.91, the lowest in the world (apart from Bhutan and Yemen and eight African countries), and in 1986, women's life expectancy at birth in Pakistan was fifty-one years, one year less than that of men. In developed countries, the World Bank report stated, the norm is for women to outlive men by about five years.

The first four months following our arrival in Islamabad in September 1981 were extremely busy ones for me as there was much to learn. In October CPAO Jim Thurber left and I was in charge until his replacement, CPAO Marilyn Johnson, arrived in early January 1982. Also during this relatively brief period, U.S. Architect Dean Philpott, who had been in charge of the construction of the new American Center during the past three years, left Islamabad having been reassigned to Washington. He was never replaced. As the senior ranking USIA officer in the country at the time, I was responsible for maintaining some semblance of supervision of that major agency building project until Johnson's arrival. After her arrival I was assigned direct supervisory responsibility for its progress for several years.

Overall program objectives of USIS Pakistan at the time consisted of six categories:

1. *U.S. Foreign Policy.* Despite increased U.S. military and economic assistance to Pakistan, Pakistan's political leaders continued to question the reliability of U.S. support. They had some reason to do so since they could not forget that in 1965, during the Indo-Pakistan war, the U.S. suspended military assistance to both sides as a means to end the fighting. Pakistan's leaders claimed this hurt them more than it did India, which had alternate sources of weapons. This perceived lack

of reliability, condemnation of U.S. foreign policy in the Middle East, and questions regarding U.S. attitudes toward India as well as the Afghanistan issue, made it necessary for USIS to constantly explain U.S. policy and actions.

2. *U.S. Economic Policies.* Conventional Third World views on North/South issues were common in Pakistan, as was the belief of a lack of dedication toward making substantial contributions to the economic development of Pakistan and other developing nations— despite the U.S. economic assistance program in Pakistan being one of the largest in the world. To offset these beliefs, USIS explained U.S. economic policies and programs and publicized major new U.S. assistance programs to Pakistan.

3. *U.S. Values.* U.S. values, society and institutions were often questioned by Pakistanis, most of whom rejected Western styles of modernization and democracy. USIS attempted to provide greater knowledge about the U.S., the democratic goals of our multifaceted society, and our human rights policies, in order to demonstrate common goals and aspirations.

4. *Narcotics.* A large percentage of all heroin imported into the U.S. in the early 1980s came from opium produced in "The Golden Crescent" of South Asia—Iran, Afghanistan and Pakistan, with Pakistan playing a leading role in its trafficking. Despite greater recognition of this problem by some Pakistanis, key officials still saw the drug problem as primarily one for the U.S. and Western nations to resolve. The vested interests of poppy growers, users, traffickers, and others who profited from illicit drug trafficking required sustained public information efforts to gain support for cooperative U.S. government and Pakistani antinarcotics programs.

5. *English Teaching and American Studies,* U.S. cooperation with educational leaders who recognized the need to halt the decline in English language proficiency in Pakistan was in our mutual interest and provided an avenue for USIS to correct misperceptions about the U.S. Many Pakistani educators, professionals, scientists, and intellectuals saw the loss of English as a threat to Pakistan's participation in international trade, science, technology, and culture. USIS assistance to Pakistani educators and institutions teaching English contributed to continuing and expanding political, economic and intellectual ties between our two peoples. Also the absence of courses in American history, literature, and society in all but a few Pakistani universities and institutes was depriving students of contact with Americans and resulted in little or inaccurate information about American culture and society. In these circumstances USIS sought to offset the dearth of

accurate information about the U.S.

6. *Nuclear Nonproliferation.* A major bilateral issue between the two countries was U.S. determination to prevent, if possible, greater proliferation of nuclear weapons, and Pakistan's concern (1) that its security might depend on nuclear parity with India which had already exploded a nuclear device and (2) that the U.S. was practicing discrimination against Pakistan by requiring full-scope safeguards as a condition for U.S. assistance to its civilian nuclear program. USIS programming sought to explain U.S. concerns and to show how controls on proliferation would lead to greater international cooperation on the peaceful uses of nuclear energy.

Because I soon became saddled with supervisory responsibility for moving the American Center building project forward, I was unable to visit the three USIS branch posts in Pakistan as frequently as I would have liked. As deputy public affairs officer I shared overall responsibility for their operations with the PAO. Eventually, however, I was able to make in-depth analyses of the branch post operations and presented my findings and recommendations about each facility and its management in a series of reports to the PAO.

Karachi, Pakistan's largest city, had been the nation's capital before the creation of Islamabad. It is the capital of Sind Province with a population, at the time, of between five and seven million. It is also the commercial, financial and industrial center of the country and its major seaport as well as being a transportation hub for the nation's highways and its rail and air systems. And Pakistan's telecommunication network is controlled from this city.

Karachi experienced a booming population growth in the 1960s and 70s, which accentuated shortages of power, water, and other essentials of modern urban areas. Its polyglot population is made up of Sindhis, Baluchis, Urdu-speaking emigrants from India, Pathans, Punjabis, Makranis and Gujratis, among others. During my assignment to Pakistan, Karachi boasted sixteen daily newspapers, including the most important Urdu daily in the nation, *Jang,* and the prestigious English-language daily, *Dawn,* as well as two radio stations and two TV channels. It was important politically as the seat of four major political parties: Pakistan Peoples Party, National Democratic Party, Jamiat Ulema-e-Pakistan, and the Pakistan Muslim League. With three universities and other educational institutions, as well as its size and importance in other ways, Karachi competes with Lahore as a center of cultural activities.

By the time of my visit to Karachi to take an in-depth look at our operations, Richard Von Glatz had replaced Paul Rappaport as the branch public affairs officer; William Jones had replaced Frank Florey as the BCAO; and the American Center director was Lee James Irwin. A fourth American position, held by Sheila Austrian who had the unwieldy title of "deputy branch public affairs officer," was about to be abolished with her imminent transfer to another post.

The staff also consisted of twenty-seven Pakistani employees in Karachi and four at a sub-post in Hyderabad, about one hundred miles inland. Numerous additional contract employees worked without the same benefits as regular employees, so my first recommendation was to eliminate as many of these contractors as possible. An excess number of employees seemed to me to be a hangover from the days when Karachi was the capital of Pakistan and the post had much greater responsibilities. When USIS Karachi was inspected later during a routine Washington inspection, the inspectors reached similar conclusions about the necessity to tighten the organization by eliminating a number of positions. One major change was to move the distribution facility of all USIS posts in the country, which had been kept in Karachi, to Islamabad where the new Wang computer system we were developing could be utilized.

The physical plant of USIS in Karachi made it one of the most impressive branch posts in the world. This was because it was housed in the building that had been the U.S. embassy when Karachi was the capital of the country. Now its embassy-like space contained, in addition to USIS, the offices of the consulate general, AID, and other U.S. government entities. The USIS library, which included a theater, was on the ground floor and had become a major cultural institution of Karachi. It escaped the destruction wrought in 1979 to the embassy in Islamabad and its sister centers in Rawalpindi and Lahore.

Lahore, a major cultural, educational, media, and political center, is the capital of the Punjab, Pakistan's most heavily populated province. About two-thirds of the country's total population lived in the Punjab. Lahore is one of the oldest cities of the Indo-Pakistan subcontinent and has more institutions of higher learning than any other city in Pakistan. It is also the site of important training centers for the Pakistan government's bureaucrats and administrators. In the early 1980s editions of all major newspapers of the country except *Dawn* were published there, as well as the government's English-language daily, *The Pakistan Times* (which was "must reading" in all embassies to see what the official line of the Pakistan government was on any given day).

The physical plant of the reconstructed cultural center and USIS offices in Lahore was now a beautiful three-story building with conference rooms, exhibit areas, a library, a theater seating 250 people, and special rooms for such things as student counseling and press conferences. Once reconstruction of the burned-out center began, Zor Engineers, a British expatriate firm in Lahore, completed the building, except for the theater, in a record-breaking eighteen months. This record is what inspired USIA to cancel its contract with the builder of the new American Center in Islamabad, after half-a-dozen years had passed and problems in its construction continued to mount. Zor Engineers was engaged to complete the Islamabad center.

The branch PAO in Lahore was Sherman Ross, an experienced, highly respected officer whose habit of shaking nearly everyone's hand upon his arrival at the office every morning endeared him to all of his employees. His American colleagues, Warren Soiffer and Alden Stallings, supervised the cultural and information programs. After a close examination of our operations in Lahore I concluded that previous cuts in personnel made before my arrival had left USIS Lahore functioning close to the bone. To make any additional personnel cuts, I argued, would require drastic and painful program reductions.

Peshawar, which I had visited much more frequently than Karachi and Lahore, is the capital of Pakistan's North West Frontier Province (NWFP). As noted earlier, it abounded with Afghan refugees who had fled from their war-torn country. Peshawar was also the seat of the Afghan "Freedom Fighters," the Mujaheddin.

The people of the NWFP are predominantly Pushtoons (better known as Pathans). They form what is sometimes called the world's largest tribal society and inhabit southern and eastern Afghanistan as well as the NWFP. Thus most of the border separating Pakistan from Afghanistan was neither controlled by the two national governments nor recognized by the local inhabitants. Tribesmen have long been accustomed to moving freely back and forth across the Pakistan-Afghanistan border in areas not far from Peshawar.

The Soviet invasion of Afghanistan made Peshawar of special interest to the U.S. The most visible effect of that invasion was the thousands of Afghan refugees who had set up camps in the NWFP, and in the massive food, shelter and medical services for them that developed primarily in and near Peshawar. Afghan refugees in Pakistan numbered between two and three million according to most estimates. Nobody really knew how many there were. The constant flow back and forth made estimates difficult.

U.S. interest in the NWFP also increased in the 1980s because of the startling growth of heroin production and trafficking in Pakistan, much of which originated in or passed through the NWFP. Large amounts of illicit heroin from this area were now entering New York and other American ports.

The State Department maintained a consular office in Peshawar while USIS was run by one American officer with the help of four nationals. A small USIS library was but a shadow of those in Karachi and Lahore. I recommended that an additional American be assigned there and noted that a secretary-receptionist position at the library/ USIS office was sorely needed. These recommendations were eventually carried out. Douglas Davidson, a young officer whose most recent tour had been as an assistant information officer in Finland, was the branch PAO in Peshawar. When his tour of duty ended he was replaced by John Dixon, an older but energetic officer who quickly adapted to Peshawar's unique environment and served USIA very well even though he was not a career Foreign Service officer. Peshawar in those days, and probably to this day, had a frontier environment that made it an exciting place to be but one in which only certain types thrive. John Dixon was one of those types.

As mentioned earlier, when the USIA Regional Architect, Dean Philpott, was transferred to Washington from Islamabad, where he had supervised the construction of the new American Center, I was left with the responsibility for seeing that construction continued. I was at the time acting director of USIS Pakistan as PAO Jim Thurber had left in October and his replacement, Marilyn Johnson, was not due to arrive until January 1982.

The day before Architect Philpott left, I asked information officer Don Jones to tape an interview with him in which Philpott was to provide us with a detailed explanation of the current status of the construction project. He was the only one with intimate knowledge of the present stage of construction. Once he was back in Washington it would be difficult to query him directly about the various aspects of the project.

Philpott was happy to oblige. His remarks were a revelation to me. We all knew that the building had been under construction for years and that problems with the construction existed, but the litany of errors and shoddy workmanship described on this occasion and later demonstrated in a walk-through with me, was almost unbelievable.

The main culprit for the lack of progress in the construction and for horrendous mistakes made in many of the elements already built, according to Philpott, was the former contractor, a Pakistani construction company known as "Supercons." Supercons' engineers were unfamiliar with many of the special items which were to be used for the building and which had been shipped to Islamabad from the U.S. They also seemed to have lacked adequate supervision of the construction. The amount of unacceptable, unsatisfactory work, which was visible even to my untrained eyes, was appalling.

There had been many arguments between Supercons' supervisors and Philpott over the years, and to see the building as I saw it in 1981, the disagreements between them were understandable. PAO Thurber was known to have had his differences with Philpott, but after having the enormity of the construction mistakes and erroneous installation of plumbing and electrical fixtures explained and demonstrated, I could sympathize with the frustrations Philpott must have suffered. So outrageous was some of the workmanship that one had to suspect that perhaps sabotage was intended, although all evidence then and later tended to indicate sheer incompetence as the villain.

In his taped recital, Philpott said the building at that stage "is principally a shell. There is a lot of work to be done." That was an understatement. The contract with Supercons had been terminated and a new contract for completion of the building had been made with the British firm of Zor Engineers of Lahore. As Philpott droned on about the problems with the building which now had been under construction for six years, he noted that "the electrical and plumbing systems are in a state of disrepair." As for the air conditioning units, "not one of the ducts in the air conditioning system connects with the pipes," and he added that the electrical connections installed by Supercons "is a Rube Goldberg type of wiring." His comments described a building under construction that had to be seen to be believed.

Some of the window glass for the center's library that had been shipped from the U.S. arrived broken. Furthermore, a large condenser for the building's central air conditioning system had been aboard a freight train in the U.S., en route to a U.S. port for shipment to Pakistan, when the train derailed. Not until the condenser was installed on the roof of the building in Islamabad, and Zor Engineers had replaced Supercons as the construction firm, was it learned that the condenser had been damaged, presumably as a result of the derailment. It would require extensive repairs if it were ever to function properly.

Another concern noted by Philpott was that the building was in a section of Islamabad with few neighbors and was surrounded by woods and fields in which birds and snakes roamed. They entered the unfinished building with some frequency.

Some bulletproof glass for the security section of the building had not yet arrived, he said, but extremely important was the fact that Supercons had installed the roof upside down! The insulation material which was intended to be on the underside of the roof to serve in insulating the interior, was facing the sky instead. It had become wet and was beginning to deteriorate. The roof was made of large, flat slabs which were fitted together. Water soon collected in various sections of the roof because its gentle slope, which should have enabled the water to run off, ran in the wrong direction in a number of places.

I was unable to pay much attention to the construction project during the first few months after Philpott left since my first priority had to be the overall supervision of USIS operations throughout the country. After Marilyn Johnson's arrival a few months later, I devoted more and more time to it. So many unique elements; my inexperience in such matters; and having to deal with so many different entities involved in the project, located not only in Islamabad but also in Karachi, Lahore, and Washington, D.C., made my responsibilities regarding the new building very time-consuming.

The government of Pakistan did not allow foreign governments to own property (other than embassies) in its new capital. An arrangement was made, therefore, whereby the building and land on which the American Center was being built became the property of the State Life Insurance Company of Karachi. Through a complicated system the building was being built to USIA specifications and being financed by USIA. The building would, for all practical purposes, belong to USIS, but the insurance company had to be involved in order to abide by Pakistan's regulations regarding its capital city. The arrangement was for USIA to pay State Life five years rent in advance, and to rent the building afterwards for twenty-five additional years. Since the U.S. had so many millions of Pakistani rupees which could be used for such purposes, many of the costs could be met by these so-called U.S. government-owned "surplus rupees" (referred to at times as "funny money").

Under U.S. Public Law 480, Pakistan was able in earlier years to repay certain AID project loans in rupees. These rupees, which totaled $119.2 million by the end of 1983, were expected to continue to generate additional rupees because of the interest earned, albeit at a declining rate, until 2010 according to calculations cited by the embassy economics officer, Ralph Boyce, in May of 1984.

Not only was this building project in sad shape after being in the hands of Supercons for some years, but the legal owner was, as noted, an insurance company in Karachi. The new contractor, Zor Engineers, had their main office in Lahore, about 350 miles from Islamabad. Further complicating the project was the fact that some officials at USIA headquarters doubted the wisdom of completing the project following the events of 1979 and the fact that the American architect was now back in Washington. The Pakistani architect, who had also been involved in planning the building, had his office in Karachi. He was always difficult to contact, possibly with good reason.

Into this maelstrom I arrived with no construction experience whatsoever and I certainly was not an engineer. I had been assigned responsibility for keeping the project on track "as a collateral duty!" I was given no petty cash fund with which to approve, at the site, petty expenses which invariably were required in a project of this magnitude. Instead, I had to cable Washington headquarters every time I wanted to spend a rupee for some small items that were considered necessary but not necessarily the obligation of the building contractor.

As months turned into years my frustration with this situation steadily rose. Long cables were drafted by me to explain what the various actors were doing in Islamabad and why things were happening, or not happening, and what was needed. I frequently had to inform Washington about what items had not arrived from the U.S. which were needed or arrived broken, or were of the wrong design. I was spending so much time drafting cables and answering queries from the office in Washington, which had overall responsibility for this project, that I began my own unique numbering system for the many cables on this subject. I did this to keep better track of developments. In about eight months I had surpassed the 150th cable with no indication that the workload would diminish. Many times I begged USIA to send a consulting engineer to see what was going on at the site and to give the post some professional advice and guidance, but my requests were always ignored or turned down. The Washington office claimed that no consulting engineers were available to be sent to Islamabad, not even one on contract, for temporary duty or a short visit.

During the following eight months the building was slowly reshaped by Zor Engineers, with whom I developed an excellent working relationship. Meanwhile, the embassy compound was slowly being rebuilt by a private U.S. contractor who had a Pakistani construction firm as a subcontractor. They worked under the on-the-job supervision of the Bureau of Foreign Buildings of the Department of State.

Architect Ich Mori was the State Department's project supervisor in charge of the embassy's reconstruction. From time to time I sought his advice and that of Don Feldt, the engineer who supervised the rebuilding of the chancery and other buildings in the embassy compound. They seemed to be much more helpful at times than the people in my own agency, but then they were here and my agency advisors were about 13,000 miles away. Although I also urged, (begged would be a better word) that the head of the Design and Technical Assistance branch, Ted Bork, visit the post for a personal consultation about our many construction problems, this too never occurred during the three years I was in Islamabad and involved in this "collateral duty."

One of the most frustrating developments concerned the question of what to do about the roof above the center's theater. The "upside down" roof problem was resolved by using additional materials, but the managers of Zor Engineers expressed concern that the roof over the theater was not properly constructed and would be a safety hazard if not redone. Thus began innumerable meetings with the representatives of the insurance company in Karachi, some held there and some held in Islamabad

The Pakistani architect who had helped design the building disagreed with Zor, claiming that the roof was perfectly all right. Nevertheless, given the suspicions raised by Zor Engineers about its safety, we could not ignore the matter. Visions of the roof caving in and killing or injuring an audience in the theater below were too terrible to contemplate. Eventually all concerned agreed that since there was a difference of opinion regarding the safety of the theater roof, the only thing to do was to conduct a load test. This would prove whether or not it was safe.

Months later the architect from Karachi came to Islamabad to be present when the test was conducted. All this was new to me, of course. Not in my wildest dreams would I have been able to predict that one day I would be visiting brickyards on the outskirts of Islamabad with a visiting architect from Karachi seeking a particular type of especially clean common brick of the type needed for the test.

The roof test was to be conducted by hauling a good number of approved bricks to the building site, each one of which was supposed to weigh a certain amount, and placing the bricks on the flat roof of the theater in various places until a certain weight was obtained. If the roof did not collapse when the required weight was reached and showed no signs of strain, the roof was considered safe. In fact, that is what happened. The roof passed the test with flying colors so at least this hurdle was crossed. One never knows what to expect. I had great faith in Zor Engineers because of the splendid, efficient job they did with the reconstruction of our Lahore center and the manner in which they had moved rapidly ahead on the Islamabad center following Supercons' terrible performance. In this instance, however, they were proven wrong in their pessimistic prediction that the roof would collapse. Nevertheless, after the test we were all relieved.

Once, in explaining my responsibilities regarding the construction of the new center, I described it as a millstone around my neck. Not only was I possibly becoming persona non grata with the committee back in Washington which had to approve the expenditures I requested (and who were tiring of my continually asking for an engineer to visit the site), but the time I had to spend on meetings concerning the building's construction, reviewing progress, drafting cables, etc. took me away from other USIS operations which, I felt, should have my attention.

"Imagine," I said, "the owner of the building is an insurance company in Karachi, the second contractor is in Lahore, the resident architect for nearly three years left eighteen months ago, and a committee in Washington, thousands of miles away, directs construction by cable." Construction started in 1979 when nearly a decade had passed since the agency first decided on building the center in Islamabad. While this was going on, USIS Islamabad was operating out of a one-family house in this nation of more than eighty-five million people!

"Conducting USIS programs here is like having one hand tied behind your back," I said, "but we shall overcome."

When I arrived in Pakistan in 1981 a heroin epidemic was just beginning to sweep that country. This was a new phenomenon for Pakistan and was caused primarily for two reasons. First, the Khomeini regime in neighboring Iran was hanging drug traffickers whenever they caught them, so heroin production there was getting more and more dangerous for producers and traffickers. Secondly, Afghanistan, a traditional source of poppies from which opium, morphine, and heroin are derived, was engaged in a civil war following the invasion by the Soviet Union. Illicit drug trafficking, like everything else in Afghanistan, was disrupted. Pakistan, which shares common borders with both of these countries, began to take up the slack.

Southeast Asia, where Thailand, Cambodia, Laos, and Vietnam share common borders, has long been known as the "Golden Triangle" because it is a major source of the heroin illicitly sold throughout the world. Less well known, but increasingly important as a source of heroin in the early 1980s, was the "Golden Crescent" of southwest Asia—Afghanistan, Pakistan, and Iran.

Long before Pakistan became part of British India, drug use was common, but opium, rather than the more devastating heroin, was the drug of choice. Opium dens still flourished in Pakistan but by 1980 they were rapidly becoming places where heroin was also obtainable. For the first time heroin labs were being established within Pakistan because traffickers could no longer depend on Iran and Afghanistan. At the same time many new poppy fields were being developed in Pakistan because of the growing demand for heroin both domestically and internationally.

Having spent four years in Peru where USIS conducted active anti-narcotics information programs, but where the problem was cocaine rather than heroin, I felt I had learned much from that experience about how USIS might contribute to anti-narcotics efforts. The type of illicit drug was of little importance in such programs, whether conducted against cocaine use and trafficking in Peru or heroin use and trafficking in Pakistan. Many similarities existed.

When illicit trafficking of cocaine first became a major activity in Peru, most Peruvians contended that this was not their problem. They viewed the narcotics problem as being that of the United States, the society where the greatest demand for cocaine existed. Many Pakistanis, from the President on down, also contended that the increased trafficking in heroin in their country was really not their problem, it was the problem of Western Europe and the U.S. In this and many other ways I saw similarities with what I had witnessed in Peru. I therefore felt that my Peruvian experience could be put to good use in dealing with this issue in Pakistan.

Shortly after my arrival in Islamabad I learned that the embassy had recently formed a Narcotics Coordinating Committee (NCC), a type of organization with which I was fully familiar since I had served on a similar committee in the embassy in Lima. The NCC planned and discussed U.S. activities designed to encourage and support host country efforts in combating illicit narcotics trafficking. The committee consisted of the deputy chief of mission as chairman and had representatives from the Drug Enforcement Administration (DEA), the State Department's antinarcotics program, the Agency for International Development (AID), and the Central Intelligence Agency (CIA). I was surprised to learn there was no representative from USIS on Islamabad's newly formed committee. My experience in Peru had clearly demonstrated that the USIS contribution to U.S. objectives in this field could be substantial. Upon expressing my concern, I was immediately made the USIS representative on that committee.

In the early 1980s the Department of State was becoming more and more attune to the need for U.S. foreign affairs involvement in antinarcotics programs. At the same time U.S. government officials in Islamabad became increasingly concerned about the flow of illicit heroin from Pakistan to the U.S. The Drug Enforcement agency estimated that about 60 percent of the total amount of heroin sold on the streets of New York now came from Pakistan.

Richard Reeves, in his book *Passage to Peshawar: Between the Hindu Kush and the Arabian Sea* (Simon & Schuster, 1984) mentions how in November 1982, the attorney general of the U.S., William French Smith, on a visit to Pakistan's Khyber Pass, was being taken through a bazaar by officials of the Pakistan Narcotics Control Board. They wanted to show how effective they were in convincing the tribes of the Northwest Frontier District to get out of the heroin business. One of Smith's companions saw some heroin on display that was for sale to anyone interested. After that incident the Pakistan government closed the Khyber District to foreigners. Four months later in March 1983, according to Reeves, in a closed session before the House Foreign Affairs Committee, narcotics control was listed as the number two priority in the State Department's briefing on the purposes of U.S. aid to Pakistan. (Number one was "the stability and security of a frontline state resisting Soviet expansionism.")

When in Peru others and I had argued that the Peruvians were being shortsighted when they contended, as they often did, that illicit drug trafficking should be more the concern of the U.S. than their concern. We often suggested to them that any country that permits illicit drug trafficking to take place unchallenged will invariably be adversely affected themselves, first and foremost by the expansion of domestic drug users and, secondly, by dislocations in their economy caused by the huge profits illicit drug trafficking provides criminal elements. Most Peruvians initially pooh-poohed such talk, until their society, and particularly their youth, became obvious victims of the illicit trade.

President Zia ul-Haq and his minister of information were on record in conversations with embassy officials as considering the illicit drug trafficking in Pakistan as being of primary importance to the U.S. They agreed to cooperate in anti-narcotics programs, but initially refused to recognize the problem as a serious one for Pakistan.

The minister of information was particularly vocal on this subject. There was no doubt among American officials that if the millions of dollars that the U.S. was beginning to pour into Pakistan in anti-narcotics efforts was to have any semblance of success, the president and his minister of information would have to be convinced that Pakistan would suffer if firm steps were not taken to attack the drug problem in their own country. Not only did the Pakistan government drag its feet on this issue, but the U.S. government was also trying to get the ambassadors of Western Europe, where the problem was also growing dramatically, to cooperate in the struggle ahead. They too needed to be educated as to the depth of the narcotics problem and its effect on their citizens as well as the rest of the world. Some success in this endeavor with western embassies was achieved due partially to the efforts of U.S. Embassy officials. Convincing President Zia and other Pakistani leaders was another story, and one in which the USIS contribution in eventually changing their minds was substantial.

After incorporating anti-narcotics programming into the Country Plan for USIS Pakistan for the first time, I launched two unique efforts that appeared to be highly successful. The goal I sought in developing these two projects, a booklet and a film, was to convince Pakistanis in general, and the president and his cabinet in particular, that the increasing amounts of illegal poppies being grown in Pakistan; the increasing number of heroin labs being created; and the illicit heroin trafficking initiated in or passing through Pakistan, were bound to create an increased demand domestically which would lead to more and more heroin addicts among Pakistanis.

The Pakistan Narcotics Control Board (PNCB), headquartered in Islamabad, was Pakistan's leading organization for combating illicit drug trafficking, It received AID funds as well as support and cooperation from the U.S. Drug Enforcement Agency. It was an undeveloped organization in an undeveloped country, with limited experience, limited expertise, limited facilities, and limited staff, especially considering the size of the problem it faced. Its director, however, was well meaning and cooperative, so the various U.S. government agencies interested in combating illicit drug trafficking and use provided all the assistance they possibly could.

USIS soon worked with the PNCB in establishing seminars to train and educate Pakistani governmental and media leaders concerning the dimensions of the growing problem for Pakistan. Techniques to better utilize the press and other outlets in efforts to educate the public concerning this issue were given a high priority. But the major project USIS undertook with the PNCB was publication of a booklet entitled *The Living Dead, Heroin Takes Its Toll*. Widely distributed in English and Urdu versions, it clearly demonstrated the toll heroin was by then taking among Pakistan's citizens. I believe that it, as much as anything, influenced the president and members of his cabinet to accept the seriousness of the growing narcotics problem within Pakistan.

The second major project we undertook was a film. This project began when a Pakistani film and television producer walked into my office and told me he had traveled throughout the country and filmed heroin addicts "chasing the dragon" in about a dozen opium dens. "Chasing the dragon" is the term used to describe heroin use in Pakistan, where, instead of "shooting up," Pakistani addicts cook the heroin by placing it on a piece of tinfoil and heating it with a lighted match. The fumes are then inhaled.

He also interviewed a number of medical doctors and others affected in one way or another by Pakistan's growing heroin epidemic. Some family members of addicts, for example, who saw a husband, son, or brother become addicted, were interviewed on film. All of the addicts were men, most in their twenties and beyond, but the harmful effects on their wives, mothers, and sisters were also dramatically shown in these interviews. The film vividly demonstrated that maintaining the habit of a heroin addict often results in the loss of jobs, family fortunes, and any semblance of former family life, not to mention the often visible physical damage to the addict with death never far away. The film made "The Living Dead" seem like a very appropriate description of heroin addicts.

A particularly sad and tragic segment of the film was an interview with a young boy who was only eleven years old and already an addict. The narrator also interviewed the boy's mother and a medical doctor who had treated him, but efforts to wean him away from heroin were useless. He was hooked. Some months later we learned that the youngster had died from complications resulting from his habit. It seemed to me that if this film could be shown to Pakistani leaders, even the most hard-hearted might be influenced to make the struggle against drug traffickers a government priority.

USIS did not have the funds to finance the production of a finished film so I turned to the Drug Enforcement Agency's chief representative in Islamabad for help. He recommended the project to his superiors in Washington with the result that the DEA financed its production.

In consultation with the producer, I suggested that the film be entitled "Heroin Hits Pakistan." As there had been few, if any, heroin labs in Pakistan until fairly recently, and as heroin was not heretofore the drug of choice among most Pakistani drug users, such a title seemed completely appropriate.

"Heroin Hits Pakistan," produced both in English and Urdu

versions, was widely viewed throughout the country, distributed by the Pakistan Narcotics Control Board and others. I urged that a Pushto version also be made which could be shown to the growers of poppies in the North West Frontier District in hopes that they would see the result of their poppy production. This was done after I completed my tour in Islamabad, and although I understand it was shown in the NWFD, it probably influenced few if any of the tribal farmers who made good profits in poppy production.

Despite efforts of the U.S. and others to induce poppy growers to raise other crops, poppy production in Pakistan continued. Just as AID programs in Peru tried to entice coca leaf farmers to grow other crops, AID in Pakistan tried to get poppy growers to switch to something else. The problem is the same in both countries. No one has yet come up with a substitute crop for coca leafs or poppies that pays more than the illicit drug traffickers will pay for their basic products. But even if the Pushto version of "Heroin Hits Pakistan" affected few farmers, I believe the film in its English and Urdu versions contributed to the thinking of the Zia government leaders. After seeing that film, they could hardly contend that Pakistanis were unaffected by the drug trafficking in their country.

On August 9, 1982, two weeks before he was to leave Pakistan, the U.S. consul general in Karachi, Richard Post, was the guest speaker at a luncheon meeting of the Rotary Club in that city. "Narcotics: A Growing Threat to Pakistan" was the title of his talk.

Post noted that "today the most conservative estimate from authoritative sources is that there are 10,000 to 15,000 addicts in Karachi alone and at least as many as 25,000 in Pakistan as a whole." About eight years later, in the spring, 1990 edition of *The Asian Drug Prevention Quarterly,* published by Development Associates, Inc., an article by Henry Kirsch noted that "Growing from just a small number of cases ten years ago," recent surveys in Pakistan reported over 1,000,000 heroin users. One wonders if our efforts and those of many others had not begun, would that figure be even greater?

USIS reproduced Post's speech as a pamphlet in English and Urdu versions and distributed it throughout the country. In his remarks Post conveyed to his Pakistani audience how heroin addicts get hooked. After the incredible euphoria of the first-time user (a fantastic "high" as it's known), very quickly the new user becomes an addict searching not for a new "high" but for relief from the intense bodily pains and cramps and spasms that set in. Heroin pains have been described as analogous in intensity to the pains of childbirth. Unlike childbirth pains, however, pains caused by heroin use can be relieved only by another dosage of heroin. If deprived of another dosage, the addict cannot sleep and can become hysterical and physically violent with risks of bodily harm to himself and others. His sole interest in life becomes the effort to secure another dose of heroin and he will do almost anything to achieve that aim.

While the booklet, the pamphlet, and the film were the most visible and possibly most effective information vehicles which USIS efforts brought to Pakistani audiences, the whole realm of USIS "tools" were brought to bear on the narcotics problem, from books and libraries to exchange programs.

Under the American Specialists Program of USIA, which brings U.S. experts to consult with foreign counterparts, Dr. Jacob Schut, M.D., director of drug rehabilitation programs at a Veterans Hospital in Texas, came to Islamabad. I escorted him on a visit to Dr. M. H. Mubbashar, director of the Drug Abuse Treatment Center at the Rawalpindi General Hospital, and Dr. Habibullah, Medical Superintendent of that hospital. Dr. Schut exchanged views with them and their staffs and we visited the wards. But as Dr. Mubbashar stated, the drug problem in Pakistan would continue to grow because even when some addicts are hospitalized like those we saw that day, they return to the same environment where they started their habit and are soon hooked again. At the time there were no rehabilitation facilities available in Pakistan. Without such facilities, recidivism would always be high.

Although all the efforts which went into combating the narcotics trafficking in Pakistan were no more successful than they appear to have been in the U.S. as this is written, more than a decade later, one can only surmise how much worse this intractable problem might be today had no effort been made, and as efforts continue to be made.

When a cable arrived informing us that Hollywood star Kirk Douglas was coming to Islamabad under USIA auspices to help publicize the plight of the Afghan refugees in Pakistan, PAO Marilyn Johnson and I shook our heads. What could a movie star do to increase world attention on the Russian invasion of Afghanistan and the plight of its people, so many of whom had fled across the border into Pakistan? How wrong we were! We had not reckoned with the power of Hollywood and the personality of one of Hollywood's most active and accomplished actors. By 1982, when he briefly visited Pakistan, Douglas had appeared in more than sixty films and many Broadway productions during his thirty-year career. He had won many awards for his acting ability and his humanitarian endeavors. USIA Director Charles Z. Wick had strong ties to Hollywood. This was probably his idea but we never learned where and how USIA-sponsorship of the visit originated.

Douglas flew from Hollywood to Manila where he boarded a Philippines Airlines plane which had sleeping accommodations enabling him to get a good night's sleep before landing in Karachi. Given the heavy schedule he insisted on keeping during five hectic days in Pakistan, it was good that he was able to get some sleep aboard that plane.

From Karachi to Islamabad, he flew aboard a special Pakistani Air Force plane sent by President Zia to pick him up at that port city. This was only the beginning of accommodations that those he came in contact with were only too willing to provide. The magic of Hollywood proved to be a powerful influence on anyone even remotely connected with one of its stars. His arrival in Karachi also immediately demonstrated that he would be the master of his program while being a guest of USIA during his visit to Pakistan.

The original plan was for him to overnight in Karachi, primarily to allow him to get a good night's rest and to shake off some jet lag before launching into a whirlwind program in Islamabad and Peshawar. He announced on his arrival, however, that he wanted to go on to Islamabad immediately, so this was arranged with President Zia's assistance. This was the same pattern which took place in the days that followed. He was the star of the show, but also his own director. While charming to talk with, especially when he regaled his listeners with stories of Hollywood experiences, he was a tyrant when it came to how his presence in Pakistan should be utilized to publicize the refugee situation. He agreed to our general plan but fine-tuned everything to meet his expectations. He was accompanied on his trip to Pakistan by Ray Peppers, the USIA desk officer for Pakistan. As the escort officer, Peppers was kept busy on a job he would never forget.

USIS had a Pakistani photographer on the staff whose photo skills were satisfactory at best and who was not always as dependable as one would have hoped. By the time Douglas arrived in Karachi, we had received so many cables and telephone calls from Washington concerning this visit that we knew it had high-level interest back at headquarters. With this in mind we began to shake off our general lethargy and low-key plans for the visit. And because PAO Johnson knew that our son Robert, a college student at the time, was in town on a short visit and that he had some experience in photography, she suggested that USIS might hire him for the five days that Douglas was in Pakistan to make sure no photo opportunities would be missed. Needless to say, Robert was delighted.

The first morning that Douglas was in Islamabad he made the usual courtesy call on the ambassador. About 9:30 a.m. the ambassador's secretary phoned and told Marilyn Johnson that Kirk Douglas was in the ambassador's office. "Where's the photographer?" she said. The regular USIS photographer was nowhere to be found, so I called home and asked Robert to rush to the embassy and go to the ambassador's office immediately to take a photo of the ambassador with Kirk Douglas, which he did. He was able to get there in about ten minutes by car. We soon learned that anywhere Douglas went he expected a photographer to be on hand. Obviously Douglas took his trip to Pakistan much more seriously than we in USIS did, at least initially.

I went to the embassy to make sure that all was going well and waited in the lobby for Douglas to pass through en route to his next appointment. The lobby was filled with embassy employees, both Pakistanis and Americans, whoever could leave their desks. Everyone wanted to catch a glimpse of this famous actor.

The elevator in the lobby opened and the first one to step out was Robert, loaded down with at least two cameras and a bag of camera gear. He looked nervous. After all, this was his first big-time experience as a photographer, so he had a right to be nervous.

Douglas stepped out of the elevator, smiled and waved at everyone while the employees applauded him, and Robert snapped photo after photo. A few days later Robert's nervousness vanished. He had been to Peshawar, Rawalpindi, and around Islamabad photographing Douglas at every stop he made, and swapping stories with the regular USIS photographer. It was amazing what the experience of a few days under pressure could do for changing an amateur into the semblance of a professional photographer. One of his photos, taken as Douglas broke bread (in this case, *nan*) in Peshawar with some Afghan refugee leaders, was later used in Kirk Douglas' autobiography, *The Ragman's Son*.

Douglas' days in Pakistan were spent attending lunches, dinners and receptions. There was also a special showing of one of his films which he attended and afterwards discussed it and answered questions from the audience.

USIA film producer Ashley Hawken, with whom I had worked on an agency anti-narcotics film many years earlier, showed up with a film crew for the filming of what later became a twenty-minute USIA produced feature entitled *Thanksgiving in Peshawar*. The film featured Kirk Douglas having Thanksgiving Day dinner in an Afghan refugee camp with Afghan refugees, thus depicting the plight of the refugees and the tragedy inflicted upon Afghanistan by the Soviet invasion.

On that Thanksgiving Day that Douglas spent eating a typical Afghan lunch at a refugee camp outside Peshawar, he returned to Islamabad in the afternoon in order to have dinner at the residence of President Zia in Rawalpindi. During the second course he became violently ill and had to leave the table. Undoubtedly the meal he had with the Afghan refugees that afternoon (which wasn't turkey) disagreed with him. After resting for some time he was escorted back to his hotel in Islamabad. By the next day he had recovered fairly well and by noon was able to continue the activities planned for him. That morning, to the surprise of everyone, President Zia showed up at the Holiday Inn in Islamabad where Douglas was staying. He wanted to make sure, the president said, that his guest of the night before was recovering all right, which he was.

Our brief experience with a Hollywood celebrity of the caliber, and ego, of Kirk Douglas was certainly a change of pace for us at USIS Islamabad. It was an exciting time because he was such an interesting, if demanding, person. The film and other publicity he generated, both in Pakistan and abroad, achieved the purpose of his visit—to publicize "the forgotten war."

Kirk Douglas' whirlwind visit to Islamabad was the most interesting one of all the visits to this distant capital by U.S. visitors, official or otherwise. Unlike La Paz, where we seldom saw official visitors, Islamabad was seldom without such visitors, except in the summer when temperatures often went above 120 degrees Fahrenheit.

There was tremendous interest in Washington concerning Pakistan, generated by the war in Afghanistan, the growing narcotics trafficking problem, and the large U.S. economic and military assistance programs to this country. Under these circumstances Islamabad became a popular place to visit. Numerous Congressional delegations, whose visits in State Department parlance were referred to as "Codels," descended upon Islamabad as did an unusually high number of foreign correspondents, scholars, and others who found Pakistan, in the early 1980s, to be an interesting place to visit. For a while we almost expected most, if not all, of President Reagan's top officials to include Islamabad on their periodic trips abroad.

The visit of Attorney General French came and went with no problems other than his advance team's dismay at some offhand remarks made by the USIS information officer who, as mentioned earlier, called the visit a "boondoggle" in the presence of some of the members of the advance team.

Two memorable visits in which I participated in making

arrangements and in providing services were those of Casper Weinberger, the secretary of defense, and George Bush, at that time vice president of the U.S. Like every important visitor during the war in Afghanistan, both VIPs were flown to Peshawar and then taken by helicopter to the headquarters of the Khyber Rifles in the Khyber Pass. After lunch and ceremonies at that historic site, the group was taken a short distance by car to a prominent peak in the pass, about a mile from the border where one could, from that height, look into Afghanistan. Its hills and valleys on the other side of the border were visible for many miles in different directions. At the very time that George Bush was being shown Afghanistan from that vantage point, Soviet bombers struck an Afghan village about five miles from the border. Some surmised later that the Soviets were sending the U.S. a message, but I, for one, was not sure what the message was. During the Bush visit the Khyber Pass was closed to normal tourists because of the drug trafficking and an incident, some months earlier, when the French Ambassador to Pakistan, while traveling in the pass, was briefly held hostage by some disgruntled Pathans, much to the consternation of Pakistan officials in Islamabad.

Always included in the itinerary of a visit to the Khyber Pass and Peshawar was a visit to an Afghan refugee camp not far from town. Only Kirk Douglas, however, ate lunch with the refugees and only he, of course, became ill as a result. Another place that was almost always visited was the local hospital where wounded Majahadeen fighters and innocent victims of the war were treated. It was most heartrending to see wounded Afghan children who had stepped on Russian land mines or had otherwise been injured and, in many cases, had lost arms or legs.

As with other visiting notables, USIS arranged press conferences for George Bush and Casper Weinberger. By the time of the Bush visit the American Club at the compound had been rebuilt. It was there that a social gathering was held which provided the opportunity for the American community to meet the vice president. Secretary of State George Shultz also visited Islamabad and received the same Khyber Pass performance, although I was traveling elsewhere at the time of his visit. Seldom did any of the official visitors at or near cabinet level manage to see Lahore or Karachi, Pakistan's two largest and, after Islamabad, most important cities, but they seldom failed to have the historic Khyber Pass included in their itinerary.

Before 1984 came to a close, my book, *USIA, Public Diplomacy in the Computer Age*, which I completed while living in the relatively quiet city of Islamabad, was published. When I received the author's copies I was pleased, of course, to see that my writing efforts had not been in vain. Ironically, although the title and contents of the book dealt with "the Computer Age," I wrote it using an old typewriter! What I was not prepared for after its publication were questions raised by PAO Johnson after she had read a few chapters.

In one instance at least, a "no" had been dropped from a sentence, completely changing the meaning. This revelation led me to closely examine the book in its entirety. Much to my dismay, while the dropped "no" was the worst printing error I discovered, I located fifty-four others. I assume the publisher had not sent me the proofs to check prior to publication (a normal practice) because I was in far-off Pakistan. After duly noting the fifty-five items and informing the publisher about them, all were corrected in the second printing. When the second edition was published in 1989, I had been able to see and correct page proofs that greatly reduced the printing errors of that edition.

By early 1984 a number of changes in the location of various offices were being made as construction at the embassy compound and the new American Center reached stages where some operations could be transferred from their temporary quarters. USIS moved into the new center and began to prepare for the opening of the USIS library. Along with the library, work on the radio studio, theater, photo lab, and some other entities in the building were nearing completion but could not yet be fully used. At about the same time the renovated embassy compound was taking final shape. The clinic was completed and moved out of its temporary quarters, as was the embassy commissary that had operated until then from a warehouse in the outskirts of the city. The rebuilt chancery also became habitable and embassy offices were moved from the AID building back to the compound.

With the completion of the embassy theater, motion pictures for the American community could now be shown there instead of at the Teen Center. Embassy apartments also became habitable and began to receive tenants. (American employees who had wanted to live in the compound had to live elsewhere until the buildings were repaired). The American Club, also rebuilt near the swimming pool at the compound, gave up its temporary quarters next to the temporary USIS offices. The house that had been used for the American Club now became the Teen Center, which moved from its old site alongside the Hansen residence.

Changes in embassy and USIS personnel happen frequently at all posts as Foreign Service personnel end their tours and replacements arrive. The numerous changes in venue for so many U.S. official activities, however, caused by the completion of many buildings in the embassy compound and about 70 percent of the new American center, was unusual. Among the changes in personnel was the replacement of U.S. Ambassador Ronald I. Spiers by Ambassador Deane R. Hinton. Both were highly respected career ambassadors. Spiers went on to become under secretary of state for administration. When Deputy Chief of Mission Barrington King, with whom we at USIS enjoyed excellent relations, was transferred to Brunei as the U.S. ambassador to that small, oil-rich country, he was replaced by Alex Rattray who returned to Islamabad. Rattray had been the commercial counselor in Islamabad when we first arrived in Pakistan and it was his old house that we had moved into upon his transfer to Karachi as the principal officer at the consulate there. Now he and his wife and daughter returned to Islamabad for a second tour, with, no doubt, mixed feelings. Many in the embassy and USIS felt, however, that he was a known element and thus welcomed his return.

There were also changes in the USIS American staff. Cultural Attaché Bob Jones was replaced by Joan Dickie. Dickie's last assignment had been on the staff of the U.S. ambassador to the United Nations, Jeane Kirkpatrick. Having lived in Manhattan during that assignment, she found Islamabad to be an extremely radical change from life in the Big Apple. Perhaps any place would have been quiet after living in New York City, but Islamabad, aside from its Islamic restrictions on cultural and social life, was still only partially constructed and many areas consisted of vacant fields and woods, so in many respects it was like living in a rural area.

Information Officer Don Jones was replaced by Frank Donovan, another "pro," but one who suffered a heart ailment. His heart condition eventually required his medical evacuation and after his return to the post, sometime after my transfer from Pakistan, he died at the post presumably from a heart attack.

My replacement, Bruce Kreutzer, was on board filling the position of administrative officer long before my tour of duty ended. But by the spring of 1984 we began making plans for our return to Washington where I was to be assigned as chief of the Media Reaction Branch in the Bureau of Programs. A Peruvian naval officer was renting our home in McLean, but he was completing a tour as naval attaché at the Peruvian Embassy in Washington so the timing was good from our point of view. Our "ninth life," my final overseas assignment with USIA, was rapidly coming to a close.

PAKISTAN POSTSCRIPT

On August 17, 1988, Pakistani President Muhammad Zia ul-Haq and the U.S. ambassador to Pakistan at that time, Arnold L. Raphel, were killed when their plane exploded in midair and crashed in eastern Pakistan, shortly after takeoff. With them were twenty-eight others, including such senior Pakistani army officers as the Pakistani chairman of the joint chiefs of staff, General Akhter Abdul Rehman, and the American military attaché of the U.S. Embassy, General Herbert M. Wassom. There were no survivors.

The crash occurred ten minutes after the C-130 military transport plane took off from a civilian airport in Bahawaipur, sixty miles from the Indian border, en route to Rawalpindi. Pakistani government spokesman Azhar Imam Zaidi said, "The plane was engulfed in a big ball of fire, somersaulted and tumbled to the ground." The group was returning from a field demonstration of the U.S. M-1 tank which Pakistan was considering purchasing.

Although the crash occurred at a time of political uncertainty for President Zia (he had dismissed his prime minister and the PM's thirty-three-member cabinet three months earlier), speculation existed that the Soviet Union, which had long been critical of Pakistan's support of the Mujaheddin, was somehow involved. Some also believed that India, Pakistan's traditional enemy, might have been involved. Indian Prime Minister Rajiv Gandhi issued an official statement of condolence and angrily dismissed such a charge. To this day no public evidence has surfaced to indicate if the plane was sabotaged by local or foreign terrorists. The cause of the tragedy remains a mystery, at least publicly.

11

The Landing

"Who remembers or wishes to record the ennuis and pettinesses of an adventure?"
—Alan Moorehead, *The Blue Nile*

In June 1984 the Peruvian naval attaché who had been renting our home in McLean with his family completed his Washington tour and moved out, leaving our house empty and ready to receive us upon our arrival back in Washington two months later.

At USIA headquarters I was assigned as chief of the small Foreign Media Reaction staff. At the time this office, which consisted of about six employees including a secretary and myself, was a branch of the Office of Research. As I was familiar with the Research Office from having worked as the chief of the Latin American branch prior to going to Pakistan, I was more convinced than ever that having the Media Reaction branch within the Office of Research was like having a pear branch grafted to an apple tree.

The normal duties of the Office of Research were to conduct polls and undertake research on long-range issues. Time was seldom of the essence. The Media Reaction staff, however, had to operate at break-neck speed every day in order to report daily on what the foreign media was saying about current U.S. policies and actions. We then condensed foreign views on specific U.S. interests to where U.S. government leaders and their aides, by reading our brief analyses, including brief translated excerpts from foreign media, could capture the tenor of public reaction abroad to U.S. programs, policies, and actions. For the Media Reaction branch, time was of the essence.

Meeting daily deadlines differed greatly from the much more leisurely pace of most of the researchers in the Office of Research who worked on long-range issues. The information we gathered had to reach the Washington foreign affairs agencies, from the White House down, as quickly as possible to be of most value.

Not only did a large difference in timing and techniques distinguish the Media Reaction office from the work of other branches of the Office of Research, but we had to provide the USIA director with an analysis of what the world press was saying in time for him to use this analysis in his briefings at the 8:30 a.m. daily meetings with the Secretary of State and other top State Department officials. After writing the director's report we prepared a more detailed analysis which formed the basis for the short daily briefings which I orally presented at a 9 a.m. meeting to the agency's associate director of programs and his key advisors. After much effort to move the Media Reaction branch out of the Office of Research, and after considerable tension developed between the head of the Office of Research and the associate director of programs, the Media Reaction office was finally transferred from the Research Office to the Bureau of Programs. Some years later, as sometimes happens in government bureaucracies, it was moved back into the Office of Research.

The daily and special reports that the Media Reaction branch issued were based on information received by cable and telephone from major USIS posts throughout the world. We noted the treatment given by leading foreign newspapers and radio and television stations to U.S. policies and actions, and how the most important media of selected countries viewed those policies and actions.

To compile this information and analyze it in time for the early morning meetings mentioned above, at least two staffers had to begin work on the process at 6 a.m. each day. Thanks to computers that enabled fast word processing, and the proven abilities of Forrest Fischer, a Foreign Service officer who had written these reports for a number of years, the daily challenge was always met. I was fortunate to be able to count on Fischer's speed, efficiency, and reliability to create the USIA Director's early morning report almost every day without fail.

Fortunately for the rest of us, Fischer liked the idea of arriving at the office at 6 a.m. This enabled him to leave work early and avoid the worst of the traffic to and from his home in Reston, Virginia, and by arriving home by mid-afternoon he could get in a round of golf every day that weather permitted if he so desired. I was happy that I seldom had to be in the office until 8 a.m., especially since I usually had to be there until late in the afternoon.

The daily reports included European media reaction on the same day that, for us, was just beginning, since European capitals are six to eight hours ahead of the U.S. If for any reason we didn't get a cable from a major European post in time for our analysis, we would phone the post and talk with the person who normally wrote the daily media report for that country. Our post in Tokyo, of course, was always a day ahead because of the time difference.

In the computer age in which we were now living, it was interesting to see how modern communications technology brought the world so much closer together. In Washington, at the USIA Press Center in the National Press Building, for example, briefings about U.S. policies, often by U.S. policymakers, would be held for foreign correspondents. Shortly thereafter, the correspondents would send their dispatches to their newspapers, many of which contained their reflections regarding the subjects discussed in those briefings. Their reports would appear the next day in European and other newspapers and in radio and television broadcasts. What they said and how they treated these policy matters would then be reflected in the cables and phone messages we received from our USIS posts. This information would then become a part of the Media Reaction reports we developed that morning for the White House, State Department, USIA and other government offices involved in foreign affairs. Thus the U.S. policy enunciations went full circle, from Washington to Europe and elsewhere and back to Washington, in a matter of hours. By means of USIA's Media Reaction reports, the U.S. government's foreign affairs community always had immediate access to global public reaction to current U.S. foreign policies.

After being on this job for a few months, I conducted a personal survey of end users of our main daily report, known as the *Daily Digest.* Although a few individual recipients in the State Department told me they found it of little or no interest (and these we quickly dropped from the approximately 200 addressees who received this report), most of the recipients with whom I talked praised it highly and said they found it very useful. My own feeling about its usefulness to the Washington foreign affairs community was confirmed following the interviews I had with a number of recipients. A USIA inspection team that later studied this particular operation, arrived at the same conclusion.

While my job as chief of the Media Reaction branch was initially interesting and challenging, it soon became routine. I missed the greater variety and excitement that so many of the other jobs I had held in USIA offered, covering, as many of them did, a great variety of interests and activities. Thus when Bob Jones, the former cultural attaché in Islamabad who was now in the agency's book division in

Washington, told me about the creation of a new job in that division, my appetite for a transfer was whetted. I knew I would miss the rather nice office I had on the seventh floor with its excellent view of the dome of the U.S. capital and a degree of freedom in my current position that I might not enjoy in filling another slot. But even if the media reaction business had been more interesting, the opportunity to be involved with books, which meant being involved with a great variety of subjects and issues, was enticing.

With my interest aroused, I immediately explored the possibility of a transfer to the new position Bob told me about. This coincided at a time with the desire of my predecessor, who had left the Media Reaction branch the year before, to return to his old job as he found his new job less interesting. With good coordination, a trait not always seen in government bureaucracies, he replaced me, thus ending my brief experience with media reaction. I was happy to move into the world of books which I felt would be a much more dynamic and potentially exciting field.

By 1985 USIA had let its traditional book translation program wither away. The time was ripe for the rediscovery of the book as an important element of public diplomacy. The agency's libraries had long been recognized as a major source of information for "telling America's story to the world." However, unlike many film, television, press, and other programs that often received enthusiastic support from the agency's top officials, book programs were often ignored by top management. This was especially true in the 1980s when major emphasis was directed toward the new, exciting, and often exotic communication technologies which were being developed at such a fast pace one could hardly keep up with them. The Computer Age was in full bloom.

There were, however, some public diplomats and others concerned with how the U.S. and its policies were depicted abroad, who believed books remained valuable public diplomacy tools. These advocates of books, when arguing that books should not be neglected, often cited the major efforts undertaken by the Soviet Union in this field. According to a book published in 1986 entitled *American Books Abroad: Toward a National Policy*, edited by William M. Childs and Donald E. McNeil, in 1982 alone the Soviets published some 74.5 million books in languages foreign to those spoken in the Soviet Union, including 11.6 million in Spanish translations. For USIA to de-emphasize book programs at a time when our greatest competitor was expanding its book programs was a cause of concern for a number of people.

Prior to the Childs-McNeil book a widely distributed study addressed this issue, supported by the publishing industry, the Center for the Book in the Library of Congress, and some concerned government officials. It was conducted by Curtis G. Benjamin, a retired president of the McGraw-Hill Book Company. Benjamin's published report became the bible for new and rejuvenated book programs of USIA.

Entitled *U.S. Books Abroad: Neglected Ambassadors,* the report noted that the study was conducted "to provide a document that endeavors to stimulate renewed and wider awareness, first, of the dire need for U.S. books in less developed countries, and, second, of possible ways and means by which this need may be met." "Less developed countries" were, of course, the targets of the massive Soviet book programs. Benjamin's analysis, published as a small pamphlet and widely distributed among government offices concerned with foreign affairs, succeeded, as intended, in stimulating a number of new U.S. government actions designed to meet the Soviet competition on the book front.

On April 4, 1984, Robert C. McFarlane, then National Security Council director, sent a memorandum to USIA Director Wick which noted: "Statistics have graphically demonstrated in Curtis Benjamin's book. . . that the United States has unilaterally disarmed in this field." Having thus, in effect, received marching orders from the White House, USIA Director Wick formed a book and library committee composed of book publishers and other interested, influential individuals from both private and governmental sectors. This committee was charged with examining the book situation worldwide vis a vis the Soviet Union's efforts and advising the Agency on how to meet the Soviet challenge in the field of books. A "U.S. Books Abroad Task Force" was also formed. With this kind of support, substantial funding flowed into the book division of USIA. Old book programs were greatly expanded and new programs created. Since additional staff was needed to supervise the new and expanded programs, the position of supervisor for the greatly expanded global book translation activities was also created.

When I expressed interest in this job the head of the book division, Jerry Prillaman, interviewed me. He seemed delighted that I wanted to fill the newly created position. Although I had never met him before, he was somewhat familiar with my philosophical ideas since some months earlier he had written a full-page review of my book on USIA that was published in the agency's in-house organ, *USIA WORLD.* (When I first read what he had written, I personally took issue with some of his conclusions about my book, especially when he seemed to more strongly defend the agency's position against some of my criticisms than I thought was justified.) On this occasion, however, I did not take him to task about this. Instead I cited my experience as a book officer in Madrid some twenty years earlier; my successful use of books in special programs in Uruguay and Bolivia; my long-standing interest in this medium; and my knowledge and experience in Latin America where major book programs were being conducted and would now be expanded. For example, the Reagan Administration was focusing so much attention on Central America, especially communist-oriented Nicaragua and strife-torn El Salvador, that a special book program called "The Caribbean Book Initiative" had been instituted. This along with many other U.S. programs and activities was designed to generate support for U.S. policies and actions and meet the Soviet competition in this field. I felt that my Latin American experience would be helpful in supervising the "Caribbean Book Initiative" and said so. A few days after the interview my transfer was approved.

There is nothing like money to make the wheels go round, so with substantial funding I had a great time creating new and expanded book programs while learning about the book business. In a way we had too much money, for as many times as we came up with new ideas on translating books, buying books, and advertising books that would contribute to our goals, we still had difficulty using all of the funds available.

By the end of the fiscal year, as with most government agencies, funds allotted to us had to be either obligated or returned to the U.S. Treasury. Although the staff of the book division was by then greatly expanded, there were still not enough individuals on board or available to review books or even book titles in search of those which were of possible interest to us. Obtaining copyrights and making the many intricate arrangements which must be undertaken in a book translation program, especially one dealing with many different publishers in different countries and in different languages, took time and effort. Since more than 60,000 new book titles appeared in the U.S. annually, the challenge of selecting titles suitable for USIA programs was formidable.

As head of the agency's global book translation program, the following two years were a blast for me. With plenty of funds available we expanded our staff and programs in Latin America, Spain, the Middle East, the Far East, Africa, and China. We began programs in Eastern Europe and developed unique ideas for getting books into Central America.

By my third year in that office, funds were beginning to dry up.

The attention span of the agency and other U.S. government offices interested in these programs was nearing its limit. By then, however, we felt we had accomplished a great deal in getting U.S. ideas through books into the minds of many people in many countries where the ideas presented in these books could be introduced, if not always adopted. In China alone, the new book program we initiated during my watch continued during and after the Tiananmen Square student riots of 1989, which unsuccessfully demanded that Chinese leaders grant greater democracy. The riots brought down a curtain on most other USIA programs in China, especially in the years immediately afterwards, but USIA's book program in that important country continued to flourish.

The power of books shows up often when leaders in almost any field reveal the influences that shaped their thoughts. On Feb. 9, 1992, for example, a *Washington Post* article by Margaret Shapiro, datelined Moscow, reported on Russian President Boris Yeltsin's inner circle of advisors. Among the "Young Turks" in that small group at that time was Gennadi Burbulis, forty-six, a former professor of Marxism-Leninism who was deputy prime minister. "One of his first recruits was Yegor Gaider, thirty-five, the economist entrusted by Yeltsin to swiftly transform Russia's moribund, centralized economy into a free market system." Shapiro then described some of Gaidar's personal history and later noted:

> When he was 12, Soviet-led forces invaded Czechoslovakia, quashing the democracy movement there known as the Prague Spring, as well as Gaidar's faith in the rightness of his country and communism. His disillusionment spread further when, several years later, a Russian language copy of Paul Samuelson's 'Economics' textbook, secretly given to him by an older friend, opened Gaidar's eyes—and mind—to the promises of a free market and capitalism.

The above is but a footnote on modern history but demonstrates how one book helped shape the mind of one influential leader. Few leaders in the world have not been influenced by the books they read.

By 1986 my "time in class" as a Foreign Service officer was catching up with me. In July of the following year I retired. The world of books that I entered for my last Washington assignment had been an interesting, challenging, and fruitful experience. The same might be said about all of my USIA assignments abroad and the other Washington interludes.

On July 4, 1987 (appropriately, I thought, for it was Independence Day), I would retire from USIA. Of course there was some trepidation on my part, for who doesn't give up the known and enter the unknown without some concern?

I had certainly enjoyed my Foreign Service career throughout the "nine lives" depicted in this epistle, and I think that my family did also. I was still enjoying my final job with USIA. Working with books, as I had anticipated, allowed me to delve into various fields that interested me. The travels connected with this final job assignment also enabled me, among other things, to attend the annual Frankfurt (Germany) Book Fair, the world's largest and most prestigious book fair, one of the man-made wonders of the twentieth century. Books published in more than one hundred countries are exhibited there at the gigantic Frankfurt fairgrounds while publishers, authors, and agents wheel and deal in that highly competitive business. There were also trips to Spain, France, and Latin America that broke me away from the Washington routine. The tonic these visits to the agency's book offices in Barcelona and Mexico City were like "paid vacations." I'm convinced, however, that the face-to-face meetings enabled by these trips contributed substantially to resolving problems and misunderstandings between headquarters and the field.

In this final job before my retirement, I also, of course, had to learn about the book business. This I did mostly by reading and asking questions of knowledgeable people. But to give this up, while still enjoying the challenges and excitement and camaraderie of professional colleagues, many of whom had become personal and family friends, was not without pangs of regret. What I didn't know at the time was that the so-called "retired life" also has its rewards, such as being your own boss; being free to determine where and what you will do and when you will do it with no obligations to any higher authority (other than, perhaps, one's spouse!); no longer having to be at the office at a certain time; and, most marvelously, no longer having efficiency reports written about you by your superiors, or, having to write any yourself!

At a gathering at the Hirschorn Museum a few months before my "Independence Day," where a ceremony celebrating the fortieth anniversary of the Fulbright Program was being held, I spoke briefly with Wilson Dizard, the author of the first book ever written about USIA, *The Strategy of Truth* and, in 2005, *Inventing Public Diplomacy:*

The Story of the United States Information Agency. He had retired some years earlier. When we talked about my favorite subject at the time, my forthcoming retirement, he said, "Al, I'll tell you one thing. There's life after USIA."

My colleagues arranged a retirement party for me that was held early in June on the eighth floor of USIA headquarters. In brief remarks on that occasion I thanked those who organized a fond farewell and added, "I'd like to especially thank my wife, Charmaine, for the strength and support she always provided me as we moved in and out of eight countries during my three-decade career with USIA." (Readers who have stayed the course will recall that my "life" in the Dominican Republic during the Civil War there was a solo act, whereas the other eight "lives" were family affairs.)

Quoting from a copy of the cable that first offered me a job with USIA some thirty years earlier while I was working in Madrid, I remarked that the offer was one I could hardly refuse, especially the salary of nearly $4,000 per annum! "Now," I noted, "more than three decades later, what we in USIA are all engaged in has become known as 'public diplomacy,' a term that didn't exist then. I still remain enthusiastic about what U.S. public diplomacy is all about. As someone once observed with regard to our mission, 'We're not selling soap,' even though there are times when it seems like we're operating in a 'soap opera' *ambiente.*"

As I came in for a landing, so to speak, at the end of my "nine lives" as a Foreign Service officer in USIA, if asked "Would I do it all over again?" I would quickly answer, "You bet your life." More importantly, I will always believe that I was privileged to have been a member of an organization that, since its establishment in 1953, contributed substantially to the foreign policy objectives of the United States as well as the economic and political development of many societies.

In the late 1990s some argued that the need for an organization of the U.S. government like USIA had passed. Others believed, on the contrary, that explaining U.S. policies and actions and the telling of "America's story to the world" would remain important because of regional conflicts that can adversely affect U.S. interests; the increased permeability of national frontiers that modern communications technology has created; and the growing economic interdependence of the nations of the world. With the abolishment of USIA as an independent U.S. government agency October 1, 1999, and the takeover of many of its functions by the Department of State, one had hoped that public diplomacy would be enhanced and not diminished. Yet as the twenty-first century rolls on, and especially after the tragedy of September 11, 2001, the demise of USIA in 1999 has resulted in the weakening of U.S. public diplomacy achievements and has occurred at a time when there is more agreement than ever that "public diplomacy has come of age." Perhaps it is time to reconsider the reestablishment of an organization similar to the now defunct USIA. Only by effectively explaining U.S. policies and actions, as expressed by U.S. officials and others, and using the experience and superb media tools which USIA developed over the years, can Americans be assured that their views will reach important audiences abroad and contribute to reducing misunderstandings.

In ending this story of nine lives, I hope I succeeded in leaving out the ennuis and pettinesses which Alan Morehead was so successful in avoiding in his great books about the Nile. And as Andy Solomon wrote in a review of *My Other Life* by Paul Theroux in the *Washington Post* (9-15-96):

> Imagination always lies at the heart of memoir. Memoir is about truth, unlike biography, which is about fact. The past is what is remembered, not what actually happened.

In a review of Jill Ker Conway's book entitled *When Memory Speaks: Reflections on Autobiography*, Francine Prose, discussing the popularity of memoirs, noted (*Washington Post* 3-1-98):

> Some of us want to be encouraged or comforted by experiences much like our own; others hope to be titillated or shocked by steamy revelations; still others want to see a lifetime transformed into art by a first-rate intellect, a charismatic storyteller, or a brilliant stylist.

And she quotes Conway's observation about the difference in how men and women approach the writing of memoirs:

> For men the overarching pattern for life comes from adaptations of the story of the epic hero in classical antiquity. Life is an odyssey, a journey through many trials and tests, which the hero must surmount alone through courage, endurance, cunning and moral strength.

As for women, Conway sees women writers as less prone to take credit for their own actions, and more likely to approach their own life story as something that happened to them. And she adds: "The family plays a major role in many autobiographies, by women and men."

Does any of this apply to *Nine Lives*? The reader can be the judge. As has been said before, "memory is a creative process" and "no recall is exactly like an earlier recall." Two individuals experiencing the same event will probably describe that event differently, especially after the passage of time. Certainly Robert, Annette, Katherine, Alicia, and Mark, to whom this book is dedicated, saw their experiences in growing up abroad differently than their father; but more remarkable, so did their mother in many instances.

All lives have their ups and downs, but if variety is the spice of life, as I believe it is, the Foreign Service should continue to attract any young person looking for a career that is as rewarding in its service to the American people as it is adventurous.

Notes

Chapter 2: Calypso in Caracas

1. "USIS" is the acronym for United States Information Service, the name used by overseas offices of the U.S. Information Agency (USIA). Before USIA was created, many of the information programs conducted by USIA were a "service" of the Department of State, from whence "USIS" originated. "USIS" was dropped briefly by many overseas posts when USIA became the International Communication Agency (ICA) in 1979, but was reinstated in 1983 when ICA reverted to its old title of USIA.

Chapter 3: Mexican Mosaic

1. I am indebted to former USIA Mexico Information Officer Earl J. Wilson for many of the descriptions of events involving the embassy and its personnel during and after the July 28, 1957, earthquake in Mexico City.

Chapter 4: Guyanese Gumbo

1. British Guiana was pronounced "British Guee-anna" by some, "British Guy-anna" by others. When the country became independent on May 26, 1966, the new nation was named "Guyana," leaving no doubt as to its pronunciation. I have used "Guiana" when referring to British Guiana, "Guyana" when referring to the newly independent country of that former British colony, and "Guyanese" as an adjective and when referring to the country's inhabitants.

Chapter 7: Murder in Montevideo

1. The *Biblioteca Artigas—Washington* was founded in 1943 as a pilot library by the American librarian Arthur Gropp under the auspices of the American Library Association and the American Council of Learned Societies. It was a privately funded public library. In 1948 the U.S. government took over the financing of the library.

In the 1960s the library had five professional Uruguayan librarians and five nonprofessionals who provided library services to some 27,000 registered borrowers in Montevideo and some 3,000 by mail to individuals and institutions in interior towns and cities. The open-shelf collection had over 24,000 volumes, about half in Spanish and half in English, with especially strong holdings in scientific and technical fields. It offered *Uruguayos* some 8,000 pamphlets on various subjects, a circulating collection of over 2,000 phonograph records and 1,500 musical scores and parts, as well as current subscriptions to some 350 periodicals (in cooperation with local universities and scientific libraries in Montevideo). Its reference collection had over 2,000 books, which were used to answer questions either in person or by mail. The library also sent book trunks containing some 150 books on a variety of subjects to institutions in the country requesting them.

Above derived from four sources:
Arthur E. Gropp, "A Portrait of Libraries in Uruguay," *Louisiana Library Association Bulletin*, Nov. 1949, p. 157

Biblioteca Artigas—Washington, unpublished annual report, 1969

Luis A. Musso, "La biblioteca Artigas—Washington de Montevideo," *Fichero bibliográfico hispano-americano* (marzo 1970), p. 5

Federico Capurro, *Una memoria mas* (Montevideo, 1970), p. 239

Abbreviations

ACAO	Assistant Cultural Affairs Officer
AFGE	American Federation of Government Employees
AID	Agency for International Development (aka USAID)
AIO	Assistant Information Officer
BNC	Binational (Cultural) Center
BPAO	Branch Public Affairs Officer
CAO	Cultural Affairs Officer
DEA	Drug Enforcement Agency
DCM	Deputy Chief of Mission
DPAO	Deputy Public Affairs Officer
FSO	Foreign Service Officer
I0	Information Officer
ICA	International Communication Agency (USIA became ICA under President Jimmy Carter; USIA name restored by President Ronald Reagan.)
IMG	Information Media Guaranty Program
JOT	Junior Officer Trainee
OAS	Organization of American States
OER	Officer Evaluation Report
PNCB	Pakistan Narcotics Control Board
PAO	Public Affairs Officer (Also known as CPAO, Country Public Affairs Officer)
PL-480	Public Law 480 (Local currencies obtained by USG from sale of U.S. surplus agricultural products and other items.
USG	U.S. Government
USIA	United States Information Agency
USICA	U.S. International Communication Agency (Acronym used by some overseas posts instead of USIS when ICA existed)
USIS	United States information Service (USIA's overseas posts)
VOA	Voice of America

About the Author

ALLEN C. HANSEN is a 32-year veteran of public diplomacy, having joined the U.S. Information Agency as an officer trainee in 1954, shortly after USIA was created. He held a variety of positions in Washington, D.C. and abroad in Latin America, Europe, and Asia. His last assignment overseas was as Deputy Public Affairs Officer in Islamabad, Pakistan (1981—84). In addition to having been the director of USIA operations in Bolivia (1970—72) and Peru (1976—80), he also practiced public diplomacy in Venezuela, Mexico, British Guiana (now Guyana), Uruguay, Spain, and the Dominican Republic. His three Washington, D.C. assignments included Caribbean desk officer for USIA at the time of the Dominican crisis in the mid-1960s; USIA Policy Officer for Latin America (1972—76); and chief of the Latin American branch of the Office of Research (1981). He retired from USIA in 1987.

After serving in the U.S. Navy in World War II and graduating from Syracuse University in 1950 with a B.A. in political science, he was a newspaper reporter for the *Perth Amboy Evening News*, Perth Amboy, N.J. before being called back into the navy during the Korean War. In 1962 he received an M.A. degree in American Studies from the University of Pennsylvania. At various times in his career he has performed such diverse roles as textbook translation officer for USIS Madrid and technical advisor for a USIA film on narcotics trafficking in Latin America. This is his fifth book.

Other books by Allen C. Hansen

USIA, Public Diplomacy in the Computer Age, 2nd ed., N.Y.: Praeger, 1989.
The Hole in the Doughnut, Growing Up in Metuchen in a Time of Innocence, Self published, 2002.
Fleet Tug Sailor, A World War II Memoir, Self published, 2004.
Campus Capers, The Life and Times of a G.I. College Student, Self published, 2006.

Index

Adair, Charles **photo #12**, 230
Allen, Lafe 221
Alliance for Progress 333
altitude illness 276–87
American Challenge, The 225–26, 272–73
Amerson, Robert 41, 42, 56
Anderson, Marian 116–17
Anderson, Orville 74
Austrian, Sheila 296

Babcock, Dwight 277, 302
Barbados 162, 348–49
Bennett, W. Tapley 167, 172, 174
Benson, Ezra Taft 23
binational centers 22, 262, 265, 268–71, 275, 319–21, 327–31, 340
Bluestein, Jerome **photo #1**
Bolivia 221, 232–33, 235–36, 243–303
Bork, Ted 402
Boyce, Ralph 400
British Guiana 103–32
Brown, Dean 381
Brown, Elizabeth 71
Brown, Kermit 186–87
Brown, Richard 182
Buchholz, Margrett 260, 303
Bunker, Ellsworth 178, 183
Burson, Ray 252, 255–56, 262
Bush, George H.W. 413
Butler, George 16, 17–19, 41, 45, 56, 59, 75

Caicedo, Harry 181, 221
Castro, Fidel 24, 103, 232, 239
Cemal, Elizabeth 382
Chatten, Robert 321
Cheatham, James 110
Chiancone, Frank 214–15, 218, 221
Childs, William M. 420–21
Colombia 308
Connett, William B. 167
Cope, John Jr. 115
Coppman, Lyle 235
Corey, Frank 128
Coy, Edward 275

Daniels, Gordon 274, 297
Darling, Ben 176
Davidson, Douglas 379, 398
Davis, Carl 221
Dean, Robert 323, 336, 340
DeSoto, Hernando 350–352
DeWeldon, Felix 337–38
Dickie, Joan 415
Dieterich, William "Jeff" 254, 276
Diggle, Arthur **photo #13**, 217, 227–28
Dixon, John 398
Dizard, Wilson 424
Dominican Republic 159–87
  Act of Santo Domingo 177
  Inter-American Peace Force 175, 177
Donovan, Frank 415
Douglas, Kirk **photo #19,** 409–13
Dunn, James C. 146

Eberle, Kyra 321
Edwards, Horace "Tex" 206, 213,
    216–17, 222
Eisenhower, Dwight 129, 141–45, 149,
    photo #8
Ellington, Duke 227, 288
Elliston, Gisela 320
Elliston, Tom 320, 344
Emmert, Fred 260, 262
Evans, David 319

family planning 306–7
Fascell, Dante 327, 343
Finney, Dean 381
Fischer, Forrest 418
Fletcher, Warren 23
Florey, Frank 312, 317, 328, 347, 365–
    66, 379, 396
Fogler, Ned 221
Fondes, Robert 30, 52, 56, 61–63, 67
Franco, Francisco 1–2, 135, 138, 142–
    153, **photo #8**

Gallagher, Jack 313
Gardner, Ava 155
Geyer, Georgie Ann 274
Gibb, Lucy 382
Gillespie, Jacob **photo #13,** 214, 227
Gomez, Frank 291–92
Guevara, Che 233
Gurvin, Anne **photo #13,** 214
Gwynne, Guy 254

Hamilton, Donald 318
Hanson, Joseph 309
Hawken, Ashley 308, 411
Hensch, Shirley 214, 221
Herath, Kent 245, 248–49, 251, 274, 290, 302
Hinton, Deane R. 415
Hoyt, Henry 230–31
Hummel, Arthur 371
Huston, Tobie 383
Hutchinson, Owen "Buck" 138
Hutchison, Barbara 311

Information Media Guaranty Program
    (IMG) 150

Irwin, Lee James 396
Islam 373–74, 376, 381, 386–89

Jagan, Cheddi 105, 114, 120, 125–26,
    129–30, 132
Jagan, Janet 114, 117
Johnson, Lyndon Baines 172, 174–77,
    179, 183, **photo #10,** 212, 219–20, 222,
    306
Johnson, Marilyn 378–79, 381–82, 393,
    398, 400, 409, 411, 414
Jones, Don 380–81, 398, 415
Jones, Gordon 236–37
Jones, Robert 380, 415, 419
Jones, William 396

Kaye, Danny **photo #11,** 227
Kendall, Harry 14–20, 41–2, 139,
    photo #12
Kennan, George F. 13
King, Barrington 415
King, Clark **photo #13,** 214
Kissinger, Henry 9, 316, 336
Kohn, Robert 339
Kreutzer, Bruce 382, 415
Kristula, Michael 276

Lane, Lyle 323, 339
Laun, Alfred 174, 180–81, 183
Lebanon 146
Lenderking, William 348
Lewis, Irving "Bud" 216
Lindsey, William 214, **Photo #13**
Llosa, Mario Vargas 305, 359, 352
Loomis, Henry 270
Lording, Elizabeth 320
Lupo, Sam 314, 341

Manapol, Perla 318–19
Mann, Thomas C. 173
Marcy, Mildred 306
Marek, Jodi 318
Martin, John Bartlow 159, 170, 177
Martin, Thomas 276
Mathes, Donald E. 264
Mclean, Malcolm 178, 181
McNeil, Donald E. 420–21

meeting of American presidents 219–22
Mexico 69–101
    July 1957 earthquake 85–92
Mitchell, Howard 228, 236
Mitrione, Daniel A. 237
Mori, Ich 400
Murrow, Edward R. 291, 311

narcotics trafficking 306–9, 345, 373–74, 394, 404–9
Newsom, David 384
Niswander, Melvin 22

Olason, Victor 346
Olberg, Weston **photo #1**
Opsata, James 23
Oram, Frank 138
Organization of American States (OAS) 170, 175, 177–78, 180–82, 184, 220–21

Pace, Vance 319, 349
Paddack, Christopher "Kit" 317, 337
Pakistan **photos ## 17, 18, 19,** 363–416
Pastor, Robert 342
Pei, I.M. 224
Peppers, Ray 410
Peru 175, 213, 233, 286, 291, 293, 301–2, 305–54, 404–5
    El Otro Sendero (the Other Path) 350–52
    El Sendero Luminoso (the Shining Path) 350
Phelan, Raymond 51, 56
Philpott, Dean 383, 398–400
Pillsbury, Phillip 157
Post, Richard 408
Preeg, Ernest 323
Prillaman, Gerald 421
Public Law 480 136, 146, 400

Raphael, Arnold I. 416
Rattray, Alex 368, 415
Ravotto, Joseph 70–72, 77–78
Reafs, Ronald 320
Reagan, Ronald 147, 342, 358

Reddish, Annica 382
Reinhardt, John 344, 357, 359
Rodman, Seldon 292
Rosenfeld, Nathan **photo #13,** 213, 217, 228, 236–37
Ross, Sherman 397
Routt, Garland 103–04, 114, 128
Rowan, Carl 179, 186–87
Rusk, Dean **photo #10**
Ryan, Hewson 175, 178

Sayre, Robert M. 212
Schwartz, Andrew 249, 291, 302
Shankle, Perry 266
Shlaudeman, Harry 334, 336, 339, 344
Shultz, George 413
Siracusa, Ernest 251, 264, 274, 292, 297
Smith, Don 331
Smith, William French 405
Soiffer, Warren 397
Spain 1–4, 133–58, 240, 352
    Pact of Madrid 146
    Radio España Independienta 151
Spiers, Ronald I. 415
Sponholtz, Conrad 329
Stallings, Alden 397
Stevens, Michael 302
Strange, Susan **photo #13**
Streibert, Theodore **photo #1**

terrorism 209, 232–43, 264, 306, 308–11, 350
Theviu, Samuel 335–37
Thomas, Lowell Sr. 288–301
Thurber, James 366, 374, 378–79, 382–83, 393, 398–99
Todman, Terry 342
Trinidad, B.W.I. 45–49, 94, 103–4, 106, 127

United Nations (UN) 146, 150, 334, 377, 415
Uruguay 175, 187, **Photos ## 10, 12, 13,** 205–44, 308, 311, 350
USIA: Public Diplomacy in the Computer Age 414

Vance, Gay   342, 344
Vaughn, Robert   173
Venezuela   10–11, 13–67, 96–101, 175, 336, 343
Voice of America (VOA)   ix, 20, 179–81, 215, 322, 359, 376, 379
Von Glatz, Richard   396

Warren, Fletcher   23
Washer, Fred   108–12
Waters, Gerald   **photo #13,** 218, 318, 320, 345

White, Barbara   157
Wick, Charles   358, 409, 421
Wilkinson, Andrew   17–18, 22, 42
Wilson, Donald   179
Wilson, Earl   78, 428
Weinberger, Casper   412-13
Winfree, John   383
Without Marx or Jesus   273
Woods, Carroll   115

Zischke, Douglas   235

CPSIA information can be obtained
at www.ICGtesting.com
Printed in the USA
FSHW02n2115120818
51377FS